Sugar, SPICE, and everything NICE

CINEMAS OF GIRLHOOD

EDITED BY

Frances Gateward and Murray Pomerance

WAYNE STATE UNIVERSITY PRESS   DETROIT

Contemporary Approaches to Film and Television Series

A complete listing of the books in this series can be found online at http://wsupress.wayne.edu.

GENERAL EDITOR

Barry Keith Grant
Brock University

ADVISORY EDITORS

Patricia B. Erens
Dominican University

Robert J. Burgoyne
Wayne State University

Lucy Fischer
University of Pittsburgh

Tom Gunning
University of Chicago

Peter Lehman
Arizona State University

Anna McCarthy
New York University

Caren J. Deming
University of Arizona

Peter X. Feng
University of Delaware

Library of Congress Cataloging-in-Publication Data

Sugar, spice, and everything nice : the cinemas of girlhood / edited by Frances K. Gateward and Murray Pomerance.
    p. cm.— (Contemporary film and television series)
    Includes bibliographical references and index.
    ISBN 0-8143-2917-9 (alk. paper)—ISBN 0-8143-2918-7 (pbk. : alk. paper)
    1. Girls in motion pictures. 2. Teenage girls in motion pictures I. Gateward,
Frances K. II. Pomerance, Murray, 1946–. III. Series.
PN1995.9.G57 S84 2002
791.43'652055—dc21   2001004774

"Sorrowful Black Death Is Not a Hot Ticket" by bell hooks is reprinted from *Sight and Sound* 4:8 (1994) by kind permission of *Sight and Sound.* "Clueless in the Neocolonial World Order" by Gayle Wald is reprinted from *Camera Obscura* 42 (1999) ©1999 Camera Obscura, all rights reserved, reprinted by kind permission of Duke University Press.

Sugar, SPICE, and everything NICE

Above all, DON'T forget that the friendship of other girls is the crown of your own success.

Emily Post, *Etiquette* (1937)

Contents

Girls II Women

Cast Types

Beyond Innocence

Acknowledgments

We could perhaps have imagined this book but we would never have compiled it without the gracious collaboration of all the authors included herein. But special thanks are offered to a number of persons whose kindness and inspiration warmed us: David Desser, Patricia Erens, Paul Kelly, Nellie Perret, Ariel Pomerance, Michael Owen of the Office of Research Services at Ryerson University (Toronto), Rod Peters of ADV Films, and Lewis M. Allen, Brandon Cronenberg, Jessica Rose-Golden, Phyllis Belkin, Jan Welsch. We are especially grateful to our colleagues at Wayne State University Press—Arthur Evans, Barry Keith Grant, Jane Hoehner, Danielle DeLucia Burgess, and Adela Garcia—and to the Unit for Cinema Studies, University of Illinois Urbana-Champaign.

Introduction

Frances Gateward and Murray Pomerance

All societies, N. O. Brown tells us Georg Simmel thought, begin with a secret and ends when it is revealed. Surely capitalist technocratic society has many secrets, including at the very least the wage and the Father, but woman's experience is a secret that is especially vital and one that has only relatively recently begun to be told. Even more deeply hidden has been the experience of the girl. It is the girl who is the most profound site of patriarchal investment, her unconstrained freedom representing the most fearsome threat to male control. That her capabilities are unexplored and that her potentialities as an adult female are undeveloped are therefore values in themselves, to be appropriated and colonized at any expense of spirit and some considerable expense of capital. When women's labor and experience is exploited to men's benefit, the girl becomes socially important as future woman, a basis for planning a continuance of exploitability. As Betty Friedan asserted in *The Feminine Mystique* (1959), womanhood and wifehood are a kind of enforced girlhood—an experience that cannot fully know itself or the way in which it is bounded. Much contemporary feminist theorizing stands on a critique of paternalist constraint of girlhood.

The control and disenfranchisement of girls is a subject that has been studied in history, education, psychology, literature, and sociology. Although there have been a number of significant essays and book-length studies on youth and film in cinema studies—*Images of Children in American Film* (1986) by Kathy Merlock Jackson, Thomas Doherty's *Teenagers and Teenpics: The Juvenilization of*

American Movies in the 1950s (1988), Jon Lewis's *The Road to Romance and Ruin: Teen Films and Youth Culture* (1992), and *Children's Films: History, Ideology, Pedagogy, Theory* by Ian Wojicik Andrews (2000)—very little has been written about the inscription of girlhood. This is surprising, given the importance girls and girl characters have played in the history of American cinema, from actresses Mary Pickford and Shirley Temple to characters like Dorothy (*The Wizard of Oz* [1939]), Carrie (*Carrie* [1976]), and Rose (*Titanic* [1997]).

Indeed, in the history of cinematic production and critical study, no systematic critical attention has been given to the fact that six of the ten highest-grossing motion pictures of all time, adjusted for inflation, are principally about adolescent girls—either their experience or the treatment they receive in male culture. It is astonishing to consider that the figure of the girl, even the aging girl who has yet failed to develop or extend an independent role in society, is both prominent and riddling in *Gone With the Wind* (1939), a film about a southern belle coming of age in the era of the Civil War; *Star Wars* (1977), an epic about charming mercenaries who come to the aid of a forsaken adolescent princess; *The Sound of Music* (1965), an account of the coming-of-age of a girl in the Nazi era at the hands of a young woman a little older but hardly more experienced than she in the ways of the heart; *Titanic*, an account of a girl's coming to terms with the social meaning of her gender onboard a fated ocean-going vessel; *Doctor Zhivago* (1965), about a pretty girl who inspires a tortured poet; and *Snow White and the Seven Dwarfs* (1937), a musical fantasy about a poor girl who makes good in the woods. These six films alone have earned more than $1.7 billion, yet "the girl" as a subject of intense and devoted analysis is missing from the literature.

For the most part in contemporary films about girls, the female subject is an exemplification—often through exaggeration—of hegemonic attitudes and values about girlhood, and the films are instructive texts rather than documents of revolution. That girls can be seen (very conventionally) as overwhelmed by shapeless feeling and as irrationally sensitive and marginal creatures is the theme of Brian De Palma's *Carrie* and Tobe Hooper's *Poltergeist* (1982), for example. Male control is hardly threatened, or even nudged, by this sort of stuff. And Randall Kleiser's *Grease* (1978) makes girls unconsciously seductive. There is certainly a body of cinematic work addressing girls and girlhood without suggesting a clear critique of patriarchy. Yet even this relatively uncritical material has not been collected for serious cinematic study.

Girls Rule!—particularly now, in the arena of American popular culture. The echo-boomers—tweeners (girls aged 8–12) and their older counterparts, teens and young women—are now the most sought-after demographic of the entertainment industries. And why shouldn't they be, given the fact that, according to Teenage Research Unlimited, teens spend over $153 billion a year, with girls spending an average of $91 per week. Unlike their male counterparts, who dedicate their income to computers, video games, and extreme sports, female youth tend to gravitate toward two activities—shopping and going to the movies. They attend in groups, often viewing the same films many times.

In fact, girls have revived the recording industry and are responsible for making the soundtrack to *Titanic* the best-selling film soundtrack of all time; for the success of boy bands (Hanson, 'N Sync, 98 Degrees, Backstreet Boys); and for the resurgence of women in pop, rock, country, and rap music, with many of the stars teenagers themselves: Lil' Kim, Britney Spears, Brandi, Mandy Moore, LeAnn Rhimes, and Christina Aguilera. The publishing world has experienced an explosion of girl magazines and in book readership for several series—*The Baby Sitters Club* for younger girls; *Sweet Valley High* for those slightly older; and for teens the action series *Fearless* (about a girl who knows no fear), *The Last Vampire* (about a five-thousand-year-old creature of the night who enrolls in high school to seek out her nemesis), and books based on the popular television series "Buffy the Vampire Slayer."

The Warner Bros. Network television program "Buffy the Vampire Slayer" is but one of the teen-targeted shows currently dominating television programming. The night is ruled not only by Buffy and her team of young monster hunters, but also by aliens in "Roswell," genetically enhanced heroines like James Cameron's Dark Angel, spell-casting witches (Sabrina), and the more everyday youth of "Moesha," "Daria," "Felicity," and "Dawson's Creek." Even younger girls have their own televised heroines in animated shows like "The Powerpuff Girls" and "Jackie Chan's Adventures" (the martial arts star is accompanied on his quest by his niece Jade).

The most profound shift in mass media has been seen in the film industry. Never before have girls been featured so prominently in commercial films produced both within and without the Hollywood system. In 1995, the shift of the industry's primary demographic from young men to young women began with the success of Amy Heckerling's *Clueless*. The following year, *Scream* appeared, the film responsible for the resurrection of the horror genre. Girls flocked to the theaters in unprecedented numbers, the first time in film history that females outnumbered males in audiences of the genre. Horror was not the only genre affected. The trend spread to romance (*Here on Earth* [2000], *She's All That* [1999], *Romeo + Juliet* [1996], *Love & Basketball* [2000]), comedy (*The Opposite of Sex* [1998], *Slums of Beverly Hills* [1998], *Dick* [1999], and *The Wedding Singer* [1998]), melodrama (*Eve's Bayou* [1997] and *Tumbleweeds* [1999]), action (*Batman & Robin* [1997] and *The Professional* [1981]), and science fiction (*Lost in Space* [1998] and *Star Wars: The Phantom Menace* [1999]). Girls are even making their presence known in films not targeted at their age groups. We have seen the release of adult-oriented, critically acclaimed films in which girls play pivotal roles, placed in dramatized situations of conflict (*Felicia's Journey* [1997], *The Ice Storm* [1997], and *American Beauty* [1999]).

What is interesting about the presence of all these films high on the lists of popular, and thus lucrative, cultural artifacts is not the specific narrative treatment girls are accorded in them but simply the fact that there are so many famous, explicit, and wildly successful films about a social category that has somehow not succeeded in inspiring substantial analysis. This book, following in the tradition of scholars like Charles Eckert, James Snead, Susan Douglas, and Carol Clover, is a modest attempt to right the balance in this regard, intending as it does at least to turn a critical eye on the character of filmic girls, films intended for girl audiences, and the issues of girlhood.

We make no assertions that this book is comprehensive. It would be presumptuous, given the body of film about girls and the lack of critical material about it, to make the claim that this collection is in any way thoroughly representative—several volumes would be needed to accomplish this. But we believe we have collected interesting and provocative analyses of material that has not been seen before in genre terms, as substantively interrelated, or as significant to those who would draft an understanding of the patriarchal culture in which we live.

To make the book more useful, we chose, with one exception, to concentrate on readily available titles, contemporary films with cultural currency within North America. We regret that we were not able to include the rich world of documentary, specifically such compelling works as *Hide and Seek* (1996), *Girls Like Us* (1997), and *Who the Hell Is Juliette* (1997); groundbreaking independent features like *Thirteen* (1997) and *Alma's Rainbow* (1993); provocative shorts such as *Two Lies* (1989) and *Monique* (1990); and acclaimed films from outside North America—*The White Balloon* (1995), *Everyone's Child* (1996), *Ponette* (1998), and *Not One Less* (1999). Instead we offer a number of highly select essays providing new insights and information, reexaminations of a few classics, and analyses of the current trends that dominate American screens, both at the multiplex and in the home. Several essays, for instance, focus on films depicting the culture's recent radical transformations of girls' socialization and identity formation.

We have divided the book into three sections to look at three broad aspects of girls and girl culture—the maturation process; the struggle to either adhere to or revolt against archetypes; and issues of power, both real and fantasized. The first section, "Girls II Women," explores issues related to the trials and tribulations girls experience in the coming-of-age process. The first two essays revisit "old favorites," providing provocative new ways to look at these classics. The remainder of the section, arranged chronologically by the films' release dates, allows us to note the way notions of coming-of-age have shifted through the years. Domestic confinement is central to the paternalistic socialization of girls. Developing a sense of independence and finding a place of one's own is certainly an important aspect of the maturation process.

In the opening essay, Ina Rae Hark explores *The Wizard of Oz*, a girl's story that has become a national institution. Her analysis reveals how the mantra "There's no place like home" is established and substantiated in this film by the effacement of a reasonable alternative destination to which Dorothy, the home-leaver, might direct herself. "Kansas," she writes, "needs to be escaped."

In Murray Pomerance's chapter on *Shadow of a Doubt* (1943), Alfred Hitchcock is revealed to have employed a deeply critical and prescient vision of the plight of girls in capitalist culture. The invisibility of masculine privilege and the cloistering of girls' experiences are shown in this film to be complementary structural elements in a social mechanism that maintains girls' subservience and inequality.

Moving on to the 1950s and the development of teenagers as a youth group, Allison Whitney explores sexual development and the girl's threat to paternalism during that decade, as made explicit in *Gidget* (1957). Ostensibly a testament to girls' freedom and exploration of identity, this film nevertheless ultimately shows, as Whitney demonstrates, that Father knows best.

An even more cutting presentation of girls as figures shaped by male culture is found in some pre–Reagan era films of the early 1980s, namely *Foxes* (1980), *Little Darlings* (1980), and *Times Square* (1980). These are explored by Chuck Kleinhans with great attention to the details of the visual construction of girls' space. There may be no social forms more vital to girls as they come into adulthood than rebellion and girl bonding.

We gratefully reprint bell hooks's powerful examination of Spike Lee's *Crooklyn* (1994), perhaps the first American feature-length film to place an African American preteen female as a protagonist. Although *Crooklyn* successfully offers images of black experience and subjectivity rarely seen in mainstream cinema, hooks argues that counterhegemonic representations by Lee are constantly undermined by stock stereotypes, in this case the subjugated black female body celebrated as restorative.

In "Clueless in the Neocolonial World Order," Gayle Wald takes a critical look at the film that opened the floodgates for Hollywood's exploitation of girl culture and girls' purses. She asks—and deftly answers—questions about the place of girls in a vast transnational consumerist world shaped and controlled by the New Right. How does the perpetual "cluelessness" of the character of Cher function to represent American preoccupation with consumerism? Why embody political incapacity in a teenage girl? Has Cher's consciousness truly been raised by the end of the film, or is she comfortable in the state of coy ignorance, intellectual paralysis, and general stupidity that allows her to enjoy race and class privilege guilt free?

In "Girlfriends and Girl Power: Female Adolescence in Contemporary U.S. Cinema," Mary Celeste Kearney brings us up to date with an exploration of female coming-of-age in the contemporary teenpic, with specific attention to four films: *Girls Town* (1996), *Foxfire* (1996), *All Over Me* (1997), and *The Incredibly True Adventure of Two Girls in Love* (1995). Coming-of-age is no longer defined by the onset of menarche and heterosexual romance. As she explains, the films recognize cultural shifts that demonstrate a valuing of feminist themes and homosocial experiences.

While film invokes broad cultural themes and depicts social conditions in dramatic settings, it also often features precisely drawn and ideologically significant character types. We can thus see on-screen not only girls' worlds but also fascinating or problematic girls, girls who call attention to issues because of the way we see them live their lives. In the second section, "Cast Types," we begin with a serious study by Linda Dittmar that focuses on girlhood and gender as performative, especially in the case of Brandon Teena in *Boys Don't Cry* (1999). Invoked here is the possibility that what girls are and what they become is a matter of consistent, supported, and institutionalized appearance, as well as the possibility that to some, appearances can be not only unsettling but also threatening.

Kristen Hatch follows with an inquiry into the political and cultural implications of the regulation of imagery about adolescent girls and their sexuality, specifically the making and remaking of the film adaptations from Vladimir Nabokov's *Lolita*. Seen in the light of the earlier *Baby Doll* (1956), Kubrick's *Lolita* (1962) is shown as a film with a complex production history. Both films are explored as studies in the ambiguous and problematic domain of the girl-woman, or fille fatale.

Next, a fascinating case study of a broadly mediated and symbolically representative filmic girl—Rose in James Cameron's *Titanic*—is presented by Lori Liggett in her essay, "Maiden Voyage: From Edwardian Girl to Millennial Woman in *Titanic*." Liggett sees Rose's rejection of her Edwardian social identity as central to her development as a person and as a symbol of women's progress toward equality in the twentieth century.

Specific filmmakers often produce in the body of their work characteristic and repetitive portraits of types; John Hughes was one such filmmaker in Hollywood film of the 1980s. Ann De Vaney explores the girls in his work, especially in *Sixteen Candles* (1984), *Pretty in Pink* (1986), and *The Breakfast Club* (1985), drawing attention to his systematic narrative limitation of their possibilities for growth and development. The reinscription of Daddy's girl is seen as a central feature of Hughes's films, a feature that had the specific cachet of attracting the attention of, and producing enjoyment for, millions of teenage viewers who were not critical of films that openly confine the body of girls.

Kimberley Roberts considers the performance of Winona Ryder in *Heathers* (1989) as a harbinger of what she calls the "angry girl" genre of the 1990s—a body of film in which teenage girl anger is specifically indicated as being a weapon against gender crime. In addition, her analysis of the film *Freeway* (1996) provides a telling discussion on the complexity of youth in relation to both gender and class.

For too many filmmakers, the filmic girl is beautiful almost by definition; it is explicitly through her good looks that her powers are contained and limited. Timothy Shary gives specific attention to what our culture defines as her opposite, the adolescent female nerd-intellectual, as exemplified in films such as *She's Out of Control* (1989), *Welcome to the Dollhouse* (1995), and *She's All That* (1999). As depicted, the nerdliness of the nerdly girl, as Shary calls her, is shown to be as suitable a device for disempowering females in our culture as is the comeliness of the beauty queen. In film, girls' nerdliness is typically associated with intellectual power, and the message is thus systematically framed for young women that to think, argue, and excel analytically limits one's chances of success in the sexual marketplace.

The third section, "Beyond Innocence," brings together essays concerning films about girls who already possess or are in the process of obtaining knowledge about the underside of life. Instead of taking the role of the passive, demure female they empower themselves to act. Some come to the realization that their position in the family, and in society at large, contains their agency. For others their emergent power reels out of control, sometimes toward the wrong ends. Miriam Forman-Brunell's "Maternity, Murder, and Monsters: Legends of Babysitter Horror" begins this section, exploring the image of one of America's most prevalent girl icons. Forman-Brunell's examination concerns the character of the adolescent babysitter in a variety of film categories, including pornography and horror. The author suggests that filmic constructions of the babysitter attempt to contain conflict, change, and fears about serious economic, sexual, and social issues.

The complex and varied girls of Japanese animation and anime's ability to transgress both borders of nation and boundaries of gender are explored by Frances Gateward. She is especially interested in the phenomenon that places females as the central figures in male-dominated genres such as science fiction. Why are these fantastical tales, often culturally specific to their country of origin, so popular with girls and youth cultures throughout the world?

Though Christie Milliken's essay concerns not works of film but works of video, it is an important contribution because it focuses on an internationally recognized experimental artist, a teenager who has seized the power to construct her own images. "The Pixel Visions of Sadie Benning" explores the confessional, autobiographical world of Sadie Benning, showing the vital importance of her work for an understanding of adolescent female queerness. Milliken demonstrates how Benning's work is linked to both popular culture and the calculated anger of the Riot Grrrl movement.

The next two chapters explore aspects of filmic girls who kill, bringing to light the way films deal with both victimhood and lethality in girls. Steven Woodward introduces us to the field of murderous minors with his essay, "She's Murder: Pretty Poisons and Bad Seeds." In his examination of films that range from 1956 to 1994, Woodward traces the trajectory of the child killer, who has gone from the tantrum-throwing adolescent girl to the cold, calculating bloodletter who kills merely because she can. Ultimately, he presents the possibility that girlhood innocence is a construction of patriarchy itself and not a gift of nature.

Corinn Columpar's study of *Heavenly Creatures* (1994) shows that innocence is a mask and that girls need to love and bond with one another. As demonstrated here, when girls are systematically blocked by hegemonic patriarchal society, the result is a violent expression that is itself a subject of social control.

The book concludes with Cynthia Fuchs's exploration of the Spice Girls in music and on film. The essay is at once a keen critique of consumerist culture as it impacts girls' lives and sells girl culture to itself, and a revelation of the flashing, worldwide surfaces girl culture creates, exchanges, transforms, and repeats.

Although the idea of collecting essays about the representation of girls and girlhood in film is exciting and new, there is also something intrinsically amorphous and elusive about the project, since all around the world this new area of exploration is being subjected to fresh forms of creative and critical attention. We should be explicit, then, in saying there are many fascinating gaps in this study, including *Eve's Bayou* (1997) and its treatment of childhood sexual abuse; Pippi Longstocking and her relation to the Swedish national image or, for that matter, the intriguing 1960s film, *Elvira Madigan* (1967); Jodie Foster and her star image; and girls possessing supernatural powers in contemporary Korean cinema. We do think, however, that some of the most important critical and theoretical issues have been raised in these pages, by both established scholars and young scholars entering the field. We see this book as a spark to further inquiry, a call to see screen girls as a central and inescapable part of the global filmic construction that is shaping, mirroring, packaging, accommodating, and provoking our cultural life.

chapter 1

Moviegoing, "Home-leaving," and the Problematic Girl Protagonist of *The Wizard of Oz*

Ina Rae Hark

The Hollywood film industry during the classical period made its profits by persuading its audience to leave home to consume filmed narratives in movie theaters. The formulaic plots of many Hollywood genres similarly indulged both protagonists and spectators in what I would call the fantasy of home-leaving. This fantasy animates such archetypal plots as those found in myths and folktales and is a basic storytelling device for propelling popular narratives. As Vladimir Propp asserts, "The structure of the tale demands that the hero leave home at any cost" (37). However, because the film industry had always had to defend itself against guardians of morality who found moviegoing an activity that in some nebulous way threatened the sanctity of the home, Hollywood films were at pains to disguise how basic the home-leaving fantasy was to many of their narratives and the audience's consumption of them.

The transformation of L. Frank Baum's *The Wonderful Wizard of Oz* into the MGM musical fantasy *The Wizard of Oz* (1939) reveals how, when processed through the studio system, even a tale about a child's quest to return home underwent substantial revisions aimed at establishing the incontrovertibility of the proposition, "There's no place like home!" and severely censuring even a passing wish to find a better life somewhere over the rainbow. The film's repeated metaphorizations of Dorothy's adventure as a type of moviegoing make it a paradigm of how the classical Hollywood film neutralizes the home-leaving fantasy in its narratives even as it appeals to that fantasy to draw spectators to consume those self-same narratives. Its unease with its female protagonist reveals the significant role gender plays in effecting such neutralizations.

25

The anxiety with which the Baum story inspired MGM is revealed in the most radical change from book to film: having Dorothy dream the entire adventure in Oz. Noel Langley, who did the adaptation and the first complete drafts of the screenplay, insisted to production executives Mervyn LeRoy and Arthur Freed "that you cannot put fantastic people in strange places in front of an audience unless they have seen them as human beings first"; Langley praised Freed for abandoning his initial concept of having Dorothy fall asleep over a book, à la Carroll's Alice, and acquiescing to his belief that "it was important to have a prologue where you see the Scarecrow and the Tin Woodman as ordinary people" (Harmetz 34–35). An MGM press release attributed to director Victor Fleming voices these same sentiments: "Fantasy can have realism. In fact, it must have realism if it is to be put on the screen as all-family entertainment" (MGM News 2).

This sounds astonishing at first. Films had often represented fantastic characters in strange places, for example, *Dracula* (1931), *King Kong* (1933), *The Bride of Frankenstein* (1935), and *The Ghost Goes West* (1936). Certainly Disney's *Snow White and the Seven Dwarfs*, the 1937 smash that had encouraged L. B. Mayer to go after the rights to *The Wonderful Wizard* in hope of achieving similar success, had done so. But Snow White lived from the outset in a fairy-tale kingdom, a place whose woods might very well house seven little men, a stepmother-turned-wicked witch, and a handsome prince. Dorothy, on the other hand, lived on a farm in contemporary Kansas, and she was not a cartoon character. For the filmmakers to assert, as Baum does, that a natural force like a cyclone could render Kansas and Oz geographically contiguous and diegetically continuous apparently struck them as akin to saying that a spectator could physically penetrate the movie screen and live within its narrative space. Indeed entering into a film is, symbolically, the very phenomenon they have Dorothy's subconscious manufacture to satisfy her desire to "find a place where there isn't any trouble"—and the very fantasy the film is determined to discredit. Therefore Dorothy's initial conviction upon awakening that she has just come back from "a really, truly live place" must fade. The return to monochrome at the end of the film is only one of several moves the producers make to contain what Leo Braudy notes as the aesthetically problematic "heightened reality of color," the Technicolor that all the original release advertising made a major selling point and through which the audience as well as Dorothy experiences the supposedly illusory Oz (61).

That films resemble dreams had long been a truism, both of film theory and of industry hype about the Hollywood dream factory. The *mise-en-scène* of *The Wizard of Oz* promotes this message throughout, or, more particularly, its corollary that dreams resemble films. A metonym for the movie screen, a window frame blown loose, strikes the blow that sends Dorothy to Oz by depriving her of consciousness. While the house is still inside the cyclone, she views images of her neighbors (including Miss Gulch transforming herself into the Wicked Witch) rear-projected behind another window/screen. The first view of Oz and Technicolor similarly appears through the door frame. The Emerald City is tricked out like a metropolitan movie palace, with a uniformed staff member in a booth to grant entrance. The passage from the wider city into the Wizard's presence suggests going from a crowded lobby, through auditorium doors, and down a darkened aisle. The Wizard creates his identity by projecting his image onto a dais that looks like the seat of a mighty Wurlitzer. He augments his ferocity by using sound and visual effects; the apparatus operated by the "man behind the curtain," which is the origin of these effects, strongly resembles the machinery in a projection booth.

Even Baum's designation of Oz's ruler as a wizard plays into the cinematic analogy. Thomas Edison, head of the first American corporation to achieve commercial dominance in the development and marketing of the cinematic apparatus and films to feed it, was nicknamed the "Wizard of Menlo Park." Skilled film technology is still frequently called "wizardry," as in "special effects wizardry." The 1939 publicists played up this connection. Columnist Irving Hoffman in the *Hollywood Reporter* referred to the film's production under the supervision of "Mervyn LeRoy, the Wizard of Metroz" (11). Several sample advertisements sent by the studio to exhibitors contained the tag lines: "A Whiz of a Wiz he Iz! Yet, with all his magic, the Old Wizard of Oz himself couldn't have worked the wonders here spread before you on the screen!" and "From the Wizards of Hollywood! . . . A movie miracle" (MGM News 4–5).

By positing Baum's really, truly live Oz as nothing but a dream, the film makes sure there's no place like home by denying that there exists any other place to which Dorothy could go. Although *The Wizard of Oz* adheres to the usual illusionism of classical Hollywood cinematic style to efface the effects of its narration and suture the spectator, to the discerning eye it simultaneously lays bare the artifice of the cinematic apparatus. Don't be seduced by Oz, it seems to say, Oz is only a movie. Underlying this "movieization" of the land of Oz is the strategy for neutralizing Dorothy's home-leaving fantasy, even though that fantasy does not at first appear to be present in *The Wonderful Wizard*. Baum's Dorothy has never articulated a desire to leave home before the cyclone sweeps her off to Oz. Yet Kansas, as the author describes its unrelieved grayness and joylessness, needs to be escaped. The Scarecrow, despite his lack of brains, intuits this immediately and asks Dorothy why she "should wish to leave this beautiful country and go back to the dry, gray place you call Kansas" (25). She responds that people of flesh and blood prefer home, "[n]o matter how dreary and gray," to anywhere else, "be it ever so beautiful."[1] Nevertheless, the journey home leads her not to retrace the distance between Kansas and Oz but to strike out on a quest, first to find the Wizard and then to conquer the Wicked Witch of the West at his behest. By compelling her to travel further away from Kansas in order to return there, Dorothy's odyssey indulges the home-leaving fantasy she denies harboring.

This activity by a female protagonist in turn raises the question of how gender differences mark fairy-tale structures and how Hollywood narratives utilize them to manage the home-leaving fantasy. Many commentators have noted that Baum's Dorothy is a girl thrust into narrative situations generally reserved for boys. Osmond Beckwith declares, "Sociologically viewed, the Oz myth as Baum created it can be considered a vast transvaluation of juvenile romantic values. Boys' adventures become girls' adventures" (243). Comparing Dorothy with Huckleberry Finn, Douglas McReynolds and Barbara Lips insist that "The search for Aunt Em is no less exciting, no less heroic, and no less dangerous than the escape from Aunt Sally: and if we will look for a usable past, for a tradition in which girls share equally with boys in the pursuit of some elusive American dream, we have to take seriously *The Wizard of Oz*" (88). In her meditation on *The Wizard of Oz* as a "mother-romance," Bonnie Friedman observes: "The boy's coming-of-age story is about leaving home to save the world. The girl's coming-of-age story is about relinquishing the world beyond home" (9). Charles Rzepka also makes this comparison: "[Dorothy] is, for Americans, the nearest female equivalent to Huck Finn" (63). Yet Dorothy's gender inevitably intervenes, requiring her to revert to dependent-child status at the end. Rzepka continues, "But she is never allowed to grow up. . . . Unlike Huck, however, and unlike the quintessential American anti-heroes, who also sought to throw off the restrictive middle-class conventions of 19th-century American society, she does not have the option of 'lighting out for the territories.' She not only can, but must go home" (63). In American home-leaving narratives, both literary and cinematic, woman as protagonist is rare; woman as protagonist who escapes either redomestication or ruin is rarer still.

Women more usually enter such narratives, if at all, to stand for the possibility of a domestic site into which wandering men can be reincorporated. If women do travel, they do so to disseminate domesticity, not escape it. "The female position, produced as the result of narrativization," according to Teresa de Lauretis, "is the figure of narrative closure, the narrative image in which the film, as Heath says 'comes together' " (140). Until that closure, woman is simply the obstacle or space through which the male subject of narrative discourse moves (de Lauretis 143).

For this reason, the screenwriters had to portray Oz, the space Dorothy moves through as female subject, as impossible for any Kansas farm girl truly to occupy or remain in. So they make Oz a dream that Dorothy experiences as if it were a movie she simultaneously watches and stars in. This dream/film serves to reinforce an already learned lesson. In the interpolated frame story Dorothy has already desired to leave home, run away, learned the error of her ways from a kindly father figure, returned repentant, and been punished by being shut out from shelter during a storm and then hit on the head by a flying window frame. But even this rebuke does not suffice. In her dream state she undergoes more perils and endlessly deferred satisfaction of her yearning to return to Kansas until she can successfully recite the catechism of home-for-woman: "I'm not going to leave here, ever, ever, again. Oh, Auntie Em, there's no place like home." Not only must she want to return, but she must repress any future desire to leave. While actual dreams express repressed fantasies through their coded dreamwork, the Oz dream becomes an educational film to serve as an instrument of this continued repression of Dorothy's home-leaving fantasy. Thus the film turns Baum's fairy tale into a fable, in Bruno Bettelheim's terms a transformation from a story that "leaves all decisions up to us, including whether we wish to make any at all," to one that "explicitly states a moral truth: there is no hidden meaning, nothing is left to our imagination" (42–43).

Lest the audience sympathize with Dorothy's need to run away to protect Toto's life and so reject this moral truth, the screenplay makes clear that a more generalized desire for escape stirs her. Her conversation with Professor Marvel reveals a dangerous preexisting inclination against the domestic site. The professor "reads" in his crystal ball a generic litany of the complaints of the frustrated adolescent: "They don't understand you at home. They don't appreciate you. You want to see other lands, big cities, big mountains, big oceans." Dorothy never adds the threat of Miss Gulch to his diagnosis; she immediately responds with heartfelt sincerity: "It's just like you could read what's inside of me." Dorothy's returning to Aunt Em will resolve the Toto problem one way or another. A full eradication of the home-leaving fantasy, however, requires the lessons of the Oz dream. The filmmakers convey these lessons by inscribing the yearning for home into the picture "by design . . . with a hatchet," as Aljean Harmetz wryly observes in her account of the making of *The Wizard of Oz* (298). Chief wielder of this hatchet, according to Harmetz, was scenarist Florence Ryerson, who, appropriately, had a prior reputation as being "good at writing warm stories for women" (47).

Under cover of the cultural code of "home," the film works, as so many classical narratives do, to deny subjectivity to woman as character and to identify her with the site of domesticity. The narrative's overinsistence on the desirability of home, however, reveals that desirability as an ideological construct far more explicitly than many other film narratives reveal their ideological constructions. The events created for the purpose of stigmatizing Dorothy's desire to go over the rainbow fail to be assimilated into the narrative structures retained from the book; the closure attained in the Oz sequence breaks open in the concluding Kansas scene.[2] The inconsistencies and contradictions within a script processed through ten writers and four directors provide ample sites for ideological rupture.

This rupture is most evident when the film, attempting a seamless inscription of Dorothy into woman's domestic space, and concomitantly tracing the destruction of the woman, Miss Gulch/ the Wicked Witch, who has usurped masculine space—the arena of the powerful gaze and patriarchal law—leaves that masculine space unoccupied. While some earlier versions of the script remedy that lack—having the Cowardly Lion be an enchanted warrior or having the Wizard's Kansas counterpart assure Dorothy that he will prevent the Sheriff from taking Toto (see Harmetz 35, 45)—in the filmed version it remains very present.

As the Kansas sequence unfolds at the beginning of *The Wizard of Oz*, it establishes the Gales' farm as home to four men who exercise no power. Uncle Henry defers all decisions to Aunt Em. Although Em performs such maternal-domestic functions as protecting chicks whose incubator has failed and baking crullers for everyone, she also bosses around the three farmhands she labels as "shiftless."[3] But even her power is inconsequential compared to that of Miss Gulch, who "owns half the county" and controls the patriarchal institutions like the bank and the Sheriff's office. While a long tradition of what Ann Kaplan calls "domestic feminism" had privileged maternal power within the boundaries of the home, in *The Wizard of Oz* the lack of a public, male-dominated agency for disseminating the mother's "highest morality" throughout the institutions of society leaves this domestic unit vulnerable to external invasion by a distinctly non-motherly woman who has usurped the male position (119). Em gives as her two reasons for not preventing Miss Gulch from taking Toto as "We can't go against the law," and that "being a Christian woman" she cannot tell Miss Gulch what she has been thinking of her for twenty-three years.

This failure of domestic female power forces Dorothy to run away from home if she is to protect her symbolic child, Toto. Unwilling to authorize her likewise adopting a male strategy (leaving home) to counter the threat posed by Miss Gulch's manipulation of patriarchal power, the filmmakers utilize the Oz "movie" to recount the "seducing" of Dorothy "into femininity," (in De Lauretis's apt formulation [137]) and the empowerment of a trio of powerless men who will obtain the falsely assumed patriarchal authority of Gulch's Ozian double, the Wicked Witch of the West, once Dorothy, as avatar of domesticity, has destroyed her.

Just as men posed no threat to Miss Gulch's authority, the Wicked Witch has little difficulty in dominating them either. She possesses a powerful gaze through a crystal ball that broadcasts images occurring at considerable distances. She commands all-male troops of flying monkeys and Winkies. Until she can be castrated—"Bring me the broomstick of the Wicked Witch of the West"—the Wizard's emblems of authority are empty show. Therefore, those who seek to challenge her from a masculine position find the Wicked Witch invincible. She is, however, susceptible to attacks from the female, domestic position. In Oz, the home gives woman power, and women who threaten or disregard it do so at their peril, as Dorothy learns instantly upon arrival when her house crushes the Wicked Witch of the East, sister to the Wicked Witch of the West. And the surviving Wicked Witch acknowledges a similar vulnerability with her visible apprehension at the advice of Glinda, the Good Witch of the South, to take care that someone doesn't drop a house on her, too.

If part of Dorothy's education in Oz serves to reconcile her to Aunt Em and the power of the maternal-domestic, it also supplies a more patriarchically compatible image of woman's public face to replace Miss Gulch's aggressive male masquerade. It does so through Glinda, the one individualized Oz character who does not have a double in Kansas.[4] This break in the detailed grounding of Dorothy's dream in events, persons, phrases, and gestures she (and the audience) experienced directly preceding the cyclone is crucial to the film's ideology. Glinda signifies the femininity that Kansas lacks. Adorned in sequin-bedecked layers of chiffon, a glittering headdress, flowing Pre-Raphaelite waves of hair, and kewpie-doll makeup, she exemplifies the "to-be-looked-at-ness" Laura Mulvey defines as projected by the male gaze onto the female figure (203). Further, Billie Burke brings to the role her high-pitched infantile voice, as well as her legacy of playing "addled matrons—what she called 'my silly women'—who had their basis in her own personality" (Harmetz 127) and of being the widow of Florenz Ziegfeld, whose "erotic spectacle" Mulvey specifically designates as an instance of using "Woman displayed as sexual object" as a leitmotif (203). Dorothy's assumption that witches must be old and ugly reveals a Kansas-derived equation of womanhood with sterility and lack of attractiveness. In Oz all women are assumed to be witches—"Are you a good witch or a bad witch?"—but a "good" one can, and should, look like a showgirl.[5] Dorothy's makeover in the Emerald City accordingly moves her coiffure and cosmetics in the direction of Glinda's style.

While Dorothy is clearing out masculine space by dispatching the usurping Wicked Witches through her assumption of traditional female positions, she is simultaneously liberating her three male companions from their literal or figurative paralyses and setting them up to move into that now unoccupied territory. While Dorothy must renounce home-leaving as a solution to her problems, the film advocates it as the proper course for empowering her male comrades. During their travels down the Yellow Brick Road, the Scarecrow, Tin Man, and Cowardly Lion gradually discover in themselves the very qualities, necessary for their full inscription into patriarchy, in which they believed themselves deficient. It only remains for the Wizard to supply proper signifiers to translate the Scarecrow's oft-demonstrated practicality into "a Brain"; the Tin

Man's sentimental weepiness into "a Heart"; and the Lion's perseverance despite his fears as "Courage." While Baum diagnosed their problem as a lack of self-confidence, so that the characters were to internalize the Wizard's signifying placebos, the film more cynically affirms that only outward and visible signs—a diploma, a testimonial, and a medal—easily readable by the wider community of discourse, can activate the psychological signifieds. Having now entered into the Symbolic Order, Dorothy's three companions are qualified to become joint rulers of Oz, taking over from both the humbug patriarch, the Wizard, and the liquidated and displaced female annexer of patriarchal authority, the Wicked Witch of the West.

When the men demand that the Wizard fulfill Dorothy's wishes next, she immediately replies, "Oh, I don't think there's anything in that black bag for me." She has learned well her lesson that women are denied access to the Symbolic Order and the role of desiring subject. That is the significance of what she tells Glinda, the insight "she had to find . . . out for herself": "It's that if I ever go looking for my heart's desire again, I won't look any farther than my own back yard, because if it isn't there, I never really lost it to begin with." The contorted syntax foregrounds the ideology. We might expect the lesson to be that one will never have to look beyond one's own backyard in order to satisfy desire. But Dorothy, as woman, must internalize the message that absence of desire ("I never really lost it") is her lot: Friedman's apt phrase for that stigmatized female, the Wicked Witch, is "a woman who wants" (23). In keeping with the tendency of narrative toward the "territorialization of women" (de Lauretis 155), she accepts her homology with place and defines that place as home. Armed with the mantra "There's no place like home," she can activate the dormant power she has "always had" to return to Kansas.

As far as the Oz sequence goes, the film accomplishes its ends in placing woman where it wants her. It is when Dorothy reawakens in Kansas that the film's ideological project stutters. As all the characters converge at her bedside, Miss Gulch is noticeably absent. But has her threat vanished? If she returns to take Toto, can the newly energized domestic power of Aunt Em and Dorothy repel her, even though it failed in that task earlier? Will any of the men present defy her and evict her from the masculine position she has usurped? Or perhaps her very absence indicates the eradication of female pretenses to the male position as a result of Dorothy's realization that there's no place like home? When I saw the film as a child, I assumed that a real house had fallen on Miss Gulch as she rode her bicycle home in the storm, but this conclusion reflects my own desire for ideological closure as much as any provided by the film text. Leaving Miss Gulch's space vacant in the Kansas of the finale and thus opening that vacancy to such varied readings ruptures the overdetermined ideology of home as safe haven the film uses to contain Dorothy securely within the female position.

Had MGM persuaded 20th Century Fox to loan out Shirley Temple to play Dorothy, the ideological strain would have shown less. The spunky ten-year-old had signified childishness and asexuality in her films. She could without dissonance have played a Dorothy awakening to proclaim herself forever the homebound child. Sixteen-year-old Judy Garland, with her sexually charged vulnerability dominating the performance, could not.

The fairy-tale type Baum had Americanized was the one in which the "prepubertal" child—his Dorothy is about six years old—overcomes separation anxiety but is not yet ready to live apart from parental figures. Bruno Bettelheim uses "Hansel and Gretel" to exemplify this type. On the other hand, "Snow White," the basis for the Disney film whose success Mayer was trying to emulate, concerns a young girl's passage through the Oedipal stage, her resolution of the conflict with the mother over the father's affections, and her repositioning as the object of acceptable male desire. The filmmakers' alteration of Baum's silver slippers to menstrually suggestive ruby ones, for the sake of the Technicolor process, contributes further to our reading the film's narrative as a description of its heroine's emergence into womanhood. Thus Garland's Dorothy makes a perfect Snow White; we wait for her prince to come, perhaps Mickey Rooney to stroll by as, say, Zeke's nephew, promising future romance on the farm. (The two performed together in the live stage show that accompanied the film's initial release in New York.) Likewise, the narrative conventions a spectator brings to *The Wizard of Oz* suggest that the Dorothy of the dream narrative should marry the Scarecrow, the new ruler whom she will miss most of all. Of course social—and biological—conventions render that impossible; such a union would retroactively arouse perverse imaginings about the long nights along the Yellow Brick Road. Yet after the film has spent so much time bringing Dorothy through puberty, its denial that her escape from her childhood home, and the maturation it signifies, ever took place is an even more perverse resolution.

This diegetic imbalance resurfaces in the film text's parallel project of situating Dorothy as both female spectator and object of the male gaze, where once again the absence of qualified candidates for the male position undermines the film's inscription of Dorothy into femininity. The film begins with Dorothy gazing anxiously behind her down an empty country road, a space she correctly fears Miss Gulch will soon fill. In both Kansas and Oz, close-ups of Dorothy frequently show her raptly looking up at the sky—or persons framed against it—projecting "the image of the longing, overinvolved female spectator" Mary Ann Doane discerns in Cecilia, the 1930s working-class woman obsessed with the movies whom Mia Farrow portrays in Woody Allen's 1985 *The Purple Rose of Cairo* (2). Garland also frequently holds her hands above her waist, giving the character an appearance of defensive apprehension. (While the necessity to carry the basket over her arm dictates some of these poses, Garland appears ready to ward off blows when not so encumbered as well.) Her gaze, therefore, does not invite spectatorial identification. Significantly, she is required to relinquish even this powerless mode of seeing in order to regain the domestic site: as well as clicking her heels together and repeating to herself, "There's no place like home," she must close her eyes.

Any male matched with Dorothy in shot/reverse shot should therefore easily become the relay for the look of the spectator in the diegesis. But there is amazingly little shot/reverse shot matching in the film. Dorothy's close-up gazings mostly receive in reply medium shots of her companions, or close-ups of rainbows, or Toto—he mediates her exchange of looks with the Scarecrow at their first meeting, for example. The only two characters who consistently match her gaze are the Wicked Witch, whose usurpation of this as well as all other masculine positions it is the narrative's main purpose to remedy, and the various characters played by Frank Morgan. Textually the film does identify Morgan (in both the Professor Marvel and Wizard roles) as the bearer of the look and articulator of the Law of the Father. But the narrative so consistently links him to fraud and connivance that this identification hardly solidifies the concept of legitimate patriarchal authority. Having succeeded in the all-too-familiar operations of stripping the female position of subjectivity and spectatorial power, the film comes up short on the masculine side of the binary.

It is only fortuitous that in recasting Baum the filmmakers neglected to bring off their masculinist project completely. Minor changes in the Kansas scenario or in editing the scenes involving

Dorothy and her companions could have smoothed over its gender ideology as so many other classical Hollywood narratives do. But gender issues aside, the additional containment strategy of using moviegoing as an analogy through which to stigmatize Dorothy's home-leaving fantasy would still have doomed the film's wider ideology of domesticity to inevitable rupture. Once the shape of the narrative was set at the end of the long process of scripting, shooting, and editing, *The Wizard of Oz* passed from being a story in the making to being a product for marketing and consumption. Successful sale of any 1930s cinematic commodity depended on arousing the desire to leave home for the movie theater in as many moviegoers as possible. There is no way out of the contradiction of enticing patrons to a movie that informs them that staying home (Kansas) is always preferable to going to the movies (Oz).

A survey of the advertisements for the film reveals the magnitude of that contradiction. They do not sell the entire *Wizard of Oz* with its Kansas bookends; they sell the Oz film within the film. They tempt the consumer with all those features of the dream world that the narrative marks as unreal and necessary to reject: "glorious Technicolor," "Gaiety . . . Glory . . . Glamour," the massive technical achievement that resulted in the spectacle of Oz. One busy lobby card invites the spectator to assume Dorothy's subject position: "Don magic red slippers (presented by the beloved Good Witch), whirl from the Everyday with Dorothy and Toto, the wonder dog—first exciting stop . . . Munchkinland." Nowhere on this card, or in any of the other ads, do we learn that the film's theme is "There's no place like home," that it contains monochrome sequences, or that it ends, not in the marvelous Emerald City, but in the dreary Kansas Dorothy has never really left. And when this card gives the credits for Ray Bolger, Jack Haley, Bert Lahr, Margaret Hamilton, and others, it lists their Oz identities, not the Kansas ones the end credits insist on. Many factors doubtless contributed to *The Wizard of Oz*'s net loss of a million dollars during a first release that saw it do phenomenal opening business in the Emerald City–style urban movie palaces only to "slow in the hinterlands and actually r[u]n out of steam" in the Kansases of the nation (Schatz 268).

It is difficult to imagine that the explicit equating of moviegoing with a censured antidomesticity did not also contribute to the film's initial lack of success. The solution to this problem was ultimately found in new technology for the domestic consumption of cinematic narratives. Taking in the narrative of Dorothy's fantasy, viewers comfortably ensconced in their living rooms would not be guilty of Dorothy's sin—thinking that there are better alternatives beyond their own backyards. In other words, for unproblematic consumption of *The Wizard of Oz*, there's no place like home, and, indeed, the film became a virtual icon of the Hollywood canon, alluded to in countless succeeding films, only after it began showing annually on television in 1956: that is, after it became possible to view it without leaving home to do so.

Notes

1. Although this passage does appear in the novel, and Baum's Dorothy does utter the last line, "And oh, Aunt Em! I'm so glad to be at home again!" (132), the "no place like home" theme does not have the centrality for Baum that it does for the filmmakers. For instance, Dorothy does not have to pass a catechism on the subject before she can get the silver shoes to carry her back to Kansas.
2. For a more thorough survey of the changes from novel to film than space permits here, see Street, "Wonderful Wiz."
3. Em's character underwent a series of revisions from that of a wicked stepmother type, who originally was the one to threaten Toto, to a more maternal, nurturing figure. But contradictory traces of her various selves remain in the finished film.
4. Baum's Witch of the North is a little old woman with white hair, a face "covered with wrinkles," and a stiff gait (12). Clearly the actress playing Aunt Em could have doubled for her. The filmmakers, however, chose to combine her identity with that of Baum's Glinda, the Good Witch of the South, and give her Glinda's appearance as "both beautiful and young. . . . Her hair was a rich red in color and fell in flowing ringlets over her shoulders" (128).
5. Mervyn LeRoy had had the idea to cast Gale Sondergaard as a glamorous "fallen woman" Wicked Witch, but he later told her that "the people around me" insisted on an "ugly, hateful witch" to conform to children's expectations (Harmetz 123). Margaret Hamilton once told an interviewer that L. B. Mayer himself was the one to insist on the equivalence of wickedness and unattractiveness.

Works Cited

Baum, L. Frank. 1983. *The Wonderful Wizard of Oz.* In *The Wizard of Oz. The Critical Heritage Series,* ed. Michael Patrick Hearn, 7–132. New York: Schocken.

Beckwith, Osmond. 1983. "The Oddness of Oz." In *The Wizard of Oz. The Critical Heritage Series*, ed. Michael Patrick Hearn, 233–46. New York: Schocken.

Bettelheim, Bruno. 1976. *The Uses of Enchantment.* New York: Knopf.

Braudy, Leo. 1976. *The World in a Frame: What We See in Films.* Chicago: University of Chicago Press.

de Lauretis, Teresa. 1984. *Alice Doesn't: Feminism, Semiotics, Cinema.* Bloomington: Indiana University Press.

Doane, Mary Ann. 1987. *The Desire to Desire: The Woman's Film of the 1940s.* Bloomington: Indiana University Press.

Friedman, Bonnie. 1996. "Relinquishing Oz: Every Girl's Anti-Adventure Story." *Michigan Quarterly Review* 8 (winter): 9–28.

Harmetz, Aljean. 1977. *The Making of The Wizard of Oz.* New York: Knopf.

Hoffman, Irving. 1939. "Tales of Hoffman." *The Hollywood Reporter*, 28 June: 11.

Kaplan, E. Ann. 1987. "Mothering, Feminism and Representation: the Maternal in Melodrama and the Woman's Film, 1910–1940." In *Home Is Where the Heart Is*, ed. Christine Gledhill. London: British Film Institute.

McReynolds, Douglas J., and Barbara J. Lips. 1986. "A Girl in the Game: *The Wizard of Oz* as Analog for the Female Experience in America." *North Dakota Quarterly* 54 (spring): 87–93.

MGM Studio News. 1939. 14 August: 2–7.

Mulvey, Laura. 1986. "Visual Pleasure and Narrative Cinema." In *Narrative, Apparatus, Ideology: A Film Theory Reader*, ed. Philip Rosen, 198–209. New York: Columbia University Press.

Propp, Vladimir. 1968. *Morphology of the Folktale.* Trans. Laurence Scott. 2nd ed. Austin: University of Texas Press.

Rzepka, Charles. 1987. " 'If I Can Make It There': Oz's Emerald City and the New Woman." *Studies in Popular Culture* 10, no. 2: 54–66.

Schatz, Thomas. 1988. *The Genius of the System: Hollywood Filmmaking in the Studio Era.* New York: Pantheon.

Street, Douglas. 1984. "The Wonderful Wiz That Was: The Curious Transformation of *The Wizard of Oz.*" *Kansas Quarterly*, 16 (summer): 91–98.

chapter 2

"Don't understand, my own darling": The Girl Grows Up in *Shadow of a Doubt*

Murray Pomerance

Hitchcock's women, in particular, have been the subject of much unperceptive comment, some observers claiming (like Mulvey) he was misogynist, some (like Modleski) that he was feminist, some like Wood, to some extent) that he was both. He has been shown to have been obsessed with a certain physical type; to have fallen in love with his leading actresses; and to have been interested sensually and philosophically in the workings of female sexuality and the experience of women. By "women," critics and viewers alike have intended to mean: Grace Kelly, Ingrid Bergman, Eva Marie Saint, Janet Leigh, 'Tippi' Hedren, Joan Fontaine, or Kim Novak.

This focus on (obsession with) women has been attributed frequently to biographical forces. Alfred Hitchcock's biographer Donald Spoto, himself never a man entirely freed of opinion, gives an apt enough description of the filmmaker's childhood as a time of emotional siege, filled with penchants and fastidious curiosity, and, most illuminating for the context that supports the present analysis, marked by withdrawal from boys. He spent time in the arms of his loving mother, for whom he would pine imaginatively upon her absence; at St. Ignatius School, where he first tasted the arcane delicacies of Jesuit education; and at work as a diligent young man at Henley Telegraph and Cable Company. Through all of this, it seems to the reader of *The Dark Side of Genius*, the other young men who surrounded him, threw him jibes, and called him Cocky, did not succeed in offering sufficient benisons of male friendship to provoke the formation of the sorts of bonds that might forbid or alienate the softer touches of female warmth. (I suspect these boys were like the ones in my own childhood, busy, like little Roger [Charles Bates] in

39

Shadow of a Doubt, counting the number of steps from here to the drugstore and back [649].) It could be argued then that Hitchcock had an affinity for girls; and it could be surmised in general that affinity breeds understanding. Such a syllogism, salient and stimulating at once, I take to be one aspect of the underframe of François Truffaut's including in his *Hitchcock,* on a page adjacent to the *Los Angeles Times'* report of Hitchcock's death, a portrait of the filmmaker in drag.

While Hitchcock's sexuality, sexual morality, and sexual politics have been the subject of some general discussion (see at least Douchet; Rothman; Chabrol; and Corber), and while his film plots have been treated in real—if misleading—depth as framings of grown "girls" unable to fully be and act as women (to name only five, Constance Peterson, Marnie Edgar, Lisa Fremont, Melanie Daniels, and 'Madeleine Elster' [see Modleski, Sterritt, and Paglia), very little attention has been given to the explicit presence of girls *per se* in Hitchcock films. There is, to be sure, not such a small number of straightforward girl characters to look at; and if frequently enough these characters appear only briefly, we may find they nevertheless contribute overwhelmingly to the meanings of the films. Consider Pat Martin (Priscilla Lane) and also the seamy Siamese twin girls/women (Jeanne and Lynn Romer) in *Saboteur* (1942)—the former triggers the complication of the plot by refusing to trustingly respect her blind father's wisdom, the latter threaten doom for the hero and heroine at a crucial moment because of their unbridled cupidinousness); or the gabby irresponsible vacationing college girls in *The Lady Vanishes* (1938) (Margaret Lockwood, Googie Withers, and Sally Stewart); or the victimized Barbara Morton (Patricia Hitchcock) in *Strangers on a Train* (1951); or David Kentley's fiancée Janet (Joan Chandler) in *Rope* (1948), a multifaceted foil for the two murderers and a constant reminder of the banality and sweetness of their absent victim; or the two young French Canadian babysitters in *I Confess* (1953) (theirs is the witnessing, the surveillance, upon which the conviction of Father Logan depends); or the nymphomaniac Mary Carmichael (Rhonda Fleming) in *Spellbound* (1945) (a first clue to the off-centeredness of Green Manors); or Cathy Brenner (Veronica Cartwright) in *The Birds* (1963) (the figure for whose benefit all of the plot is set in place); or the unnamed girl studying the painting of Carlotta Valdes in Gallery 6 of the Palace of the Legion of Honor in *Vertigo* (1958) (*for the viewer* the first incontrovertible sign in the film of the circularity of time); or the jazz dancer Miss Torso (Georgine

Darcy) in *Rear Window* (1954) (our perduring clue to the darker side of "Jeff" Jefferies's personality); or Eve Gill (Jane Wyman) in *Stage Fright* (1950); or wiry Danielle Foussard (Brigitte Auber) in *To Catch a Thief* (1955) (the girl as professional); or Dr. Koska's charming, but bizarre and riddling daughter, in *Torn Curtain* (1966). There is the kidnapped Betty Lawrence (Nova Pilbeam) in the original *Man Who Knew Too Much* (1934), and in the 1956 remake there are the two girls in the lobby of the Albert Hall, gawking at (and drawing our attention to) the visiting prime minister as he walks up the stairway to his death. There is the unnamed new Mrs. de Winter in *Rebecca* (1940), quintessentially a girl in order that she may be quintessentially vulnerable.

Shadow of a Doubt (1943), however, is all but a treatise on girlhood and the vulnerabilities associated with it in the frame of the heterosexist and patriarchist hegemony of America in the 1940s. While no synopsis of Hitchcock does his work any real justice, this condensation of the story will assist the reader who is unfamiliar with the film:

> In order to escape a pair of investigators who are tailing him, Charlie Oakley (Joseph Cotten) flees westward to his older sister's family in Santa Rosa, California, where he is welcomed with open arms by the entire community. Particularly enchanted by him is an adoring niece (Teresa Wright), named after her uncle and living in the flush of adolescent girlhood. Gradually she begins to suspect that her beloved Uncle Charlie may be wanted by the police for a series of widow killings. Her suspicions are echoed by a young and handsome detective (MacDonald Carey). Meanwhile, back East, another suspect is arrested and the inquiry is officially closed.
>
> But now aware of young Charlie's serious doubts about him, Uncle Charlie twice tries to murder her in the house. She threatens to reveal what she knows if he does not leave town, and finally steps aboard the train for New York with him to say goodbye. He holds her until the train is moving and struggles to push her onto the tracks. He falls instead and is crushed to death by a passing train. The townsfolk pay respectful tribute to him at his funeral, and certainty of his guilt remains a secret bond between young Charlie and her detective suitor.

This film, then, is a tale of a sensitive and philosophical girl, Charlie Newton, growing up in a middle-class family and encountering for the first time the perplexing and chilling syndrome of malevolence, duplicity, and societal *charaderie.* As we meet her she is still innocent enough, for example, not only to meditate on the state of her soul and the soul of her family—"We're in a terrible rut"—but to be anxious about the soul's prospects in the shadow of doubt that is the vagary of contemporary civilization: "How can you talk about money when I'm talking about souls. We eat and sleep and that's about all. We don't even have any real conversations."

This is no anticommercialist diatribe but a setting of commercial concerns in a higher and broader context; and Charlie's characteristic *innocence*, far more than a failure to understand or closing off of sight, is a refusal and failure to surrender moral concerns in the face of her father's raises from the bank, and of the "dinner, dishes, and bed" that are all her mother has to look forward to. It is, of course, a particular and productive *bed* Charlie is acknowledging: conjugal, yet also toilsome, since in it life is made and in it, too, the exertions of the well-socialized, highly patriarchalized, commercial commitments of the day are slept away in recuperating dreams.

Young Charlie is not herself the nexus of *Shadow of a Doubt*, however. In the most central heart of darkness of this film, organizing and generating much of the bizarre characterization and many turns of the coiling story that catches and implicates Charlie, reside, interpenetrate, and confront one another two deeply strange images that carry us far outside the entrapping shell of the Newton family even as they reflect, and in many ways explain, its structural form: the cloistered girl and the invisible man.

The first image is of a creature profoundly fascinating to us, even as she fails spectacularly to fascinate herself. She is also in some ways perfectly Hitchcockian—in the precise sense of being, if not like typical characters in typical Hitchcock films then like "Hitchcock" himself (that character revealed to us through the agency of certain privileged documentation): cloistered, doubting, an all-seeing, all-retaining commentator. I am referring *not* to young Charlie, to Ann, her younger sister (Edna May Wonnacott), or to the mother of these two, Emma (Patricia Collinge), a personnage who is girlish in the extreme, flatterable, giddy, detached from the mechanism of the day-to-day even as she is imprisoned in its surfaces, but to Louise Finch (Janet Shaw), Charlie's former classmate and friend. Louise has taken a job serving tables at the *'Til-Two* bar on Main Street, and it is her privilege to come upon Charlie at the precise, awkward moment when—her uncle having tried to cajole her into complicity with his true, and unsavory, position in life—Charlie is on the verge of returning a ring he gave her:

CHARLIE: How could you *do* such things? You're my uncle, my mother's brother. We thought you were the most wonderful man in the world. The most wonderful and the best.
UNCLE CHARLIE (*sternly*): Charlie, what do you know?
She puts the ring he gave her on the table between them. Louise reenters with the drinks.
LOUISE: I'm sorry I was so long. We're awful busy. *She sees the rings and draws in a breath, picks it up.* Whose is it? Ain't it beautiful! I'd just die fer a ring like that. Yessir, fer a ring like that I'd just about die. I love jewelry—*real* jewelry. Y'notice I didn't even have to ask if it was real. Y'can tell. I can.

I will return to the provocative and repeating mantra, "What do you know?" since it surely constitutes a signal and central element of the meaning of the film. But what must fascinate any viewer burdened with a desire to navigate the plot of *Shadow of a Doubt* is the inclusion in this scene of Louise *as a foregrounded character*, since her ostensible function is merely to fill out the decor of the restaurant and thereby add verisimilitude. We come to know her in many ways, however: as a person who does not hold a job, a high school student without much promise, and a girl who knows how to look at a man or, indeed, a fancy ring.

There is no girl in Hitchcock quite as dumbfounding as this girl, lumpen, sullen, retreated, and depressed, a punctum of vaguely stifled sensibilities and dampened prospects with no trail in the past or eroticized charge for the future, whose every vocalization is a sigh of loss and whose every gesture is a limp surrender. She exists in the moment, but only in the moment, couched behind a vision that looks through the exterior surfaces of things and unravels all mystery, yet to no effect. We have the unmistakable sense that Louise's knowledge of the bond between the two Charlies is unfathomably deep and instantaneously true and that she has seen it so many times it holds no excitement for her. It seems to be through Louise's quick knowledge, indeed, that we can verify young Charlie's suspicions and know for ourselves that the uncle is a cad. Her presence suggests in a flash a domain of ineffable sadness, despair, and reality against which young Charlie's every affectation of emotion and concern is suddenly hollow—as hollow as her uncle's, to be sure.

By her manner this young waitress is something of a demi-mondaine and in some ways (though her freshened and immature appearance belies this) no longer exactly young. As Uncle Charlie

Louise's uncanny, defeated eyes, shifting from one Charlie to the other Charlie, tell the story of her own gluttonous imagination.

talks about his travels and mistakes, the lighting turns him into a grown *boy*, and so in this respect he affiliates with Louise; she is his proper double and mate in the film. Her enslavement as a wage laborer in the "'Til-Two," her exposure to the exigencies of adult life in its precincts, and a certain history, if not of sexual encounter then at least of sexual imagination, fostered, no doubt, by the conceptual efforts required of her as an audience understanding the tiny dramas played out at the tables she serves, have conjoined to produce in this young woman an emotional development far in advance of that of the romantic Charlie. While Charlie hopes, Louise is resigned. Little Ann Newton dwells in the imaginary phantasmagoria of *Ivanhoe*, but compared with Louise, Charlie is herself not so far away from this two-dimensional, fictive kind of life. Her uncle, indeed, has deduced this about her:

UNCLE CHARLIE: You live in a dream, you're a sleepwalker, blind. How do you know what the world is like? Do you know the world is a foul sty? Do you know if you ripped the fronts off houses you'd find swine? The world's a hell, what does it matter what happens in it? Wake up, Charlie, use your wits, learn something.

As Louise watches Charlie and her uncle negotiate the footings upon which they may relate one to another, she looks with eyes that have seen men and women in every phase of negotiation; and for her, the two people at the table are hardly other than what they could seem to be to strangers out at night and unfamiliar with the relationship of blood that unites them: a couple at a readable stage in the fluid history of a dramatic and sexualized encounter. Louise's canny, defeated eyes, shifting from one Charlie to the other Charlie, tell the story of her own gluttonous imagination, her own contacts, her animal attention, her ressentient class consciousness typified by repressed desire for what cannot be had. In commenting that she is surprised to see Charlie in a place like this, Louise, who does not have benefit of the social capital that could elevate her above the environment, is commenting not only on Charlie's presence in the bar, but also on Charlie's ostensible involvement in activity that may be normal for this place but is hardly normal for her—relations with men, indeed, sexual relations. Although the putative sexuality of the encounter between the Charlies may be titillating for us, it is a humdrum commonplace for the waitress, an onlooker now bereft of romantic fantasy and utterly well-socialized to the mundanity of sexual relations, strategies, and outcomes as played out on a daily basis in front of her in this place. It is therefore with comprehension, but without excitement, that she regards Charlie and Charlie. Her resignation to a station in life—as a female, as unprivileged, as a marketable commodity—is palpable in her movement, her expression, her tone, her businesslike demeanor, and the way in which she shows by her dully glowing eyes that the fairy-tale romanticism of her own girlhood is chambered far off in the most distant interior remove of her dungeon. We sense this repression vaguely at a telling moment in which she ogles the ring Charlie is holding and says she would die for a thing like that.

The *mise-en-scène* spikes our attentiveness to this girl and our tendency to take her seriously and affiliate with her position. Hitchcock has set the bar encounter as a play-within-a-play, in which young Charlie's encounter with her uncle is played out before the

waitress as a contained and artificial encounter, some of the prepa-
rations for which we have seen and the deep motive and backstage
tensions of which we are increasingly in a position to fathom. The
onstage viewer of all this, the waitress, is thus *not* part of a mocked-
up scenario—the conversation between the Charlies—of which we
have sufficient views to be certain it is in some important way false,
and is thus, herself, relatively true. We take her seriously, seduced
into the scene by her obsessive attentiveness to the Charlies. We see
the Charlies through her, mythically over her shoulder though in
fact from a matching position at the opposite side of the table, and
she is therefore in some ways a model for the expected audience of
the film.[1]

This brief moment is more than a foreshadowing of the fact
that a woman *did* die for that ring. It suggests, too, how the appeal of
the ring is—for someone not necessarily unintelligent but certainly
uneducated, and therefore uncapitalized and vulnerable—an agency
of powerful men. It allows us to imagine that in her dependence if
not in her class origin, the waitress is the germ that became Charlie's
mother, Emma,—a person whose expressiveness is diluted by the
sacrifices she has made in service and whose far-off romantic past is
very similar to the waitress's long-lost hopes of, perhaps, falling in
love, being carried away, and never having to work in such a place as
the "'Til-Two." The 'Til-Two is the Newton marriage, a ceremony
of serving and cleaning, and Uncle Charlie's sitting at table with
young Charlie there is his visit to the family in microcosm. The
general dilutness of Emma Newton's expression is emphasized by
her momentary and uncontrolled inflammation as she receives the
fur collar from her brother; and later emphasized again, horrifically,
in the crestfallen and despairing apathy with which she regards him
when he has announced that he is leaving Santa Rosa. "We were
so close when we were young," she drones: "You know how it is.
Sort of forget you're you. You're your husband's wife." If the Newton
household, which has contained and sedated Emma, is in actuality
not 'Til-Two, it is certainly a similar place of service and reduction,
a residuum of the charms and hope-laden deficiencies of girlhood-in-
patriarchy that Charles Oakley's self-serving visit has reinvoked and
that will now be blotted out again in a dull return to the security and
charmlessness of married life.

The dramatic reason Charlie Newton is at a table in this bar,
then, is so that in the moment of morally evaluating the grown man
who is her uncle, she may be confronted with what she is in dan-

ger of becoming, what she has perhaps already started to become—
her own mother, as reflected in the presence of Louise. Distracted
by another, openly moral play-within-a-play—the tale of the Merry
Widow strangler and her own uncle's key performance therein—she
can use her wiles and courage to overcome a childish infatuation
with Oakley. This is to little avail, however, since her attentions will
be turned in the end not away from what Charles Oakley represents
but toward the detective Jack Graham, a man no less self-serving
than Oakley, nor less handsome, and who will soon, it seems, become her husband. Surely no less devoted a husband to her than Joe
(Henry Travers) is to her mother, he will dutifully provide for her
edification and containment a world in which she, too, can bury her
childhood dreams.

The waitress is reduced by the pressures of work, not the duties
of marriage. Already in her adolescent years she is but a shadow of
her own rich girlhood, a person educated in life beyond her years,
a shell. Bedazzled by jewelry, servile of temperament, knowledge-
able of her station, she is the prototype of all the other women
we meet and hear about in this film, *except* the early, too hope-
ful, morally sensitive Charlie Newton (who will come round). What
is provocative about the characterization of the waitress is its hon-
esty. When the fantasies of dreamy girlhood have been swept away
by economic press, a young woman in 1943 America had only two
choices—entrance into a marriage contract (that is, working in a
male-dominated institution while masquerading in an aestheticized
"femininity") or entrance into a labor relation at face value. The
waitress eschews the masquerade of femininity—she is pretty, but
hardly young Charlie's equal, and without class, the basis and rationale for investing in appearance. No matter what she does to prettify
herself she will never be good enough. In the middle class, by contrast, one can be on display even as one is busy at work. Mrs. Potter,
the aging widow—indeed, the aging girl—who meets Charles Oakley
at the bank, is a case in point: on display as a beauty, indeed, *to cover*
her being at work on the hunt.

But it is male *ocularity* that can provide a view of the territory,
a warning of dangers, a navigational aid toward steadily improving
service, and a fixation on sites of potentially great reward. If Mrs.
Potter's intent is to settle herself institutionally (as wife and then
inheriting widow, merry or otherwise), Charles Oakley's is to extract
value without the commitment of settling. His visual scan, his opti-
cal acuteness, couples with the unseeing gaze of his intended objects

that is intrinsic to the hegemonic control male dominance insists on (Mulvey). Charles is devastated, in this respect, that young Charlie may have *seen* something. Similarly, a close look at the already settled Emma Newton suggests that she is all but blind to the realities of power and strategy that surround her. The scene in which, oblivious to a range of clues the viewer sees easily and directly, she bakes in order to entertain the federal "statisticians" (detectives) who want to know about her family life evidences this "blindness." Louise, on the other hand, has eyes that focus, dart left and right, that catch every potential opportunity to earn reward or to see other people's strategic moves. Though her uncle calls her "blind," Charlie Newton's ocularity in *Shadow of a Doubt* is intermediate between Louise's and her mother's. It is because she is *not* blind that she manages in the end to see enough to save herself.

If the perceiving girl is one glyph waltzing through this film, a companion figure—in many ways its opposite and the generator of much of the concern and trouble of the plot—is the invisible man. All of the males—the detectives, the minister, the traffic policeman, Herb the neighbor, Joe Newton, little Roger, and the bank manager—act in such a way as to keep motive secret; they are "invisible" at a fundamental level, unreadable, unpredictable. The policeman, for example, suddenly behaves like a repressive schoolteacher. One detective behaves like a photojournalist, the other like an abashed boyfriend from the basketball team. For a bank teller above thinking of himself as an embezzler, Joe Newton is eager to accept an expensive watch as a gift from a brother-in-law he doesn't know too well. For all his dignity, the bank manager proceeds very quickly to business once Charlie Oakley has permitted himself to be recognized as a man who knows the world and who knows money dealings: one suspects the manager may have something to hide. Indeed, the difference between the superficial reading of all these men, a reading made in conventional and morally upstanding terms perfectly congruent with the social charade, and a questioning of their surface in terms of underlying motive and vested interest, is precisely the gap between Charlie Newton as innocent reader and Charlie Newton as informed adult. We can wonder what she will begin to suspect of *all* men in the postdiegetic universe she inhabits after the ending of this film. Such a reading, too, is what her uncle refers to as "ripping off the shutters" to reveal the swine. Just as she learns to see the handsome uncle from the East as a potential criminal, she is made capable of seeing the noble policeman as a busybody, the dignified bank manager as a potential thief, the sanctimonious minister as a codger, and so on. To repeat, this analytical view is what she learns not only from the inscription on the ring but from her friend Louise, just as Louise is ogling it. Under our sociable facades, we are cupidinous. Underneath their statuses and their dignities, men are decodable in terms quite different from the surfaces in which they costume themselves for the societal dance.

But even if men are generally secretive, Charles Oakley is invisible in a way that the other characters in this story are not—plainly and technically so. Since a moment in his early boyhood, he has forbidden others to photograph him and is thus—in this filmic self-reflexivity by which his refusal to be pictured is, among other things, the subject of the picture we are looking at—the epitome of a man who can be known but never recognized. Twice we are confronted directly with his invisibility: at the beginning of the film, as he strolls right past a pair of detectives waiting to nab him on a street corner in the East, and later, with his choreography of dodging the view camera of Fred Saunders (Wallace Ford) and then finally seizing the man's film when a picture has successfully been shot. He is altogether a man whose actions are known without being seen; indeed, young Charlie does not witness him in any criminal involvement and forms all her conclusions on the basis of an equivocal newspaper article and a monogrammed ring. Thus, although *Shadow of a Doubt* poses in many ways as a film about a crime and also a film about a family being disrupted, it is at its deepest a film about a man who cannot be seen and a girl who cannot forgo attempting to see the world.

What it is that girls in general, and Hitchcockian girls par excellence, cannot quite manage to see of men is not their presence or, plainly enough, what men do but what men mean by what they do—their motive. It is, then, the ultimate business of men that is abstracted from the girl in Hitchcock: attempting to comprehend Mitch Brenner's hidden motive, for example, Melanie Daniels drives to Bodega Bay, inciting the action of *The Birds*. In *Shadow of a Doubt*, the hidden affairs of men are thematized by the game Joe Newton and Herb Hawkins engage in night after night, trying to come up with ways of "committing the perfect murder." The staging of the interaction between the two men is curious and fascinating: Herb seems incapable of visiting his friend Joe *except* while Joe is at the dinner table, as though he cannot figure out, after all these years, what time the Newtons dine—or as though he does not care.

He enters like a terrified dog, creeping into the dining room, and then confabulates with his friend while Joe sits finishing his meal, drawing Joe away from conversation with his family—especially Emma and Charlie—and into a conspiratorial bubble. This bubble, virtually sketched on the screen through Hitchcock's blocking of the action for camera, is the male preserve that the intellect of the young girl must not penetrate, the sacred shanty in which the male battle for dominance is—in this case figuratively and playfully—acted out.

As a late Victorian himself, Hitchcock would have been eminently familiar with the closeting of girls, or *jeunes filles.* The Newton household is a kind of *jardin cloissonné,* in fact, a perfectly symmetrical cell in which the *jeune fille* can be delighted by beauty (fiction) while remaining ignorant of the business of the world. While Charlie is more vivacious than the recalcitrant and narcissistic Ann and more enthusiastic than the world-weary Emma, it cannot really be said that she is better informed. All three females in the house are ignorant in their ways, and the mother cannot be better described, once her brother has come back into her life to charm her back to childhood, than Henry James does Aggie in *The Awkward Age*: "She knows nothing—but absolutely, utterly: not the least little tittle of anything." The *jeune fille* is described by Nellie M. Perret, in a prescient and deeply informative essay (1979), as a creature "beatifically irradiated by her nescience," a cultured and beautified tabula rasa, "the young woman into whose 'delicate' ear is whispered the refrain, 'Don't understand, my own darling—don't understand.' " And further, for Perret, it is a paradoxical truth that the *"jeune fille's* 'golden' ignorance—the absence of consciousness which defines her as an object designed for reverence . . . is precisely that quality which would make her presence most 'awkward' for the circle of adults into which she is to be introduced." Knowledge, we may recall, is the treasure Uncle Charlie is convinced his niece lacks, the subject of his taunt in the bar that she is blind, ordinary, and a dreamer of peaceful, stupid dreams. If the knowledge withheld from the *jeune fille* is men's knowledge, men's business, it is clearly, among other things, sex, which is to say, men's way of hiding themselves from the probe of women's eyes, of probing without being probed themselves. Without knowledge of how things are done, Charlie, like her mother, is forced to meander through philosophical pastures, catching conceptual butterflies, as it were, and being charmed by the mists of pure speculation. She does not see what is in front of her eyes, partly because it does not show itself. Yet her eyes never rest.

The girl Charlie, caught in the process of becoming a woman, is the paragon of opticality, say, reading. Ann's textual obsessiveness prepares her to become an adolescent like Charlie, who reads the world. And if growing into womanhood in American society is a process of coming to terms with men and all they represent, Charlie's problem, as a type and as a character, is just that men are the hardest texts to read. The one man she comes most dangerously close to—most dangerously because he is both malevolent and fabulous, not merely male—is Charles Oakley, the man of all men in her life who is least readable, "the most wonderful man in the world, the most wonderful and the best." In place of direct reading and straightforward exegesis, then, Charlie is forced—as are we—to substitute the surmise. However, surmising without a great deal of experience (compared, say, with her girlfriend in the bar), she can never have certainty (what she will think is certainty) until the climactic moment on the train, when it is far too late.

If *Shadow of a Doubt* shows Charlie Newton beginning her ocular play with a delirious incapacity, and then developing instinct and shrewdness and alacrity in response to the pressure of (male-induced) events, it is an essay on the girl's learning to detect in men what they have secreted against detection. Her mother's retreat into bland acceptance and mystification in the presence of her seductive brother is a retreat into the past. Young Charlie is then the true detective in the film, and Jack's detective role is hardly more than a cloak he wears against the chills of careerlessness in a competitive postwar world. One has the distinct sense, by film's end, that he will cheerfully abandon this career for something more stable in Charlie's company—a career, indeed, that will cede to her the rights of detection at least in the domestic sphere. The girl does more than become a detective as she becomes a woman, however.

The film also shows in Charlie a keen moral sense developing into a capacity to equivocate, weigh in a balance, and compromise against the need to place oneself on faultless moral ground. In that strange early moment when Charlie meditates, "Our family has gone to pieces, we're in a terrible rut," she is talking, too, about modern civilization. "Our family" is all of us. It is certainly true in moral terms that the development of our civilization has been a fall and that our society is an entrenchment—this is a theme one finds consistently in Hitchcock. Charlie's receptivity to this fact is what draws our attention to her, and what makes Melanie Daniels at the end of *The Birds,* and Marnie Edgar sobbing in her mother's arms, and

Judy Barton climbing the nuns' tower, and Eve Kendal clinging to the crag in Rapid City, and Jo McKenna listening to the sopranos sing, "The storm clouds broke and drowned the dying moon"—Charlie's Hitchcockian relations all.

The fall of boys, this film would suggest, is from gloriously awkward presence (Roger) into manly camouflage (Uncle Charlie). But the fall of girls is into a ceremony of recognition. In the bedroom scene, with her father powerless to address her, Charlie is beginning to see—beginning with the broadest, most sweeping, least particular, and least real view—and therefore to know how artfully to use the eyes, and therefore to find men's elusiveness alarming, and therefore to hope. Ultimately, in her hoping is her girlhood. What is it she hopes for? Plainness above all, and clarity, presentation, exteriority—that the world will show itself and endure consistent with its display. She hopes that people—Jack at least—will say what they are and be faithful in this saying. Given the structure of gender relations to which her cultural affiliation subjects her, this film argues, hope is her trap. She hopes that when this nightmare is done, things will be what they look to be—that, in short, it will be a worthwhile activity to employ one's sight in the capture, or at least comprehension, of this elaborate life. What is profound about *Shadow of a Doubt* is that a story has formed around Charlie Newton's hope like a crystal. What is tragic is that at story's end her hope is undiminished and her commitment to hoping unquestioned. The motive force continues to reside with men and in men's elaborate secrecy, a cache deeper than can, at least in this narrative, be fathomed. Charlie, ready for a future with Jack Graham, is still, and always to be, a girl.

NOTES

1. See Goffman, *Frame Analysis*, 474.

WORKS CITED

Chabrol, Claude. 1954. "Histoire d'une interview." *Cahiers du cinéma* 39 (October): 39–44.

Corber, Robert J. 1993. *In the Name of National Security: Hitchcock, Homophobia, and the Political Construction of Gender.* Durham: Duke University Press.

Douchet, Jean. 1959. "La Troisième clé d'Hitchcock." Part I: *Cahiers du cinéma* 99 (September); Part II: *Cahiers du cinéma* 102 (December).

Goffman, Erving. 1974. *Frame Analysis: An Essay on the Organization of Experience.* Cambridge: Harvard University Press.

Modleski, Tania. 1988. *The Women Who Knew Too Much.* New York: Methuen.

Mulvey, Laura. 1975. "Visual Pleasure and Narrative Cinema." In *Narrative, Apparatus, Ideology: A Film Theory Reader,* ed. Philip Rosen, 198–209. New York: Columbia University Press.

Paglia, Camille. 1998. *The Birds.* London: British Film Institute.

Perret, Nellie M. 1979. "The *Jeune fille* in the Novels of Henry James." Unpublished paper, University of Toronto.

Rothman, William. 1982. *Hitchcock—The Murderous Gaze.* Cambridge: Harvard University Press.

Spoto, Donald. 1983. *The Dark Side of Genius: The Life of Alfred Hitchcock.* New York: Ballantine Books.

Sterritt, David. 1993. *The Films of Alfred Hitchcock.* New York: Cambridge University Press.

Truffaut, François. 1985. *Hitchcock.* New York: Simon and Schuster.

Wood, Robin. 1989. *Hitchcock's Films Revisited.* New York: Columbia University Press.

chapter 3

Gidget Goes Hysterical

Allison Whitney

This essay will examine how the problematic transformations in gender roles and social taxonomies that accompanied the creation of the teenager in 1950s North America are expressed in *Gidget* (Paul Wendkos, 1959), a film targeted at the teen girl market. Although the plot and characterization in *Gidget* are essentially inane, it was a significant film for teenage girls in the late 1950s, enjoying great popularity and establishing Sandra Dee as a model for clean teenage living—free of drugs, alcohol, and other vices, sexually inhibited, and respectful of one's parents. In his *Teenagers and Teenpics: The Juvenilization of American Movies of the 1950s*, Thomas Doherty establishes categories for teenage films, defining *Gidget* as a "clean teenpic," a film that represents a safe, palatable type of teenager who does not threaten the social order (179). However, even an apparently benign film such as *Gidget*, about a girl who dreams of becoming a surfer, carries with it substantial cultural anxiety about the new phenomenon of teen identity and is a perfect example of how the North American struggle to ascribe cultural meaning to the teenage girl was expressed in 1950s popular cinema.

Although many teenpics of the 1950s expressed American society's fears of teenage behavior through exploitation narratives, *Gidget* conceals its fear-mongering under its status as a clean teenpic. In *Cool: The Signs and Meanings of Adolescence*, Marcel Danesi describes the "split personality" of the teenage persona, which by the late 1950s projected two conflicting images of teen identity, the first being rebellious, nonconformist, and sexually aggressive, the second being "toned-down and socially more acceptable," challenging neither parental authority nor traditional sexual mores (21). This division was borne out in genre distinctions among teen films, ranging from "wild" accounts of juvenile delinquents to the "mild" antics of clean-living teens who made their parents proud (Staehling 230).

"She acts sorta teenage, just in-between age . . ."

So begins the Gidget themesong, about a girl "in-between" child-hood and adulthood who will discover her teenage self during a sum-mer at the beach.[1] *Gidget* was the first in a long series of beach/surfing movies produced for the teen audience, a genre that came to include such titles as *Beach Party* (1963) and *Beach Blanket Bingo* (1965). The beach setting was popular in part because of its poten-tial for visual spectacle: swimming, surfing, and sunbathing pro-vide ample opportunity to photograph young tanned bodies in the semi-nudity of bathing suits. More important, the symbolic poten-tial of the beach zone is closely related to the liminal nature of teen identity. Teenagers are boundary figures, positioned in a twilight zone of uncertainty about their childlike freedoms and innocence and their desires for adult responsibility and carnal knowledge. The coastline is a boundary zone, lying between the safe civilization of land and the dark dangerous chaos of the ocean. The beach is for-ever in a state of flux, continually reshaped by the warring powers of nature's winds and tides and civilization's encroaching beachfront development. The protagonists of teenpics congregate in this space because it facilitates the representation of cultural anxieties about teen boundary transgressions. In order for teenagers to mature into heterosexual, chaste, and responsible workers and consumers in the capitalist economy, they must try to establish a new equilibrium of social roles to replace the traditional time lines of personal develop-ment.

The Story

Gidget recounts the summer vacation of seventeen-year-old Francie Lawrence (Sandra Dee), a bookworm, musician, and tomboy who becomes a surfer and acquires the nickname "Gidget," meaning girl midget. We first meet her in her bedroom, where her buxom friend Patty (Patti Kane) is demanding that she come to the beach for a manhunt. Gidget reluctantly joins her friends at the beach but soon finds that her lack of physical maturity proves a liability in efforts to attract men.[2] Gidget decides instead that she wants to join a surfing gang under the leadership of Kahoona (Cliff Robertson), a self-described Korean War veteran and beach bum who shocks Francie with accounts of his counterculture lifestyle. Gidget soon falls in love with a surfer named Moondoggie (James Darren), and by the end of the film she is wearing his fraternity pin.

Gidget's narrative is unremarkable, but Gidget's trials and agonies on the road to successful teenagerhood reveal the enormous anxiety of American society over the volatile development of teenage girls. In detailing Gidget's summer of transformation, *Gidget* touches on the struggle to enforce heterosexuality while preventing sexual expression, the construction of femininity as masquerade, racial and class dynamics, popular understandings of Freudian psychology, and the rise of 1950s consumerism.

Oedipus and All That

The emergence of the teen phenomenon was accompanied by a popular interest in scientific, anthropological, and especially psychoanalytic explanations for teenage behavior. In an era of atomic science, the space race, and antibiotics, science was popularly regarded as society's saving grace, providing a new means of social control.[3] The use of biological and psychological theories to explain the teenage phenomenon serves to pathologize the terrifying and violent transformations of the teenage body while seeking to establish a new set of rationalized social boundaries that might contain and regulate the teenage experience. The popularity of bastardized interpretations of psychoanalytic models of human development grew out of this desire to reduce the complexities of the adolescent psyche to a system of easily understood rules and models. Freudian psychoanalysis entered the American popular discourse of psychology in the 1950s, leading to new ways of understanding behavior, particularly as it relates to sexuality.[4] Although popularized accounts of psychoanalytic theory grossly simplify complex models of development, new understandings of the existence of the unconscious, Oedipal dynamics in relationships and family interactions and the concept of psychosomatic illness or hysteria had a revolutionary effect on how the average person interpreted human behavior.

Gidget contains several references to popular theories of teen psychology. For example, Gidget feigns an Oedipal fascination with Kahoona in an effort to make Moondoggie jealous, explaining, "Oh, I know, Oedipus and all that, it's called a father complex." Further, Moondoggie lives out his own Oedipal drama, ranting about his plans to forsake his father's bourgeois priorities and become a surf bum. At several points in the narrative, characters express their anxieties about the troubling boundary transgressions of Gidget's personal development through what amount to hysterical symptoms. Freud and Breuer's (1991) theory of hysteria describes it as a somatic expression of a repressed trauma; when an event is too terrible to be expressed or remembered verbally, its cathexis migrates through the body until it manifests as a physical symptom. For example, when Gidget's father (Arthur O'Connell) comes home to discover that his daughter has been out manhunting, her mother (Mary La Roche) tries to calm him by explaining that this is to be expected because "the female matures earlier than the male." Regardless of this psycho/scientific explanation, her father is so upset that he is struck with a headache and has to lie down. Gidget's mother begins to massage his head while he explains that he fears the breakdown of the family's Oedipal dynamic[5]:

> MOTHER: Can't you see, Russ? She went because she had to, a girl needs love.
> FATHER: Well . . . *I* love her!

The father's traumatic realization that his love is no longer sufficient to satisfy the maturing female's needs is thus expressed somatically.

Gidget experiences her own hysterical interludes when she begins to discover sexual feelings. In fact, Gidget's mother describes the beginning of adult sexuality as though it were a trauma: "Like being hit on the back of the head with a sledgehammer." Later, when Gidget is recovering after her surfing initiation, a highly sexualized ceremony in which she feels like she has been hit with a sledgehammer, she actually touches the back of her head as though this new sexual affect were expressing itself as an injury—and a cranial one at that. In spite of her apparent good health and physical strength, Gidget convalesces for two weeks from this "injury," which is described inconsistently as near-drowning, sunstroke, and/or tonsilitis. Gidget's illness is mutable and migratory because it is essentially an hysterical reaction to the awakening of sexual desire.[6]

Both Gidget and her father are so overwhelmed at the realization of her burgeoning sexuality that they are unable to address their fears directly; they must convert these traumatic feelings into physical symptoms. The explicit location of these traumatic processes in the body represents society's difficulty in defining and accepting the new set of powers and functions now associated with the adolescent body. As an adult child, the teenage body is in flux, at once sexualized yet apparently free of social responsibility and uncontained by the sexual mores meant to keep adult sensuality in check. Thus, the teenager inhabits what is essentially a new bodily category, one whose energy and drives are derived from the contradictory forces it encounters in the teenage boundary zone. Although the potentially explosive qualities of teen sexual energy are not detailed as explicitly in *Gidget* as they are in more exploitative films of the time, the fact that this film is peppered with references that indicate a bastardized understanding of psychoanalytic theory points to an overriding concern in 1950s culture about the transformation, sublimation, and employment of young people's sexuality, and a desperate need to establish a new set of psychological criteria with which to understand and control the teen phenomenon.

"I'm No Dame!"

The teenage body is by definition in a state of transformation, and Gidget's evolving relationship with her body, particularly as a female athlete, is very telling of the difficulties of defining the parameters of teen female sexual identity. Excluded from conventional teenage girl activities, Gidget tries to gain access to the surfers' social group by learning to master a surfboard. She achieves some success, but her newfound athleticism does little to advance her status as a teenage girl, for the surfers continue to regard her as jail bait or as one of the guys rather than as a prospective date.

It is important to understand that surfing was an unconventional activity for girls in the late 1950s. In fact, in the film's surfing scenes, Gidget is played by a man wearing a woman's bathing suit, which suggests that female surfers were a true rarity in 1959. The surfers are aware that athleticism is incompatible with conventional female roles, and they explain to Gidget that "surfing's not for dames." Gidget insists, "I'm no dame!" thereby relinquishing her claim on established categories of female identity in order to pursue her interests, while Gidget's friend Patty laments that "she's more fish than dish," more of a sea-bather than a sunbather. Since she insists on being active and regards physical strength and endurance as valuable qualities, Gidget does not fit into conventional notions of sedentary and domestic 1950s femininity, and her competence as a surfer creates an unfavorable comparison with more passive girls. For example, when she tries to get Moondoggie's attention by surfing alongside him, she discovers that he is more interested in Joanne, an "ultrafeminine" girl in a tight sweater who watches the boys admiringly from the beach. Gidget is threatened by Joanne's rivalry, and they have a brief confrontation:

> MOONDOGGIE: Hey, Joanne, this is the kid I was telling you about. She's only been surfing for a little over a month.
> JOANNE: Oh, really? It must be wonderful if you like that sort of thing. Of course, Moondoggie can tell you I'm not the outdoor type.
> GIDGET: Then maybe you better get out of the sun before you melt.

Gidget's problem is that she wants to be active, vital, dynamic, and carefree, while her female friends are determined to be popular teenage girls and therefore devote their energy toward putting themselves on display. Gidget wants to live through her body, while her friends and mother know that a socially acceptable woman can do no such thing. They are willing to quite literally "suffer and be still," to endure physical discomfort and boredom, and deny themselves the visceral and psychological freedoms of childhood in order to take on prescribed passive roles. Gidget's mother makes the case for passive femininity when she assures Gidget that one of the nice things about being a woman is that "it's not up to you, it's up to the young man" to take the active role in pursuing a mate (indeed, in pursuing anything). She explains further that the highest achievement for a woman is "to bring out the best in a man." The teenage girl soon learns that her body is an object that must conform to a feminine iconography, that using her body in active pursuits is incompatible with that iconography, and that her only goal in life should be to accommodate the goals of men. Gidget finds this selection of passive roles—the reclining bathing beauty, the hapless female, or the girl who's "not the outdoor type"—unacceptable as models. Imitating them would require that she relinquish control of her body, her feelings, and her thoughts.

Because Gidget is athletic, her relationship with her body becomes more and more complicated when she starts to develop sexual feelings. When she describes surfing to her parents, she talks about it as the most exciting experience she has ever had, jumping on the sofa to demonstrate and shrieking that surfing is "the ultimate." At this point in the film, Gidget has experienced surfing only once, and in that instance she was semiconscious, lying on Moondoggie's surfboard after a near-drowning experience. Why, therefore, would a girl want to take on an activity she associates with near death?

When compared to her peers, Gidget (left) is "more fish than dish."

The answer is in the film's representation of surfing as a sublimated sexual act and as a marker of masculinity. In the scene where Gidget is rescued, the position of the characters on the surfboard has clear sexual connotations—Gidget is spread-eagled on her front, and Moondoggie climbs on the board behind her. Gidget's enthusiastic description of surfing points to a contradiction in her position on sexuality. She is identified as masculine in that she wants to do things like surfing and swimming, which are male activities and not for "dames," and she is furious when her father suggests she go on a date with a boy, even going so far as to describe physical contact as disgusting. And yet Gidget describes her first pseudosexual contact with a man as a thrilling experience and one she wishes to repeat. It is possible that Gidget wants to become a surfer in order to attain a position of power, to conquer her fears of the ocean. However, this is a conflicted goal because such power is identified as masculine. Mastering a surfboard and skimming along the surface of the ocean, a territory that clearly symbolizes the sexualized side of the beach boundary zone, places Gidget in an active role and affirms her status as an athlete. However, she can never be truly satisfied with this role because, as is reiterated by her friends and Joanne, it estranges her from established ideals of femininity.

In addition to the threat of masculinization, Gidget's foray into the world of ocean sports leaves her vulnerable to unwanted sexual advances. Gidget's first surfing lesson is conducted by a surfer whose beach name is, significantly, Loverboy (Tom Laughlin). The lesson quickly deteriorates as Loverboy tries to grope Gidget but Moondoggie intervenes and sends her home with a warning that the surfing scene is too dangerous for girls. Gidget persists, however, and when she is initiated into the surfing community, the surfers pick her up and run into the ocean shouting, "She's asking for it!" with clear sexual connotation. Surfing is a perilous activity because it allows Gidget to transgress both gender categories and codes of sexual conduct. If Gidget ventures into the sexualized ocean she may be consumed by it and drown or be seduced, or, even more disturbing, she may master it and take on a position of activity and subjectivity reserved for males. The threat that Gidget will attain too much male expertise is kept in check when, during the initiation, she nearly drowns for the second time. This additional near-death experience highlights the pitfalls of female sexual exploration but also ensures that in spite of her new status as a surfer, Gidget remains passive in relation to her male friends. Still, her development as an athlete ensures that her gender identifications remain unstable; Gidget discovers her heterosexuality through her interactions with male surfers but at the same time transgresses her gender role by refusing to be passive. She becomes at once a woman and one of the guys.

Faking It

Gidget soon finds that to become a woman requires that one assume an unnatural persona. When she asks her mother, "Do you think there's anything weird about me? . . . Why don't I like dates?" she is assured that she is simply "too genuine to pretend anything you don't feel yet." Gidget will eventually mature and develop sexual feelings, but her mother's comments also suggest that she will soon learn that femininity is a masquerade, or even a form of deception.

Rather than experience womanhood as an awakening of erotic power, Gidget will discover that being a woman means expressing things one does not genuinely feel and concealing one's true sentiments.

Gidget's difficulties as a teenage girl stem from her initial inability to fake it, and thus she finds it impossible to fit securely into a prescribed gender or sexual role. Gidget learns the value of exhibiting false emotions when she offers to pay Hot Shot, one of the surfers (Robert Ellis), to escort her to the luau and pretend to be in love with her in order to make Moondoggie jealous. Though it is strange that a cute and likeable teenager like Gidget would have to pay people to be in her company, her strategy indicates that success in romantic relationships requires that one recognize the roles and scripts of heterosexual courting as contrived and inauthentic. Gidget's plan backfires when Hot Shot, unaware that Moondoggie is Gidget's true love interest, backs out of the job and gets Moondoggie to take his place. Once at the luau, Moondoggie asks Gidget for pointers on how to fake romantic interest and create a sexualized display. His curiosity is significant because although he has far more sexual experience than Gidget, when it comes to faking sexual feelings he is forced to ask this naive and inexperienced girl for help, making it clear that this type of falsehood is specific to femininity.[7] The struggle for the teenage girl is thus to construct an identity based on lies rather than genuine desires.

Gidget's Queer Interludes

Gidget's summer in the beach boundary zone proves difficult and dangerous. When she follows her interests into the male and highly sexualized world of surfing, it nearly costs her her life, places her in constant sexual peril, and threatens to destroy her femininity. However, Gidget's development is no less problematic when she leaves the boundary zone and goes back to the apparent security of her bourgeois home where she spends time with her friend Betty-Louise (Sue George), known as "B. L." B. L. may be read as a lesbian presence and a counterpoint to the construction of femininity that is causing Gidget so much trouble. B. L.'s hairstyle, clothing, and posture are compatible with the codes of 1950s butch lesbianism, but other elements of her behavior encourage a queer reading as well. While Gidget's voluptuous "ultrafeminine" friends bemoan Gidget's immaturity, B. L. does not see a problem with Gidget's behavior or state of mind and defends Gidget's lack of interest in manhunting

or dating. B. L. is exempt from the manhunt because she "has social
security" by wearing a man's fraternity pin; however, we never see
"Buck," the pin's supposed owner. And one may wonder, if B. L.
really has a serious boyfriend, why is she spending her entire summer
in Gidget's bedroom?

In a film full of sexual tension, the most explicitly sexual scene
takes place when B. L. is helping Gidget practice surfing techniques.
Gidget places her surfboard on her bed and balances on it while B. L.
bounces on the mattress. While vigorously shaking the edge of the
bed, B. L. apologizes for the ways her friendship has obstructed Gidget's knowledge of men, claiming that she has been a bad friend for
praising Gidget's academic performance and her interest in classical music instead of encouraging her to pursue boys. It would seem,
therefore, that their relationship is a barrier to Gidget's heterosexual
development. Even B. L.'s attempts to help Gidget become popular
among the surfers have unforeseen consequences; by helping Gidget
become a better surfer, she ensures that Gidget will move further
away from the passive feminine ideal embodied by the other teenage
girls in the film.

B. L.'s presence offers a point of covert identification for lesbian
audiences, but she also mediates viewers' desire for and identification with Gidget, a function that may be further understood in relation to lesbian theories of spectatorship. Teresa de Lauretis's "Film
and the Visible" offers examples from several lesbian-themed films
where female characters who watch other women's performances
take up what she calls a lesbian subject position, diegetically representing the female spectator (228). B. L. clearly occupies such a position as the only female (apart from Gidget's mother) who regularly
sees Gidget in private. Indeed, she alone fully appreciates Gidget's
emotional state, physical prowess, and desirability. Meanwhile, the
surfers initially ignore Gidget as a sexual entity, looking past her in
favor of her more voluptuous contemporaries, while Gidget's parents, particularly her father, are perennially blind to her devices and
desires. Thus, like the film viewer, B. L. holds a position of exclusive
spectatorial privilege, privy to Gidget's attempts to hone her own
performance of femininity through coyly sexual surfing drills and
bust enlargement exercises.

In *Star Gazing*, an in-depth study of women's identifications
with Hollywood stars, Jackie Stacey asserts that homoeroticism is
a vital component of women's experience of visual pleasure (29). Indeed, as Gidget's closest friend, B. L. mediates the viewer's access

to Gidget's intimate life in a way that evokes butch/femme codes, implying an erotic motivation for female spectators' identification with Gidget herself and with Sandra Dee. Given the volatility of teen identity and the potential influence of star personae on teens' self-definition, it is significant that the process of spectatorial identification is explicitly eroticized in queer terms and subsequently denigrated as both homosocial and antisocial. Within the film's larger heterosexist project, the implication of homosexuality in female audiences' identification with Gidget is made visible through B. L., who functions as both a spectatorial mediator and a cautionary figure, indicating that even if Gidget stays home, safe from the physical and sexual hazards of the ocean, she remains vulnerable to "sexual degeneracy."

When Gidget is out in the public sphere, trying to establish her identity as an outdoor type, she is subject to many dangers, mostly associated with the threat of male sexuality. However, the alternative is to stay indoors and participate in what amounts to a lesbian dynamic with B. L., hardly an "acceptable" option for a 1950s teenager. Thus, the spaces on either side of the beach boundary zone are as dangerous as the beach itself, indicating that teenagers cannot simply opt out of the struggle for teen identity by choosing to inhabit one area over another. Without the insecurity of teenagers like Gidget, teetering between interior and exterior spaces, the dialectic at the heart of the teen phenomenon would collapse, as would the profitable teen economy balanced upon that phenomenon. Therefore, it is imperative that Gidget's home life provide her with as many gender troubles as does the public sphere.

Money and Meat

By 1957, two years before *Gidget*'s release, "the new teenage consumer market was worth over thirty billion dollars a year" in North America (Danesi 139). Industries from clothing to entertainment encouraged teenagers to compensate for their personal angst about their physical, emotional, and social development by consuming more and more products, from cosmetics to movie tickets. It is therefore no coincidence that money plays a central role in Gidget's navigation of teenage life.

If the economic function of the American teenager is to consume teen-targeted commodities, then it is no coincidence that money plays a central role in Gidget's navigation of teenage life. As is mentioned above, Gidget offers to pay Hot Shot twenty dollars to be her date at the luau to arouse Moondoggie's jealousy. Gidget thereby literally purchases a facade of sexual maturity, making it clear that teen identity is not only a marketing ploy but a commodity that can be bought and sold. When Gidget first shows an interest in surfing, the surfers tell her she needs twenty-five dollars to buy a used surfboard. Gidget asks her father for the money, and it appears that Gidget uses her father's love to manipulate him and his pocketbook. This suggests a fear among parents that teenagers will exploit them by extracting favors with emotional blackmail and that the emotional structure of the family is itself a financial agreement, that personal relationships cannot be estranged from the capitalist system.

Gidget's ability to provide cash affords her a place on the beach and access to teen social circles. Gidget frequently buys her way onto the beach by purchasing food for the surfers and even offering to steal food from home and bring it to the beach. Initially, Kahoona refuses to allow her to attend the luau because he regards her as a child, fearing the naive Gidget will be overwhelmed by the sexual energy and wild party behavior. Gidget persists, however, and manages to secure an invitation and a date through offers of meat and money. In a comical scene, Gidget tries to sneak out of the house with a sack full of food and drops it on the floor; her outraged father holds up a leg of lamb and shouts, "Do you think this is what the young man of today wants?!" Gidget's defiant response is to say, "The man I'm after sure does want something else, and I'll see he gets it!" This is a rather strange comment, because it has already been established that Gidget's date is to be all appearance and no action, but it serves to make a clear link between the teenage female body, meat, and money, both as markers of sexuality and as commodities. Gidget offers these commodities in exchange for an illusion of sexual maturity and social standing. Teenagers are thus not only a consumer group, but a group that consumes and is consumed by teen identity itself.

Hawaiian Drums and Surf Bums

Although Gidget's capitalist, social-climbing strategy of purchasing friendships may not seem ideal, the film presents the alternative, the vaguely socialist anti-work philosophy of the surf bum, as equally unsatisfactory. This alternative is represented by Kahoona, a character whose influence on teenagers is seen as potentially dangerous because he is an economic rebel who claims to have opted out of 1950s materialism. Living in a makeshift shack on the beach, he appears to have no financial responsibilities or consumer needs. Gidget is very confused to discover that he is a surf bum and asks timidly, "This might sound very naive of me, but, when do you work?" The idea that someone could exist outside the mainstream economy is highly disturbing, since it suggests that youthful rebellion could have real repercussions in the social structure, alter the boundaries between social classes, and allow teenagers to establish a set of identities independent of consumer culture.

Kahoona's persona as a free spirit/beach bum is associated with his claims of identification with primitive societies. His frequent references to life among the natives of South and Central America and Hawaii suggest a connection between preindustrial civilization and teen/beach culture. It becomes clear that the surfers fancy themselves connected to these "exotic" cultures, particularly Hawaiian culture, as is apparent in surfing names such as "Kahoona" and "Waikiki," the drum music they play on the beach, and their reference to the beach party itself as a luau. Indeed, the sequel to *Gidget*, titled *Gidget Goes Hawaiian* (1961), sees her visit Hawaii for a surfing holiday.[8] Kahoona's persona as a precapitalist rebel begins to collapse, however, when he confesses that his stories of going native were fabricated and that the native masks adorning his shack were simply purchased "in Acapulco for fifty pesos," suggesting that his "other" ethnicity is more display than substance and that regardless of one's ideals, the capitalist economy is inescapable.

Any possibility of a class commentary or a statement against 1950s materialism is entirely negated in the final scenes of the film when Moondoggie is revealed to be Jeffrey Matthews, a suit-wearing law student, and Kahoona turns out to be a commercial pilot named Burt Vail. We make these discoveries when Moondoggie/Jeffrey shows up at Gidget/Francie's house to take her out on a blind date arranged by their respective fathers. They drive to the beach where they find Kahoona dismantling the shack where he had lived during the summer and discover that he has renewed his pilot's licence. Thus, before he can inspire any genuine rebellion against consumer culture, Kahoona moves out of the beach's liminal space and returns to a professional life, literally tearing down the infrastructure he had established in the boundary zone.

Father Knows Best

In melodramatic films like *Gidget,* it is common for the ending to be somewhat implausible or unsatisfactory. "The happy end is often impossible, and, what is more, the audience knows it is impossible" (Nowell-Smith 73). Douglas Sirk called these endings "emergency exits," where the enormous upheavals represented in the text are neatly solved in the final sequence.[9] *Gidget* employs such an emergency exit when Gidget's problems of sexuality and gender identity, the questioning of capitalist consumption, and the suggestion of cultural miscegenation are suddenly and inexplicably solved, thanks to the collaborative efforts of the fathers of Gidget and Moondoggie. Gidget is transformed from a sexually confused tomboy into a bouncy and ultrafeminine teenage girl who wears her boyfriend's fraternity pin on her fluffy white sweater while she stumbles along the beach in her high-heeled shoes. It seems as though without pause and without reason Gidget has forgotten everything that happened to her over the summer—all of her troubles with athleticism and femininity are quickly overcome and transformed into pure female delight in the sort of happy ending we can see with Dorothy Malone caressing the symbol of an oil empire in Sirk's *Written on the Wind* (1954). Moondoggie is similarly transformed from a moody rebellious youth, in danger of sinking into anti-capitalist counterculture, into a respectable future lawyer. Meanwhile, Kahoona never was a true surf bum, and it appears that his rebel persona and the suggestions of non-white ethnicity were just a masquerade.

As a clean teenpic, *Gidget* concludes by telling us that Gidget's summer of trial was actually an illusion, and the solution to a happy teen life, for both girls and boys, is to abide by traditional family structures and obey one's father. Even after the anxieties associated with teen identity have been thoroughly rehearsed, the narrative resolves all these issues by reassuring us that bourgeois patriarchy is still the code of the land and that its corresponding social boundaries remain intact. This message is reinforced visually, for once the main characters have been relegated to socially acceptable positions either through paternal control or by virtue of employment, they suddenly appear out of place on the beach by virtue of their clothing and behavior.

The sudden resolution of Gidget's identity problems functions as an object lesson for teenage girls. If a girl is careful not to transgress the boundaries of feminine behavior and keeps her body, intellect, and emotions in check, then her teenage years will be relatively tranquil. For a female teenage boundary figure to achieve this balanced position, her process of maturation should proceed under the close supervision of her father, who may closely monitor her appearance, the company she keeps, and her financial resources. By following her father's instructions to go on a traditional arranged date, Gidget effectively gets what she wanted all along—a date with Moondoggie. Therefore, the message of *Gidget* is that one can avoid the terrible conflicts, humiliations, and brushes with death that plagued Gidget's summer by relinquishing control of one's life to paternal regulations and distancing oneself from the symbolic disruptions of the beach boundary zone Daddy fears.

NOTES

1. "Gidget," lyric by Patti Washington, music by Fred Karger.
2. As is common in films and television programs about teenagers, the actors are often much older than the characters they are playing. In *Gidget,* the actors playing Gidget's friends were in their twenties, while Sandra Dee was an actual teenager in 1959.
3. The idea of the teenager as an object of scientific study is not uncommon in 1950–60s teenpics. For example, much of the narrative of *Beach Party* (William Asher, 1963) centers on the research of Professor Sutwell (Robert Cummings), an anthropologist who sets up shop in a house on the beach to study teen behavior. The professor watches beach-going teenagers through telescopes and eavesdrops on their conversations with listening devices. He compares their dancing and courting antics to the behavior of exotic birds and "savage races," alluding to the fear that teenagers might threaten the society's racial taxonomies, particularly through music and dance. The study of teenagers in narratives like *Beach Party* never seems to produce much in the way of explanation for their behaviors, instead serving to characterize teen identity as aberrant, exotic, foreign, and uncivilized.
4. Although psychoanalysis was certainly practiced in the United States before the 1950s, psychoanalytic theory became more widely understood after World War II, when psychoanalysis became central in American psychiatric training. In addition, books on psychoanalysis, including collections of Freud's case studies, often attained best-seller status in the 1950s (Walker 4, 7).
5. It is interesting to note that the father's psychosomatic ailment is treated with pressure on the temples. In *Studies on Hysteria,* one of Freud and Breuer's suggested treatments for hysterical patients was

placing pressure on sensitive areas of the head. This was a controversial notion at the time and was rarely employed in practice, but it does indicate that pressure on the surface on the body is related to the release of unconscious anxieties. Significantly, the first American edition of *Studies on Hysteria* was published in 1957, just before *Gidget* was in production.

6. Studies of film melodrama have produced a substantial body of work demonstrating the relationship between psychoanalytic concepts, particularly hysteria, and melodramatic narratives. A significant product of this scholarship is the critical strategy of "reading against the grain," which regards the perceived emotional and syntactical excesses of melodrama as hysterical symptoms, pointing to the text's repressed ideological content. Relevant texts include Thomas Elsaesser's "Tales of Sound and Fury: Observations on the Family Melodrama," in *Home Is Where the Heart Is: Studies in Melodrama and the Woman's Film,* ed. Christine Gledhill (London: British Film Institute, 1987), 43–69, and Mary Ann Doane's *The Desire to Desire: The Woman's Film of the 1940s* (Bloomington: Indiana University Press, 1987).

7. Thanks to Ann Bernardo for pointing out Gidget's employment of feminine falsehood at the luau.

8. In *Gidget Goes Hawaiian* (Paul Wendkos 1961), the film is peppered with exoticized references to Hawaiian culture, from scantily clad hula girls to lascivious "native boys" who, confusingly enough, speak with Japanese accents.

9. For more on Sirk's commentary on melodramatic endings, see Douglas Sirk, *Sirk on Sirk: Interviews with Jon Halliday.*

Works Cited

Danesi, Marcel. 1994. *Cool: The Signs and Meanings of Adolescence.* Toronto: University of Toronto Press.

de Lauretis, Teresa. 1991. "Film and the Visible." In *How Do I Look?: Queer Film and Video,* ed. Bad Object-Choices, 225–76. Seattle: Bay Press.

Doherty, Thomas. 1988. *Teenagers and Teenpics: The Juvenilization of American Movies in the 1950s.* Boston: Unwin Hyman.

Freud, Sigmund, and Joseph Breuer. 1957. *Studies on Hysteria.* New York: Basic Books.

Nowell-Smith, Geoffrey. 1987. "Minnelli and Melodrama." In *Home Is Where the Heart Is: Studies in Melodrama and the Woman's Film,* ed. Christine Gledhill, 70–74. London: British Film Institute.

Sirk, Douglas. 1971. *Sirk on Sirk: Interviews with Jon Halliday.* London: Secker and Warburg for the British Film Institute.

Stacey, Jackie. 1994. *Star Gazing: Hollywood Cinema and Female Spectatorship.* London: Routledge.

Staehling, Richard. 1975. "From Rock around the Clock to the Trip: The Truth about Teen Movies." In *Kings of the Bs: Working within the Hollywood System, An Anthology of Film History and Criticism,* ed. Todd McCarthy and Charles Flynn, 220–51. New York: E. P. Dutton.

Walker, Janet. 1993. *Couching Resistance: Women, Film and Psychoanalytic Psychiatry.* Minneapolis: University of Minnesota Press.

chapter 4

Girls on the Edge of the Reagan Era

Chuck Kleinhans

In 1980, the election year that led to the end of both the Carter presidency and the Iranian hostage crisis, three remarkable girl culture films appeared. *Foxes* (Adrian Lyne), a hip melodrama, portrays the lives of four sixteen-year-olds from dysfunctional Los Angeles families. *Little Darlings* (Roland F. Maxwell), ostensibly a summer-camp comedy, depicts a contest between a tough working-class girl and a privileged rich kid to lose their virginity. From intense rivalry, the pair move to bonding as best friends. *Times Square* (Allan Moyle) also joins a street-smart teen with a rich girl as they escape authority, live by their wits on the street, and produce a grassroots teen girl rebellion against an urban renewal real estate deal. Taken together, these films capture a social and historical moment, a liminal space for female teens poised between the post-Vietnam, post-Watergate period and the "Reagan renewal."

By viewing them as girl culture films, I mean to stress that while boys and men appear, the films are primarily about white young women bonding, expressing the situation of girls in a group or pair, and showing the world from their perspective. I want to validate these films by considering them: recalling *Foxes*, a film often remembered by women who saw it when it was first released but neglected today; remembering *Little Darlings*, often referred to as "Little Dykes" in the 1980s lesbian community; and rediscovering *Times Square*, which bombed in its own time but is amazingly prescient today with the Disneyfication of West 42nd Street in Manhattan. I also want to reflect on some questions of reading the way these films express the independence of young adolescent girls—or the lack of it—in relation to a past history and social moment as well as cinematic expression.

Context

Because they are examples of commercial entertainment cinema, these films must be placed in relation to their times and understood in the context of other girl/teen films. Such films narrate three general (if often overlapping) age phases of representation and story. First, we find films of female childhood played out by juvenile actors and bounded by a preadolescent time frame (for example, *The Little Princess* [1939]). Then there are films of early adolescence such as those discussed here. Third are dramas of the later teen years and early adulthood when girls become fully mature adults (for example, *Ruby in Paradise* [1993]). Within the Hollywood system, these age groupings fulfill two obvious functions. On the one hand, they signal narratives that tend to be keyed to specific audiences, in this case girls and young women. On the other hand, they provide appropriate narrative frames, since the teen years as a time of transition provide a bedrock for creating cinematically effective drama, conflict, and change. Further, given the Hollywood production system, we can recognize in U.S. cinema distinct patterns dictated by the evolving star system, ranging from the perennial girlhood of Mary Pickford to the (often delayed) cinematic development of female juveniles such as Shirley Temple and Judy Garland. And audiences have the experience of watching such girl stars as Elizabeth Taylor, Hayley Mills, Jodie Foster, Brooke Shields, and Drew Barrymore grow up.

The historical development of a distinct U.S. teen culture in the post–World War II era adds another dimension. In *The Road to Romance and Ruin: Teen Films and Youth Culture*, Jon Lewis surveys films of the 1970s and 1980s and finds that

> teen films all seem to focus on a single social concern: the breakdown of traditional forms of authority: patriarchy; law and order; and institutions like the school, the church, and the family. . . . By and large, the teen film presides over the eventual discovery of viable and often traditional forms of authority . . . in effect, the restoration of the adult authority informed rather than radicalized by youth. (3)

Lewis concentrates on films that represent youth culture primarily through institutions that highlight teens. Most teen films show mixed-gender groups—such as *Grease* (1978), *Fast Times at Ridgemont High* (1982), and *The Breakfast Club* (1985)—or concentrate on primarily male groups, such as *Porky's* (1981) and *Revenge of the Nerds* (1984). Other writers have broadened the scope of teen films. For instance, William Paul's *Laughing Screaming* elaborates teen horror (for example, *A Nightmare on Elm Street* series [1984–89]) and gross-out comedies (for example, *National Lampoon's Animal House* [1978]). We could expand the male teen category by adding military basic-training stories (*Platoon* [1986]; *Full Metal Jacket* [1987]) or reformatory movies (*Bad Boys* [1983]). Some films concentrate on female characters' point of view, such as the slasher horror genre (*Halloween* [1978]; *I Know What You Did Last Summer* [1997]) so well analyzed by Carol Clover in *Men, Women, and Chain Saws* for the figure of the "Final Girl" who defeats the killer.

Some gals' and guys' teen films show significant actions of female leads from their young women's point of view (the sexual initiation sequences in *Fast Times* or *Valley Girl* [1983], or the sympathetic female leads of *Sixteen Candles* [1984] or *Smooth Talk* [1985]). However, these films do not show girl culture or female bonding in groups or pairs in the same way as the three films I am concentrating on. It is not until the 1990s with films such as *Mi Vida Loca* (1994), *The Incredibly True Adventure of Two Girls in Love* (1995), and *Girls Town* (1995), the spate of costume films such as *Little Women* (1994), and the various Jane Austen adaptations such as *Clueless* (1995) and *Emma* (1996) that we observe attention centered on young female culture.

More particular to the cinema, the appearance of the three films in the same year marks a pattern. Three suggests more than an accident. (The rule of thumb in Hollywood is that any significant action must be shown/spoken three times: once for clever viewers, twice to be clear to the majority, and a third time for the slow or distracted. Two could be coincidence; three is a pattern.) These films appeared on the cusp of the Reagan era, but movies are not politically clairvoyant. Given the time it takes to get scripts into production and exhibition, it would be foolish to read back directly from the fact of the conservative shift signaled by Reagan's election (in November 1980) to the precise production of meaning in these filmic narratives. However, the late 1970s was a time that embodied the contradictions of a specific historical moment, and in that way the films can be seen as exhibiting symptoms of deeper structures, some of which took on a different aspect with the shift in national executive governance. Therefore, considering the basic social fantasies embodied in these films helps us understand their uniqueness to their time, as well as that time, and also their ongoing appeal.

Fantasy

Psychoanalytically based criticism perceives fantasy as developing around deep unconscious patterns found in the mind and echoed in the text. But my interest here is in what I will call social fantasies: somewhat vague and general projections that satisfy persistent needs in specific social groups. For young people such fantasies found in creative cultural products facilitate a useful projection, a kind of modeling behavior, that is practical and needed in adjusting to life at moments when it seems difficult—and sometimes impossible—to keep physical, emotional, and intellectual levels all in sync. Jon Lewis plausibly argues that *Rebel Without a Cause* (1955) is a foundational teen culture film, and that both in story and star image James Dean functioned for a generation as the archetypal "moody (male) teenager." In our time, the remarkably successful television channel MTV has prominently maintained its teen audience base with the documentary shows "Real Life" and "Road Rules." These series have a common denominator of offering glimpses, primarily to those not yet there, of what may soon be their experience: living away from home, being sexually active, and living with others you have to learn to get along with instead of family. For middle and high school students, these shows are model situations that allow them to project their own fears and anxieties, hopes and desires, onto other characters and safely observe actions and decisions that they may not be ready for in real life, but know that they probably will experience sooner or later. The same function is served by the MTV dramatic shows such as "My So-Called Life" and "Undressed." The former (originally an ABC network drama in the 1994 season) deals with the interpersonal and emotional aspects of high school life, and the latter depicts the sexual experiences of teens. As has often been noted, other recent successful television shows have the same role and appeal: "Dawson's Creek" (small-town teen life) and "Felicity" (off to college) in a melodramatically realistic vein, and "Buffy the Vampire Slayer," "Angel," and "Roswell" in a more fantastic way. Even MTV cartoon comedy shows provide this kind of modeling: "Beavis and Butt-head" with the boredom and authoritarian atmosphere of school and fast-food workplaces, and "Daria" with the title brainy girl suffering the inanity of school sociality and her family. Of course this idea of projective fantasy does not exhaust the audience's relation to these or other works, but it is most assuredly a key part of the media appeal. In this framework, the three girl culture films I am considering also contain social fantasies. I want to consider the films in terms of the nature of those fantasies, both in their own historical moment and as they have continued to have relevance for contemporary viewers.

Foxes: Reconstituting the Family

By the time *Foxes* appeared, the notion of southern California teen culture as the cutting edge of U.S. culture as a whole was well established. In the 1950s, *Rebel Without a Cause* established the terrain in the popular cinematic imagination, and the beach party movies, such as *Beach Party* (1963) and *How to Stuff a Wild Bikini* (1965), provided a carefree teen comedy framework while the Beach Boys and other surf-sound pop music groups created an aural background throughout the 1960s. The Berkeley student movement and flower children in northern California expanded media attention. By the end of that decade journalist Tom Wolfe was covering "a new way of life out there" for eastern seaboard readers in feature journalism on southern California, in particular in his essays, "The Pump House Gang" and "The Kandy-Kolored Tangerine-Flake Streamline Baby." Trained in American studies at Yale, adopting a hip persona and a florid, highly subjective writing style, Wolfe moved against the grain of media concern with campus and antiwar protests and hippie culture, uncovering a fundamental vapidness, a youth culture not rebelling against authority but detached from absent parents.

A decade later, *Foxes* presents four young women looking for their own place in a southern California culture that, far from celebrating youthful freedom, entraps it. The girl group has a common goal to save Annie (Cherie Currie), who bounces from irresponsible drug use to physically abusive encounters with her father, a cop. Jeanie (Jodie Foster) acts as the mother to the group and to her own divorced mother (Sally Kellerman), who introduces her new boyfriend from bed when the teen is leaving for school. Madge (Marilin Kagan) is sweet, warm, and naive, while Dee (Kandice Stroh) is conventionally attractive, manipulative, and cynical.

The girls move through a gauzy Los Angeles that complements the narrative search for their own space. Rather than the hard, open, bright midday light that dominates most film images of L. A., here exteriors are shot in the early morning and late afternoon or at dusk, with a diffused light. Interiors seem oppressively small and cramped with other people. With intense exterior light softly diffused into an extremely low-key environment, extensive use of long lens close-ups increases the sense of spatial compression. The visual style matches a slow-moving narrative. Often the camera follows characters through the events, privileging visual narration as opposed to the conventional Hollywood practice of the script dominating storytelling by setting up standard plot points. And the film begins with the slow opening on the audio track of Donna Summer's pop hit, "On the Radio," which repeats during transition scenes. A song of remembrance, it creates an elegiac mood underlined by the soft visuals.

In child development class, alarmed by Jeanie's holding her baby doll upside-down while washing it, the distressed teacher scolds, "We show our babies love!" But love is exactly what these girls lack. Earlier, Annie's father handcuffed her sister at home to keep the girl from getting an abortion. Dee's divorcing parents have no time or place for her, and Jeanie's mother, now a forty-year-old trying to finish her undergraduate degree at UCLA, needs mothering from her daughter. The girls dream of getting a place of their own, a physically and emotionally separate place to escape. At first it seems that they have such an opportunity when Madge's boyfriend, Jay (Randy Quaid), an older working man, offers to let them have his place while he is out of town on business. The girls celebrate with a little dinner party, but it is invaded by other teens, including a rough bunch of guys who start a fight and trash the place. In the aftermath, Jeanie's mother decides to move out with her new boyfriend and Madge faces Jay's anger and frustration. When the girls offer to pay for all the damage, Jay yells that they could work years waitressing at Denny's before they could come up with that much money, a moment that underlines the girls' limited economic options. Annie's father confines her in a hospital, but the druggy teen escapes and runs off. Eventually Annie ends up with a couple who pick her up, intending to engage her in a sexual escapade, but in the aftermath of a traffic accident, she dies. The film ends with Madge marrying Jay, and a now college-bound Jeanie taking the wedding flowers to Annie's grave, finishing the elegiac tone of the entire narrative.

Foxes presents a world where girls must negotiate a situation governed by dysfunctional adults who have all the power: physical and institutional in the case of Annie's cop father, and economic for the other girls. There are no happy solutions to the situations they face: Annie dies—more from poor judgment under distress (taking the ride) than any self-destructive impulse. Madge finds her Mr. Right, and for a moment the girls seem to have, as Dee calls it, "a place of our own . . . a family, sort of," but they cannot prevent outsiders from wrecking it. Madge and Dee revert. Only Jeanie, the motherly leader, pushes on, remembering Annie and looking forward. The film is bittersweet. Reality intervenes in living as an adult, and aspirations cannot be met without paying dues. One could read the conclusion in terms of Lewis's postulate of a fundamental conservatism in the endings of teen films, but I would argue that the film's ending validates the near-utopian fantasy of the girls finding their own space and way. Within an overall elegiac mood, the film overturns Wolfe's counterintuitive position that the new way of life for teens rests on an extreme vapidness in individuals. *Foxes* shows the social situation of girls unable to transcend their larger social situation, but the film concludes it is not their fault. Jeanie is the object lesson—she carries on by learning to adapt and solve problems with the options she has at hand.

Little Darlings: Contested Bonding

Little Darlings contrasts Angel (Kristy McNichol), a working-class girl, tough on the surface, living with her single mom, to Ferris (Tatum O'Neal), a fifteen-year-old private school student and daughter of wealthy (and divorcing) parents. The pair meet on their way to a girls' summer camp. Against a typical high-key, comedic *mise-en-scène,* the campers engage in sports activities, camp songs, and a comic food fight. Angel and Ferris's initial antipathy turns to intense rivalry when a sexually active teen who has been modeling for television commercials challenges the pair to lose their virginity. Encouraged by the other campers, Ferris schemes to entice a high school teacher working as a camp counselor (Armand Assante), while Angel is attracted to Randy (Matt Dillon), a boy from a nearby camp. Filled with hyper-romantic illusions, Ferris pursues but is (predictably) gently turned away by her inappropriate love object. However, she gives the other girls the false impression that the pair did make love.

Meanwhile, narratively cross-cut with Ferris's adventures, Angel awkwardly pursues Randy. She paddles a canoe to his camp across the lake and gets him to come away with her. Angel gives him bootlegged beer to turn him on but he passes out. The next encounter takes place in a dark abandoned boathouse with chiaroscuro lighting underlining the tension. Angel's hesitation, awkwardness, and actual modesty turn Randy off (though not before his hunky teen body is displayed wearing briefs). Finally, in another boathouse meeting, she overcomes her nervousness and tentativeness, but instead of experiencing sex as a consummation and blossoming of an emotional relation, Angel concludes, "I feel so lonesome." Returning to her camp mates, Angel denies anything took place. Later she breaks off the relation with Randy explaining, "We started in the middle." At last, sadder but wiser, Angel and Ferris tell each other the truth and bond. Arriving back from camp, Angel introduces Ferris to her mom as "my best friend." The camera freezes them in a close two-shot smiling at each other.

Little Darlings contains two different fantasies. For Ferris it provides the overt fantasy of romance with a handsome older man (presented as a mild and comic delusion in O'Neal's excellent performance). For Angel it balances pleasure (her aggressively gazing at Randy's body, reinforced by shots of him from her point of view) with realistically awkward and hesitant emotional scenes. Although Randy is clumsy and somewhat confused by Angel's mixed signals, he is not mean or careless with her. After sex and her revelation that it was her first time, he tries to talk with her and reestablish their relation. Later he argues they could start over from the beginning. Although the film seems conservative on one level, actually it contains a different fantasy within a cautionary tale. Essentially *Little Darlings* recommends that girls resist peer pressure and manipulation, that they try to avoid being what they are not or are not ready to be, and it urges the reward of emotional life as "best friends" as an adequate substitute, at least at this stage of life. Of course, it is precisely this same-sex bonding that allows the further fantasy of a lesbian love between the two. This is reinforced by bookended sequences: initially Angel is seen lighting up a cigarette and then having a taller boy verbally come on to her. She responds by unhesitatingly and swiftly kicking him in the groin. And in the final shot the gal pals have their arms around each other as they smile into each others' faces. Even without taking the story to an active homoerotic fantasy, the film endorses holding on to homosocial girl friendship.

Times Square: Breaking Away

Times Square opens at night on West 42nd Street, in the 1970s the notorious Manhattan neighborhood of porn shops, X-rated movie theaters, strip bars, sex shows, and other lowlife venues. Among the druggies, pimps, and disco dolls, sixteen-year-old Nicky (Robin Johnson) appears as a street-savvy runaway, a street musician with a guitar and amp. Loud, brash, destructive, and aggressive, she is carted off to a psychiatric hospital where she shares a room with another distressed teen, conventionally feminine rich girl Pamela (Trini Alvarez), thirteen, daughter of an unctuous widower, the mayor's commissioner to clean up Times Square. The girls bond and escape the hospital. They steal an ambulance, establish homeless quarters in an abandoned wharf, steal food, wash auto windows for change, set up a three-card monte game, comically attempt a mugging, and escape a pursuing cop. Throughout this section, the girls' fun, energetic, and rebellious spirit is encouraged by the denizens of Times Square who support, rather than threaten, the pair. Upbeat contemporary music adds to the mood. (Producer Robert Stigwood was a major record executive who produced *Saturday Night Fever* [1977] and *Grease* [1978]. The soundtrack features The Talking Heads, Lou Reed, Patti Smith, Suzi Quatro, The Cars, The Ramones, The Pretenders, and The Cure.)

Nicky takes Pamela to a bar where waitresses dance topless. Pamela is hired on, though she will not undress. Her first performance starts awkwardly, but quickly her sheer energy takes over and wins the crowd, to the pride of a now-very-butch-looking Nicky with tied back and slicked-down hair. The pair quickly become midtown, street-culture icons, especially as the very femme Pamela's picture appears on "missing child" posters, and they draw the attention of late-night DJ Johnny LaGuardia (Tim Curry)—who has been mocking the attempts to clean up Times Square by picturing the campaign as a moralistic response by uptight official elite culture against the vibrant, earthy, creative perversions at society's bottom. With the runaway pair now dubbed the Sleaze Sisters, and amplified throughout the city by the DJ, Nicky believes she can become famous. When the pair begin a guerrilla theater gambit by dropping television sets off roofs, Pamela begins to have misgivings, seeing the destructive aspect of Nicky's manic behavior. "We're going to crash," she warns. When Johnny LaGuardia shows up at the wharf hideout, bottle of vodka in hand, he and Pamela drink. Nicky arrives and mistakenly thinks they are romantically involved. She attacks, smashes things up, tears up poems Pamela had written, jumps in the river, and breaks down, calling for "Pammy."

Refitted with maintenance drugs, Nicky makes a final midnight appearance performing in Times Square. Pamela's media savvy has gathered a crowd of teen girls, dressed in black plastic garbage bags (a kind of "if they treat us like garbage, we'll be garbage" fashion statement), and Nicky, on top of a movie theater marquee, sings her signature number. As the police close in to arrest her, she leaps off into the crowd, which safely captures her in a blanket, and they all run off together into the night.

Times Square provides a pair of fantasies. The runaway rich girl learns to become self-sufficient, emotional, and expressive—to shout, to dance, to stride around enjoying herself in public space. But she also becomes more responsible, as she ends up taking care of Nicky emotionally. Although Pamela returns home to her father's domain, it is as someone who is a young adult, no longer a little girl. Nicky provides the fantasy of being able to survive on the street. The unreal aspect of this is much more obvious today: in the film the girls do not have to face rape, theft, street drug culture, lack of medical care, and brutal winter weather. But the film appeared before homelessness became a widespread phenomenon in the 1980s when Reagan calculatedly engineered the removal of social safety nets, downsizing welfare and aid programs and deliberately driving up unemployment to shape up the workforce. Today Nicky's situation would be read as an unmistakable example of bipolar (manic-depressive) disorder, and her attractive manic energy would be interpreted as self-destructive much sooner. Also, in retrospect, the film's interpretation of Times Square redevelopment is hopelessly naive. The film postulates it as "caused" by traditional morality rather than recognizing the source as business interests who long have used scare arguments about morality and crime to promote their economic agenda.

Times Square has other problems. The film bombed in its initial release (for example, playing only a week in Chicago before disappearing). In 1999 it was shown on a cable movie channel, leaving a new audience to claim it. Though not atrocious, the direction badly misses its mark in key scenes. Director Allan Moyle fails to cheat shots in the final crowd sequence, ineptly making it appear that only a handful of girls are present, rather than the thousands that the fantasy ending needs. A crucial turning point, a recognition scene between Pamela and her father, when he appears at the club to see his daughter dancing, fails to underline the parent's sudden awareness of his child's sexual potential and the changed understanding that results for both. And the Johnny LaGuardia radio figure is haltingly conceived (compared to, say, the same device in *Choose Me* [1984], *Talk Radio* [1988], *Rude* [1995] or in Moyle's *Pump Up the Volume* [1990]).

Figure 1. Gauzy diffuse light warms the opening scenes of *Foxes*.

Visualizing Girls' Space

Although projective social fantasies are solidly grounded in narration, their visual expressions often remain fixed in memory, just as the pictures in a child's book may be vividly recalled long after the story is forgotten. In these three films key moments of production design reinforce the fantasy projection of girls' space.

Of the three films, *Foxes* displays the most accomplished visual *mise-en-scène*. The opening sequence establishes a familiar teen girl scene as the camera in close-up glides slowly over the details of Jeanie's bedroom and what seems like the early morning aftermath of a sleepover (see figure 1). Gauzy diffuse light warms the markers: hair curlers, Clearasil, Twinkies, deodorant, pictures of John Travolta and

Figure 2. The dinner party at Jay's apartment.

Kiss, polaroids, and sleeping teen faces. As the radio alarm summons everyone awake, the day begins, the group stirs, and Annie is doused with water—a mildly comic representation of her recalcitrant relation to normality. The warmth of this beginning is gradually undermined. First we realize it is another school day, then that Jeanie's mother was not home the night before, and finally—explosively—that Annie's father is at the door trying to physically apprehend his runaway daughter. The utopic girls' space is vulnerable to adult instability. And against encroaching children. When Madge's parents agree to host a party for her friends, complete with beer, the annoying presence of little sister and her middle school pals destroys the fantasy.

Figure 3. Randy in the stark seduction sequence in *Little Darlings*.

While Jeanie's pickup truck gives her some safe mobility, the adult world remains dysfunctional. At the rock concert Jeanie's father holds a deeply personal discussion with his daughter in the appropriated privacy of a backstage men's lavatory. The girls' supreme fantasy space is displayed when they hold a small dinner party for a few boys at Jay's apartment (see figure 2). But the ensuing destruction again visually demonstrates the instability of girls' space.

Although *Little Darlings* transpires in the (almost) all-girl space of summer camp, it is a space controlled by adults who can be challenged only through the libidinal infantilism of a food fight. Angel finds the private space of the old boathouse to prepare for her seduction of Randy. But the appropriated place remains stark, dramatic,

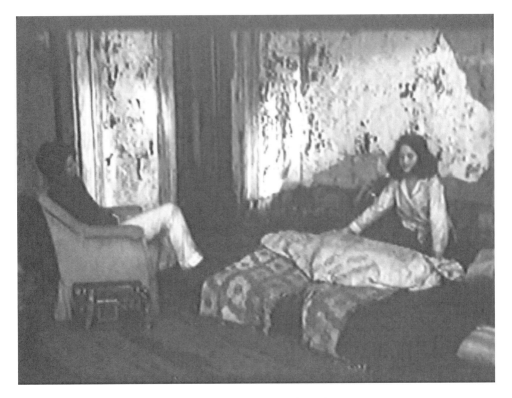

Figure 4. One of the few secure places the girls make in *Times Square.*

and "masculine," without any conventionally "feminine" conveniences or comforts such as a bed or bathroom (see figure 3).

In *Times Square,* while the Sleaze Sisters appropriate public space on West 42nd Street (as in the three-card monte game), that action is always temporary and unstable since the authorities chase them. Their only secure place is the nest they construct in an abandoned wharf (see figure 4). But when an outsider arrives, it destabilizes the relationship. While they are on the run, the only safe public space is the topless bar, itself only tangentially secure (see figure 5).

The visual depiction of a place for girls in all three films underlines that though the protagonists may find, in Virginia Woolf's phrase, "a room of one's own," these spaces are inherently temporary, contingent, and unstable—just like the girls' lives.

Figure 5. The only safe public space for the girls—a topless bar. *Times Square*

Girls on the Edge

In the 1970s, British cultural studies analyst Angela McRobbie began important work on girl culture. Although she established key
parts of the terrain based on U.K. experience, historical change and
a North American framework call for modifying some of that analysis. The initial flush of fandom for Madonna in the early 1980s,
for instance, marked a "girls just want to have fun" reclamation of
girls' space through the vehicle of music video as detailed by Lisa
Lewis. Susan Seidelman's 1982 film *Smithereens* featured a bold
post-punk female who made it seem more interesting to break away
than stay at home—a theme continued with star power three years
later in Seidelman's *Desperately Seeking Susan.* Periodic repetitions

of rebellious girl images, as with the short-lived but notable Spice Girls, marked the power of a projective fantasy of "girl power." Some try to dismiss early Madonna or the Spice Girls, or Mariah Carey, who seems to successfully recycle a teen girl image in many of her videos. But that dismissal goes along with the easy disregard for girls themselves.

In contrast, sentimental male fantasy coming-of-age films are consistently overvalued in film culture, for example *American Graffiti* (1973), *The Graduate* (1967), *Blue Velvet* (1986), and *The Lion King* (1994). The three girl culture films I have discussed here first appeared at a particular moment for girl culture. Largely ignored in a male version of cinema history (Jon Lewis does not mention them in his book), these three films have found their place in a low-key and awkward way. *Foxes* has been recently reissued on tape, highlighting Jodie Foster's continued fame, and *Little Darlings*, twenty years later, is still on the comedy shelves at my local video store, which relentlessly displays only works with a steady rental base.

It is true that the three films are all-white. People of color appear only as background—local color in *Foxes* and *Times Square* and totally absent from *Little Darlings* (which also—and without any explanation or reflection—has all the happy campers singing a Christian hymn together). But the films also have no noticeable product placements and other trappings of High Concept filmmaking. They stand as some of the last examples of mainstream Hollywood film before the full force of blockbuster-driven economics struck. In that sense they are interesting as examples of the quirky offbeat style and stories allowed in the aftermath of the studio era and before "different" meant only Sundance-auteurist.

The late 1970s were peculiar times for girls. The Women's Movement was more than a decade old in 1980, but it seldom spoke well to the issues of teen girls. Although feminism expanded the material conditions for girls by addressing reproductive rights and sexual abuse of children, the image of the women's movement as depicted in mainstream media and in some cases actual practice often conveyed a male-bashing rhetoric, downwardly mobile counterculture lifestyle, and proscriptive standards of behavior and appearance. For girls in the process of freeing themselves from the constraints of childhood, second-wave feminism often negated key concerns of girls becoming women in areas they wanted to explore: dress, cosmetics, grooming, heterosexual activity, and teen culture— especially in music and dance. At a time when the two new music expressions were punk and disco, *Ms.* magazine feminism seemed stuck hopelessly in folksong.

The decade of the 1970s was also a period of economic uncertainty. High inflation and high unemployment rates meant girls were still in the typical position of having vastly fewer options than their male peers. It was also the time of the last big push for the never-to-be-passed Equal Rights Amendment. There was actually a teen girl in the White House—Amy Carter—but many tsk-tsked at her relatively liberal interests (such as ecology) and actions (she appeared once on "Saturday Night Live"). In this somewhat bleak landscape, few noticed what would become in the next twenty years the most important face of teen feminism: girl sports. Gymnastics, ice skating, track and field, and tennis, for example, produced Olympic stars and world champions while little-noticed Title IX mandated equitable treatment for women in school athletics. This created the material and cultural foundation for later triumphs such as women's soccer in the late 1990s. Twenty years earlier, these three films, like the teens in *Foxes*, stand in an awkward relation to 1980 culture—unable to find their own place but depicting a difficult, strained, and often unjust situation that called out for change.

NOTES

This essay developed out of an independent study on girl culture with Laura Vazquez and Janie Hayes—they taught me a lot. Julia Lesage and Kathleen Karlyn discussed the films and issues with me as well. Dave Tolchinsky and Jon Lewis gave valuable feedback.

WORKS CITED

Clover, Carol. 1992. *Men, Women, and Chain Saws: Gender in the Modern Horror Film.* Princeton: Princeton University Press.

Lewis, Jon. 1992. *The Road to Romance and Ruin: Teen Films and Youth Culture.* New York: Routledge.

Lewis, Lisa. 1990. *Gender Politics and MTV: Voicing the Difference.* Philadelphia: Temple University Press.

McRobbie, Angela and Jenny Garber. 1976. "Girls and Subcultures." In Ken Gelder and Sara Thornton, eds. *The Subcultures Reader.* New York: Routledge, 1997.

McRobbie, Angela. 1990. *Feminism and Youth Culture: From Jackie to Just Seventeen.* Cambridge, MA: Unwin Hyman.

Paul, William. 1994. *Laughing Screaming: Modern Hollywood Horror and Comedy.* New York: Columbia University Press.

Wolfe, Tom. 1965. "The Kandy-Kolored Tangerine-Flake Streamline Baby," in *The Kandy-Kolored Tangerine-Flake Streamline Baby.* New York: Farrar, Straus & Giroux.

Wolfe, Tom. 1968. *The Pump House Gang.* New York: Farrar, Straus & Giroux.

chapter 5

Sorrowful Black Death Is Not a Hot Ticket

bell hooks

Hollywood is not into plain old sorrowful death. The death that captures the public imagination in movies, the death that sells, is passionate, sexualized, glamorized and violent. Films like *One False Move, True Romance, Reservoir Dogs, Menace II Society, A Perfect World* bring us the sensational heat of relentless dying. It's fierce— intense—and there is no time to mourn. Dying that makes audiences contemplative, sad, mindful of the transitory nature of human life has little appeal. When portrayed in the contemporary Hollywood film, such deaths are swift, romanticized by soft lighting and ele- giac soundtracks. The sights and sounds of death do not linger long enough to disturb the senses, to remind us in any way that sorrow for the dying may be sustained and unrelenting. When Hollywood films depict sorrowful death, audiences come prepared to cry. Films like *Philadelphia* advertise the pathos so that even before tickets are bought and seats are taken, everyone knows that tears are in order, but that the crying time will not last long.

The racial politics of Hollywood is such that there can be no serious representations of death and dying when the characters are African-Americans. Sorrowful black death is not a hot ticket. In the financially successful film *The Bodyguard,* the sister of Rachel Marron (Whitney Houston) is accidentally assassinated by the killer she has hired. There is no grief, no remembrance. In most Hol- lywood movies, black death is violent. It is often trivialized and mocked—as in that viciously homophobic moment in *Menace II So- ciety* when a young black male crack addict holding a fast-food ham- burger while seeking drugs tells the powerful drug dealer, "I'll suck your dick," only to be blown away for daring to suggest that the hard gangsta mack would be at all interested. Pleased with the killing, he laughingly offers the hamburger to onlookers, a gesture that defines the value of black life. It's worth nothing. It's dead meat.

Even black children cannot be spared Hollywood's cruelty. Audiences watching the film *Paris Trout* witness the prolonged, brutal slaughter of a gifted southern black girl by a powerful, sadistic, racist white man. The black males who are her relatives are depicted as utterly indifferent. Too cowardly to save or avenge her life, for a few coins they willingly show the lawyer who will defend her killer the blood stains left by her dragging body, the bullet holes in the walls. Her life is worth nothing.

Violent Slaughter

Audiences are so accustomed to representations of the brutal death of black folks in Hollywood films that no one is outraged when our bodies are violently slaughtered. I could find no Hollywood movie where a white child is the object of a prolonged, brutal murder by a powerful white male—no image comparable to that of *Paris Trout*. Yet no group in the United States publicly protests against this image—even though the film is shown regularly on Home Box Office, reaching an audience far wider than the moviegoing public, finding its way into the intimate spaces of home life and the private world of family values. Apparently the graphic representation of the murder of a little black girl does not shock, does not engender grief or protest. There is collective cultural agreement that black death is inevitable, meaningless, not worth much. That there is nothing to mourn.

This is the culture Spike Lee confronts with his new film *Crooklyn*. On the surface, the movie appears to represent issues of death and dying in black life as though our survival matters, as though our living bodies count, yet in the end the usual Hollywood message about black death is reaffirmed. Lee has made a film that is both provocative and controversial. To introduce it to consumers who do not take black life seriously, advertisements give little indication of its content. Huge billboards tell consumers "The Smart Choice is Spike Lee's hilarious *Crooklyn*," suggesting that the film is a comedy. The seriousness of the subject matter must be downplayed, denied.

Expecting to see a comedy, moviegoers I talked to were not so much disappointed as puzzled by the fact that the comedic elements were overshadowed by the serious representation of a family in crisis that culminates with the mother's death. When the movie ended, the folks standing around the theatre in Greenwich Village were mostly saying: "It wasn't what I expected. It wasn't like his other films." But *Crooklyn* differs from Lee's previous work primarily because the major protagonist is a ten-year-old-girl, Troy (Zelda Harris). Positively radical in this regard—rarely do we see Hollywood films with Black female stars, not to mention child stars—*Crooklyn* invites audiences to look at the Black experience through Troy's eyes, to enter the spaces of her emotional universe, the intimate world of family and friends that ground her being and gives her life meaning.

Lee's magic as a film-maker has been best expressed by his construction of an aesthetic space wherein decolonized images (familiar representations of blackness that oppose racist stereotypes) are lovingly presented. But this radical intervention is most often framed by a conventional narrative and structure of representation that reinscribes stereotypical norms. The laughing darky family portrait that advertises *Crooklyn* is just one example. Moviegoers want to see this image rather than those that challenge it. This contradictory stance tends to undermine Lee's ability to subvert dominant representations of blackness. His radical images are usually overshadowed by stock characterizations and can easily be overlooked, particularly by audiences who are more accustomed to stereotypes. Even progressive, aware viewers may be so fascinated by the funky, funny "otherness" of typical Spike Lee black images that they refuse to "see" representations that challenge the conventional ways of looking at blackness.

J. Hoberman's review of *Crooklyn* in *Village Voice* is a perfect example of the way our standpoint can determine how we see a film that highlights issues of death and dying—to his mind's eye, "the grittier specifics of the Lee family drama" are exemplified by arguments at family dinners and witty disagreements over television programs. Indeed, he saw the movie as having "no particular plot;" never mentioning the mother's death, he did not see the film as constructing a context in which this event, more than any other, leads to a ten-year-old black girl's coming of age. Hoberman is more engaged with the comedic aspects of the film, especially those that center on the eldest child in this family of four boys and one girl, Clinton (Carlton Williams), the character who most resembles Lee himself. Not unlike other moviegoers I talked to, Hoberman seems more fascinated with the antics of Spike Lee, controversial film-maker, than with the content of this film. By deflecting attention away from *Crooklyn* and on to Lee, Hoberman and the others do not have to interrogate the film on its own terms. To do that would require looking at *Crooklyn*'s treatment of death and dying, and the way this aspect of the film fails to excite and challenge our imagination.

Play and Pleasure

Crooklyn is most compelling in those moments when it offers fictive representations of black subjectivity rarely seen in mainstream cinema, depictions that counter both racist stereotypes and facile notions of positive images. The property-owning, artistic, progressive 70s black family portrayed is one that dares to be different. The Carmichaels in no way represent the conventional black bourgeoisie: they are not obsessed with being upwardly mobile, with the material trappings of success. Counter-cultural—a mixture of the nationalistic movement for racial uplift and a bohemian artistic subculture—they represent an alternative to the bourgeois norm.

The father Woody (Delroy Lindo) is an aspiring jazz musician and composer, the mother Carolyn (Alfre Woodard) a non-traditional school teacher. Their five children are all encouraged by the progressive, hands-off parenting to be individuals with their own interests, passions, and obsessions. These are not your average kids: they take a democratic vote to see which television show will be watched and are made to participate equally in household chores. Though black nationalist in thinking shapes the family politics, the world they live in is multicultural and multi-ethnic—Italians, Latinos, gays and straight, young and old, the haves and have nots are all part of the mix. This is the world of cultural hybridity and border crossing extolled by progressive contemporary critics. And much of the film depicts that world "as is" not framed by the will to present images that are artificially positive or unduly negative.

Beginning in the style of a fictive documentary (enhanced initially by the cinematography of Arthur Jafa), the film's opening scene offers a panorama of visual images of black community that disrupts prevailing one-dimensional portrayals of urban black life. Highlighting scenes of play and pleasure, the beauty of black bodies, the faces of children and old men, we see joy in living as opposed to the usual depictions of racial dehumanization and deprivation. These representations signal heightened creativity, an unbridled imagination that creates splendor in a world of lack, that makes elegance and grace so common a part of the everyday as to render them regular expressions of natural communion with the universe.

Northerners in Drag

This opening sequence acts like a phototext, calling us to be resisting readers able to embrace a vision of blackness that challenges the norm. Lee engages in a politics of representation which cultural critic Saidiya Hartman describes in "Roots and Romance," an essay on black photography, as "a critical labor of reconstruction." She explains, "It is a resolutely counterhegemonic labor that has as its aim the establishment of other standards of aesthetic value and visual possibility. The intention of the work is corrective representation." At rare moments the camera leads—to catch sight of such empowering images. Seduced by this initial moment of radical intervention—by the way it shifts paradigms and requires new ways of seeing—the enthralled viewer can sit in a daze of delight through the rest of the movie, failing to experience how the cinematic direction and narrative structure counteract the initial subversive representations.

A distinction must be made between oppositional representations and romantically glorifying images of blackness which white supremacist thinking as it informs movie-making may have rendered invisible. Visibility does not mean that images are inherently radical or progressive. Hartman urges cultural critics to ask necessary questions: "Simply put, how are redemptive narratives of blackness shaped and informed by romantic racialism, the pastoral and sentimental representation of black life? How is the discourse of black cultural authenticity and Afrocentrism shaped and informed by this construction of Africanism and do they maintain and normalize white cultural hegemony?" *Crooklyn* is offered as a redemptive narrative. The counterhegemonic images we see at the beginning serve to mask all that is "wrong" with this picture.

From the moment we encounter the Carmichaels at their dinner table, we are offered a non-critical representation of their family life. Shot like docu-drama, these early scenes appear innocent and neutral; the ethnographic day-in-a-life style of presentation demands that the viewer see nothing wrong with this picture. The camera aggressively normalizes. These family scenes are presented unproblematically and so appear to be positive representations, fulfilling Lee's quest to bring to the big screen "authentic" black aesthetic subjects.

Since Spike Lee's cinematic genius is best revealed during those moments when he documents familiar aspects of rich black cultural legacy wherein collective internal codes and references that may or may not be known to outsiders converge, it is easy to overlook the fact that these counterhegemonic representations are constantly countered in his work by stock stereotypical images. When these are coupled with Lee's use of "animal house" type humor appropriated from mainstream white culture, a carnivalesque atmosphere emerges that seems directed toward mainstream, largely white, viewers. This cultural borrowing, which gives the movie cross-over appeal, is most evident in the scenes where Troy travels south to stay with relatives in a Virginia suburb. Though the cinematography didactically demands that the audience detach from a notion of the "real" and engage in the "ridiculous and absurd," these scenes appear stupid, especially the mysterious, not really comical, death of the pet dog Troy's aunt dotes on. Lee works overtime to create a comedic atmosphere to contrast with the seriousness of the Carmichael household, but it does not work; the switch to an anamorphic lens confuses (no doubt that is why signs were placed at ticket booths telling viewers that this change did not indicate a problem with the projector). In these scenes Lee mockingly caricatures the southern black middle class (who appear more like northerners in drag doing the classic Hollywood rendition of southern life). Lee gives it to us in blackface. It is predictable and you can't wait to return home to the Carmichael family. However, while he strategically constructs images to normalize the dysfunctions of the Carmichael family, he insists on making this family pathological. This attempt at counterhegemonic representation fails.

Anyone who sees the Carmichael family without the rose-colored glasses the film offers will realize that they are seriously dysfunctional. The recurrent eating disorders (one of the children is coercively forced by verbal harassment to eat to the point where on one occasion he vomits in his plate); an excessive addiction to sugar (dad's pouring half a bag of the white stuff into a pitcher of lemonade, his ice cream and cake forays, his candy-buying all hint that he may be addicted to more than sugar, though he is not overtly shown to be a drug-user); the lack of economic stability, signified by the absence of money for food choice, shutting of the electricity, as well as dad's mismanagement of funds, are all indications that there are serious problems. By normalizing the family image, Lee refuses to engage with the issue of psychological abuse; all interactions are made to appear natural, ordinary, comedic, not tragic. The autobiographical roots of *Crooklyn* may account for Lee's inability to take any stance other than that of "objective" reporter; working with a screenplay written collaboratively with his sister Joie and brother Cinque, he may have felt the need to distance himself from the material. Certainly emotional detachment characterizes the interaction between family members in the film.

Joie Lee stated that to write the screenplay she "drew from the few memories I have of my mother," who died of cancer when she was 14. Yet the children in *Crooklyn* are much younger than this and are clearly deeply ambivalent about their mother. Portrayed as a modern-day Sapphire with direct lineage to the "Amos n' Andy" character, Carolyn responds to economic crisis by constantly nagging and erupting into irrational states of anger and outrage that lead her to be mean and at times abusive. Even though the problems the family faces are caused by Woody's unemployment, he is depicted compassionately as an aspiring artist who just wants to be left alone to compose music, always laidback and calm.

Sexist/racist stereotypes of gender identity in the black experience are evident in the construction of these two characters. Although Carolyn is glamorous, beautiful in her Afrocentric style, she is portrayed as a bitch goddess. Her physical allure seduces, even as her unpredictable rage alienates. In keeping with sexist stereotypes of the emasculating black matriarch, Carolyn usurps her husband's authority by insisting that as the primary breadwinner she has the right to dominate, shaming Woody in front of the children. These aspects encourage us to see her unsympathetically and to empathize with him. His irresponsibility and misuse of resources is given legitimacy by the suggestion that his is an artistic, non-patriarchal mindset; he cannot be held accountable. Since Carolyn's rage is so often over-reactive, it is easy to forget that she has concrete reasons to be angry. Portrayed as vengeful, anti-pleasure, dangerous, and threatening, her moments of tenderness are not sustained enough to counter the negatives. Even her sweetness is depicted as manipulative, whereas Woody's "sweet" demeanor is a mark of his artistic sensibility, one that enhances his value.

As the artist, he embodies the pleasure principle, the will to transgress. His mild-mannered response to life is infinitely more compelling than the work-hard-to-meet-your-responsibilities ethic by which Carolyn lives. Being responsible seems to make her "crazy." In one scene the children are watching a basketball game when she encourages them to turn off the television to do schoolwork. They refuse to obey and she goes berserk. Woody intervenes, not to offer reinforcement, but rather to take sides. Carolyn becomes the bad guy, who wants to curtail the children's freedom to indulge in pleasure without responsibility. Woody responds to her rage by being physically coercive. Domestic violence in black life is sugarcoated—portrayed as a family affair, one where there are no victims or abusers. In fact, Carolyn has been humiliated and physically assaulted. But her demand that Woody leave makes him appear the victim and the children first attend to him, pleading with him not to go. Her pain is unattended by her male children; it is Troy who assumes the traditional role of caretaker.

In contrast to Carolyn, the ten-year-old Troy is concerned with the traditional notions of womanhood. Her mother expresses rage at not being able to "take a piss without six people hanging off my tits," repudiating sexist thinking about the woman's role. Flirtatious and cute, Troy manipulates with practiced charm. It is she who advises her dad to take Carolyn on a date to make up. Troy embodies all the desirable elements of sexist-defined femininity. Indeed, it is her capacity to escape into a world of romantic fantasy that makes her and everyone else ignore her internal anguish. When she lies, steals and cheats, her acts of defiance have no consequences. As the little princess, she has privileges denied her brothers; when her mother is sick, it is only Troy who is sheltered from this painful reality and sent down south.

In the home of her southern relatives, Troy meets a fair-skinned cousin who is portrayed as conventionally feminine in her concerns, though she is eager to bond with her guest. By contrast, Troy assumes a "bitchified role." She is hostile, suspicious, until charmed. Representing the light-skinned female as "good" and Troy as "bad." *Crooklyn*, like all Lee's films, perpetuates stereotypes of darker-skinned females as evil. While her cousin is loving, Troy is narcissistic and indifferent. When she decides to return home, it is her cousin who runs alongside the car that carries Troy away, waving tenderly, while Troy appears unconcerned. This encounter prepares us for her transformation from princess to mini-matriarch.

Taken to the hospital to see her mother, Troy is given instructions as to how she must assume the caretaker role. Contemporary feminist thinkers are calling attention to girlhood as a time when females have access to greater power than that offered us in womanhood. No one in the film is concerned about the loss of Troy's girlhood, though her brothers remain free to maintain their spirit of play. Clinton, the eldest boy, does not have to relinquish his passion for sports to become responsible; he can still be a child. But becoming a mini-matriarch because her mother is sick and dying requires of Troy that she relinquish all concern with pleasure and play, that she repress desire. Sexist/racist thinking about black female identity leads to cultural acceptance of the exploitation and denigration of black girlhood. Commenting on the way black girls are often forced to assume adults roles in *In The Company of My Sisters: Black Women and Self-Esteem,* Julia Boyd asserts: "Without fully understanding the adult tasks we were expected to perform, we filled shoes that were much too big for our small feet. Again, we did not have a choice and we weren't allowed to experience the full developmental process of girlhood." Lee romanticizes this violation by making it appear a "natural" progression for Troy rather than sexist gender politics coercively imposing a matriarchal role via a process of socialization.

Television Times

Carolyn did not make gender distinctions about household chores when she was well, and the movie fails to indicate why she now has an unconvincing shift in attitude. As if to highlight patriarchal thinking that females are interchangeable, undifferentiated, the film in no way suggests that there is anything wrong with a ten-year-old girl assuming an adult role. Indeed, this is affirmed, and the mother's dying is upstaged by the passing of the torch to Troy. The seriousness of her illness is announced to the children by their father, who commands them to turn away from their gleeful watching of "Soul Train" to hear the news (even in her absence, the mother/matriarch spoils their pleasure). Throughout *Crooklyn* Lee shows the importance of television in shaping the children's identities, their sense of self. While the boys panic emotionally when they hear the news, bursting into tears, Troy's feelings are hidden by a mask of indifference. That the children obey their father in their mother's absence (not complaining when he tells them to turn off the television) suggests that he is better able to assume an authoritative parental role when she is no longer present. Woody's transformation into a responsible adult reinscribes the sexist/racist thinking that the presence of a "strong" black female emasculates the male. Carolyn's death is treated in a matter-of-fact manner; we learn about it as the children casually discuss the funeral. We never see the family grieve. Troy, who is emotionally numb, only confronts the reality of this death when she is jolted from sleep by what she imagines is her mother's raging voice. Bonding with her father in the kitchen, her suppressed grief does not unleash tears; instead she vomits. This ritual cathartic cleaning is the rite of passage that signals her movement away from girlhood.

Taking her mother's place, Troy is no longer adventurous. She no longer roams the streets, discovering, but is bound to the house, to domestic life. While the male children and grown-up dad continue to lead autonomous lives, to express their creativity and will to explore, Troy is confined, her creativity stifled. Since she is always and only a mother substitute, her power is more symbolic than real. We see her tending to the needs of her brothers, being the "little woman." Gone is the vulnerable, emotionally open girl who expressed a range of feelings; in her place is a hard impenetrable mask. Just as no one mourns the mother's death, no one mourns the erasure of Troy's adolescence. In their book *Failing at Fairness: How America's Schools Cheat Girls,* Myra and David Sadker document the pervasiveness of a "curricular sexism" that turns girls into "spectators instead of players." Troy becomes a spectator, standing behind the gate looking out at life, a stern expression on her face.

Silent Losses

Though dead, Carolyn reappears to reassure and affirm her daughter. This reappearance is yet another rejection of loss. The controlling, dominating mother remains present even when dead, visible only to her girl child, now the guardian of patriarchy who gives approval to Troy's subjugation. Powerful black mothers, who work outside the home, the film suggests, "fail" their families. Their punishment is death. When she is dying Carolyn gives lessons in sexism to her daughter in a way that runs counter to the values she has expressed throughout the film (she does, however, encourage her daughter to think about a work future, if only because it is her own career that ensured the family's economic survival).

The Sadkers conclude their introductory chapter, which exposes the way sexist socialization robs girls of their potential, with a section called "Silent Losses" that ends with the declaration: "If the cure for cancer is forming in the mind of one of our daughters, it is less likely to become a reality than if it is forming in the mind of one of our sons." Whereas *Crooklyn* attempts to counter racist assumptions about black identity, it upholds sexist and misogynist thinking about gender roles. Order is restored in the Carmichael house when the dominating mother-figure dies. The emergence of patriarchy is celebrated, marked by the subjugating of Troy, and all the household's problems "magically" disappear. Life not only goes on without the matriarch, but is more harmonious.

Crooklyn constructs a redemptive fictive narrative for black life where the subjugation of the black female body is celebrated as a rite of passage which is restorative, which ensures family survival. Whether it is the grown woman's body erased by death or the little girl's body erased by violent interruption of her girlhood, the sexist politics embedded in this movie has often gone unnoticed by viewers whose attention is riveted by the exploits of the male characters. In failing to identify with the female characters or to bring any critical perspective to these representations, audiences tacitly condone the patriarchal devaluation and erasure of rebellious black female subjectivity the film depicts. Oppositional representations of blackness deflect attention away from the sexist politics that surfaces when race and gender converge. The naturalistic style of *Crooklyn* gives the sense of life-as-is rather than life as fictive construction.

Lee is indeed fictively re-imagining the 70s in this film and not merely providing a nostalgic portrait of the way things were. In his ahistorical narrative there is no meaningful convergence of black liberation and feminist politics, whereas in reality black women active in nationalist black power groups were challenging sexism and insisting on a feminist agenda. In *Crooklyn* Lee's aggressively masculinist vision is diffused by excessive sentimentality and by the use of Troy as the central embodiment of his message. Writing about the dangers that arise when excessive emotionality is used as a cover-up for a different agenda, James Baldwin reminds us that: "Sentimentality is the ostentatious parading of excessive and spurious emotion. It is the mark of dishonesty, the inability to feel." Such emotional dishonesty emerges full force in *Crooklyn*. The focus on Troy's coming of age and her mother's death is a non-threatening cover for the more insidious anti-woman, anti-feminist vision of black family life that is the film's dominant theme.

It is used to mask the repressive patriarchal valorization of black family life, in which the reinscription of sexist idealized femininity symbolically rescues the family from dissolution. Death and dying are merely a subtext in *Crooklyn*, a diversionary ploy that creates a passive emotional backdrop on to which Lee imposes a vision of the black family that is conservative and in no way opposed to the beliefs of white mainstream culture. The aspects of the film that are rooted in Lee's own life-story are the most interesting; it is when he exploits those memories to create a counter-worldview that will advance patriarchal thinking that the narrative loses its appeal.

Women's Work

Testifying that writing this script was cathartic, that it enabled her to confront the past, Joie Lee declares: "The emotional things that happen to you as a child, they're timeless, they stay with you until you deal with them. I definitely cleaned up some areas in my life that I hadn't dealt with before—like death." But the film Spike Lee has made does not confront death. In *Crooklyn*, death and dying are realities males escape from. There is no redemptive healing of a gendered split between mind and body; instead, *Crooklyn* echoes the patriarchal vision celebrated in Norman O. Brown's *Life Against Death*, where the hope is that "unrepressed man" "would be rid of the nightmares . . . haunting civilization" and that "freedom from those fantasies would also mean freedom from that disorder in the human body."

The messiness of death is women's work in *Crooklyn*. Expressing creativity, engaging pleasure and play is the way men escape from the reality of death and dying. In the space of imaginative fantasy, Lee can resurrect the dead female mothering body and create a world where there is never any need to confront the limitations of the flesh and therefore no place for loss. In such a world there is no need for grief, since death has no meaning.

chapter 6

Clueless in the Neocolonial World Order

Gayle Wald

Seldom has a contemporary US "teen flick" risen to the levels of both critical and commercial popularity attained by Amy Heckering's 1995 film *Clueless,* an Americanized and updated version of Jane Austen's novel *Emma.*[1] One of four Austen film adaptations released in US theaters in the space of two years (the others were *Sense and Sensibility* [1995], *Persuasion* [1995], and a much-hyped version of *Emma* [1996] featuring Gwyneth Paltrow), *Clueless* not only attracted generally high critical regard in the mainstream and independent film press, but in its video version the film became a fast best-seller, particularly among the young female teenagers who were its primary target audience. Indeed, in a year that also witnessed the release of Larry Clark's frankly dystopian *Kids,* a movie with which it was frequently contrasted in reviews, the fate of *Clueless* seemed almost as charmed as that of its protagonist, the ever fortunate Cher Horowitz. Modeled after Austen's heroine Emma Woodhouse, Cher lives a life that appears as orderly and abundantly provided for as her overstocked clothes closet, as seen in the film's opening sequence: untouched by the social and familial conflict, drugged-out confusion, or sexual turmoil that characterize other cinematic depictions of adolescence, including Heckerling's own classic *Fast Times at Ridgemont High* (1982). Or as cultural critic Cindy Fuchs observed in a review in the *Philadelphia City Paper,* "As 'teen movies' go, *Clueless* is obviously, self-consciously, lightweight: there are no suicides, no violence, no generational battles . . . no class or money angst . . . no racial conflicts . . . no sexual crises . . . The world of the film is ideal, shimmering, stable."[2]

It is this "ideal, shimmering, stable" world of *Clueless* and of its protagonist Cher (played winningly by Alicia Silverstone) that I seek to interrogate in this essay. More precisely, I am interested in using *Clueless* to explore the role of cinematic representation in the construction of national and cultural citizenship, as well as to examine the gender, race, and class dimensions of the national narratives produced by a contemporary Hollywood film explicitly addressed to an audience of adolescent and pre-adolescent US girls. The impetus for my inquiry into *Clueless* emerges, at least in part, from silences and elisions in the critical literature on nation, empire, and US cinema.

While scholars have recognized the status of US films as global commodities (i.e., commodities whose paths of dissemination mirror the paths of global capital), mediating the production of national narratives for "foreign" as well as domestic audiences, they have been reluctant to interrogate how notions of nationhood and national identity circulate in films that do not explicitly promote jingoistic fantasies of US global supremacy. At the same time, they have often failed adequately to theorize the gendering of nationalist discourses in US cinema, overlooking in particular the possibility that these may be voiced, embodied, or symbolized by female protagonists whose sphere of influence is more likely to be the home than the boardroom or the battlefield. Yet while *Clueless,* a clever adaptation of an English comedy of manners, would seem quite remote from the innumerable Hollywood action and suspense films that wear their nationalist desire on their sleeves, primarily calling upon women to establish the heterosexuality of male heroes, this essay argues that it is no less likely a site for the production or negotiation of national narratives and fantasies.[3] Rather, what we find in *Clueless* is a representation of national citizenship that is inextricably tied to, and mediated through, the representation of commodity consumption, heterosexual romance, and class and gender "cluelessness."

Fuchs's useful oxymoron of a world at once "shimmering" and "stable" anticipates my method of reading *Clueless* as a film structured around contradictions, especially concerning Cher's status as a privileged First World "consumer citizen." Like *Emma, Clueless* centralizes the narrative of its protagonist's development from eager orchestrator of others' social affairs to object of her own heterosexual romance, a process depicted as both inevitable and desirable, particularly insofar as it corresponds to Cher's loss of a cluelessness that inures her to her privileged place in the "real" world. At the same time, in pursuing this narrative end—one dictated by the precedent of Austen's text as well as by the exigencies of market and genre—*Clueless* subsumes or deflects many of the questions raised by its portrayal of Cher's national and class agency. In so doing, I argue, the film situates the subjectivity of its protagonist at the intersection of competing narratives of gender; for while it represents Cher as a "First World" girl who deploys her cluelessness in order to "innocently access power," it also suggests that such cluelessness stands in the way of her "successful" gendering according to the demands of the marriage plot.

In this essay I engage the following questions: How does *Clueless* envision citizenship, and more particularly how does it use the alibi, of a critique of "clueless" citizenship to justify and enable a certain gender narrative? How does the film construct Cher's identity through her pursuit of commodities, and how is this representation related to US cultural fantasies of consuming the world? How does the film use the character of Cher to construct the nation, or national/imperial desire, as itself innocent or clueless? In rendering Cher's cluelessness a narrative obstacle to heterosexual romance, what light does the film shed on the power relations implicit in its own "girling" of national discourse? As these questions imply, in my analysis *Clueless* is characterized by a degree of ideological and narrative ambiguity that I also find in its heroine, who is neither entirely clueless about her social location nor entirely capable of constructing an alternative to the imperatives of heterosexualization and romantic coupling that largely determine the direction of the film's ending. This reading of Heckerling's film in turn contributes to my larger argument about the ways that conventional narratives of gender ultimately frustrate the capacity of economically privileged First World women to realize their complicity with neocolonial relations of domination, on the one hand, and to recognize the mutuality of their experience with the manifestly different experience of economically disadvantaged and/or Third World women, on the other. As *Clueless* helps to illustrate, the "proper" gendering of economically privileged First World women will depend, to one degree or another, on their cluelessness about (read: ignorance about as well as "innocence" with regard to) the various interests through which their own privileged identities are established. As the term "clueless" itself suggests, First World women enjoy their privileges from a subject-position that paradoxically denies them status as political and intellectual agents, thereby diminishing their ability to resist conventional scripts of both gender and nation.

In what follows, I develop my argument about *Clueless* by framing it within the context of the issues raised by Heckerling's "Americanization" of Austen's text. In invoking such a term, I do not mean to argue that Cher is simply Emma Woodhouse temporally and geographically transposed from the nineteenth century to the twentieth, and from the English countryside to Southern California. In order for *Clueless*'s representation to "work" in the ways that I am suggesting it does, Heckerling's film must account, at the levels of both spectacle and narrative, for shifts from a colonial to a neocolonial order and for the different identity-formations that emerge or recede in the wake of such shifts. Here I am interested in the ways that the film effects a "translation" of Emma, the unwitting heiress of British imperial and colonial enterprises (although she herself has never visited the English seaside), into Cher, a "citizen" of Beverly Hills named after the eternally youthful and ambiguously "ethnic" star of contemporary infomercials, and the beneficiary of a late twentieth-century "global" economic order. My essay thus begins by demonstrating how *Clueless* establishes Cher's identity in and through a tacit discourse of "First World-Third World" economic and social relations. After showing how *Clueless* represents Cher's citizenship in terms of her privileged relation to commodities, as well as both implicitly and explicitly to the labor (and bodies) of Third World women workers, I go on to show how the film forwards the ends of the romance plot by gendering her within the context of her vulnerability to sexualized violence, significantly staged within a symbolically "Third World" locale where Cher cannot hold on to her class privilege. In so doing, I argue, Heckerling's film traces the process through which Cher subtly sheds cluelessness in order to embrace a more acceptable form of domestic virtue, though she initially resists it.

As I suggested in my opening reference to the recent handful of Jane Austen film adaptations, I see *Clueless* as implicated within a larger discourse of US nostalgia for an imagined and romanticized English past. Here *Clueless* might be seen, however, as a potentially liberating departure from the customary translation of British literature classics into cinematic postcards, realist works that strive to authentically represent the habits, speech, manners, and dress of the English landed gentry, the class that served as Austen's primary source of artistic inspiration. Modeled after a string of commercially successful productions by the UK producer-director team Ismail Merchant and James Ivory (including 1986's *A Room With a View*), these "faithful" cinematic translations of Austen's novels circulate within the context of US national fantasies of pre-industrial England as a site of authentic social and cultural tradition. Whereas in films such as *Emma* and *Pride and Prejudice* the consumerist pleasures of the rich are endorsed under the premise of historical accuracy, in *Clueless* a space is opened up for the interpretation of consumption as a specific social practice, one shaped by factors of gender, race, nation, and class. In eschewing the high minded seriousness and patent nostalgia of these more "faithful" Austen adaptations, *Clueless* also insinuates its own self-consciously clueless appropriation of a classic or high cultural text into a more commercially marketable representation. Perhaps more importantly, in relocating *Emma* to a Southern California location more readily associated in the US cultural imaginary with a postmodern lack of historical depth, Heckerling's script plays with ideas of temporality and tradition that are intimately linked to the ideology of Empire, in particular to the notion that imperial power may be duplicated and extended through the establishment of "domestic" traditions in various "foreign" outposts, which may or may not be seen as sustaining their own cultures and traditions.

First World Girls Just Wanna Have Fun

The plot of *Clueless* can be summarized as follows: Cher Horowitz, the most popular girl in her class at Bronson Alcott High School, decides along with her best friend Dionne to devote her considerable energy, imagination, and resources to "bettering" the social standing of Tai, the slightly grungy, somewhat déclassé new girl at school. Cher herself takes little interest in high school boys, with their gawkiness, social immaturity, and goofy ways of dressing, but she has high aspirations for Tai, whom she hopes to set up with Elton, the only boy Cher deems worthy of attention. Not surprisingly, these apparently altruistic intentions backfire when it becomes clear that Elton is merely using Tai to ingratiate himself with Cher. A scene in which Elton tries to force himself sexually on Cher and in which she is subsequently mugged by a stranger establishes her vulnerability and her need for male protection, and yet Cher initially bumbles in this regard by pursuing a romance with the new boy Christian, ignorant of the fact that he is gay. Eventually, however, Cher comes to realize that she has fallen in love with Josh, the hunky and sensitive older guy who has been living under her father's roof with her all along. On the one hand, this realization is achieved conventionally, as Cher learns to pattern her own desire after the desire displayed

by Tai, who has meanwhile recuperated from her disastrous pairing
with Elton and redirected her libidinal energies toward Josh. On the
other hand, while Cher's attraction to Josh is necessary for the film
to achieve closure and to gratify audience expectations, it is not altogether narratively predetermined or determining of the film's meaning. In particular, *Clueless* allows room for some equivocation in its
portrayal of the marriage plot by introducing unresolved Oedipal am-
biguities: to wit, the detail that Josh is Cher's father's ex-stepson (the
child of the woman he married after Cher's mother died, and whom
he has since divorced). This ambiguity, however minor, carries over
into the film's ending, a wedding scene in which Cher predictably
catches the bridal bouquet that portends her own imminent marriage
to Josh. While the penultimate moments of the film show Cher and
Josh passionately kissing, in the final shot Cher turns to address the
camera directly, offering a mildly sarcastic "as if," a phrase through
which she perhaps signifies her own mild disbelief at this conventional turn in her "fate." The General Public song "Tenderness" (exemplary of the film's retro 1980s soundtrack) kicks in as the credits
roll.

    Clueless establishes the contours of its overlapping national,
class, and gender narratives early on, in a scene that not only ensures Cher's status as a likeable and admirable film heroine, but
also organizes its representation of Cher's gender identity through
its portrayal of her loyalty to "American" values of inclusion and
social equality. In this scene (also one of the film's most humorous),
Cher delivers a speech before her high school debating class on the
subject of Haitian immigration to the United States. Assigned to argue in favor of Haitian immigration, Cher reveals in both her logic
and her delivery how the principle of US altruism toward economically downtrodden or disadvantaged Third World nations is premised
on the very assumptions about "correct" femininity and domestic
virtue that Cher herself must negotiate if she wants to have a romantic relationship with Josh. That is, by emphasizing Cher's cuteness as
she delivers the speech, *Clueless* offers the construction and revision
of "feminine" domestic virtue as the rationale for the expansion and
revision of American national identity. As she speaks, moreover, we
hear the strains of the national anthem, soft at first, as they swell
to an increasingly audible crescendo that coincides with her own
rhetorical crescendo. Given its importance to my argument about
Clueless's own construction of national desire, I quote the "Haiti"
speech in full:

> So OK, like, right now for example, the Haitians [pronounced "Hay-
> teeins"] need to come to America. But some people are all, "What
> about the strain on our resources?" Well, it's like when I had this
> garden party for my father's birthday. I put R.S.V.P. 'cause it was a sit-
> down dinner. But some people came that, like, did not R.S.V.P. I was
> totally buggin'! I had to haul ass to the kitchen, redistribute the food,
> and squish in extra place settings. But by the end of the day it was,
> like, the more the merrier. And so, if the government could just get to
> the kitchen and rearrange some things we could certainly party with
> the Haitians. And in conclusion, may I please remind you that it does
> not say R.S.V.P. on the Statue of Liberty![4]

As is rather obvious, Cher's speech—not to mention Silverstone's
wonderful performance of it—is calculated to win her the admiration of the film's audience as well as her own audience of classmates
(who respond to the speech with cheers and applause as Cher, ever
gracious, curtsies and bows). The speech scene not only serves to establish how gender is produced in and through ideologies of nationhood and national identity, but how narratives of national identity
may be framed within the context of (or even serve as the rationale
for) ideologies of domestic female virtue. Cher's voicing of a solidly
liberal position on Haitian immigration additionally prefigures her
compatibility with Josh, who lectures Cher about the environment
and who, in contrast to Cher's father, wants to become a lawyer to
fulfill his dreams of some day being an advocate for social justice.
The only one who is apparently unpersuaded by Cher's speech is Mr.
Hall, the debate teacher, who gives Cher a grade of C+ (a mark she
later contests). Mr. Hall is never given an opportunity to explain his
indifference to a performance whose cuteness and charm is so apparent to everyone else (both within and without the world of the
film), but one suspects that his frustration derives from Cher's inability to "read" Haiti properly—to understand the plight of would-
be Haitian immigrants from a viewpoint informed by the history of
US-Haitian relations. As it stands, Cher rationalizes Haitian immigration through an analogy that hints at her proficiency not in history but in husbandry—a proficiency that is confirmed in the scene
immediately following this one when Cher's father praises her for
looking after him so well.

Yet as the speech hints, here, too, Cher's performance of domestic virtue is inextricable from her role as a consumer of domestic labor, and from her obliviousness to the discrepancy between
her parable and the problems that Haitians and Haitian immigrants

actually face. As viewers might be led to surmise, in other words, the only way that "real" immigrants attended her father's fiftieth birthday party were as laborers in the kitchen. Moreover, the garden party scenario merely fosters a simulacrum of parity between the poorest and richest nations in the Western Hemisphere without really addressing the sources of such yawning economic disparity; as long as US citizens (those who R.S.V.P.'d) do not object to a redistribution of the abundance of food and space that they already enjoy by virtue of their power, the Haitians (the unanticipated guests who lack the civility to respond to the invitation) can be accommodated at the table.

Here the notion of "sharing" (a pun on Cher's name?) is put forward not only as a form of inclusive, and therefore more ethical, national consumption, but also as the sign of renegotiated social relations between First World and Third World nations. The Haiti speech thus operates on a number of different levels: it ingratiates Cher to the viewing audience, pairing her cluelessness about US-Haitian relations with the audience's affection for her as a liberal advocate of the sort of democratic values associated with national symbols such as the Statue of Liberty; it legitimates gendered domestic virtue as both a principle of international diplomacy and the means by which she can win the approval of her father and then later of Josh; and it establishes altruism (gift-giving) and communitarianism as the logical paradigms of First World-Third World relations, and by analogy of the gendered relations within the "domestic" (i.e., the national/public and home/private) spheres.

Cher's Haiti speech enacts a dialectical relationship between cluelessness and innocence that provides the basis for her privileged subjectivity within a neocolonial world order, as well as the footing for much of the film's comedy. In many ways, too, it is a condensation of *Clueless* itself: both are charming, both are performative, and both manage to keep viewers diverted while also tacitly reinscribing conventional narratives of gender, class, and nationality. Both are also ironic, in the sense that both invite audience dis-identification and distance. After Cher delivers her speech, for example, her debating opponent and social nemesis Amber complains that in talking about her father's garden party, Cher hasn't followed the teacher's instructions, which were to talk about Haiti. Amber misses the point, of course; but on another level her grievance models the mistake of reading the scene of Cher's speech too literally, as though she really were an exemplary defender of Haitian liberty and Northern-

Southern solidarity. Insofar as Amber is Cher's antagonist, that is, we understand her objection to Cher's speech as exemplifying her own (mock?) cluelessness, whereas Amber's refusal/inability to voice the "con" side of the argument (that Haitians should be prohibited from immigrating to the United States) hints at Cher's success at using ber cluelessness to silence opposition to her speech's liberal narrative.

Cluelessness and Consumer Citizenship

In addition to illustrating the ironic rhetoric of *Clueless*, the Haiti speech correlates to the anticipated trajectory of Cher's transformation from romantically disinclined arranger of others' affairs to the eager subject of her own romance narrative. Like her father's fiftieth birthday party, which turned out to be a success after signs of potential disaster, so *Clueless* must work to avoid the potential "disaster" of an unrealized heterosexual narrative by securing her femininity within a patriarchal and paternalistic system. In order to be made a heroine, that is, Cher must be made to recognize and also surrender to the bounded nature of her own gender identifications.

Given the film's deployment of the Haiti speech as a kind of preamble to its own narrative development, we might ask what kind of gender, class, and race "citizenship" the film subsequently imagines for Cher. In pursuing this line of questioning, we find a conflation of national citizenship with highly specific gendered and classed forms of commodity consumption. Whereas in *Emma* the protagonist's innocence is coupled with her enjoyment of material comforts supplied by the British colonial endeavor (as Edward Said has argued in discussions of Austen's work), in *Clueless*, Cher's cluelessness about social relations is coupled with her ability to enjoy a certain gendered consumer "agency."[5] From its opening shots, *Clueless* quite literally frames Cher's image within an ever-shifting panorama of commodities that lend her world an air of prosperity, convenience, and abundance, signifying the presence of wealth that is never actually displayed (in part because the characters buy goods on credit).

The spectacular nature of Cher's identity as a possessor of things suggests a breakdown in the conventional binary distinction between the "private sphere" of the home (where commodities are enjoyed) and the public sites of commodity exchange; Cher's bedroom, the quintessential private sphere of bourgeois girls, is less a private space than an extension (or even a domestic "colony" of) the Galleria, the quintessential Southern California commodity palace, which is significantly also the place where Cher feels most "at home." Just as *Clueless* portrays Cher as seamlessly assimilated into this world of commodities, so commodity consumption is perfectly integrated into Cher's moral universe; when she and Dionne jokingly refer to the affliction they call "buyer's remorse," for example, they mean regret over the purchase of an unwanted item, not regret over the fact of consumption itself. Consumption is not merely an "activity" in which Cher and her girlfriends engage; it is also a sign through which their gendered and classed identities are made and re-made through the mediation of a purchasable relationship to commodities. In *Clueless*, consumption is additionally a primary means of sociability among girls, who alternately "bond" over shared (or similar) purchases or fan social rivalries through competition over the possession of specific items (e.g. a particular party dress).

As a subject who manifests class agency primarily through consumption (in part because her gender and youth preclude any direct access to the means of production), Cher might be said to belong to the "consumer elite," that recent "class" of national subjects which has emerged, according to Gayatri Spivak, within the context of reordered power relations of the global economy of late twentieth-century capitalism.[6] As the phrase implies, "consumer elite" designates an identity-formation that arises in a context in which consumption has become a sign of agency in and of itself. Yet as Arjun Appadurai argues, under such terms consumption is less a manifestation than a chimera of agency: a "fetish" constructed through the discourse of an integrated system (or global economy), which in turn conceals the increasing concentration of power over production.[7] In Appadurai's terms, the consumer elite is thus the "definitive citizen" of a world order in which consumption is not only increasingly divorced from production, but has actually taken the place of production within the social imaginary.

Neither Spivak nor Appadurai situates the emergence of this "new" fetishism of the consumer in terms of a specific discourse of gender or nationality; indeed, Spivak's discussion locates the emergence of a "consumer elite" within the context of Indian decolonization and the social, economic, and political re-orderings that characterize the transition from "Empire" to "Nation." In many ways, however, their respective depictions of consumption as a site of contradiction—a space of agency and non-agency alike—correspond to Cher's subject position as a gendered and classed underage "citizen" of Beverly Hills. For Cher, consumption signifies ambiguously. It is, on the one hand, an extension of nationalized class privilege that hinges on the "Third World-ization" of production, as well as a form of leisure or "play" that signifies her privileged relation to both gendered domestic labor (i.e., shopping isn't a chore) and the global gendering of commodity production. Yet it is also inevitably bound up with Cher's performance of femininity (i.e., a properly classed, heterosexual, virginal femininity), and hence associated with the loss of gendered agency (even as such displays of femininity win Cher a degree of approval both at school and at home). Given the trajectory of the romance plot, which requires that Cher begin to question the terms of consumption in order to endear herself to Josh, who is critical of her attachment to clothes and shopping, it is particularly significant that Cher's profligacy as a consumer is paired with her failure to accurately read the social: for example, to realize that Elton likes her and not Tai. This conflation of consumption with cluelessness in turn portends the film's representation of romance as the rationale for the revision of Cher's gendered identity.

Clueless's representation of its protagonist's consumer identity is further complicated (albeit not in ways that are immediately or easily readable) by its coding of Cher as Jewish. Cher's Jewishness is signified both explicitly, through her possession of a recognizably Jewish last name[8] and more subtly, through references to ubiquitous nose jobs and stereotypical markers of "Jewish" ethnicity (e.g., the neurotic family; the characterization of Mel Horowitz as a fast-talking, high strung attorney), as well as through occasional puns (e.g., the fact that it is a character named Christian who is an inappropriate love-object for Cher). Perhaps not incidentally, Jewishness is also part of the discourse of teenage fandom around Silverstone, a "known" Jewish actress whose "all-American" blonde prettiness does not immediately signify as such.[9]

Although the film carefully avoids lapsing into anti-Semitic typecasting—for example, coding consumption as a particularly "Jewish" pastime—nevertheless Heckerling's translation of *Emma* into a Jewish American "princess" complements the film's re-visioning of national identity in terms of specifically "American" narratives of the upward economic mobility of immigrants. In terms of such nationalized class mythologies, Cher's Jewishness may be thus said to render her quintessentially American, the implication being that her father has risen to a position of authority within WASP society on account of professionally acquired wealth rather than ancestry.[10]

Cher's Jewishness abets the film's narrative of a "multi-cultural" American nation (already established in the Haiti speech scene), in which racial/ethnic subjects are treated as equals by the white majority, and in which immigrants are capable of ascending the ladder of social and economic success. What this adds up to, in fact, is a portrayal of a Bennetton-esque American "diversity" that forwards the film's own nationalist subtext. For example, the film works to dissuade the audience from questioning Cher's social privilege by representing it within the context of harmonious "race relations," as symbolized by her friendships with a pointedly diverse group that includes Dionne, her African American best friend, and Tai, whose class and ethnic differences (the latter less clear cut) are coded through her vaguely "New York" accent. Like *Independence Day* (1996), a film that packaged its blatantly nationalist agenda (i.e., Americans saving the world from itself) in the guise of a domestic diversity embodied by its black and Jewish male leads (Will Smith and Jeff Goldblum), thereby contributing to the export of "US multiculturalism" itself as a global and imperial commodity, *Clueless* works to convey the impression that Cher's cluelessness with regard to national identity is justified because it is shared among a racially and even economically "mixed" group of teenagers. *Clueless*'s innovation, in this regard, is to portray the American public high school—rather than the US Armed Forces—as the site that best illustrates the equality-in-diversity that is a hallmark of the liberal "multicultural" nation-state. This is not to say, however, that such portrayal of the American nation as welcoming and inclusive, not colonizing or racist, renders the film monolithic in its national discourse or negates the possibility of a critical subtext. For example, in making the comic excessiveness of Cher's wealth clear (recall the spectacle of her hyperbolically overstocked and tidy clothes closet), the film encourages young viewers to revel in their superiority to her class cluelessness, and thus to establish an ironic distance from her and her friends, who are otherwise shown to have the same menstrual cramps, to suffer the same sexual insecurities, and to blunder incompetently through the same mindless homework assignments. Young audiences of the film are similarly meant to feel pleasure in their recognition of Cher's cluelessness when she offers to donate ski boots and gourmet food items to a charity drive for a homeless shelter, or in their awareness of Cher's ignorance when she complains to Josh that she has trouble understanding Lucy, the Horowitz family's Salvadoran maid, because Lucy speaks "Mexican." As this remark about Lucy implies, however, the film's narrative of a "multicultural" and class-transcendent American nation (a narrative that co-exists with its portrayal of distinctions in wealth and status) is repeatedly undermined by references to "Third World" subjects or locales who are not easily assimilable to it. As I have been suggesting, to read *Clueless*'s national narrative entails we will need to read into some of the film's most "clueless" moments, paying attention to its formulation of relations between the "First" and "Third" worlds. Such relations in turn shed light on the film's construction of Cher as a gendered "First World" subject. For example, Cher's reference to Lucy, an immigrant domestic worker, not only complicates the film's narrative of the United States as a welcoming "domestic" space for all of those who seek to establish themselves within its borders, but it is also instrumental in situating Cher as a gendered subject who occupies a position of national, racial, and class privilege relative to other gendered subjects within the patriarchal "private sphere." Even as her remark displays her ignorance and a national obtuseness that viewers can laugh at, it also points to the fact that within the confines of the home, she enjoys a comfort and freedom that are contingent on Lucy's labor. Indeed, the only time domestic work is deemed appropriate for Cher is when she is directly engaged in ministering to her father (e.g., his garden party), when such work ceases to signify as domestic labor and instead becomes re-coded as filial duty. In contrast to Lucy's labor, which is naturalized within the domestic sphere, Cher's own service for her father is simultaneously assumed on account of her gender and transformed on account of her social and economic privilege. It is important to keep in mind, moreover, how such distinctions between women who simultaneously (if unequally) perform domestic work within the patriarchal household are themselves mediated through particular imperial or neocolonial discourses. What initially appears to be an isolated, "domestic" conflict ("domestic" here maintaining its dual signification as both the feminized, private sphere and the masculinized public sphere of the nation itself) may thus be governed by specific national discourses about "foreigners." Here, for example, Cher's comment about Lucy illustrates her general indifference to national distinctions among Spanish-speaking immigrants and to household "help"; yet it also speaks to her ignorance of the history of US intervention in El Salvador. The point is not merely that we do not expect a character like Cher to know about this history, but that her own raced and classed gender privilege is enabled through this not knowing.

As long as she maintains her cluelessness about the particular histories of Salvadoran domestic workers in the United States, in other words, Cher can also remain the untroubled beneficiary of Lucy's labor—labor that not coincidentally also affords Cher a privileged mobility within and outside of domestic spaces. In effect, to remain ignorant/innocent of US relations with El Salvador (or for that matter Haiti) means that Cher can remain ignorant/innocent of her own relations with Lucy, and thus of her own position within a gendered economy of national, race, and class privilege.

First World-Third World Encounters and the (Re)construction of Gender

While the conventions of the romance narrative require that Cher be "rewarded" for her compliance to a patriarchal script of gender in her acquisition of a boyfriend, it is significant that the film cannot bring about such narrative closure without the intervention of a scene of gendered violence that is itself inscribed by issues of First World-Third World relations. In particular, the scene in question stages a paradigmatic "encounter" of the gendered First World subject with the violence and disorder of the "street," as Cher, abandoned by Elton on the way home from a party (notably after fending off his unwanted sexual advances), is mugged in a deserted parking lot while making her way home from a distant neighborhood. The location of the mugging scene is significant because it offers a symbolically "Third World" locale as the site in which Cher's class privilege does not "work" to guarantee her safety and agency as a woman, as it does in the "First World" domestic sphere. Although in her immediate response to the mugging Cher continues to insist on her classed invulnerability to gendered violence (she frets loudly at the loss of her cellular phone and the state of her muddied designer dress), at the same time *Clueless* undercuts her comic interpretation of the mugging scene by using it to lay the groundwork for the refashioning of her gender identity and thus for her gradual acquiescence to the romance plot. The scene begins to serve such a legitimizing function with regard to gender when Cher calls Josh, himself in the middle of a date, to ask him to drive out to pick her up. On the one hand, the phone call situates Cher within a gendered economy of power and mobility, in which women are victims and men rescuers, and in which Cher's plea for help constitutes a form of passive consent—if not an active invitation—to romantic courtship. Yet on other hand, the scene serves a complementary function in engendering masculine desire, providing the first occasion in which Josh sees Cher not as a spoiled Beverly Hills brat, but as a "woman."

The mugging poses the most obvious danger to Cher; yet it is additionally dangerous within the context of *Clueless*'s efforts to "domesticate," or otherwise rhetorically tame, the questions the assault raises. By immediately recuperating it as comic, and by using it to initiate the anticipated romance narrative between Cher and Josh, the film avoids having to explicitly contemplate the chastening effects of such violence on Cher's gender identity. In narrative terms, the mugging could itself signify as a moment of crisis, in which Cher might be led to question her own social and ideological alliances, and yet instead it becomes the moment when she recognizes that her interests lie in following a patriarchal script of femininity. In a sense, we might therefore conclude, the scene represents two distinct, if related, kinds of violence: a real violence whose effects are disavowed, and a symbolic, or rhetorical violence that is necessary to the film's expected narrative closure.

The film's disciplining of gender through the romance plot becomes particularly clear in its representation of the effects of her newfound interest in Josh on her previous enthusiasm for shopping. Whereas at the beginning of *Clueless* Cher's identity is defined almost entirely through her role as a consumer (of goods, labor, and other people's romantic pleasure), gradually she learns to re-conceptualize her desires, realizing that fulfillment lies not merely or only in the possession of material goods but in the possession of a boyfriend. This shift in Cher's relation to consumption is ironic, if only because Cher is accustomed to finding in shopping— an activity which, significantly, she is more likely to associate with leisure and feminized sociability than with domestic labor—a form of surrogate agency. As she reasons, even when she has a particularly "bad" day at home or at school, spaces where she is expected to submit to paternal/patriarchal authority in a fashion becoming her gender (i.e., to be a "good girl"), she can make herself feel better by going shopping. At the mall, Cher submits only to the authority of her own desires; whereas home is a space of generational and gendered conflict, the mall is contrastingly a space of perfect equivalence between want and its fulfillment.[11]

Insofar as shopping is a form of gendered and classed agency for Cher, it becomes all the more ironic that her habits of consumption are represented as inconsistent with the expression of erotic desire for Josh, who, brimming with paternalistic college affectation (he reads Nietzsche, eschews popular culture, and at one point dons a black beret), deems her interest in items such as clothes, make-up, and exercise videos frivolous. At his suggestion, Cher even takes it upon herself to engage in charitable activities, such as helping to organize a food drive; she also makes a point of dressing down in his presence and of wearing make-up less conspicuously. However, these apparently more ethical forms of consumption that Josh stands for are ultimately revealed to be a different form of domestic virtue to which Cher must accede if she wants to have a romantic relationship with him. The film wants viewers to applaud Cher's transformation by contrasting her behavior in the mall, where her habits of conspicuous consumption make visible her cluelessness to her class privilege, with her behavior around Josh, where she is noticeably more self-conscious and self-critical.

Heckerling underscores these changes in Cher's attitude and appearance with a more sparing use of voice-over in the scenes that feature Josh and Cher, thereby signifying that Cher sheds superficiality and gains in interiority as she becomes closer to Josh. Here again, however, the film is somewhat ambivalent. While their romantic attachment is presented as a happy confluence of romance and social convenience (after all, they not only share the same house but the same class status) the incestuous overtones of their attachment enforce a sense that Josh and Cher are potentially mismatched.

Clueless and the Reel World Order

As the film's resolution makes clear, Cher's cluelessness serves conflicting ideological functions. On the one hand, it is inextricably linked to her agency as a gendered and classed First World subject. Being clueless means that Cher is spared the burden of critical self-consciousness that falls to subjects who cannot peremptorily assume that others will greet their presence with warmth and appreciation, or who take for granted a certain freedom of self-expression and/or movement. It also invests her with an aura of gendered innocence that she can draw upon in negotiations with more powerful and/or authoritative figures, from her father to her debate teacher to the man who mugs her. On the other hand, to the degree that it signifies ironically, her cluelessness opens up a space for audience critique of Cher's class and race privilege. In this sense cluelessness offers a means for "clued in" viewers to realize a critique of the national prerogatives that Cher's social and economic entitlement assumes—but only to a degree, since it never actually threatens the terms of stable audience identification with Cher as a likeable protagonist. Finally, and insofar as it is construed as an impediment to the development of a successful heterosexual romance narrative, Cher's cluelessness represents that quality that she must shed in order to become a more conventional cinematic heroine. For Josh to like her, in other words, she must demonstrate through example (rather than mere suggestion) that her cluelessness is merely an aspect of a performance of femininity that she uses to ward off potential romantic suitors.

My attempt to map the ideological function of cluelessness in Heckerling's film finally suggests that cluelessness may be a metaphor for ideology itself, specifically that "system of ideas" around issues of gender and class that Cher must shed in order to be rewarded, with Josh's (and the audience's) love by the end of the film.[12] Yet even if "cluelessness" constitutes the terrain upon which Cher acquires subjectivity and consciousness, nevertheless, the fact that the film pairs her relinquishing of cluelessness with her embrace of gendered domestic virtue remains deeply problematic, suggesting that the "price" of her insight is submission to the heterosexual romance narrative. Here, too, cluelessness becomes a rhetorical strategy of the film itself, which requires that the audience similarly assent to the revision of Cher's gendered identity, even if we do not welcome the film's insistence on romantic coupling as a narrative climax, insofar as this revision is conflated with her growth in self-consciousness. Just as through her attraction to Josh, Cher learns to construct her femininity in conformity with his interests and desires; so, too, the audience is led to order its desire in conformity with the romance plot and with the attendant "gendering" of the cinematic heroine, who wins our approval and admiration for having gained in "humanity."

Here *Clueless*'s own status as a cultural commodity becomes particularly salient. In the US, where it had its biggest audience, *Clueless* was an unanticipated hit, grossing $57 million at the box office and spurring a weekly television series. *Clueless*, a film that was originally based on a pilot for a television show, became a moderately successful Fox television series featuring many of the members of the film cast, but with the notable exception of Silverstone, the film's greatest asset. (Here it is notable that the TV show locates Cher in a "pre-Josh" period, allowing for the formulation of plots centering on Cher, her friends, and their various "clueless" adventures, rather than the determining "master-plot" of heterosexual romance.) In turn, the commercial success of the film, and,to a lesser degree, its TV spin-off, have been widely credited with sparking a trend in the marketing of films specifically to teenage girls, who are perceived by industry executives as an "emerging" and highly profitable audience.

Yet while *Clueless*'s commercial viability and the marketing trends it has encouraged might attest to the "consumer power" of US teenage girls (and could conceivably be a harbinger of such power), they also raise questions concerning the cinematic construction (or reproduction) of national, race, and gender identities, both "domestically" and abroad. In a recent *New York Times* article, for example, Joe Roth, the chairman of Walt Disney Studios, reasoned that film executives are eager to target teenage girls because they may be counted on to generate increased profits for multinational corporations: "They're easier to market to, compared to the older audience, because their tastes are very specific," he is quoted as saying. "They come to a movie over and over again if they like it. They don't work; they don't have families to raise. They're available consumers with money."[13] Roth's notion of teenage girls as an audience of "available consumers" who "don't work" is telling, not only for its emphasis on girls' perceived docility and therefore their commercial exploitability, but for its conflation of "girlhood" itself with leisure and commodity consumption. Moreover, insofar as his vision of what girls "want" is predictably market-driven, it is difficult to read his allusions to "girl power" (à la the English pop group the Spice Girls) as anything but cynical. According to Roth, girls are being rewarded for their loyalty and dependability as consumers with their "own" films; and yet if *Clueless* is what they want, films like *Titanic* are what they are (and dependably will be) given.

I have hastened to add this account of *Clueless*'s ongoing influence within the US film industry in order to outline potential intersections between the discourse of marketing and the discourse of gender, as well as to suggest connections between the apparent "spending power" of "First World" girls and the representation of gendered agency in Heckerling's film. In *Clueless*, as I have argued, Cher is made to realize the bounded nature of her own gender identifications, which are themselves structured in and through the film's narrative of First World-Third World relations. Hence notions of classed and gendered domestic virtue may be recuperated as the rationale for the expansion of national identities, as the winningly patriotic conclusion of Cher's Haiti speech demonstrates. They also serve as the ideological machinery driving Cher's transfer of libidinal energy away from consumption and instead toward heterosexual coupling, such that she does not need to be "convinced" to like Josh, but eventually comes to recognize romance as the object of her "own" desire. Given that (at least by the *New York Times* account) *Clueless* and Cher are paradigmatic, respectively, of the kind of commercially visible movies and "empowered female, teen characters" that Hollywood sees girl audiences as "wanting," then the highly touted consumer "agency" of US girls may be no less problematically tethered to the embrace of conventional gender and class narratives cloaked in the rhetoric of the charming, the cute, or the clueless.

NOTES

For their helpful suggestions, comments, and encouragement on various versions of this essay, I would like to thank Patricia White, Andrea Levine, You-me Park, Rajeswari Sunder Rajan, Ann Cvetkovich, and Brigid Nuta.

1. Although the conditions of cultural production and authorship of novels and films are quite different, for the sake of argument I will take Heckerling to be the "author" of *Clueless* throughout this essay. In the film credits, Heckerling is cited as director, screenwriter and executive producer.
2. See Cindy Fuchs, "Clueless," http://wwwinform.umd.edu:8080/EdRes/Topic/WomensStudies/FilmReviews/clueless-fuchs. Like her literary precursor Emma Woodhouse, Cher Horowitz may be said to live "in the world with very little to distress or vex her." Jane Austen, *Emma*, rpt. 1816 (New York: Signet, 1964), 5.
3. For an excellent example of such an analysis, see Lynda Boose, "TechnoMuscularity and the 'Boy Eternal': From the Quagmire to the Gulf," in Amy Kaplan and Donald E. Pease, eds., *Cultures of United States Imperialism* (Durham: Duke University Press, 1993), esp. 587–91.
4. My source for this quote is "Movie Quotes for *Clueless* (1995)," http:Hus.imdb.com/cachehitle-more/quotes+19091.
5. Edward Said, *Culture and Imperialism* (New York: Vintage, 1994), 89.
6. Spivak discusses the effect of such shifts in "Woman in Difference," an essay that focuses on the representation of subaltern women in the fiction of Mahasweta Devi. See Gayatri Chakravorty Spivak, *Outside in the Teaching Machine* (New York: Routlege, 1993). In particular, she argues that nationalist discourses of development and progress, specifically those that emerge in the context of post-independence India,

conceal the ongoing oppression and domination of subaltern women, a gendered identity produced under the sign of "Empire" and "Nation" alike. The relatively unchanged status of subaltern women—which can be inferred, in part, from Devi's fiction—belies the post-colonial narrative of national "progress" measured in terms of democratization, secularization, and capitalist development (80). Indeed, as Spivak concludes, signs of national "progress" can produce radically different results for subjects who occupy different social locations within the national imaginary. Hence even if such measurements could assess the impact of decolonization and independence on the lives of poor, socially despised Indian women, the effects of the transition from "Empire" to "Nation" could not be properly understood in abstract, universal terms, because "Empire" and "Nation" are both constitutive of the identities that also "inhabit" them.

7. Arjun Appadurai, "Disjuncture and Difference in the Global Cultural Economy," in Bruce Robbins, ed., *The Phantom Public Sphere* (Minneapolis: University of Minnesota Press, 1993), 186.

8. In "High School Confidential," an interview with Heckerling, *Rolling Stone* cites the name of Silverstone's character as "Cher Hamilton," a divergence which is perhaps attributable to discrepancies in the press material, but which is nevertheless interesting as a potential "Anglicization" of Cher's Eastern European Jewish surname. R. C., "High School Confidential," *Rolling Stone* (9 September 1995), 53.

9. For example, Silverstone's "Jewish" identity is frequently noted on web sites devoted to her, and Silverstone periodically is identified as/identifies herself as Jewish in interviews with the entertainment press.

10. The film does contain one mildly disparaging reference to "Persians," or to the Persian Jews who constitute a small but visible minority of Jewish immigrants in Beverly Hills. *Clueless*'s ambivalence about Cher's Jewishness mirrors the coding of much "American" comic narrative as "Jewish" humor, as in the television show "Seinfeld."

11. This conflation of domesticity and consumption contrasts with the separation of the public, entrepreneurial sphere (the site of commodity production and purchase) and the private, domestic sphere in *Emma*. For Cher, commodity culture constitutes an alternative form of domesticity, domesticity embodied in the mall. In constructing the mall as an extension of the domestic, *Clueless* references the mall's place within late twentieth-century US culture as a surrogate public sphere—or more precisely, a fetish of the public (complete with an architecture that conventionally includes fountains, benches, tree-lined pedestrian "avenues," and quaint storefronts) that orders everyday social life even as the "real" public sphere is increasingly controlled by private interests. The mall's link to the street—the old and perhaps

obsolete public sphere—is made explicit, for example, in a scene in which Tai is attacked in the Galleria by a group of rowdy boys who threaten to throw her over a railing.

12. Antonio Gramsci, *Selections from the Prison Notebooks,* ed. and trans. Quintin Hoare and Geoffrey Nowell Smith (New York: International Press, 1971), 377.

13. See Bernard Weinraub, "Who's Lining Up" *New York Times*

Works Cited

Appadurai, Arjun. 1993. "Disjuncture and Difference in the Global Cultural Economy." In Bruce Robbins, ed., *The Phantom Public Sphere.* Minneapolis: University of Minnesota Press, 186.

Austen, Jane. 1964. *Emma.* New York: Signet.

Boose, Lynda. 1993. "TechnoMuscularity and the 'Boy Eternal': From the Quagmire to the Gulf." In Amy Kaplan and Donald E. Pease, eds., *Cultures of United States Imperialism.* Durham: Duke University Press.

Fuchs, Cindy. 1995. *"Clueless." Philadelphia City Paper.* http://www.inform.umd.edu:8080/EdRes/ Topic/WomensStudies/ FilmReviews/clueless-fuchs

Gramsci, Antonio. 1971. *Selections from the Prison Notebooks,* ed. and trans. Quintin Hoare and Geoffrey Nowell Smith. New York: International Press.

Said, Edward. 1994. *Culture and Imperialism.* New York: Columbia University Press.

Spivak, Gayatri Chakravorty. 1993. *Outside in the Teaching Machine.* New York: Routlege.

Weinraub, Bernard. 1998. "Who's Lining Up At Box Office? Lots and Lots of Girls." *New York Times,* 23 February: B4.

chapter 7

Girlfriends and Girl Power: Female Adolescence in Contemporary U.S. Cinema

Mary Celeste Kearney

The representation of female adolescence in U.S. cinema changed dramatically during the last decade of the twentieth century. Most significantly, many recent films focusing on teenage girls no longer ground their themes of transformation in an ideology of heterosexual romance. Instead, such films incorporate contemporary feminist themes, especially the need for girls to develop confidence, assertiveness, and self-respect apart from boys and through same-sex relationships. Moving beyond the depiction of girls' heterosexual awakenings in order to explore their homosocial experiences, these films significantly challenge the conventional female coming-of-age narrative upon which previous films about adolescent girlhood were based.

By exploring the portrayal of teenage girls in several films from the 1990s, my aim is to shift critical analyses of representations of adolescent and female subjectivity in new directions.[1] My first objective is to challenge theories about the depiction of adolescence in film, which heretofore have been gender blind and predominantly male biased.[2] In addition, I want to broaden the field of feminist film criticism, which typically has ignored issues of age and, therefore, girls.[3] Central to my project is an examination of transformations in the ideologies of gender and generation and the effect of such changes on representations of female coming-of-age in contemporary U.S. cinema.

Female Coming-of-Age and Early Representations of Female Youth

Adolescence and coming-of-age are relatively recent concepts, having emerged during the late nineteenth century as a result of the industrialization of the United States and appeals to youth to move to urban centers and participate as laborers in modern society (Kett 144–72). As much as some girls participated in this migration and labor effort, coming-of-age was attributed primarily to male youth, whose entrance into adult life through labor outside the home made possible their social and financial independence from parents. Unlike male adolescence with its dominant connection to the public sphere, female coming-of-age was defined as a private matter related to a girl's maturing body during pubescence, a life stage signified particularly by the onset of menstruation, which, during this time, typically occurred around fifteen years of age (Brumberg 289). Rarely discussed in mixed company, a girl's menarche was mediated socially through public rites of passage, such as debutante cotillions, which indicated that she was ready for marriage and, more important, physically capable of reproduction. A girl's change in generational status, therefore, was linked primarily to her involvement in a committed heterosexual relationship and her adoption of the roles of wife and mother.

Because the amount of time between a girl's onset of menstruation and marriage was fairly minimal prior to the twentieth century, sometimes as short as a few months, female coming-of-age meant the swift transformation of a girl into a woman (Welter 3). Despite this quick shift from child to adult status, however, women experienced a prolonged state of dependence, one which was extended by marriage rather than curtailed by it (as was the case for boys). Limited by few opportunities for labor outside the domestic sphere, teenage girls rarely had the privilege that boys did: a stage of social and financial independence.

Prior to the 1930s, many films relied on the traditional female coming-of-age process by depicting girls transforming quickly into women through heterosexual romance.[4] Even working-girl characters, like Betty Lou in *It* (1927), had as their primary objective finding men whose proposals of marriage would ensure their ascension to adulthood and, they hoped, a higher socioeconomic class. As Sumiko Higashi argues, "The work experience of the silent movie heroine . . . lasted only until her wedding day. . . . In fact, the nature of

[her] employment was not even important inasmuch as work represented a background for romance" (102–3). Although these working-girl characters projected a new form of modern femininity linked to the public sphere, by constructing female coming-of-age primarily through their involvement in romance, such films reproduced the stereotypical association of females and the private sphere. Moreover, by depicting girls' swift transformations into women, these films reaffirmed the child/adult binary, which had formed earlier notions of generational (and gendered) subjectivity.

The Emergence of a Female Youth Culture and Female Teenpics

With U.S. participation in World War II, adolescents were encouraged again to become part of the American workforce, a situation that dramatically increased their disposable income. Recognizing the potential spending power of young wage earners—who, unlike most adults, did not have many financial obligations and thus spent their money more freely—manufacturers began to make special appeals to those in their teens. This new focus on teenagers as a consumer class gave rise to the emergence of a youth culture distinct from adult, mainstream culture.[5] American youth culture was formed largely through teenagers' interactions with mass media forms of entertainment (especially popular music, magazines, and movies), which were produced with adolescent tastes in mind. For example, in contrast to earlier films about young people, which focused on the impending experiences of adulthood, coming-of-age movies produced in the early 1940s foregrounded the unique experiences of adolescence. These teenpics broadened the traditional view of youth by depicting young people in nonfamilial activities and environments, especially high school, which after the war became the primary institution associated with teenagers.[6]

Integrated into public society through their role as laborers yet still constructed primarily as future wives and mothers, teenage girls of the 1940s began to receive attention as a niche market of consumers whose lifelong shopping habits could be molded and fixed if properly catered to by advertisers and manufacturers. Tapping into the burgeoning female youth culture of this period, films typically portrayed teenage girls as sub-debs or bobby-soxers, stereotypes based on a group of white, middle-class, suburban female adolescents who came to signify all-American wholesomeness during the late war years and immediate postwar period (Rosen 237–41).[7] Girl-oriented films such as *Miss Annie Rooney* (1942), *Janie* (1944), and *Junior Miss* (1945) introduced many of the narrative and representational conventions that came to be associated with female teenpics, particularly a high-school-age female protagonist and a comedic coming-of-age plot that revolved around her pursuit of heterosexual romance (often with an older male). These early female teenpics depicted the protagonist and her girlfriends wearing trendy clothing, sporting fashionable hairstyles, mouthing the latest teenage jargon, and engaging in activities newly associated with female youth, such as babysitting, gossiping on the telephone, and beautifying themselves with cosmetics. In keeping with the postwar association of teenagers and high school, 1940s films that focused on adolescent girls moved beyond the rituals traditionally associated with female coming-of-age by relying on school-related events, such as dances and fraternity pinnings, to signify a girl's maturation.

Despite their placement of girls in nondomestic contexts, these early female teenpics typically ignored the transformative effects of the war economy on gender roles and relations in U.S. society. Instead, such films reproduced traditional ideologies of female subjectivity by privileging girls' desires for heterosexual romance and by commenting consistently on their future roles as wives and mothers. Indeed, such films helped reaffirm the primary message being sent to adult women during the postwar period: "A woman's place is in the home."

Transformations in the Female Coming-of-Age Process

Over the past fifty years, traditional notions of female coming-of-age have been troubled greatly by a variety of transformations in American society and female anatomy. For instance, improvements in nutrition and health have resulted in girls experiencing menarche at a much younger age than one hundred years ago, typically around eleven or twelve years old (Brumberg 289). Associated with this decrease in the average age of menarche is a similar decline in the average age of sexual initiation, a decline that has accelerated since the 1960s due to the increased availability of effective and inexpensive contraception, as well as a liberalizing of social mores about premarital sex and female sexuality.

The noticeable declines in the average ages of menarche and sexual initiation have resulted in significant changes not only in girls' physical experiences of pubescence but also in their social experiences of adolescence and femininity. Most significantly, transformations in female physiology have contributed to female adolescence being drawn out to its lengthiest state ever. A girl's age at menarche used to be fairly close to her age at marriage; during the latter half of the twentieth century the distance between those two experiences has widened considerably, as girls are menstruating at younger ages and many women are forming committed relationships and having children much later in life, if at all. This situation has provided girls with a much longer period to experiment with a variety of identities, lifestyles, and interests, including those that take them beyond the realms of domesticity and heterosexual relationships.[8]

This does not mean, however, that girls today are taking more time to mature emotionally and socially. Indeed, the early maturation of female bodies has contributed to girls being treated as sexual beings at younger ages than perhaps ever before. Moreover, as the bodies of female youth are signifying maturity at younger and younger ages, girls are required to become street-wise long before their mothers were. Forced to recognize the power imbalances that structure our society, girls must learn and practice the strategies that will help them survive in an environment that is often hostile to both females and the young.

New Developments in Girl-Oriented Cultural Texts

These radical transformations in the physical and social experiences of teenage girls have made the differences between female childhood, adolescence, and adulthood increasingly difficult to discern. In turn, changes in our society's ideologies of gender and sexuality have blurred the boundaries between masculinity and femininity and thus transformed both the ways in which girls are socialized and the expectations they have for the future. For example, the popularization of liberal feminist ideas about women's equality with men has altered significantly the ways in which girls dress, behave, and interact with others. One effect of this phenomenon is that female youth are no longer seen as abnormal for wearing clothing or participating in activities traditionally associated with males. Furthermore, girls are encouraged to develop into assertive and independent individuals capable of taking care of themselves. Thus, most female adolescents today see marriage and motherhood as only two of the many options of lifestyle and labor available to them in the future.

It is no wonder, therefore, that the stories of teenage girlhood produced by the mass media have also changed dramatically. For instance, Angela McRobbie has found that heterosexual romance no longer serves as the primary ideology structuring magazines produced specifically for female youth. As she argues, "A new climate prevails where dependency on boys and romance has given way to a new, more confident, focus on the self" (183). Extending McRobbie's argument to the representation of female adolescence in audiovisual media, I would argue that heterosexual romance no longer works as the primary ideology grounding cinematic portrayals of teenage girlhood. While many contemporary films continue to place female youth in the role of girlfriend or sexual fantasy figure (especially studio-produced teenpics that focus primarily on male adolescents), since the early 1990s there has been a significant increase in the number of films about teenage girls that do not privilege heterosexual romance narratives.[9] Indeed, many recent movies focusing on female youth subordinate both boys and romance and instead foreground girls' development of individual identities and same-sex friendships.

McRobbie argues that this shift in the ideological perspectives of girl-oriented media texts is partly the result of the popularization of feminist ideas, and of the greater presence of feminists working in the culture industries (165). In spite of the relatively low ratio of females to males in the film industry today, the increase in the number of women producers, directors, writers, and studio executives over the last three decades has allowed female and, at times, feminist perspectives to gain more legitimacy and screen time. In addition, recent transformations in the industrial practices of film production, distribution, and exhibition have allowed previously marginalized artists and perspectives to reach audiences. For instance, the rise of the independent film community since the early 1980s has provided feminists with a more supportive environment in which to create their films. More importantly perhaps, the emergence of alternative forms of film distribution and exhibition (for example, video, laserdisc, and DVD, as well as cable and satellite delivery systems for television) has resulted in a market that is more open to nonmainstream films and has made narrowcasting to smaller, niche audiences more promising than ever before.

As a result of the popularization of feminist ideologies and the transformation of the film industry over the last several decades, the cinematic world of girls has been altered considerably, particularly by filmmakers who have attempted to move past traditional female coming-of-age narratives. Their films have broadened the spectrum of female adolescence beyond the white, middle-class, suburban, heterosexual stereotype of teenage girlhood consistently reproduced by the Hollywood studios.

The Effects of Feminism on Contemporary Films about Teenage Girls

The influx of females and feminist ideas in the film industry has not resulted in uniform ways of representing women and girls. In addition to the widely divergent sensibilities brought to the filmmaking process via filmmakers' various subjectivities and ideological perspectives, different sociopolitical contexts have shaped the ways in which female and feminist perspectives are communicated to audiences. For example, during the last twenty years two trends in the representation of female empowerment have emerged that can be related to two different strategies for female liberation advocated by second-wave feminists. On the one hand, some films explore woman power through a singular adult female character who not only inhabits male-oriented genres and roles but also exhibits traits typically associated with masculinity, particularly independence, leadership, and physical strength. Introduced in science fiction/action films like *Alien* (1979), these physically empowered female heroes continue to appear in contemporary films, such as *Terminator 2: Judgment Day* (1991), *The Long Kiss Goodnight* (1996), and *The Matrix* (1999) (Tasker 65–88). The emergence and popularity of this cinematic perspective on woman power can be understood as a result of the popularization of liberal feminist ideas, especially women's equality with men on male terms, as well as the continued hegemony of patriarchal ideologies of subjectivity.

On the other hand, some woman-power films depict two or more females who gain confidence through and find support in same-sex friendships. Although this type of narrative was typical of 1940s woman's films, it did not reemerge fully until the late 1980s/early 1990s with films such as *Steel Magnolias* (1989) and *Thelma & Louise* (1991). More recent chick flicks, such as *Boys on the Side* (1995), *Waiting to Exhale* (1995), and *The First Wives Club* (1996), continue this theme by focusing on women's empowerment through their relationships with other women, which are often formed as a result of the friends' similar mistreatment by men (Tasker 137–60).

This perspective on woman power is resonant of cultural feminists' insistence on women's essential difference from men (particularly the privileging of emotional intimacy and relationships), as well as their advocacy of female liberation outside the company of men.

It is not surprising that these two narrative approaches to female empowerment are also apparent in contemporary films focusing on teenage girls. Beginning in the late 1970s, independent slasher films, such as *A Nightmare on Elm Street* (1984), presented their heroes as singular female adolescents capable of besting the psychokillers threatening their communities. Labeled "Final Girls," because they outlived the films' other characters, these teens were masculinized through their embodiment of the hero role, as well as through their names, clothing, and physically assertive behavior (Clover 35–41). Like the first wave of contemporary woman-power films, these early girl-power movies constructed their protagonists according to liberal feminist and patriarchal ideologies of subjectivity. Thus, such films often subordinated, if not outright ignored, themes about the importance of girls developing identities independent from boys and forming supportive relationships with other female youth. Indeed, the protagonists of Hollywood's first girl-power movies, *Buffy the Vampire Slayer* (1992) and *The Next Karate Kid* (1994), typically learned their combat skills and moral sensibility from older men whose presence on screen helped contain the potential threat of representations of female empowerment. Moreover, much like the characters in liberal feminist woman-power films, these girls' physical powers were used primarily to restore a sense of order in the patriarchal public sphere rather than in their own lives.

Although the Final Girl character was resurrected, reshaped, and mainstreamed in the mid-1990s with *Scream* (1996) and *I Know What You Did Last Summer* (1997), several other recent films about teenage girlhood have moved beyond representations of the solo girl hero by exploring the empowerment of female youth through same-sex relationships. This new approach to girl power is no doubt the result of a changed understanding of contemporary female adolescent psychology. Since the early 1980s, feminist scholars have brought attention to the noticeable decline in girls' self-esteem upon their entrance to puberty.[10] Public discourse about the "confidence gap" experienced by adolescent girls (Orenstein) increased considerably in the 1990s, especially following the publication of AAUW's 1991 report, *Shortchanging Girls, Shortchanging America,* and Mary Pipher's 1994 best-seller, *Reviving Ophelia: Saving the Selves of*

Adolescent Girls. As a result of these studies, girls today are encouraged to develop identities independent of boys and heterosexual romance, a goal many believe is achieved best through single-sex social and educational environments.

In addition to women advocates for female youth, a community known as Riot Grrrl, which is made up of young feminists with a radical edge, has been championing girl power since the early 1990s (long before the Spice Girls decided that this was a catchy marketing slogan). Although operating on the margins of society, Riot Grrrls' pro-girl ethos and reshaping of girlhood as a powerful position of social, political, and cultural agency have helped shift public attention toward female youth.[11] Moreover, this community's girl-only meetings and activities have provided many female adolescents with a supportive environment where they can bond with other like-minded girls and come to terms with the difficult experiences of teenage girlhood, such as homophobia, sexual abuse, and body-image problems.

In keeping with Riot Grrrls' vision of female empowerment, several independent films from the mid-1990s—particularly *The Incredibly True Adventure of Two Girls in Love* (1995), *Foxfire* (1996), *Girls Town* (1996), and *All Over Me* (1997)—portray coming-of-age as a homosocial process, wherein girls gain confidence, assertiveness, and self-respect through each other. These films' privileging of same-sex relationships over heterosexual romance is unique in the history of U.S. cinema. Although films about preteen girls, such as *Now and Then* (1995), *The Baby-Sitters Club* (1995), and *Gold Diggers: The Secret of Bear Mountain* (1995), often portray the transformative power of female friendships, most mainstream representations of female adolescents suggest that girls must leave their same-sex friendships behind as they enter womanhood (a position naturalized in such films as heterosexual). Thus, contemporary studio teenpics that feature groups of adolescent girls, such as *The Craft* (1996) and *Jawbreaker* (1999), typically pit friends against each other in battles over control, power, and boys, leaving girls estranged from, rather than supported by, one another.

Film narratives that downplay, ignore, or eliminate girls' relationships with other girls suggest an unwillingness to explore the homosociality of female youth and its possible effects. This no doubt arises from the fear that girls' same-sex bonds might be understood as homosexual and therefore as offensive to conservative viewers and, more important, financial backers. However, as Tasker argues,

"It is not the case that the portrayal of female friendship *necessarily* involves the suggestion of lesbianism. Nonetheless, both women's friendships and cinematic portrayals of lesbianism operate in a shared terrain which involves female characters acting in a space not defined by male characters or by a narrative progress towards heterosexuality" (153). What appears to be threatening about films that privilege girls' relationships with one another, therefore, is not female bonding per se but the marginalization or absence of males and heterosexuality from such narratives.

This is not to say that boys and heterosexual issues do not play a significant role in films that focus on girls' relationships. For example, the young female protagonists of *All Over Me*, *Foxfire*, *Girls Town*, and *The Incredibly True Adventure of Two Girls in Love* form bonds not only out of their love and respect for one another but also as a result of their similar experiences of disrespect by males and/or straight people. In these four films, the oppression of females by men and heterosexuals (in the form of sexual abuse and homophobia) is an important catalyst for girl power. Thus, such films provide new images of female adolescence that are as disturbing in their depiction of the various problems teenage girls face as they are inspiring in their themes of female empowerment and solidarity.

The Films: Girlfriends and Girl Power

Girls Town focuses on four girlfriends from Hackensack, New Jersey, who are about to graduate from high school and move into adult life: Nikki (Aunjanue Ellis) and Emma (Anna Grace), who are college bound; Angela (Bruklin Harris), who wants to be a poet like her idol, radical African American lesbian feminist activist Audre Lorde; and Patti (Lili Taylor), a single mother who has been held back in school and dreams of working in a garage.[12] The film begins with scenes of the girls hanging out and attending school together; however, the majority of its narrative centers on how Nikki's suicide affects her three friends. Attempting to understand why Nikki killed herself, Angela, Emma, and Patti obtain her journal and discover that she was raped. This revelation leads to the unveiling of the other girls' hidden troubles, including Emma's date-rape the previous year and Patti's tolerance of her ex-boyfriend's abuse. Confused about how to cope with these problems, Angela suggests that they move beyond talking and fight back against the violence and misogyny they experience.

Following this bonding experience, Patti, Emma, and Angela each develop an assertive attitude that allows them to act on their intolerance of misogyny. For example, the girls aggressively vandalize the car of Emma's abuser by scratching its paint, puncturing its tires, and breaking its windows. In addition, they spray paint the word "RAPIST" on the hood, an act that not only outs this boy as violent toward females but equates the damage of a teenage boy's most prized possession (his car) with that of a girl (her body). The friends also create a "door of shame" in their school bathroom to warn other girls about abusive males, and they pawn the stereo, guitar, and television of Patti's ex-boyfriend, thereby obtaining for her daughter the money he failed to provide for child support. The ultimate demonstration of the girls' unified intolerance of misogyny comes during the film's climax, which depicts Angela, Emma, and Patti publicly confronting Nikki's rapist.

Much like *Girls Town*, *Foxfire* demonstrates the need for female adolescents to develop a strong support system by communicating intimately with their girlfriends and standing up for themselves and each other in the face of adversity, especially misogyny. The film's primary characters are united through their sexual harassment by one of the male teachers in their Portland high school. His victims include Rita (Jenny Lewis), a shy student without many friends, and Violet (Sarah Rosenberg), a sexually confident girl. Rita and Violet are incited to face their abuser by Legs (Angelina Jolie), a homeless orphan who has arrived recently in their town. Two other characters are also inspired by Legs: Maddy (Hedy Burress), a well-adjusted girl who functions as the film's primary character; and Goldie (Jenny Shimizu), an Asian American girl whose self-destructive drug addiction is presented as the result of her adoptive father's neglectful and abusive behavior.

While the characters in *Girls Town* retaliate against misogyny, the girls in *Foxfire* are less vengeful. Instead, they are depicted defending themselves against their teacher's sexual abuse. Presented as a mixed blessing, the girls' defensive action against the teacher leads to both their suspension from school and their further bonding, especially when they must defend themselves against a group of male students who threaten to rape Maddy if the girls don't drop the charges against the teacher, who also serves as the boys' coach. When Legs needs a place to stay, the girls take her to an abandoned house on the outskirts of town, which they quickly convert into

their own hangout. It is significant that the only girl in a heterosexual relationship, Maddy, withdraws from her boyfriend to spend
more time with her new friends. In a scene that cinematically and
thematically resembles the bonding scene from *Girls Town*, the *Foxfire* girls form a circle and tattoo each other, thus formalizing their
solidarity via a permanent mode of signification popular among contemporary youth. Unfortunately, despite the characters' creation of
this empowered and supportive female community, the end of *Foxfire* finds the girls distant from one another, especially Maddy and
Legs, whose sexual desire for one another is cut short by the latter's
psychotic behavior and subsequent departure from Portland.

   Although *Foxfire*'s conclusion demonstrates some filmmakers' apprehensions about depicting teen homosexuality as a possible, and positive, result of homosocial bonding, two recent films—
All Over Me and *The Incredibly True Adventure of Two Girls in
Love*—make full use of the theme of female empowerment through
same-sex friendships in their portrayals of girls' emerging lesbian
identities. A bittersweet tale of love and loss, *All Over Me* focuses
on two best friends, Claudia (Alison Folland), a larger-than-average
red-headed teen, and Ellen (Tara Subkoff), a skinny bleached-blond.
Although "Claude" and Ellen live near each other in Manhattan's
Hell's Kitchen, Ellen spends most of her time at her friend's home,
particularly in Claude's bedroom, a safe space where the girls fanta-
size about forming a rock band.[13]

   Despite their close ties, the girls find that their friendship begins to disintegrate when Ellen develops a relationship with Mark
(Cole Hauser), a possessive, macho boy who keeps her well supplied
with alcohol, cocaine, and sex. The more involved Ellen becomes
with Mark, the more isolated Claude feels. Looking outside her relationship with Ellen for emotional support, Claude eventually develops friendships with several gay youth, who offer support through
the rough patch of self-discovery that helps Claude come to terms
with her lesbianism. Ellen, however, is not supportive of her friend's
new assertions of homosexuality, especially when she understands
herself to be the object of Claude's desire. Their friendship suffers its
most drastic blow when Claude reports to the police Mark's involvement in her gay neighbor's murder. Although it is not depicted as an
act of retaliation against her own abuse, Claude's decision to inform
the police of Mark's homophobic violence is constructed as a significant step in her self-acceptance as a lesbian. Following the demise
of her friendship with Ellen, Claude becomes involved romantically

with Lucy (Leisha Hailey), a musician with whom she can bond emotionally and physically, as well as pursue her dreams of forming a band.

Whereas *All Over Me* ends with Claude's entry into a lesbian relationship, the narrative of *The Incredibly True Adventure of Two Girls in Love* is a full exploration of a first-love romance between two female adolescents. On the surface, the girls' love story does seem incredible; although they each live in a female-centered environment, they represent two extremes of female adolescent (and lesbian) subjectivity: the tomboy (butch) and the girly girl (femme). Randy (Laurel Holloman) is a short-haired white teenager who lives with her lower-class all-lesbian family, works part-time in a female-run gas station, and privileges getting high and listening to music over her schoolwork. Randy's independence and assertiveness are signified through her mobile, rollerblading body, her masculine attire, and her love of loud rock music. Although she lives in a gay-friendly household, Randy is treated as an outcast at her school, where she endures homophobic insults daily.

In direct contrast to Randy, Evie (Nicole Parker) is a popular, smart, and upper-middle-class African American girl who lives with her divorced mother and hangs out frequently with her white girlfriends. In addition to her location within a context of considerable material wealth, Evie is constructed as culturally sophisticated through her love of opera, Walt Whitman, and gourmet food and wine. Portrayed as conventionally feminine through her clothing and hair, Evie is also depicted as dependent and passive. For example, she is too scared to put air in the tires of her Range Rover, a task the street-wise Randy accomplishes with ease.

Reaffirming the cliché that opposites attract, Randy and Evie meet and fall in love, though hardly without negative repercussions. Although Evie has broken off a heterosexual relationship before meeting Randy, she ultimately loses her three closest girlfriends when she informs them that she is in love with Randy. Meanwhile, Randy's grades worsen as she spends more time with Evie; eventually she finds that she cannot graduate. Despite these obstacles, the girls persevere in their relationship, and their sexual desire for one another is realized finally on the night of Evie's eighteenth birthday. When Evie's mother comes home and is horrified to find her daughter and Randy in bed, the girlfriends run away and hole up in a local motel. They emerge after repeated pleadings by Randy's family, Evie's mother, and their friends to come out, yet they do so only after swearing to each other that their love is forever. The final image of the girlfriends embracing one another in the presence of the people closest to them is an extremely affirming message for gay youth.

Moving toward a New Form of Female Adolescent Subjectivity

Exploring the theme of female adolescent empowerment, *Girls Town, Foxfire, All Over Me*, and *The Incredibly True Adventure of Two Girls in Love* suggest that there is a strong need for girls to place boys on the side (if not out of sight) in order to develop independent, confident, and assertive identities. To communicate this message visually, each of these films locates its characters in primarily female-dominated environments. For example, *Girls Town* presents Angela and Nikki as the only daughters of single mothers, while Patti and her daughter live in her grandmother's house. In addition, the characters of *Girls Town* are shown gathering in places off-limits to males, especially the girls' restroom of their school. *All Over Me* and *The Incredibly True Adventure of Two Girls in Love* take this girls-only theme a step further by reconfiguring the bedrooms of female youth as places of lesbian bonding. In *Foxfire*'s more utopian (yet conflicted) vision of female bonding, the girls create an alternative home in an abandoned house that isolates them not only from boys but also from their families and the rest of their community.

In addition to these films' visual constructions of female environments, the inclusion of diegetic and soundtrack music by assertively feminist performers helps reinforce their girl-centered themes. Moreover, the inclusion of music by female rock and rap artists, such as L7 and Queen Latifah, signifies the extent to which these musicians function as powerful role models for many contemporary girls. Indeed, *The Incredibly True Adventure of Two Girls in Love* foregrounds Randy's admiration for Riot Grrrl bands, such as Bikini Kill, while Patti Smith functions as Claude's idol in *All Over Me*. In addition, *All Over Me* features a real-life female rocker (Hailey of the Murmurs) as Claude's lover and depicts a women's rock group (the Coochie Band, which includes Hailey and Mary Timony of Helium) being enjoyed by an all-female audience. The use of feminist music and the portrayal of female musicians in films focusing on teenage girls are notable attempts to move beyond the formula of studio-produced female teenpics, which continue to rely predomi-

Girl-bonding in *All Over Me.*

nantly on male-created music for their soundtracks and portray male figures as girls' primary role models and objects of desire.[14]

It is interesting that despite the attempts to feminize their girl characters through these visual and musical strategies, *Girls Town, Foxfire, All Over Me,* and *The Incredibly True Adventure of Two Girls in Love* subvert the traditional feminine *mise-en-scène* of female teenpics through a simultaneous masculinization of their protagonists. For example, the girls are often depicted engaging in activities typically associated with males (performing music, playing sports, working at manual jobs), wearing traditionally masculine clothing (pants, work boots, baseball caps), and inhabiting male-dominated spaces (street corners, sports fields, gas stations). As much as these female characters learn to privilege a pro-female ethos and feminine characteristics, such as caretaking and emotional intimacy, they often exhibit traits conventionally associated with masculinity, particularly rage and physical assertiveness. Thus, while depictions of female bonding through emotional intimacy and solidarity move the theme of empowerment beyond its conventionally masculinist connotations, these films nevertheless suggest that in a society where homophobia, child abuse, and sexual violence are on the rise, girls need to get in touch with their anger and develop more confidence in their physical capabilities.

Given these films' message that female youth need to develop and exhibit attributes traditionally associated with femininity *and* masculinity to survive in today's society, their representations of teenage girls subvert the two-gender system that grounds the ideologies of not only patriarchy and heterosexuality but also liberal and cultural feminism. In doing so, such films signify an important turning point not only in the media's representation of girlhood and female empowerment but also in our society's understanding of gender and subjectivity.

NOTES

1. This article originated as part of my dissertation, "Girls, Girls, Girls."
2. For example, see Considine, *The Cinema of Adolescence* and Lewis, *The Road to Romance and Ruin*. Although Clover (*Men, Women, and Chain Saws*) analyzes representations of teenage girls in horror films, her primary interest is the reception of such films by male adolescents.
3. An obvious exception is Scheiner's historical overview of cinematic representations of female adolescence, "Are These Our Daughters?"
4. Such films include *Daddy Long Legs* (1919), *True Heart Susie* (1919), *Are Parents People?* (1925), *The Little Firebrand* (1927), and *Sweet Sixteen* (1928).
5. The term "teenager" entered common usage by 1939.
6. It is not surprising that the world depicted in these early teenpics was distinctly white, heterosexual, middle class, and suburban.
7. The term "sub-deb" (from "sub-debutante") was coined in 1919 to describe a young girl about to become a debutante; by the 1940s, it was used to describe a girl in her mid-teens. "Bobby-soxer" was coined in 1944 and associated primarily with a group of white, middle-class, female adolescents who developed a distinct clothing style (including bobby socks) and particular entertainment tastes, especially the crooning of Frank Sinatra. See also Scheiner, "Are These Our Daughters?" especially chapter 4, "The Bobby-Soxer Meets the War."
8. This phenomenon is especially true for middle-class girls who, by attending college, extend their financial dependence on parents and postpone full-time work, as well as the roles of wife and mother.
9. Recent teenpics that demonstrate this tendency include *Can't Hardly Wait* (1998) and *American Pie* (1999).

10. Carol Gilligan is one of the pioneers of this type of research.
11. Analyses of Riot Grrrl's cultural and political significance include Gottlieb and Wald; Leonard; Rosenberg and Garofalo; and Kearney (1997 and 1998, "Don't Need You").
12. Departing from the white, suburban milieu of most teenpics, *Girls Town* constructs its characters as members of a racially and economically diverse urban community.
13. In contrast to studio-produced female teenpics that use loud rock music as a signifier of dysfunction, such as *The Next Karate Kid* and *Mad Love* (1995), *All Over Me* presents the consumption and production of rock music as positive activities for girls' identity formation and creative expression.
14. Studio-produced teenpics that continue this formula include *Clueless*, *The Craft*, and *Jawbreaker*.

WORKS CITED

American Association of University Women. 1991. *Shortchanging Girls, Shortchanging America.* Washington, DC: AAUW.

Brumberg, Joan Jacobs. 1993. "Learning to Menstruate the American Way, 1850–1950." In *Girls, Girlhood and Girls' Studies in Transition*, ed. Marion de Ras and Mieke Lunenberg, 287–311. Amsterdam: Het Spinhuis.

Clover, Carol. 1992. *Men, Women, and Chain Saws: Gender in the Modern Horror Film.* Princeton: Princeton University Press.

Considine, David M. 1985. *The Cinema of Adolescence.* Jefferson, NC: McFarland.

Gilligan, Carol. 1982. *In a Different Voice: Psychological Theory and Women's Development.* Cambridge: Harvard University Press.

Gottlieb, Joanne, and Gayle Wald. 1994. "Smells Like Teen Spirit: Riot Grrrls, Revolution and Women in Independent Rock." In *Microphone Fiends: Youth Music and Youth Culture*, ed. Andrew Ross and Tricia Rose, 250–74. New York: Routledge.

Higashi, Sumiko. 1978. *Virgins, Vamps, and Flappers: The American Silent Movie Heroine.* St. Albans, VT: Eden Press Women's Publications.

Kearney, Mary Celeste. 1997. "The Missing Links: Riot Grrrl—Feminism-Lesbian Culture." In *Sexing the Groove: Gender and Popular Music*, ed. Sheila Whiteley, 207–29. London: Routledge.

———. 1998. "'Don't Need You': Rethinking Identity Politics and Separatism from a Grrrl Perspective." In *Youth Culture: Identity in a Postmodern World*, ed. Jonathon S. Epstein, 148–88. Cambridge: Blackwell.

————. 1998. "Girls, Girls, Girls: Gender and Generation in Contemporary Discourses of Female Adolescence and Youth Culture." Ph.D. diss., University of Southern California.

Kett, Joseph F. 1977. *Rites of Passage: Adolescence in America, 1790 to the Present.* New York: Basic Books.

Leonard, Marion. 1997. " 'Rebel Girl, You Are the Queen of My World': Feminism, 'Subculture' and Grrrl Power." In *Sexing the Groove: Gender and Popular Music,* ed. Sheila Whiteley, 230–55. London: Routledge.

Lewis, Jon. 1992. *The Road to Romance and Ruin: Teen Films and Youth Culture.* New York: Routledge.

McRobbie, Angela. 1991. "*Jackie* and *Just Seventeen:* Girls' Comics and Magazines in the 1980s." In *Feminism and Youth Culture: From "Jackie" to "Just Seventeen",* ed. Angela McRobbie, 135–88. Basingstoke: Macmillan.

Orenstein, Peggy. 1994. *School Girls: Young Women, Self-Esteem, and the Confidence Gap.* New York: Anchor Books.

Pipher, Mary. 1994. *Reviving Ophelia: Saving the Selves of Adolescent Girls.* New York: Pantheon.

Rosen, Marjorie. 1973. *Popcorn Venus: Women, Movies, and the American Dream.* New York: Coward, McCann, and Geoghegan.

Rosenberg, Jessica, and Gitana Garofalo. 1998. "Riot Grrrl: Revolutions from Within." *Signs: Journal of Women in Culture and Society* 23 (spring): 809–41.

Scheiner, Georganne. 1990. "Are These Our Daughters?: The Image of Female Adolescence in Film, 1920–1970." Ph.D. diss., Arizona State University.

Tasker, Yvonne. 1998. *Working Girls: Gender and Sexuality in Popular Cinema.* London: Routledge.

Welter, Barbara. 1976. *Dimity Convictions: The American Woman in the Nineteenth Century.* Athens: Ohio University Press.

chapter 8

Performing Gender in *Boys Don't Cry*

Linda Dittmar

> Feared, trapped . . . and spliced open under the private
> auspices of those experts on truth . . . her body is killed
> off by the brutal ignorance of a society which works hard to
> display—while she feverishly reaches out to maintain—her
> manhood in all its sordid and mutated glory. Remarkably
> enough, she does not die in vain.
>
> SUE GOLDING[1]

A nagging challenge this essay faces from its readers is, "Why include attention to a film about a *boy* in a book about *girlhood*?" Most obviously, discussion of *Boys Don't Cry* (1999) has a legitimate place here because the youth it concerns was biologically female. The film is based on the true story of Brandon Teena, who lived as a young man but was born a girl (Teena Brandon) and was murdered at age twenty-one as a woman. But, since the film's rendition of this story suggests that biology may not be destiny after all, there are other reasons for including this essay in this particular book. Most important, *Boys Don't Cry* fits in here because it mounts a forceful critique of our culture's notions of girlhood. Instead of being about a girl, this disturbing, courageous, and widely screened film questions the very essence of "girlhood" and thus challenges the notion of fixing any gender or sexual difference. As such, it ends up addressing difficult, contentious questions regarding gender identity as they are being fought over in legislatures and courts as well as homes, churches, school and college campuses, laboratories, hospitals, places of employment, prisons, back alleys, barracks, and bars.

The passion behind these battles devolves on society's heterosexually based understanding of gender identities, romance, and sexuality. At stake here are queer modes of being our society sees as ranging from sinful and criminal to repellent, taboo, and "sick." *Boys*

Don't Cry counters this prevailing view with its sensitive, loving treatment of the dilemmas faced by transgendered and transsexual youth, including the abjection that propels their assailants. In this respect, to tell Brandon's story is to illuminate a long history of violent assaults on gays, lesbians, and other queers whose sexuality eludes traditional "male" or "female" gender delineations. As Brandon's assailants would have it, the girl "Teena" was beaten, raped, and murdered because she passed as a man. In so doing, she usurped a range of male privileges, including the right to be empowered through physical displays of strength, male camaraderie, and the love of women. But as the film would have it, Brandon chose to *be* a man, not simply *pass* as one. Thus, the contribution this film makes to the discourse of girlhood is, precisely, that it challenges the limits of gender delineation and proposes a more flexible and indeterminate model of being than normative, binary positions.

To discuss Brandon's sexual identity, gender, and therefore place in a society where a binary, heterosexual definition of "male" and "female" is the norm is to enter murky terrain. How does one assimilate the idea that somebody lives as a man but dies as a woman? How does one relate to a person whose sense of self is so definitively at odds with biology? How do we make sense of this sentence, voiced by Brandon's girlfriend, Lana, in an interview: "He tried to kill himself because he thought he was a lesbian, but then it was proven that he just had a sexual identity crisis, he wasn't a lesbian" (Minkowitz, 29)? Is Lana right to use the word "he" here, and am I right to follow suit and if so, does an essay about the film *Boys Don't Cry* fit into a book about filmic representations of girlhood?

The first challenge Brandon Teena poses, then, is on the level of vocabulary. Our language resists being "queered." With the exception of the nonhuman "it," our pronouns insist on a binary, masculine/feminine organization of knowledge. Inevitably, the pronouns we apply to Brandon take a stand on people's right to self-determination as it comes up against society's need to protect its established institutions. The following discussion responds to this problem by referring to Brandon as male when the film has him seen as male, which is most of the time. It treats Brandon as a female on those few occasions when characters or the film treat him as female. In this, my usage articulates respect for Brandon's masculine self-perception.[2] Furthermore, with awareness of transgendered and transsexual people entering public discourse, and with masculinity and femininity now seen as diversely distributed across individuals, even the terms "homosexual," "lesbian," and "hetero-sexual" are proving simplistic in their binary organization of identities. Thus, though Brandon objected to being labeled "lesbian" (that is, female), he lacked, tragically, an alternative concept by which to position himself outside prevailing categories. ("Queer," which does acknowledge the range of non-normative sex and gender formations, is a subcultural term, urban, activist, mostly middle class, and un-available to a small-town working-class youth like Brandon.[3])

Still, in themselves, the politics of language and ignorance would not be that important if it were not for the resulting practical politics of fear and hate. The homophobia and misogyny behind Brandon's murder are not simply a function of inadequate vocabulary and poor understanding.[4] They exist on a continuum of primitive, atavistic fears and hates that people secrete in the face of any exception to normative values. Jews, blacks, gays, women, communists, anarchists, disabled people, immigrants and foreigners, ethnic minorities, religious minorities, people living with AIDS, those living in poverty: these are the "things that go bump in the night" of the collective unconscious, the "demons" that some see as threatening to bring about the collapse of the social order. The targets of hate may shift over time, but the designated Other is always made to inhabit the desolate no-man's-land between dominant notions of humanity and "monstrosity," between pathetic deformity and "sinful abomination." Posed as objects of horror and terror, such Others end up targets of violence because it is hard for societies to accept difference, especially when what they fear threatens to expose their own fragility. Protecting the privileges guaranteed by established norms, societies perceive difference as a "deviance" that threatens what the prevailing consensus asserts is "natural," "right," and "God-given."

Though we cannot address the genesis, psychology, and politics of such hate in any depth here, it is important to weave Brandon Teena's story into such broader practices of social disenfranchise-ment and thus into a broader understanding of social accountability. Certainly *Boys Don't Cry* is about gender and homophobia, but it is also about social class and human aspirations. Brandon was "trailer trash," a gay high school acquaintance tells a reporter. His last girlfriend, Lana Tisdel, describes her family to a reporter in these terms: "In Falls City you have the high class, the middle class, and the scums, and we are the scums" (Minkowitz 28). Underneath the film's vast and visually beautiful skies, so often punctuating the action as a reminder of nature's magisterial expanse, live human beings whose horizons close in on them in ways that extend beyond gender anxiety. Thus, while the film's plot guides us to read Brandon's life and death as a tragic consequence of rampant homophobia and patriarchal sexism, its setting and cinematography guide us to read this life through the lens of geography, history, and social class as well.

Accordingly, *Boys Don't Cry* contains two intertwined narratives. Most immediately, it concerns the blinding and potentially murderous terror with which our society protects male privilege within its heterosexist social order. As such, it is a film about gender, homophobia, and patriarchal power. But it is also a film about the crumbling of that power and about the violence social disenfranchisement breeds more broadly. In this sense the circumstances surrounding the plot inscribe additional subtexts through the film's ancillary action, its treatment of social power, and its cinematic "language"—*mise-en-scène*, photography, editing, soundtrack, lighting, etc. Brandon is murdered because he destabilizes male/female distinctions and thus poses a radical threat to received notions of family, nation, and masculine power. But he is also murdered because of other contingencies, notably the brutalizing and dysfunctional life in a small Midwestern farming community that is stranded, at the end of the millennium, in the material and spiritual poverty of dead-end lives.

We shall return to the issues of "trailer trash" and "scum" as they frame *Boys Don't Cry*, but first we need to look more closely at the primary claims this film makes through its focus on gender and sexuality. Most obviously, *Boys Don't Cry* foregrounds gender as its primary concern through its close elaboration of Brandon's process of establishing, cultivating, and defending his male identity. From the first "rites of passage" sequence, where we see Teena in Lincoln, Nebraska, getting a boy's haircut, packing a sock in her jeans, donning a large cowboy hat, and going to the skating rink to pick up girls, to Brandon's arrival and eventual death in rural and impoverished Falls City, Nebraska, the film draws us to the enigma of gender identity. We know that Brandon is biologically female; the first sequence has established this fact definitively. At the same time, we do see him as male; the plot affirms that Brandon can "pass" successfully (Peirce) and Hilary Swank's androgynous performance is truly compelling. Brandon is attractive to women, is taken for a peer by men, and is accepted as Lana's boyfriend by Lana's mother. Though his masculinity is still tenuous in the skating rink episode in Lincoln (where his date's irate brother assaults Brandon as a "dyke" in a fury prophetic of the extreme danger Brandon will continue to court), by the time he arrives in Falls City he has mastered the role. He proves a feisty barroom fighter, a daredevil "bumper skier" on a pickup truck, a reckless driver, and a romantic lover who can win the heart of the morosely independent Lana.

Though the film's narrative insists on Brandon's masculinity as its central concern, it also invites audiences to dwell on the very indeterminacy of Brandon's gender. Like Lana's mother, whom we watch touching and scrutinizing Brandon's face quizzically, we too find ourselves puzzling out this person's gender. It has us scrutinize his every gesture, wonder how he can pee standing, worry when he gets his period, marvel at how his dressing (breast binding, jeans, layered loose shirts) transform him into a male, and examine his lovemaking for give-away signs. How could she, Teena, pull it off? How could Lana fall for it? How could all involved fall for it? And why are we inclined to do so, too, despite the evidence?

Not only are the script and acting of *Boys Don't Cry* incredibly supple in this regard, the production is, too. Here camera focus and placement, image cropping, editing, lighting, music, ambient sounds, and the like at once help construct Brandon's masculinity as a convincing identity position and preclude definitive knowledge. The use of highly masculinized *and* feminized country western music, the tight interior spaces that constrain expansive ("masculine") movement, the chiaroscuro of the darkly lit scenes to which both the lovemaking and the violence are relegated, the prevalence of cropped close-ups and fast editing that at once "show" and derail knowledge at potentially "telling" moments, the importance of frenzied speed in the filmed action, and Hilary Swank's body language keep the question of gender identity alive. Even toward the end of the film, when Brandon's biological makeup becomes a definitively known fact, the film continues to define him as "he"—a practice that instructs the viewer to do likewise. Lana does so most pronouncedly, but even Tom Nissen, one of his two assailants, calls Brandon "little Dude" shortly after the rape that precedes the murder.

This unclarity is most obviously anchored in the film's treatment of Brandon and Lana's lovemaking scenes. Here is the film's opportunity to "tell all," but here is also its opportunity to repress viewers' access to what one might learn from the sex act. We see Brandon's sex-specific paraphernalia when his friend, Candice, searches his belongings—the bunched socks, the dildo, and the tampax are all in a jumble. But it is not clear how, exactly, he gives Lana her orgasm in the second lovemaking scene, and that scene builds on the first, which does not yield much information either. In both instances the camera disguises the actual sex by focusing on Brandon's and especially Lana's ecstatic faces and by having much of the scene in close-ups that crop the images and have body parts obscure the intercourse. Though one could attribute this roundabout strategy to the problem any non-pornographic film has about the limits of good taste, ratings, and access to theatrical screenings when it attempts to portray sex acts, the film's coy camera and editing are also an opportunity to circumvent full disclosure of both Brandon's sexuality and Lana's credulity.

This unsettling irresolution carries over even into the film's most painful moments of heterosexually motivated assaults on Brandon—his rape and murder—if in fact one can call those "heterosexual." At issue are the Christmas Eve scene, when Nissen and John Lotter forcibly expose Brandon's genitals to prove his femaleness to themselves and Lana, and the New Year's Eve scene, when they rape and a few hours later kill him. In the first instance, the men's exposure of Brandon's pubis in the face of his desperate resistance and piercing shame comes across as a scene of castration. Though we know that he is not literally castrated, the melee of scrambled close-ups, the erupting sounds of fighting and screaming, the absence of a penis on his slim "masculine" body, and his excruciating psychic pain in the scene all create that effect. We know that a desperately resistant person's genitals are being assaulted, if only by the gaze (John's, Tom's, the camera's, and our own), but we read the sequence as a symbolic castration because the display of Brandon's "lack" threatens what de Lauretis calls his "body ego" (243). While the film goes to great lengths to accept Brandon's self-definition as male, the exposure aims to humiliate Brandon, forbid him any further access to women, and assert the absolute rule of "The Law of the Father."

Brandon's rape is also redolent with visual and conceptual ambiguity. It is significant that at first the film narrates it through a series of flashbacks intercut with his testimony at the police station, including a sustained focus on the tape recorder by way of stressing the regulatory and public context of the account. This cross-cutting does diminish after a while, but not before it is established enough to constitute a norm of audience reception of this particular sequence. One of the functions of the editing is to put forth a critique of the role law enforcement personnel play in Brandon's victimization. Another is to note the failure of Brandon's language to convey an assault he is too traumatized to articulate. But this disrupted account, especially given its somewhat blurry transitions into memory, also enforces a discontinuous mode of reception. As a narrative strategy it may reflect Brandon's wrenching shifts between unbearable memory and present consciousness, but it also creates an epistemological turmoil that shuttles the audience between comprehension and distress.

This state of fluid and partly intuitive reception affects the ways one might read the "facts" of the rape. Brandon is raped both prone and from behind (though probably not anally)—that is, in a mix of heterosexual and gay codes. Further, his rapists are men whose defense of proper gender boundaries is marked by a questionable surplus of emphasis. Although this surplus does not specifically indicate a homosexual impulse, it blurs boundaries all around. On the one hand, this scene's rendition ascribes to John and Tom a certain fleeting gentleness toward Brandon after the rape, almost as if he is a "girl" they like but have to discipline "for her own good." At the same time, the film makes a point of showing the rape from behind in some detail. Folded into this treatment is the suggestion of a more complicated impulse than just putting a "woman" in "her" place. Does Tom also rape Brandon as a boy (that is, from behind)? And does John's position as the dominant, "alpha" male in relation to Tom further eroticize the situation? The intimate bonds that characterize heterosexual male friendship throughout the film—the punching that is also touching, the scuffling that allows for embrace—suggest an intimacy that puts the men's own sexuality in question. Here, as in many films focused on male bonding (for example, road movies, boy bike movies, combat films, urban delinquency films, and porn that uses women as relays between men), contact plays a more complicated role than heterosexual formulas would have us believe. Homosocial bonds become a means of repudiating homosexual desires, and Woman becomes a token of exchange, a vehicle for the forbidden touch, among men.

The fact that Brandon is barely out of adolescence further complicates matters. The film's opening attention to his rite of passage concerns a transition into adulthood as well as masculinity in ways the film does not ultimately probe in depth. Brandon's agitated comments about a sexual difficulty, possibly medical, come across as brief, muddled, and ill-informed. Mostly the film treats his trangendered persona as an incontrovertible necessity even as it leaves the notion of an authentic, essential nature unresolved. I do not mean to question Brandon's self-definition, but its contradictory male/female

Brandon Teena further victimized by the police.

formation emphasizes the conflicting roles of personal desire and social will in the production of identities. Puberty and adolescence are crucial in this regard as a period of heterosexual self-formation played within or against social expectations. Most important to our purposes is the disproportionate shame and loss of agency many girls experience in the process of becoming adult women, in contrast with boys for whom claiming an adult body and sex are common modes of empowerment (Martin). Seen in these terms, Teena's embrace of a masculinity is compelling, be it a "choice" or "true nature." Being a man, not simply masquerading as one, lets Brandon disavow the injuries of femalehood and gives him a tremendous sense of agency. He can display physical prowess, take up space in a crowded room, drink and scuffle with men, romance women, initiate sex with women, and so heal for himself the narcissistic injury to which girls are so often destined. Being a man lets him articulate a fuller, more assertive and dynamic self than would be possible for him as a woman.[5]

The difficulty *Boys Don't Cry* keeps forcing on viewers devolves on their wish to settle matters once and for all in a film that refuses to allow it. The film explicitly frames Brandon's story in the testimony of the opening sequence, where Teena turns herself into a simulacrum of a boy, except that the simulacrum is so persuasive that it is hard to remember the pretense. The film at once registers and suspends the examining nurse's empathetic recognition of Brandon's femaleness after the rape, and it chalks up the knowing leer of Falls City's sheriff to crude prurience rather than treating it as a guiding view.[6] It lets the ambiguity of Lana's mother's close look at Brandon fade off, and also fades the cropped and edited sequences of Brandon and Lana's lovemaking and the murky visibility of the exposure and rape scenes. Further, in a strange twist on all the above, the film's last love scene, just after the rape, shows Lana and Brandon moving to a mutuality that suggests *lesbian* sex, in contradistinction to everything that preceded this moment, including the unlikelihood of any sex, however loving, so soon after a rape.

Ultimately *Boys Don't Cry* lets Brandon's identity remain elusive. As we take in the reiterated if not consistent acceptance of his manhood by all the principal characters, and as we review his various indicators of masculinity (even if put in doubt at certain moments) the ill fit haunting the relationship between knowledge and understanding is something we will not let go. This ill fit extends to the inconclusive representation of the lovemaking, too. After she posts bail to get him out of jail where he landed (in the women's ward) for speeding, carrying false identification, and evading a prior summons in Lincoln, Nebraska, Lana tells Brandon "I want to touch you the way you touch me." But in what sense is that possible? Inevitably, we keep seeing Brandon with a kind of double vision.

This instability of knowledge is at the heart of the human dilemma that concerns Brandon's life and the spectatorial dilemmas *Boys Don't Cry* constructs to convey it. As viewers, we are drawn to combing the film for give-away signs—the girlish gesture, the curve of a hip, the nongenital intercourse with Lana, the point of entry during the rape—so as to settle this undecidability. Ironically, to make a settlement is to become complicit in the very binarism the film's sympathetic portrayal of Brandon aims to challenge. We still rummage for a simple either/or answer, a clear-cut male/female notion of gender, a stable place in the cultural regulation of sexualities. We once more reveal our lingering inability to live with the permeable boundaries of queer identities. Unlike the film *The Crying Game* (1992), where the male character's passing for a woman is sprung on viewers only toward the end of the action, here the "secret" is revealed from the start. *The Crying Game* uses its sustained obfuscation and eventual surprise to challenge its protagonist's and audience's capacity for flexible, inclusive acceptance, while *Boys Don't Cry* uses its diagnostic voyeurism to establish a state of sustained ambiguity. It presupposes knowledge but precludes definitive categories. Its loving treatment of Brandon's personal appeal advocates acceptance but does not fully eliminate the tradition-based wish to pigeonhole runaway sexualities.

Ultimately, the questions stirred up by the film do not end with, "What does it mean to be a 'Man'?" but include, "Why does it matter?" Is gender an essential human (and animal) quality, inscribed in bodies and lodged in specific biological attributes (a penis, a big Adam's apple, a low voice, large hands, and the like)? Is it a role, a mode of behavior, that can be grafted onto what our system of classification considers male or female bodies? Were we to call Teena a masculine woman rather than a "he," the problem would diminish. She would be seen as a butch, a baby bull dyke, not as a man. But Brandon refuses such definitions, and *Boys Don't Cry* respects the resulting ambiguity. He wants to literally redesign his body, not merely cross-dress to disguise it, but as long as he has not accomplished that, what is he, and does it matter?

It matters to Minkowitz, it seems. As partly an object of private fantasy in line with a particular scenario, her Brandon is mostly a female desired for her masculine qualities: "Everybody wants her. . . . Brandon looks to be the handsomest butch in history—not just good looking, but arrogant, audacious, cocky—everything I look for in a lover" (27). For recent scholarship on body identities Brandon's self-definition matters in a different way. In this context Brandon/Teena's gendered identity is important symbolically, in that it helps originate a critique of society's deadly effort to regulate erupting subjectivities and radically resistant bodies by forcing them back into binary social formations. "The body must be understood through a range of disparate discourses," Elizabeth Grosz writes. "There are other ways in which sexually specific corporeal differences may be understood than those developed in more conventional and scientific representational contexts" (20).[7]

Such tangled evocations of runaway genders, non-normative desires, and "deviant" sexualities as they bump up against conventional social organization are hardly unique to *Boys Don't Cry*. They can be found across fiction films ranging from *Last Exit to Brooklyn* (1989), *Trash* (1970), *Some Like It Hot* (1959), *La Cage aux folles* (1978), *The Kiss of the Spider Woman* (1985), *The Crying Game*, *The Adventures of Priscilla, Queen of the Desert* (1994), or *Ma Vie en rose* (1997) to reportorial and poetic documentaries like *The Queen* (1966), *Paris Is Burning* (1990), *Looking for Langston* (1988), or *Tongues Untied* (1991). However, this brief list is about male-to-female transgendering, not the obverse. Filmic representations of female-to-male (FTM) transgendered or transsexual themes are rare and less radical. During the Hays Hollywood Production Code (1932/34–1962) such themes were compromised, encrypted, and ultimately reclaimed back into patriarchal heterosexuality or killed. Their few, short-lived, and underexamined lesbian or queer gestures mainly served as a vehicle for male desire and a mark of a purely temporary female autonomy (Straayer). Women's resistance to gender expectations, when it is depicted, is often ridiculed or demonized.

Halberstam's survey of mostly mainstream films (175–230) suggests that they include a small cluster of lesbians, including some butches, but not of FTM characters. A few more forthright but rarely screened renditions include k. d. lang's role in *Salmonberries* (1992), Queen Latifah's in *Set It Off* (1996), and the documentaries *Storme: Lady of the Jewel Box* (1987), *Outlaw* (1994; dedicated to Brandon Teena and Marsha P. Johnson), and *You Don't Know Dick: Courageous Hearts of Transsexual Men* (1996).[8] Of these, only *You Don't Know Dick* is about postoperative FTM transsexuals. It should come as no surprise, then, that queer and feminist scholarship (together with other progressive work) take such qualified representations as reflecting the belief that any threat to masculine hegemony, however slight, is a threat to the established social, political, and economic order. (This is especially applicable to FTM transitions. Male-to-female transvestites and transgendereds incur a loss in social status that invites ridicule, not erasure.) Any ambiguity seeping into gendered identity, any enigma about social positionality, is a crack in our social fortification.

Ironically, the anxiety enigmas provoke also fuels their seductiveness. Uncanny objects of contemplation, their unresolvability occupies a kind of twilight zone where knowledge is at once yearned for and withheld. Such unresolvability renders revolutionary desires conceivable; it opens up a space for liberatory, defiant, and subversive impulses. The pathos or humor in some of the films named above is, precisely, that they place knowledge in a maze of uncertainties. The appeal of some others is that the fantasies they embody lead us to probe our own hidden selves. In *Boys Don't Cry*, where the plot and even Swank's appearance closely replicate a highly publicized actuality, the focus is ultimately not simply documentary or epistemological. Thematically, it is all that, but the viewing experience it constructs also brings to light the active complicity of our own desires. The film does normalize the unresolvability of Brandon's gendered and sexual identity and his claim to autonomous self-definition as basic human rights, but its appeal and box-office success are also owed to its seductive rendition of fantasy. That the fantasy is ultimately indeterminate, that the film leaves Brandon's position within sex and gender compartments unresolved, ushers us into the haunting realm of barely named desires.[9]

Over the last three decades, a considerable body of cultural theory, including feminist and subaltern film studies, has focused on questions of identity, agency, and desire. Resting in part on other post-structuralist inquiries into the construction of meanings, this work has been deepening our understanding of ways individual and communal identities are an effect of construction and ideology. Key here is the idea that identity is, in part, an artifact that defines access to social goods and that people do have choices—political choices—about negotiating their place in society. This activist reading of social positionality encourages us to read Teena Brandon's age, race, social class, location, education, and biology as signifiers of a range of disenfranchisements she is struggling to resist. Thus, while the hold *Boys Don't Cry* has on its audiences may well be indebted to the way it sets up compelling positions for identification, self-discovery, and pleasure (on the level of both plot and cinematic rendition), the political energy of this film has to do with its move toward dismantling society's seemingly unassailable definitions of identities (and hence privileges and power relations) as unchangeable states of being.

This point is all the more evident in light of recent theories of performance as further refinements of this line of thought. Moving beyond the debate over "construction" versus "essence" (1970s–1980s) the notion of "performativity" has emerged out of queer activism and scholarship in the post-Stonewall and AIDS era and in the wake of performance and conceptual art. Though the constructionist view never assumed a passive subject, in that we all participate in our formation, the emphasis on performance is more active. The very theatricality implied by this word helps define identity as a deliberate articulation of a self-willed persona meant for public display. It comes across as assertive and even defiant—extravagant, cathartic, revolutionary, and carnivalesque (Bakhtin). Treating identity both as a site of personal fantasies and desire and as a composite of stock modules and variations, the performative view also evinces an ironic postmodernism regarding the derived and mirroring effects of such artifice.

The scene where Teena sets out to become a man is emblematic of her move toward displaying the performative resonance of attire, posture, and fetish objects. Respecting Teena's own perspective, this sequence is neither ironic nor camp, which it could have easily been. There is intensity, passion, and thrill here, as we see Teena assume her new persona so fully that we ourselves let her dissolve into Brandon, albeit with considerable help from the film's director, Kimberly Peirce. The very "truth" *Boys Don't Cry* sets us up to seek proves to be, at once, a mirroring and usurping of societal values (that is, Teena performs masculinity as a power position), a ritualized fulfillment of personal desires, and an interventionist political challenge to hetero-patriarchy. The emphasis here is on the shaping and display of fluid, actively willing, engaged identities. We see a self being produced as an effect of a deliberate, agency-driven performance of social codes. This self has a specific corporeal constitution that cannot exist outside gender, seeing that we are all deeply embedded in gender relations, but it is nonetheless a self that lays claim to autonomy through its performance of the codes of masculinity and, so, bends essence to its will.

This view of identities as constituted through performance should help us understand what a film about a "boy" is doing in a book about cinemas of girlhood. That is, once we accept Brandon's conviction that he is male even though we also know that biology has marked him as female, we can move toward interrogating any and all definitions of gender from a radically skeptical perspective. Putting aside whatever viewing desires we may experience—to be Brandon Teena, to possess him or her (as each of us may incline), or to reclaim Brandon the young man into a more embracing definition of normalcy—*Boys Don't Cry* encourages us to keep a more flexible understanding of gender. If there is one service this film performs in helping us explore cinemas and ideals of girlhood, it is that it has Teena and Brandon unite in a layered presence, a palimpsest of possibilities.

Though the ambiguity that perpetually attaches to Brandon's identity—and, thus, to our own viewing relations to the film—shapes the appeal of this film, other social forces also affect the film's plot and rendition. This point becomes clear when we compare Brandon's story to the 1998 brutal murder of Matthew Shepard in Laramie, Wyoming.[10] Both died as a result of hate crimes perpetrated by disadvantaged working-class youths in provincial Midwestern settings, except that Matthew, unlike Brandon, was an openly gay college student. Educated, economically secure, privileged by sex and gender (as a male-identified person), at ease with his identity and poised to move forward in society (and doing so in the late 1990s, when the outlook for openly gay people seemed to be improving), he was better off than many queers, including Brandon. One way to measure the difference in their empowerment is to note that Matthew's mother became an activist, thus continuing to support him, while the mothers of Brandon and Lana could not quite accept Brandon's sexuality.[11] Whatever his gender position, Brandon had significantly less access to economic, intellectual, familial, and thus social resources.

Though *Boys Don't Cry* includes no such class comparison as Brandon's and Matthew's, its treatment of social class, economics, ignorance, and the resulting entrapment is very much to the point.[12] Its physical location and personal dramas suggest a film of the post-Vietnam, as well as the post-Stonewall era.[13] Its settings in particular resonate as signifiers of the desolation of all the lives involved—the flattened horizons, the eerie hulk of a canning factory scarring the landscape, the alienating monumentality of the courthouse as the "temple" regulating civic order, the harried functionality of shabby homes, the meager affection and desperate snatches of joy these places provide, the reiterated presence of high-tension towers, the use of cars as social centers as well as a means of reckless transportation, and more. This is a landscape where neglect and entrapment are intertwined with the characters' longings for mobility and escape. The escape Lana and Brandon unrealistically envision is the honky-tonk glitz of singing karaoke in Memphis.

Accordingly, much of the film's action takes place in constricted spaces framed and filmed as restraints on characters' movement or, noir style, shrinking the expanse of the image's frame (with doorways, corridors, furniture, cars, etc.). Agency is enacted here mainly through rage and violence, be it in "bumper skiing" on pickup trucks, drag racing in speeding cars, passing around bottles of beer, or displaying bravado. It is a form of agency, a kind of freedom, which the film ascribes emphatically to a masculinity that appropriates violence as the only way men can reclaim power. Bodies—especially those of men—in constant frenetic motion are deeply encoded here in their class position within a derelict town where a canning factory, a convenience store, a hospital, a prison, and a courthouse seem to be the only employers and institutions at hand.

This overdetermined representation of working-class lives in America's "heartland" radically shapes the particular version of homophobia that is the plot's central concern. It is no accident that the institutional locations it shows signify both civic/economic regulation and body regulation in the senses elaborated by Foucault. It is also significant that the cramped interior spaces (bathrooms, bars, cars) and bleak nocturnal wastelands are standard settings for surreptitious and transitory male sexual encounters. *Boys Don't Cry* weaves queerness and class dynamics into a tight fabric, infusing it with a vision of how embedded each character is in social and personal abjection. In a sense, what is most at stake here are the injuries of systemic ignorance and the politics of knowledge. The violence, the boredom, the inarticulateness, the time "done" in prison, and even the nurse's ultimate silence are all symptomatic of the fact that the much-touted prosperity of the 1990s has left this "trailer trash" and "scum" behind. The myriad assaults inflicted on these bodies (epitomized by John's and Tom's self-mutilation) are all signifiers of profound disenfranchisement and self-hate.

Given this grid of disenfranchisements within our social order, it is hardly surprising that the film's men, including law enforcement officers, are guilty of a range of abusive behaviors. Abuse, after all, is an accepted code for power. It is also not surprising that Brandon reaches for masculine efficacy to reclaim his own personal agency in the face of the multiple injuries his world assigns him as a woman, and a working-class one at that. But perhaps what is most noteworthy about Brandon's performance of masculinity is his proclivity for romance, for protecting women, and for the empowerment he gets from caring. The Brandon we see picking up a girl at the skating rink in Lincoln and the Brandon we later see with Lana hinge masculinity on chivalry, not abuse. He establishes a tough and fearless persona early on, but it is a knightly persona in its performance of masculine rites. His generosity with money and gifts he cannot afford harkens back to fables where courtship leads to living happily ever after. Perhaps this boy-girl, trailing behind him forged checks, thefts, speeding tickets, evaded court summonses, and broken hearts is, after all, made of sugar and spice and everything nice.

NOTES

1. Golding is talking about a nineteenth-century female hermaphrodite. We have now a substantial body of scholarship about current theories

on race, ethnicity, criminality, prostitution, gender, sex "deviance," etc., and their historic antecedents. See Cartwright, Gilman, Lulvani, McClintock (1995), Terry, and others.

2. See Middlebrook regarding Billie Tipton—a musician who lived as a man. Minkowitz mostly uses "she" for Brandon. See Halberstam for the naming of gender/sex/body identities and "gender dysphoria" (chapters 1, 4–5, esp. 118–20).

3. "Queer" signals militancy, notably AIDS–related activism, including publications from the 1990s on transgender and transsexuality, such as Feinberg, Devor, Cromwell, Prosser, Halberstam, and Burana and Due. See also Nestle and de Lauretis.

4. The terms "lesbian" and "dyke" capture the homophobia here, but Brandon's gender-crossing also suggests a gender instability that extends to John and Tom. "Misogyny" refers to their panic about being feminized and their hatred of Brandon for embodying their own fears of symbolic castration and physical lack.

5. Though the real Teena suffered incest and rape, at issue are generic, routine injuries (Martin, de Lauretis), reflecting a broadly shared dilemma. Cf. Sue Friedrich's *Sink or Swim* (1990), Julie Zando's *Let's Play Prisoners* (1988), and the videos of Sadie Benning.

6. Minkowitz cites the police and district attorney's homophobic handling of the case—a claim supported by the documentary, *The Brandon Teena Story* (1998). *Boys Don't Cry* includes a segment of the police record. It is cited more fully in the documentary.

7. Cf. Butler, Halberstam, Sedgwick, Singer, and Straayer.

8. For a more comprehensive discussion see Straayer 1996.

9. Note again the quote above from Minkowitz (27) and Golding. Cf. also the seductive power of James Dean, Montgomery Clift, and Marlon Brando as gay icons.

10. Matthew Shepard died Monday, October 12, 1998, from severe injuries due to a brutal beating and torture.

11. *Boys Don't Cry* and *The Brandon Teena Story* depict this reluctance. While Brandon's obituary described him as "buried in men's clothing, wearing her favorite cowboy shirt and black cowboy hat," a correction was entered noting that he was buried in "shirt purchased in the women's section of a local store."

12. Race was more than peripheral in Brandon's life, though this all-white film sidesteps this issue. Lana's family had interracial ties and for awhile sheltered an interracial baby. Her sister's black boyfriend was murdered with Brandon and Brandon's friend, Candy, in Candy's house.

13. The Stonewall riots, where transvestites and gays stood up to police harassment in New York City, June 1969, marked the start of contemporary queer activism.

Works Cited

Bakhtin, Mikhail. 1984. *Rabelais and His World.* Bloomington: Indiana University Press.

Bell-Metereau, Rebecca. 1993. *Hollywood Androgyny.* New York: Columbia University Press.

Burana, Lily, Roxie, and Linnea Due, eds. 1994. *Dagger: On Butch Women.* Pittsburgh and San Francisco: Cleis Press.

Butler, Judith. 1990. *Gender Trouble: Feminism and the Subversion of Identity.* New York: Routledge.

———. 1993. *Bodies That Matter: On the Discursive Limits of "Sex."* New York: Routledge.

Cartwright, Lisa. 1995. *Screening the Body: Tracing Medicine's Visual Culture.* Minneapolis: University of Minnesota Press.

Cromwell, Jason. 1999. *Transmen and FTMs: Identities, Bodies, Genders, and Sexualities.* Urbana: University of Illinois Press.

de Lauretis, Teresa. 1994. *The Practice of Love: Lesbian Sexuality and Perverse Desire.* Bloomington: Indiana University Press.

Devor, Holly. 1997. *FTM: Female-to-Male Transsexuals in Society.* Bloomington: Indiana University Press.

Feinberg, Leslie. 1996. *Transgender Warriors: Making History from Joan of Arc to Rupaul.* Boston: Beacon Press.

Foucault, Michel. 1977. *Discipline and Punish: The Birth of the Prison.* New York: Pantheon.

Gilman, Sander L. 1986. "Black Bodies, White Bodies: Toward an Iconography of Female Sexuality in Late Nineteenth-Century Art, Medicine, and Literature." In *Race, Writing, and Difference,* ed. Henry Louis Gates, Jr., 223–61. Chicago: University of Chicago Press.

Golding, Sue. 1991. "James Dean: The Almost-Perfect Lesbian Hermaphrodite." In *Stolen Glances: Lesbians Take Photographs,* ed. Tessa Boffin and Jean Fraser, 197–202. London: Pandora Press.

Grosz, Elizabeth. 1994. *Volatile Bodies: Toward a Corporeal Feminism.* Bloomington: Indiana University Press.

Halberstam, Judith. 1995. *Female Masculinity.* Durham: Duke University Press.

Lulvani, Suren. 1995. *Photography, Vision, and the Production of Bodies.* Albany: SUNY Press.

Martin, Karin A. 1996. *Puberty, Sexuality, and the Self: Girls and Boys at Adolescence.* New York: Routledge.

McClintock, Anne. 1995. *Imperial Leather: Race, Gender, and Sexuality in the Colonial Conquest.* New York: Routledge.

Middlebrook, Diane Wood. 1998. *Suits Me: The Double Life of Billy Tipton.* Boston: Houghton Mifflin.

Minkowitz, Donna. 1994. "Love Hurts." *The Village Voice,* 19 April: 24–30.

Nestle, Joan. 1992. *The Persistent Desire: A Femme-Butch Reader.* Boston: Alyson Publications, Inc.

Parker, Andrew, and Eve Kosofsky Sedgwick, eds. 1995. *Performativity and Performance.* New York: Routledge.

Peirce, Kimberly. 2000. "Putting Teena Brandon's Story on Film: Francesca Miller Interviews the Director of *Boys Don't Cry.*" *The Gay and Lesbian Review* 7 (fall): 39–40.

Prosser, Jay. 1998. *Second Skins: The Body Narratives of Transsexuality.* New York: Columbia University Press.

Sedgwick, Eve. 1990. *Epistemology of the Closet.* Berkeley: University of California Press.

———. 1993. *Tendencies.* Durham: Duke University Press.

Singer, Linda. 1983. *Erotic Welfare: Sexual Theory and Politics in the Age of Epidemic.* New York: Routledge.

Straayer, Chris. 1996. *Deviant Eyes, Deviant Bodies: Sexual Re-orientation in Film and Video.* New York: Columbia University Press.

Terry, Jennifer. 1995. "The Seductive Power of Science in the Making of Deviant Subjectivity." In *Posthuman Bodies,* ed. Judith Halberstam and Ira Livingston, 135–61. Bloomington: Indiana University Press.

chapter 9

Fille Fatale:
Regulating Images of Adolescent Girls, 1962–1996

Kristen Hatch

The ad campaign openly wondered, "How did they ever make a movie of *Lolita*?" Only five years earlier, in 1955, before it became a best-seller, the book had been banned in the United States and Europe and rejected by U.S. publishers due to its controversial subject matter. But Stanley Kubrick had translated Vladimir Nabokov's novel into a film, which MGM would distribute. The film earned not only a Production Code seal and an acceptable rating from the Legion of Decency but a tidy profit as well. Although many critics reported that, in fact, MGM *had not* made a movie of *Lolita*, Stanley Kubrick's success in creating a commercially viable film of the infamous novel about a middle-aged man's sexual obsession with a young girl seemed proof that Hollywood was at last beginning to break free of the conservatism that had so shackled its creativity.[1]

Today, Nabokov's novel is required reading in college courses; the Production Code has been scrapped in favor of a rating system that is intended to protect filmmakers from the necessity of cutting their films for anything other than aesthetic purposes; and the Supreme Court has determined that film is a form of speech, guaranteed protection under the First Amendment.[2] Yet, when Adrian Lyne made an R-rated film of the novel in 1996, the nearly unanimous response among American distributors was that it was too controversial a project to be profitable in the United States, even after Lyne edited the film, with a lawyer at his side, to ensure that it conformed to the Child Pornography Prevention Act that was passed earlier in the year.[3] Child protection groups in the United States and Europe protested the film, sight unseen, and a heated debate ensued, in which the merits of censoring the tale of a man obsessed with a pubescent girl were weighed against the damage that censorship would do to the First Amendment. Two years after its completion, the film was finally seen by American audiences on the cable network Showtime.

Although the difference between the responses to the two *Lolita*s defies the common perception that American society, Hollywood in particular, has become steadily less restrictive regarding sexuality since the 1960s, it also appears to confirm our sense that we have become increasingly enlightened regarding the problem of child sexual abuse since that period, when child victims of incest and molestation were regarded as sex delinquents (see Jenkins). Although the heightened sensitivity to erotic images of girls reflects an increased awareness of the nature and extent of child sexual abuse, a consideration of the debates surrounding the mainstream films that have faced accusations of child pornography suggests that there is far more at stake than children's physical safety. The debates serve to reinforce the ideal of childhood innocence and to reassert the role that adults play in maintaining it. In the face of the radical social changes of the latter half of the twentieth century, particularly the redefinition of womanhood and the diminishment of patriarchal authority, the controversies surrounding these films serve as a means of reinforcing women's maternal role and of articulating concerns about men's sexuality.

For the most part, film audiences in 1962 perceived Humbert Humbert's interest in his stepdaughter to be a normal, if atypical, response to a sexually precocious girl. Responding to a journalist from the *New York Herald* following a screening of the film, viewers regardless of age or gender, have little trouble making the characters and their actions conform to their understanding of adult and children's sexuality:

> Mrs. Juanita Harper, 27: It could happen in real life. I wasn't shocked though. . . . Mrs. Anna Casa, 42: There are lots of girls like that one, lured on by men. . . . Mrs. Barbara Puleo, 24: I think it was the mistake the mother made, having all those men around her, that accounted for the daughter. The girl never had any supervision. . . . Miss Virginia Venturini, 15: I think the girl took over the older man and I felt sorry for him. . . . Albert Scarkilli, 48: The story is understandable, a middle-age man goes overboard for a young girl. I would say she took him over. . . . Charles Puleo, 27: This was something that could happen to anybody. I felt sorry for the stepfather—an older man hooked up with a girl like that.

Likewise, the reviewers found hardly anything shocking about the film, largely because the age of the title character had been raised from twelve to fourteen.[4] *Time* conjectured that "Older men have often pined for younger females. This is nothing new on the screen" ("Humbert"). The *New Yorker*'s was a fairly typical response: "The story isn't so altered as to be downright wholesome, but neither is it any longer perverse" ("Little Girl").

How is it that in 1962 the story of an older man's affair with his fourteen-year-old stepdaughter could be considered neither "new" nor "perverse"? When we consider the context in which the film was released, it becomes clear that these responses arise not from a willingness to countenance child abuse as much as they do from a very different manner of defining relationships between adolescent girls and adult men. At the time, a girl was understood to reach sexual maturity through her relationship to an older man, usually her father. Such an understanding of girls' sexual development served to reify the patriarchal order, placing the father at the center of female sexuality. Rachel Devlin examines theories of girls' Oedipal attachments in psychoanalytic literature and the manner in which these theories were adopted by the juvenile courts and popular culture, arguing that the father/daughter bond was central to the understanding of adolescent girls' sexual development during the postwar period. Helene Deutsch, whose *Psychology of Women* formed the basis for much of the psychoanalytic understanding of women's sexuality during this period, understood a girl's erotic desire for her father to be essential to the development of a healthy adult sexuality: "The woman who is harmoniously erotic, who is most 'feminine' and represents the best achievement of her Creator [remembers] a figure to which in her early youth she attached her great yearning and readiness to love, and through which she unconsciously preserves her faith to her first love object, her father" (Devlin, 92).

However, the possibility of incest was introduced when a girl's erotic attachment to her father was perceived to be central to her psychological well-being. In the extreme, some analysts looked on an actual incestuous relationship between father and daughter with a degree of approval. For the most part, however, the psychiatric community simply ignored the possibility of sexual contact between fathers and daughters, creating, argues Devlin, an unresolved tension between the necessity of this erotic attachment and the impossibility of its fulfillment by virtue of the incest taboo.

Throughout the 1940s and 1950s, Hollywood studios released

countless films that depicted adolescent girls awakening to sexual maturity through their association with a much older man, conforming to the popular understanding that a girl's sexuality was properly developed in relation to a patriarchal family structure. In them, the girls invariably grow up outside the traditional nuclear family, and their attachment to an older man is attributed to their need for a father figure. Melodramas of the period explore the dangers that arise from a girl's failure to confine her Oedipal crisis to the family, a failure that is usually precipitated by her mother's refusal to renounce her own desires in favor of her maternal role. In *Mildred Pierce* (1945), Veda (Ann Blyth) has an affair with her stepfather while her mother is preoccupied with running a restaurant; in *Imitation of Life* (1959), Susie (Sandra Dee) pursues her mother's long-time suitor Steve Archer (John Gavin) while her mother Lola Meredith (Lana Turner) focuses on her stage career; and in *Where Love Has Gone* (1964), Joey Heatherton plays a fourteen-year-old who shares a lover with her mother (Susan Hayward), whose voracious sexual appetite drove away the girl's father. Likewise, in comedies like *It's a Date* (1940) and its remake, *Nancy Goes to Rio* (1950), a girl (Deanna Durbin and Jane Powell, respectively) and her mother (Kay Francis and Ann Sothern) compete not only for the same role in a play but for the same man as well. The girl's desire is perceived to be a natural outcome of her growing up without a father and her mother's unwillingness to forego a career in favor of motherhood. In the comedies, the problem is happily resolved when the mother trades her career for marriage, the daughter takes the part in the play, and her love object becomes her stepfather, safely confining the girl's developing sexuality within the boundaries of the family.

Clearly, the reception of Kubrick's *Lolita* was informed by these familiar narratives of adolescent girls lost on their way to sexual maturity, their misplaced Oedipal attachments pointing to the absence of a strong father figure in their lives. However, Nabokov's novel had threatened to vitiate these Oedipal readings by acknowledging the possibility of the middle-class man's desire for the girl, rather than attributing the affair solely to her misplaced Oedipal attachment. Kubrick's film of *Lolita*, subjected to the conventions of commercial cinema and the scrutiny of the Production Code Administration, reinstates the details of the more familiar narratives of adolescent sexuality, reemphasizing the necessity of the nuclear family for the well-being of maturing girls.

In his correspondence regarding the film, Geoffrey Shurlock, then director of the Production Code Administration, betrays an uncertainty as to what constituted perverse or normative sexuality between an adult man and a teenage girl. Writing to Warner Bros. Executive in Charge of Production Jack Warner, he suggests "the subject matter, 'an elderly man having an affair with a twelve-year-old girl' would *probably* fall into the area of sex perversion prohibited by the code" (Shurlock, emphasis added). In the end, the Production Code Administration compelled two changes that were designed to eliminate the suggestion of perversity from the story. Lolita's age would be raised from twelve to roughly fourteen and Humbert would no longer be attracted to young girls in general, but to Lolita in particular—tactics that focus the story on her delinquency, not his uncontrolled desire. Kubrick's film had originally included a montage of pubescent girls, over which Humbert would give his famous definition of the nymphet, "Now I wish to introduce the following idea. Between the age limits of nine and fourteen there occur maidens who, to certain bewitched travelers, twice or many times older than they, reveal their true nature which is not human, but nymphic (that is demoniac); and these chosen creatures I propose to designate as 'nymphets' " (Nabokov 16). Instead, at Shurlock's insistence, the film suggests that the middle-aged professor is instantly and unexpectedly seduced by the image of Lolita lounging in her bikini. The original passage had made it clear that the nymphet exists in the eye of the beholder: "A normal man given a group photograph of school girls or Girl Scouts and asked to point out the comeliest one will not necessarily choose the nymphet among them. You have to be an artist and a madman . . . in order to discern at once, by ineffable signs . . . the little deadly demon among the wholesome children; she stands unrecognized by them and unconscious herself of her fantastic power" (Nabokov 17). Instead, the film suggests that Lolita's seductive qualities—her bikini, sunglasses, and hula-hooping hips—arise from her unchecked participation in a commodity culture newly directed toward teenage girls. Lolita therefore can be read as a "typical" teenager, whose developing sexuality is expressed through her Oedipal desire for her mother's lover and who is led astray by virtue of the fact that her biological father is not available to see her safely to maturity, not only by restraining her access to these corrupting commodities but by becoming the focal point of her romantic fantasies.

The "nymphet" displays her seductive charms in the 1962 version of *Lolita.*

Lolita's mother, Charlotte Haze, is reluctant to relinquish her own pleasures in favor of motherhood, resenting her daughter's budding sexuality. As played by Shelley Winters, her well-rounded physique, accentuated by tight-fitting costumes, suggests a love of bodily pleasures. Indeed, rather than securing a father for her daughter by marrying Humbert Humbert, she plots to keep him to herself by sending Lolita away first to summer camp and then to boarding school. Once again, competition between mother and daughter renders the older man a prize, the conquest for which will demonstrate the adolescent girl's usurpation of her mother's position. There is little wonder, then, that audiences perceived the film as "nothing new."[5]

Likewise, the film transforms Humbert into a benign father figure rather than the obsessive pedophile that Nabokov had invented. In an effort to make Humbert a more likeable character, his machinations to seduce Lolita—his plans to drug her and rape her in her sleep—are eliminated altogether. And their relationship is confined almost entirely to the home. Much of the novel depicts a cross-country journey, in which Humbert drags his increasingly resistant charge from one motor lodge to another. For reasons of economy, the film does not depict their travels; their affair takes place within a comfortable middle-class home. Because the single-family home is closely associated with traditional family organization, this change subtly shifts the meaning of their relationship. Relocated into the familiar arena of the family romance, it takes on the contours of the Oedipal attachments already common to Hollywood.

This is not to say that audiences were unmindful of the potentially unsettling eroticism embodied in the image of an adolescent girl. Six years earlier, Carroll Baker's performance as the nubile title character in the film *Baby Doll* (1956) had deeply challenged American mores.[6] Baby Doll was explicitly erotic, and her appeal was patently perverse. Although the Production Code Administration (reluctantly) approved the film, the Legion of Decency condemned it, prompting widespread debate regarding the virtues of the film. Although the Legion had condemned the film because "it dwells almost without variation or relief upon carnal suggestiveness" (Legion of Decency), the reviewers tended to focus on the shock value of Baby Doll's infantile eroticism. Her erotic image was understood to be vaguely threatening. At nineteen, Baby Doll is hardly too young to be married, particularly by the standards of 1950s American society. Nonetheless, in commentary on the film, she was consistently referred to as Archie's "child bride," connoting the moral decay of the old South. Further, in their attempts to identify what it was that was so perverse about the film, reviewers invariably cited the opening sequence, in which Baby Doll lies sleeping in her crib, sucking her thumb, as her husband spies on her through a hole he has bored through the wall.

Baby Doll shocked because the film invited its audience to share in the pleasure of looking at an infantilized girl. Just as *Lolita* referred to a tradition of film narratives in which adolescent girls compete with their mothers, so *Baby Doll* bore some resemblance to popular films in which a girl is transformed into a woman through the awakening of sexual desire. Leslie Caron had achieved stardom through a series of films—*Lili* (1953), *Daddy Long Legs* (1955), and *Gigi* (1958)—in which she played girls transformed into women by their love for older men. However, while Caron's films had remained safely chaste, merely implying that this transformation was based on the girl's developing sexuality, in *Baby Doll*, sexual desire is made explicit. The result is a guilty pleasure. The audience runs the risk of succumbing to the forbidden image of the girl's erotic awakening: "[T]here are scenes of intimacy—specifically in the awakening womanness of Baby Doll through the ardent attentions of [Eli] Wallach—that are as embarrassing to watch as they are mesmerizing" (Scheur).

In *Baby Doll*, reviewers recognized a departure from the familiar image of the adolescent girl, one in which her sexual appeal was made explicit and, as a consequence, dangerous. The *Los Angeles Times* described her as "an entirely new kind of *femme fatale*—the antithesis of the Marilyn Monroes of today and the slinky vamps of yesterday . . . the very quality that makes her sex so potent is that it seems so unconscious" (Scheur). Three years later, in an article for *Esquire,* Simone de Beauvoir described this new character, in the person of Brigitte Bardot, as an "erotic hoyden," linking her to the long tradition of Hollywood vamps and femmes fatales (de Beauvoir 10). She attributes the evolution of this *fille fatale* to women's changing gender roles: "The adult woman now inhabits the same world as the man, but the child-woman moves in a universe which he cannot enter. The age difference re-establishes between them the distance that seems necessary to desire. At least that is what those who have created a new Eve by merging the 'green fruit' and the 'femme fatale' types have pinned their hopes on" (10).

Twenty years later, Hollywood films were replete with images of *filles fatales* whose frankly erotic appeal more closely resembled that of Baby Doll or Nabokov's Lolita than they did the innocent charms of Leslie Caron. Melanie Griffith, Nastassja Kinski, Tatum O'Neal, Linda Blair, and Jodie Foster had all achieved stardom through a sexual precocity that led them to be labeled at one point or another as a new incarnation of Lolita. However, American society was far from comfortable with this new image of female adolescence. Simultaneous with the rising popularity of Hollywood's new breed of *filles fatales* was a radical shift in the interpretation of child sexual abuse. In his overview of twentieth-century construction of what we now call child sexual abuse, Philip Jenkins argues that the orthodoxies we take for granted—that child molesters abuse children compulsively and repeatedly, that molestation will escalate into violence and murder, that sex with adults will cause lasting damage to children—only began to emerge in the mid-1970s. Before that, as we have seen, the child was perceived to be culpable in his or her own abuse. Further, whereas in the 1960s the courts and the popular media had downplayed the adult's role in the molestation of children, attributing such acts to feeblemindedness or impotence on the part of the adult, beginning in the mid-1970s the child molester was redefined as the worst sort of criminal. This revolutionary change came about when two opposing political movements coalesced to reframe child sexual abuse as a pervasive and pressing problem. Right-wing moral crusaders, led by Anita Bryant, invoked the specter of pedophilia to galvanize opposition to the burgeoning gay rights movement. On the other side of the political spectrum, feminists referred to the abuse of children in their campaigns against rape and pornography. In 1977, the same year that Anita Bryant brought the "Save Our Children" campaign into the national spotlight, Gloria Steinem published a cover story for *Ms.* magazine, denouncing child pornography as an outgrowth of masculine desire to dominate, and the Kildee-Murphee Bill was passed, prohibiting the manufacture, distribution, and possession of child pornography.[7]

It was in this context that Louis Malle's first American film, *Pretty Baby* (1978), was released.[8] A storm of controversy greeted the film, which was about a twelve-year-old girl (Brooke Shields) living in a New Orleans brothel at the turn of the century. Condemnation of the film was swift and impassioned. Child welfare groups threatened to take the child actress out of her mother's custody; the television show host Rhona Barrett warned audiences that the film was an example of child pornography; and *People* did a cover story with headlines that read, "Brooke Shields, 12, stirs a furor over child porn in films" ("Brooke"). While the film earned an R rating in the United States, it was banned in two Canadian provinces and in Queensland, Australia. The British Board of Film Censors deferred, approving the film pending the passage of the Protection of Children Bill, which would provide severe punishment to anyone profiting from child pornography.

The controversy surrounding *Pretty Baby* suggests that more than Shields's innocence was at stake. Childhood in general seemed to be under threat as a result of the changes engendered by the women's movement. The debates about the film served to reaffirm both childhood innocence and women's role as the caretaker. What is interesting about the response to *Pretty Baby* is the degree to which it centers on the question of the effect that the adult (implicitly male) gaze would have on the child. Where once narratives of intergenerational desire had served to confirm the necessity of the patriarchal family structure for the development of a mature heterosexual identity, such films now betrayed a distinct fear that adolescent girls were increasingly vulnerable to corruption. And, where once men's self-control had been assured, masculine desire became a powerful and dangerous force. No longer was an adult man responsible, by virtue of his role as father, for the development of a girl's sexuality. Instead the girl was susceptible to his dangerous gaze. The publicity that preceded the release of *Pretty Baby* included a *Playboy* cover story that described the film as "1978's Naughtiest Film" and included a "Pretty Baby pictorial" ("Pretty"). Unlike most of the pictorials that appear in *Playboy*, the photographs were merely publicity stills for the film. However, the suggestion that the young girl's image was being exploited in pornography was compounded by rumors that more explicit photographs would appear in *Penthouse*. It is significant that Shields's image should appear in the magazine that, Barbara Ehrenreich has argued, represents the middle-class, adult male rebellion against his breadwinning role. Now that her image had appeared within the folds of a magazine whose distinct purpose was to undermine the ideal of the patriarchal nuclear family, a pubescent girl was no longer protected from adult men. What was apparently troubling about the film was the degree to which it rendered Shields an erotic object for the adult gaze, that her public display of childhood sexuality was performative. Acting sexy for the benefit of the adult gaze, she became sexy in fact.

The discomfort generated by the film's publicity—the fear that Shields was being exploited for the gratification of male desire—was compounded by the film's narrative. *Pretty Baby* is roughly based on the photographs of E. J. Bellocq, a turn-of-the-century photographer who worked in the Storyville district of New Orleans. The film depicts Bellocq (Keith Carradine) as becoming increasingly entranced by a child, Violet (Brooke Shields), who was born in the brothel. Within the film, Malle reproduces a number of Bellocq's frank documentary photographs of Storyville prostitutes. In the original photographs as well as Malle's reproductions of them, the prostitutes appear to be actively presenting themselves for the camera, participating in the creation of their own image with varying degrees of coquetry and defiance. One of Bellocq's more well-known images is of a young prostitute reclining nude on a divan. Malle chose to use Violet as the subject in his re-creation of this photograph. The image, never reproduced in the publicity for the film or even captured by Bellocq within the film's narrative—because Violet refuses to remain still—was circulated in the American imagination through stories about the filming of the scene that appeared in the press. In the published descriptions of the sequence, the photograph becomes pornographic. Thus, oddly, it was the press that created an erotic image of Shields (albeit one that existed only within the imagination), whereas Malle had created a study of a child who refuses to be captured and defined by the adult gaze.

Shields's image challenged the popular understanding of childhood innocence, thereby generating a great deal of discomfort on the part of adults. She was often described as a sort of freak of nature, an unnerving half woman/half child. Malle himself explained, "There's something disturbing about her . . . with this face of a woman, the body of a child" ("Pretty"). But if the image of Brooke Shields suggested that girls' sexual development was threatened by the decline of the nuclear family, it also pointed to the degree to which adults themselves imbued the child with sexual meaning. She was a creation of the spectator's own imagination. Like Garbo's Queen Christina, she presented a blank visage, and adults projected their own desires onto it. The girl's agent explained that, to encourage an erotic pose, photographers would tell her to " 'Do your no smile face,' and the sex just oozed from her" (Peer and Gelman). However, this oozing sex was understood to derive not from the child, but from the adults who gazed upon her. *Newsweek* described her as a "libidinal tabula rasa onto which men and women alike can project their fantasies" (Peer and Gelman).

The debates surrounding *Pretty Baby* turned on the question of girls' sexual development. What had seemed so assured in a period when the patriarchal family was perceived to be a guarantee of healthy sexual development was now understood to be under threat; girlhood had become a period of precarious innocence. *Newsweek* noted that "Violet (and Brooke Shields herself) . . . raise questions about innocence and corruptibility that are . . . at the heart of our culture today" (Kroll 106). In a *Vogue* article, Molly Haskell warned, "What is titillating for audiences may be damaging to . . . children. They are not allowed to mature according to the normal stages of childhood (if such even exist anymore) during which sex is repressed or sublimated into non-sexual activity" (128). And a *Good Housekeeping* article wondered, "Can [Brooke's] childishness survive the job she'll be doing for Louis Malle as a prostitute? Can childhood, no matter how stable the child, survive such experiences?" (Frank 99).

Likewise, in countless letters to the editor, readers expressed concern that the very idea of a normative girlhood, which had once seemed so assured, was now thrown into question. Not only did

Shields's erotic image indicate that harm had been done to her, but its circulation suggested that childhood itself was at risk of becoming corrupted. The psychoanalytic discourse that had popularized Oedipal theories of adolescent development gave way to a feminist-inflected theory of a "cycle of abuse," whereby the victim of a sexual crime is in danger of becoming sexually corrupt. *Ms* reported a young mother complaining, " 'I don't even know what kind of damage this movie could do, but I wouldn't want my ten-year-old daughter to see it' " (Braudy 28). The very concept of a normative girlhood seemed to be at risk. One woman, writing to *People,* asked facetiously, "You say that Brooke 'remains a very normal little girl.' I have a 13-year-old daughter and she has never appeared nude in an R-rated film, never been asked by *Playboy* what 'good in bed' means to her, and, amazing as it may seem, never been offered a part in a Swedish lesbian movie. Could it be that my child is not normal?" ("Letters" *People*).

If adolescent girls' sexuality was perceived to be in jeopardy, adult women were blamed for leaving them vulnerable to the male gaze. In this way, the debates that the film incited served as a means of reinforcing women's role in caring for children, regardless of the expansion of their role within the public sphere. It is interesting to note the degree to which commentary surrounding *Pretty Baby* echoes the underlying principal of the films of an earlier generation, in which Mildred Pierce and her career-minded cohorts were judged to be indirectly responsible for their daughters' delinquency. Girls' innocence was understood to be imperiled by the changes initiated by the women's movement and the sexual revolution. The pursuit of sexual pleasure on the part of adults had left girls defenseless against masculine desire. "The problem is not with [children], it is with us, adults who have in effect become children. By refusing to grow up and assume the voice of moral authority, by insisting on instant gratification, we too often compete with children on their ground" (Haskell 128). More than that, women were to blame for the disintegration of the nuclear family as a safe harbor for girls' sexual development. Feminist and traditionalist women alike blamed the women's movement for the increased sexualization of young girls. A *Mademoiselle* article complained, "The obsession with children is part of the backlash against women's demands for equality. It's as if these men are saying that if they can't keep us tied to the bedpost, they'll desert us for girls too inexperienced to break the chains" (Coburn 100). In the pages of *Good Housekeeping*, on the other hand, it was bad mothering that led to the corruption of innocent girls. An article on Hollywood's new crop of child stars notes that the mothers of Brooke Shields and Jodie Foster were both divorced and ends by asking mothers to put a stop to this sexualization of children, to reassert the family as the center of a girl's erotic development: "Isn't it about time . . . that mothers make their voices heard?" (Frank 99).

Although these commentaries suggest that women's neglect of their maternal role posed a threat to girlhood innocence, that innocence seemed to be restored by displacing the child's desire onto her mother, Teri Shields. In much of the publicity surrounding Brooke Shields, Teri is described as greedy and ambitious, using her daughter to secure her own ends. She is a figure of drunken excess, of uncontrollable desires, who serves as a convenient foil for her disciplined daughter. Teri Shields was held responsible for the too-intimate knowledge of Brooke's body, having announced the onset of the girl's first menstrual period during the filming of *Pretty Baby.* The official view, handed down by a Los Angeles judge, was that if audiences perceive sexuality in Brooke Shields's image, it is because her mother put it there. Ruling that nude photographs, taken of the child when she was ten, could not be withdrawn from circulation, the judge explained that Teri had forfeited Brooke's innocence to her own ends, having "chosen to engender an image of Brooke Shields which is sexually provocative and exciting while attempting to preserve her innocence" (Peer and Gelman).

Vincent Canby, in his review of *Pretty Baby,* conveyed the majority view that "the movie will delight a lot of Humbert Humberts among us, though [it's unlikely] it will create any new ones" (17). Eighteen years later, Adrian Lyne's *Lolita* was greeted by the precise opposite response, igniting a storm of controversy as intense as the one that had surrounded *Pretty Baby.* In Britain, child protection groups claimed that the film "appears to glamorize pedophile behavior [and] makes sexual abuse of children into entertainment" (Dunckley). London's *Daily Mail* waged a virulent campaign against the film, with headlines warning that the film's message was that "paedophilia is fun" (Maddox). In Germany, the film was denounced as "an attempt to promote pedophilia" (Van Gelder) and in Australia, several Members of Parliament regarded the film as "an endorsement of pedophilia" and demanded that it be banned in that country (Murdoch). In the United States, where the Child Pornography Prevention Act had just been signed into law, no distributor would pick up the film. It took two years of determined effort on the part of the film's director, stars, and producers to give the film its American debut.

At that point, newspapers were crowded with editorials and letters to the editor complaining that the film would inspire adult men to become pedophiles.

If *Pretty Baby* was perceived to pose a danger to girls' sexual development, positioning pubescent girls as the object of a sexualized male gaze, *Lolita* was understood to be a threat to the stable sexuality of adult men who were imagined to be at risk of being transformed, en masse, into pedophiles. And, while the controversy surrounding *Pretty Baby* invoked the necessity of good mothering, that on *Lolita* turned on the perceived crisis in fatherhood. American families are no longer modeled on the patriarchal family structure that was so central to the understanding of girls' sexual development in the 1950s and 1960s. The near disappearance of the family wage, upon which men's authority within the home was based, the increased divorce rate, and the broadening of the definition of "family" to include gay and lesbian parents have contributed to the redefinition of male gender roles in what historians have begun to describe as a "post-patriarchal" era (Stacey; Gordon and Hunter). Dislocated from their patriarchal role within the family, men's sexuality is a source of concern, as is their relationship to children. The debates surrounding *Lolita* articulate this need, redrawing the boundaries of acceptable sexual practices.

No longer the guardian of a girl's developing sexuality, the middle-class adult male is perceived to pose a potential danger to her by virtue of his failure to control his own desires. Adrian Lyne inadvertently articulated the problem when he described the film as seductively erotic: "It's sexy, isn't it? . . . You can get so used to the subject matter. Then you have to pinch yourself and remember it's appalling" (Chamberlain). But men were not trusted to pinch themselves into awareness of their moral responsibilities. One *Vogue* reader responded to the *Lolita* controversy by complaining, "I continue to be amazed by men's timeless argument that they cannot control their sexual impulses and should not be expected to do so" ("Letters" *Vogue*). When *Esquire* ran a photograph of Lolita (Dominique Swain) on its cover, provocatively sucking her finger in a pose somewhat reminiscent of Baby Doll's, an angry reader accused, "The real reason Lolita is on your cover is that she turns men on" ("Letters" *Esquire*).

And if much of the anger over the highly sexualized representations of Brooke Shields was displaced onto her mother, in the case of *Lolita* Lyne received the blame for the discomfort caused by the film. Bad parenting was no longer to blame; it was the middle-aged man's unwillingness to curb his sexual appetite. In the popular imagination, Lyne's *Lolita* threatened to redefine sexual relations between adult men and young girls from deviant to acceptable, just as the director had helped to do with other sexual activities that were no longer forbidden but newly defined as excitingly naughty. The film's critics made much of the fact that Lyne's previous films included *9 1/2 Weeks* (1986), *Indecent Proposal* (1993), and *Fatal Attraction* (1987), which variously describe sexual experimentation within the upper-middle classes, broadening the boundaries of acceptable, though risky, sex play for the bourgeoisie to include such practices as illicit sex, bondage, and prostitution. (What the critics failed to note was that each of these films also reaffirmed the primacy of traditional monogamy by having the characters renounce these activities after a period of experimentation.)

If in *Pretty Baby*, the girl was understood to be vulnerable to the male gaze, central to the controversy surrounding Lyne's film was the perception of the adult male as vulnerable to the onslaught of erotic images of girls in popular culture. The danger of the film was explicitly visual; Lolita would "no longer be hidden inside the pages of a book but displayed in all her sexual explicitness, 10 feet high in living color" (Marks 70). Her image poses a danger to viewers, "who spend more than two hours ogling the girl as much as Humbert does [and] are, on some level, as sick as he is" (Katz 35). Nabokov had warned against making a film of his book on the grounds that it would require a young girl to act the part and "you would have to teach the child things no child should be taught" ("Lolita's Creator"). He explained to *Life* magazine, "It was perfectly all right for me to imagine a 12-year-old Lolita. . . . She only existed in my head. But to make a real 12-year-old girl play such a part in public would be sinful and immoral and I will never consent to it" (Bunzel). When Lyne brought the title character to the screen, the concern was no longer for the performer's well-being but that any visual representation of the affair between Humbert and Lolita would reinforce the pedophile's perspective, rendering Lolita an erotic object rather than the victim of abuse. A number of reviewers expressed their discomfort over the idea of rendering the familiar story in visual terms with a repeated refrain: "It's one thing to read Humbert saying that Lolita 'arrived in her Sunday flock stamping, panting, and then she was in my arms, her innocent mouth melting under the pressure of dark male jaws,' and quite another to see Lolita bound up the stairs, wrap her legs around his waist and plant her tongue in his mouth" (Katz 35). "It is one thing to read Humbert's memoir and hear him describe Lolita as a coquette. . . . It is quite different to see Ms. Swain roll over in bed and kiss Mr. Irons passionately, to whisper in his ear, to act seductive. Putting the action in front of a viewer makes it real, even though we are still confined to Humbert's skewed perspective" (James).

Clearly, then, the controversy surrounding *Lolita* suggests much more than concern about the well-being of children in contemporary society. Although it may be tempting to dismiss the very different receptions of the two film versions of *Lolita* as resulting from the demise of Hollywood's Production Code or from an increased sensitivity to the problem of child sexual abuse, it is clear that the changing public response to sexualized images of children over the latter half of the century corresponds to a changing perception of the middle-class family as a site for maintaining social order. Whereas an affair between a middle-aged man and a fourteen-year-old girl was once read as a sign of the necessity of maintaining the patriarchal family structure as a space that would encourage the healthy sexual maturation of the adolescent girl, such an affair is no longer understood in terms of the girl's misplaced Oedipal attachment. Rather, it is taken as evidence of the degree to which childhood innocence has become imperiled. Whereas once the father was understood to guide a girl's sexual development, he is now perceived as vulnerable to her sexualized image; no longer able to protect the bourgeois family from the corrupting influences of the world at large, he is now prone to them. In this understanding of his susceptibility to the erotic image of the girl we see reflected contemporary fears about the decline of the patriarchal family.

NOTES

1. The Production Code, which was a set of guidelines to which the Hollywood studios had agreed to conform in an effort to protect themselves from church-led boycotts and state-mandated censorship, was enforced through the Production Code Administration (PCA) beginning in 1934. The PCA office, headed first by Joseph I. Breen and later by Geoffrey Shurlock, monitored content of every feature-length film produced by the studios, from the earliest stages of story development through the final cut. However, in the 1960s, the Production Code no

longer served to protect Hollywood's investments but had actually begun to stand in the way of profits; no longer vertically integrated, the studios were vulnerable to competition not only from television but from foreign and art-house films as well as the drive-in circuits, which were unencumbered by the studios' system of self-censorship. In 1968, the Production Code was finally replaced by a National Motion Picture Rating System.

2. In 1952, the Supreme Court (in *Joseph Burstyn, Inc. v. Wilson, Commissioner of Education of New York, et al.*) ruled that First Amendment protections of free speech extend to the medium of film. The case was brought before the courts after the state of New York refused to permit Roberto Rossellini's *The Miracle* (1948) to be shown on the grounds that it was sacrilege.

3. The Child Pornography Prevention Act (1996) defines as child pornography any image that appears to be of a minor engaged in sexual activity. Although designed to curtail the circulation of erotic images of children on the Internet, the law effectively renders pornographic any film that suggests a minor engaged in sex, regardless of whether a body double is used, as is the case in *Lolita.* Although the legal community contends that the law is overly broad and therefore of dubious constitutionality, it has not yet been challenged.

4. It is interesting to note that Adrian Lyne's Lolita was also fourteen, though his Humbert was a decade younger than Kubrick's.

5. In fact, Rachel Devlin makes a convincing argument that Nabokov's novel was, in part, referencing the popular Broadway plays of the 1940s—*Junior Miss* (1945) and *Kiss and Tell* (1945) among them—in which the relationships between adolescent girls and their adoring fathers are governed by an erotic bond.

6. Based on a Tennessee Williams play, *Baby Doll* takes place on the day before Baby Doll's twentieth birthday. The day is significant because she has promised to consummate her year-long marriage to an older man, Archie Lee (Karl Malden), when she turns twenty. However, while Archie Lee is on a futile quest to keep his cotton gin from going out of business, Baby Doll is seduced by the man whom Archie blames for his business's failure.

7. Prior to 1977, the manufacture of child pornography was illegal only insofar as it documented child abuse; its sale and possession were otherwise subject to the same obscenity laws that restrict other pornographic material.

8. Malle could not have chosen a worse time for the release of *Pretty Baby.* Production on the film began just as Roman Polanski was convicted of the rape of a thirteen-year-old girl, a conviction that would inspire a number of social commentators to attribute to Hollywood what seemed to be a newly emerging trade in children.

Works Cited

Beauvoir, Simone de. 1972. *Brigitte Bardot and the Lolita Syndrome.* New York: Arno Press.

Bird, Robert S. 1962. "The Provocative Lolita a Film: Why Nobody Is Shocked." *New York Herald,* 15 July. PCA File for *Lolita,* Margaret Herrick Library of the Academy of Motion Picture Arts and Sciences, Beverly Hills.

Braudy, Susan. "Not Such a Pretty Baby." 1978. *Ms.,* April.

"Brooke Shields, 12, Stirs a Furor Over Child Pornography." 1978. *People,* 18 May.

Bunzel, Peter. 1962. "Yes, They Did It: Lolita Is a Movie." *Life,* 25 May. PCA File for *Lolita,* Margaret Herrick Library of the Academy of Motion Picture Arts and Sciences, Beverly Hills.

Canby, Vincent. 1978. "Malle's *Pretty Baby* Is Perverse and Poetic." *New York Times,* 9 April, II: 17.

Chamberlain, Lesley. 1996. "*Lolita* Is No Apologia for Paedophiles." *Times,* 14 August: Features section.

Coburn, Judith. "The Intelligent Woman's Guide to Sex." *Mademoiselle* April 1979: 100.

Devlin, Rachel. 1998. " 'Their Fathers' Daughters': Female Adolescence and the Problem of Sexual Authority in America, 1941–1964." (Dissertation, n.p.)

Dunckley, Cathy. 1998. "Uncut *Lolita* Is Cleared for 18 or Older in Britain." *Hollywood Reporter,* 25 March; *Lolita* (1998) clippings, PCA File for *Lolita,* Margaret Herrick Library of the Academy of Motion Picture Arts and Sciences, Beverly Hills.

Ehrenreich, Barbara. 1984. *Hearts of Men: American Dreams and the Flight from Commitment.* New York: Doubleday.

Frank, Elizabeth Pope. 1977. "What Are They Doing to Our Children?" *Good Housekeeping,* August: 99.

Gordon, Linda and Allen Hunter. 1998. "Not All Male Dominance Is Patriarchal." *Radical History Review* 71 (Spring): 71–83.

Haskell, Molly. 1979. "The Sexy Baby Turn-On." *Vogue,* January: 128.

"Humbert Humdrum & Lullita." 1962. *Time,* 14 June. PCA File for *Lolita,* Margaret Herrick Library of the Academy of Motion Picture Arts and Sciences, Beverly Hills.

James, Caryn. 1998. "A Movie America Can't See." *New York Times,* 15 March, II: 1.

Jenkins, Philip. 1998. *Moral Panic: Changing Concepts of the Child Molester in Modern America.* New Haven: Yale University Press.

Katz, Alyssa. 1998."Television Program Reviews: *Lolita.*" *The Nation,* 24 August: 35.

Kroll, Jack. 1978. "Alice in Brothel-Land." *Newsweek,* 10 April: 106.

Legion Of Decency. 1956. Memorandum, 13 December. Production Code Administration Files for *Baby Doll*, Margaret Herrick Library of the Academy of Motion Picture Arts and Sciences, Beverly Hills.

"Letters to the Editor." 1997. *Esquire*, May; *Lolita* (1998) clippings, PCA File for *Lolita*, Margaret Herrick Library of the Academy of Motion Picture Arts and Sciences, Beverly Hills.

"Letters to the Editor." 1978. *People*, 19 June: 1b.

"Letters to the Editor." 1997. *Vogue*, February; *Lolita* (1998) clippings, Margaret Herrick Library of the Academy of Motion Picture Arts and Sciences, Beverly Hills.

"Little Girl, Big Girl." 1962. *New Yorker*, 23 June. PCA File for *Lolita*, Margaret Herrick Library of the Academy of Motion Picture Arts and Sciences, Beverly Hills.

"Lolita's Creator—Author Nabokov a 'Cosmic Joker.'" 1962. "*Newsweek*, 25 June. PCA File for *Lolita*, Margaret Herrick Library of the Academy of Motion Picture Arts and Sciences, Beverly Hills.

Maddox, Brenda. 1998. "Movie Reviews: *Lolita*." *New Statesman*, 24 April: 40.

Marks, John. 1996. "Lolita, a Girl for the '90s." *US News and World Report*, 14 October: 70.

McGuigan, Cathleen. 1981. "Newsmakers." *Newsweek*, 23 November: 101.

Murdoch, Blake. 1999. "*Lolita* Will Not Get Rating Review." *Hollywood Reporter*, 13 April; *Lolita* (1998) clippings, Margaret Herrick Library of the Academy of Motion Picture Arts and Sciences, Beverly Hills.

Nabokov, Vladimir. 1991. *Lolita*. Ed. Alfred Appel, Jr. New York: Vintage.

Peer, Elizabeth and Eric Gelman. 1981. "The Two Faces of Brooke." *Newsweek*, 9 February: 80.

"Pretty Baby Pictorial." 1978. *Playboy*, March: 35.

"Protesting *Lolita*." 1997. *New York Times*, 30 December: E1.

Scheuer, Philip K. 1956. "*Baby Doll* Bold and Offbeat Film". *Los Angeles Times*, 25 November, PCA file for *Baby Doll*, Margaret Herrick Library of the Academy of Motion Picture Arts and Sciences, Beverly Hills.

Shurlock, Geoffrey. Letter to Jack Warner. 11 September 1958. Production Code Administration file for *Lolita*. Margaret Herrick Library of the Academy of Motion Picture Arts and Sciences, Beverly Hills.

Stacey, Judith. 1998. "What Comes after Patriarchy? Comparative Reflections on Gender and Power in a 'Post-Patriarchal' Age." *Radical History Review* 71 (Spring): 63–70.

Van Gelder, Lawrence. 1997. "Footlights: Protesting *Lolita*." *New York Times*, 30 December: E1.

chapter 10

Maiden Voyage:
From Edwardian Girl to Millennial
Woman in *Titanic*

Lori Liggett

> Woman never exists without her image, the history of
> women always involves a figurative dimension. Women are
> symbols. . . . And it was by starting to change these images
> that they change themselves, for they knew that the image
> was a trap.
>
> FRAISSE AND PERROT 5

It has been said that the three most written about events in history
are the story of Jesus Christ, the assassination of John F. Kennedy,
and the sinking of the Titanic. We have seen a frenzied revival of
Titanimania due to the discovery of the sunken ship in 1985 in a
watery grave two and a half miles beneath the surface and, more
recently, with the release of James Cameron's film phenomenon, *Titanic* (1997). The film has grossed well beyond one billion dollars
worldwide, topping the charts for a record fifteen weeks and garnering eleven Academy Awards. The $200 million epic (the highest pro-
duction cost of any film to date) has been hailed as a technical masterpiece, a monumental achievement in the history of moviemaking.
It was perceived by many to be a tribute to humankind's mastery
of technology as the new millennium dawned. But much the same
acclamation heard in praise of the film once described the building
of the ship itself nearly a century ago. It was a triumph of engineering, setting new standards in turn-of-the-century opulence. After ten
years in the building stage, Titanic represented the achievements of
an era—the combined power of Anglo-Saxon imperialism, industrialization, and market capitalism—at their pinnacle. The ship was
believed to be unsinkable. Even before the fateful demise in the icy

waters of the North Atlantic on April 15, 1912, the legend of the Titanic had already begun.

Interest in the Titanic disaster had not waned by the end of the twentieth century when Cameron's film was being shot. The ship has been the subject of countless books and articles, several previous films, television movies, and even theatrical productions. There are Titanic archival collections, Titanic societies devoted to preserving the memory of the wreck, monuments, museum collections, traveling exhibits, and memorabilia. Many historians and cultural scholars have delved into Titanica fact, fiction, and myth to analyze and interpret why the event continues to play such an important role in our historical collective conscience. Since the Cameron film premiered on December 19, 1997, thousands of newspaper and magazine articles have been written about it, and there are hundreds of websites devoted to the movie and its stars. In addition, recent research continues to unearth how the legend has been culturally and socially constructed by various divergent groups since that morning in 1912 when the sun rose on a world shocked to learn of the ship's horrific fate (see Heyer; Biel). More than 1,500 people died, while only 705 survived the wreck. Today it still represents the worst maritime disaster during peacetime (Heyer 2).[1]

While most of the film's critics typically lauded the extraordinary technical accomplishments showcased on the big screen, many ridiculed the plot for placing two fictional young lovers central to our understanding of a historical event. In seeking answers to the film's heretofore unheard-of popularity, many asked, "What is this film?" It is part disaster film, part romantic drama, part action-adventure flick. It is a fictive period piece and a docudrama. It is a lesson in history that both dispels and perpetuates many myths about humanity, nature, and technology in a rapidly changing Western society. It is true and factual; it is legend and allegory. Repeat business for the three-and-a-half-hour film is responsible for its astronomical financial success, which has surpassed records set by such legendary blockbusters as the *Star Wars* trilogy (1977, 1980, 1983), *E.T. the Extra-Terrestrial* (1982), and *Jurassic Park* (1993). The film's largely female fandom encouraged Cameron to dub *Titanic* "my chick flick" (Murray).

While *Titanic* has made an international star of the actor who portrayed the hero Jack Dawson (Leonardo DiCaprio), the female of the duo (British actor Kate Winslet) was largely neglected or soundly criticized for her portrayal of the spoiled American debutante, Rose

Bukater Dewitt.[2] One must delve beneath the surface of the love story to discover the cultural complexities facing Winslet's character in the film. As Rose, she has entered into a realm of a new type of girl heroine—not an archetype of past film genres, such as the sacrificing, dying, tragic victim played by Greta Garbo in *Camille* (1937). She is neither the oppressed and unscrupulous female of film noir nor the fetishized girl-spectacle of musicals, nor the typical wife-girlfriend-daughter-mother appendage to the lead male actor found throughout Hollywood films of the 1950s and 1960s. Nor is she the buff heroine of recent sci-fi and action films (including those directed by Cameron). Winslet does not sacrifice her woman's body or her femininity to morph into a male hero with female genitalia. Her Rose is mentally and physically strong, intelligent, willful, decisive, and unapologetic in her possession of a womanly body.

Embodied as Rose, the heroine develops through multiple constructions that resist status quo representations of onscreen women and enable us to examine cultural implications of gender. Rose exhibits protean qualities, bridging the historical and cultural gap between the Victorian lady archetype and the emerging "Votes for Women" social reformer. She undergoes a life-altering transformation—from girl/daughter/fiancée to Woman—and in this process provides a means for viewers to understand the historical challenges and changing attitudes of the society from which she came.[3]

Is Rose *real*? Undoubtedly the film character is a fiction, but could she possibly represent real women who existed during the time of the Titanic disaster? What are we to make of her bifurcated identity within the film, situated as we are between the three-day story of a seventeen-year-old girl (Winslet) and a lifelong story, full of memories, of a one-hundred-year-old woman (played by eighty-seven-year-old actor Gloria Stuart)? Does the story of Rose expand beyond the tale of doomed love and the lost innocence of an era which, according to most, is the film's heart? Linda Seger suggests in *When Women Call the Shots* that the emergence of a heroic female model in film requires a redefinition of "the myth of the heroine" (165). Calling on new-breed heroines to be active, motivated, and in charge, rather than passive, submissive victims who are defined by men in movies, Seger shows how a heroine is not necessarily required to conquer the problems at hand (as is expected of a male hero); she can become empowered by internalizing a situation and eventually be transformed by it (165–66). Within the context of *Titanic*, I will explore the historical incarnation and transformation of Rose—her onscreen multiple representations that defy strict temporal and spatial boundaries and accepted notions of beauty.

As the mysteries of the new millennium loom ahead, not unlike the enormous iceberg waiting silently in black waters for the Titanic, we find ourselves living in a culture in which information, images, sounds, emotions, and concepts come to us through mass-mediation. As a result, we have learned to read and interpret our culture by mapping political and historical events, changing ideologies, and cultural phenomena through representational bodies, such as those of cultural icons like Marilyn Monroe and John F. Kennedy. In *American Monroe: The Making of a Body Politic*, S. Paige Baty examines our mass-mediated existence by examining the cultural significance of Marilyn Monroe in particular. She suggests that we can read and interpret the latter part of the twentieth century through the representational body of the actor/model; that these types of individual representative characters can symbolize for us a multiplicity of values, visions, aspirations, and achievements (10).

While Marilyn Monroe has evolved into one of the most identifiable global icons, that icon represents the transformation of a real person who died nearly four decades ago (1962) into a representation of a life that has come to signify various aspects of American culture, past and present (Baty 8–9). Rose is not unlike Monroe. Once a representative character transforms into a cultural symbol, she is available for commodification and public consumption through iconographic, representational, reconstituted rememberings. These are all part of our postmodern cultural landscape, which is both material and metaphorical and into which we insert ourselves, as occupants of this space, by literally buying (into) the mass-mediation (37). Theories of time also take on different meanings through the mapping of the representative and continually transformable body— what Baty calls the "mediatrix" (a term originating in the Latin *matrix*, for womb, and suggesting a creation that springs from the media alone). Baty says, for instance, that "Marilyn [Monroe] serves as both a reminder of the time in which she lived and as expression of the times that have followed. . . . In her various cultural incarnations, she assumes the traces of the decades in which she is reproduced, and her body is made over into a product of the times" (58). Visual reproductions of the representative character manifest a multiplicity of meanings, and "suddenly the world is a series of surfaces begging for an image [which] proffers presence, the suggestion of history, through its transparent body" (13).

Rose in *Titanic*—neither the Old Rose nor the Young Rose but the concept that is "Rose"—is also a character like this, symbolizing the Titanic disaster itself. As a concept, she is open to mass-mediation through endless interpretations—all based on the real historical referent of the disaster. Just as Marilyn Monroe is reproduced on bedsheets and toasters, reinterpreted by each new generation while at the same time representing a real past historical moment, in *Titanic* Rose is not fixed in time, either 1912 or 1997, but gains multiple identities, calling up many things to cultural consumers both within the film and beyond its borders. She is now a doll, available at Toys R Us; her dresses from the film have been reproduced; and there is a novel being written about her post-Titanic life. Perhaps someday people will think about the Titanic tragedy without visualizing Rose, but for the time being, her image has come to represent the historical moment of the Titanic's sinking for a whole generation of young moviegoers.

The Titanic tragedy is also a representative event because it has been ingrained in our collective consciousness through myriad mass-mediated material rememberings. Though the ship appears deceptively three-dimensional, its essence is that of an endlessly reproducible media artifact. The sinking and resinking of this icon easily obliterates the catastrophe of the actual event, one that represented an almost incomprehensible loss of life and the curtailment of personal stories we will never know. These stories—real or potential media content—are not insignificant as cultural entities. Over the years, attempts to portray the massive loss of life in an intimate manner have been dependent on various culturally constructed "memories" of the individuals—indeed, the aristocratic individuals—onboard. Yet the diversity of the passengers aboard the ship represented a microcosm of Edwardian society as a whole, illustrating the enormous gap between the upper crust and the masses. There are more than two thousand such stories that could be told, of people who all died together, social classes intermingling as the frosty bodies bobbed toward a blue death under a moonless, starlit sky.

For *Titanic* to successfully portray the enormous terror of that night and the massive loss of life, it required an individual upon whom to inscribe the details of the event, someone who could act as representative of an entire segment of humanity at a specific historical moment. Cameron, known for casting strong women to play lead roles (Linda Hamilton, Sigourney Weaver, Jamie Lee Curtis—

although they are most often acted upon by the male-dominated narrative), chose a woman through whom to retell and interpret this tragedy. (Jack is tangential to the story of Rose.) It is through the transformative body of Rose, while the character of Rose is a signifier, calling into question the ideology of an era, that the historical significance of the tragedy and the intricacies of the event are perceived. If, unlike Monroe, Rose never existed in history, as a character she does embody a hybrid of individuals aboard the ship. By film's end, she is an historical construction of the culture in which the tragedy took place and, perhaps even more intriguing, of our own present: a synecdoche. Through the two primary constructions of Rose, Young and Old, this particular mass-mediated rendering of the Titanic disaster collapses time and joins past, present, and future to dictate our understanding of an historical event.

To go further, Rose is not only intended to represent a generation of Western women undergoing tumultuous cultural changes in 1912, but is clearly situated as a physical, fleshly representation of the ship. The extreme transformation she personally experiences in the story—from oppressed, cloistered, proper girl from the dominant class to the bedraggled, uncorseted, even loose woman who willfully denies her good name—is a metaphor for the demise of the ship. That is why the bodily changes she undergoes are so important as representations of both the changing attitudes of women (which threatened the patriarchy) and the changing "attitudes" of the ship. It is ironic that she and her generation of Progressive Era women survive but the ship does not. This symbolizes the death of an era dominated by imperialism. The sinking of the Titanic has always been viewed by historians as the event that shook the confidence of the industrialists and ended the Gilded Age as well as being an indirect harbinger of World War I. Rose therefore signifies a whole cultural and political ideology of an era that was questioned at its very core with this event.

Rose dominates the narrative in a series of descents in search of self-knowledge and ascents of conversion and, in the process, becomes transformed. Through this process, she emerges as a heroine born of mass-mediation in which themes of temporality and spatiality, of power and propriety, of historical continuity and social control, are questioned, reinterpreted, and redefined—not only influencing what we know/believe about history but also shaping how we might view our own future.

Cameron's *Titanic* looms upon the movie screen to evocative strains of a somber, haunting Gaelic melody, revealing its story in antique sepia tones of a bygone era. As the Titanic prepares to leave port for her maiden voyage across the Atlantic, there are faraway cries from the lucky ones on deck who are waving enthusiastic good-byes to their families and friends on shore, whom they will never see again. Then the screen becomes dark with ominous black angry waves, and the past becomes the present, with only a distant bea-con of bluish-white light to illuminate the ocean's depths. Aboard a submersible is a crew of ocean salvagers who have been hired by a corporate consortium to uncover the valuable secrets hidden in the wreckage.[4] At the film's beginning, the issue of salvaging the wreck has already been determined, and commerce has won out over historical sentiment or ethical responsibility. With the aid of ultra-modern remote control technology, the all-male crew penetrates the Titanic's hull and enters the cavernous ship for the first time since she sank. Mysterious underwater creatures now inhabit the great beauty, making their own her still intact crystal chandelier in the grand ballroom. Hundreds of unbroken plates emblazoned with the "RMS Titanic" insignia and a child's doll still remain in the interior of the ship, while thousands of other objects fill a debris bed nearly one square mile in diameter.[5] Many of these material remainders are amazingly well preserved after decades underwater, but there is a sadness accompanying the realization that although so many per-sonal belongings survived the disaster, so few people did—a painful testament to the hardiness of material culture in the face of the fragility of human life.

All such objects, large and small, are of utmost importance to Titanophiles, the few remaining living survivors, ancestors of de-ceased passengers, and historians. But in the film, the fictive search is for one item only: a fifty-six-carat blue diamond necklace pur-ported to have a Louis XVI provenance, which was given by Cal Hockley, Pittsburgh steel heir, to his young fiancée, Rose Bukater Dewitt, aboard the Titanic. However, when Hockley's safe is recov-ered from the wreck, all that spews forth are decades-old mucky, rusty, water-soaked papers, and an illustration of a beautiful young woman, lounging contemplatively with her eyes fixed confidently on all who gaze back, defiantly wearing the ostentatious necklace that symbolizes her class—and nothing else. "The Heart of the Ocean," a sign of wealth, male power, prestige, and craven greed, hangs heavily around the delicate neck of a girl.

The drawing, sketched by a young steerage-class, vagabond art-ist, Jack Dawson, is of his beloved Rose on the night the ship sank. Apparently a siren of the deep, the female staring out at us from this drawing—a girl who stared at Jack in 1912 and now a memory staring at the elderly Rose—is not only the wearer of a fabulous jewel, not only the center of attention for the male gaze (Jack's and Cameron's), but most important a figure who will later be able to recount the names and histories of all the people soon to disappear on this ship—indeed, the tale itself. As the Rose of the drawing peers out from beneath the water that has silenced her for decades, an elderly woman with clear blue eyes stares back into the shimmering pool. "Wasn't I a dish?" she asks the salvagemen, eccentric and doddering and everything their scientific world is not, covered in pottery dust, accompanied by a pet goldfish and an array of framed photographs wherever she goes. Old Rose represents the culmination of a woman's lived experience. Now, although the story of how her life unfolded has yet to be detailed, the saucy old lady assumes control of the retelling of the Titanic tragedy from the male crew.

It is her memory that writes the story of Titanic and interprets the meaning of its demise for the crew—and for us. She listens and watches intently as a computer-generated, forensic analysis of the sinking is neatly detailed for her, noting that "the actual experience of it was somewhat different." Technology cannot capture human memories or emotions. In a subversion of linear time, Old Rose returns for one final descent of self-discovery to the wreckage. When she emerges her final transformation will be complete. But in the meantime, she puts names and faces, stories and insights, to the myth of the Titanic. This is the beginning of the emergence of Rose as interpretable and reinterpretable icon—first in the present, then historically as the narrative journeys back to the past through her recollections. Through this final expedition, Rose redefines who she was and is by metamorphosing the "Heart of the Ocean" into an object of resistance and defiance to all who would control her through it.

At the onset of her journey, and like her mother and the others in her party, Rose is both hyperconscious about and completely ignorant of class distinctions. Her form emerges from her limousine at quayside, first one perfect, gloved white hand, then a foot, then the wide brim of her navy hat."I don't see what all the fuss is about," she comments. She is impeccable in appearance, unimpressed at the sight that stands before her, and indifferent to the claims that "God himself could not sink this ship." Meanwhile the scene is a flurry of last-minute activity. The cars of first-class passengers are being hoisted onto the boat, and thousands of pounds of luggage are being carried by Titanic porters. As the Bukater Dewitt/Hockley party embarks unencumbered onto the huge ship, steerage passengers are going through an inspection line for lice. They are guided to the lower decks, an area where aristocrats' dogs will be walked to relieve themselves. The ship represents the stratification of Edwardian society, which is delineated by economic class and ethnic heritage. Most of those in steerage, coming from all over the globe, are heading to America to start a new life and carrying with them all their worldly possessions. For the wealthy, it is the opportunity to revel in man's finest hour and relax in first-class luxury for several cool, blue, April days. In accordance with her station in life, Rose ascends to the upper deck and her predetermined future.

From the moment of this first ascent, the narrative becomes a series of allegorical ups and downs in which Rose undergoes several self-discoveries and learns something about the world external to her own. With each ascent from below, she becomes transformed and is finally able to not only understand the fundamentals of her own gendered and class oppression but also discover a means to defy it and, ultimately, conquer it.

At their first dinner aboard the enormous liner, for example, Rose and the other women are regaled with stories about the size, stability, luxury, and strength of the ship, as White Star manager J. Bruce Ismay claims, "She's the largest moving object ever made by the hand of man in history. Willed in solid reality." Rose, disinterested, puffs defiantly on a cigarette. Her mother admonishes her for this behavior, and Cal promptly removes the cigarette from between her delicate fingers. Silently outraged, Rose draws an analogy between the male infatuation with size and Dr. Freud's analysis of the male's preoccupation with his own anatomy. Cal comments that he must begin minding more closely what she reads, and then he orders her meal for her. This is perfectly acceptable conduct to all at the table except for Rose and an American tourist, Margaret Tobin Brown ("Unsinkable Molly Brown"), who wryly questions: "Are ya gonna cut her meat for her, too, Cal? She's a pistol—I hope you can handle her!"

Through the narration of Old Rose, we come to understand that Young Rose was viewing her life at this moment as though it had already passed, that she was standing on a precipice with no one to pull her back, no one to care. We see her act on these emotions literally, as she attempts to throw herself off the stern of the ship. Jack Dawson must pull her back. Although Jack is sincere in his attempt to save her, it becomes evident that what she is really running from is a life in which she is not in charge; that he, indeed, is helping her continue that life. She says to her rescuer: "Don't presume to tell me what I will and won't do, you don't know me." Clearly, Rose is speaking about all those around her who dictate to her, but she is also commenting on the fact that she has never really been given the opportunity to know herself.

It becomes evident during the extended attempted suicide scene that women are considered to be "alien" to the mechanization and technological prowess of the age. As he tries to convince Rose not to jump, Jack describes an ice-fishing experience he once had and implies that she may not be familiar with the sport. She becomes indignant, and he comments, "Sorry, you just seem like an indoor girl." As a proper, educated young lady, Rose would have been sequestered most of her life within the walls of domesticity. The ship, although a self-contained space, represents a freedom she has never experienced. After Rose is rescued by Jack, she claims that she was just trying to see the boat's huge propellers. "Women and machinery do not mix," claims the master-of-arms with superiority, and all onboard seem to agree. It is clear that to have women aboard the ship means keeping them in the sitting rooms surrounded by paintings or cloistered together at proper teas. The open decks, the bowels of the boiler room, and certainly the steerage deck below are no place for well brought-up ladies. Later, when they begin to fall in love, Rose stands with Jack on the rail of the bow, arms outstretched, reaching toward the red horizon of the West and a life of hopefulness and dreams. (Jack softly sings to her a popular song from 1911, "Come Josephine in my flying machine, up she goes, up she goes, . . ." and Rose exclaims, "I'm flying!")

The journey of the Titanic can be viewed as one of cultural crisis and liminality. It is between Old World traditions and New World possibilities, from post-Victorian, Edwardian Great Britain to Progressive Era America, with human technology pitted against nature. Upper-class women posed a unique threat on the ship because their virtue was considered to be the cornerstone of white patriarchal dominance. What happens when different classes are allowed to share the same encapsulated physical space, even if separated by decks? In the character of Rose, we are able to explore the possibilities. Onboard, she experiences personal anxiety that represents prevailing cultural fears about the changing, dichotomous social roles of females, "tensions between real and ideal, virtue and vice, public and private, body and soul, and subject and object" (Vallone and Nelson 6).

To repay Jack for saving Rose from falling overboard, Cal invites him to dinner in the first class dining salon on the second night of the trip. After dinner "The Masters of the Universe" (as Rose refers to them)—John Jacob Astor, Benjamin Guggenheim, and Sir Cosmo Duff Gordon—leave the womenfolk and retire to drink brandy, smoke cigars, and talk about business and politics. Jack: "Wanna go to a real party?" Deciding to "make it (each day) count," Rose ascends the grand staircase to meet him under the clock, the same timepiece whose every click is foretelling that there is not much time left for the ship and her occupants. Rose and Jack then descend to the lower deck. The decision to accompany Jack represents a critical turning point for Rose as she begins to defy traditional notions of conformity at every opportunity. For the first time in her life, she interacts with people not of her class or ethnicity. With each subsequent foray to the lower decks, she begins to challenge her own disenfranchisement, represented by the conditions of the upper deck.

Many other films and novels have employed the problematic narrative device of well-heeled Anglos journeying into the mysterious realm of the lower classes only to emerge later more enlightened and humane. This important romanticization of the poverty and labor of marginalized groups is not critically explored within Cameron's film. Although this strategy is central to the plot—reinscribing Rose's class and ethnic privilege—it also renders a visual means to explore the character's dramatic transformation from post-Victorian female ideal to Progressive Era "New Woman," and from girlhood to womanhood, during a short period of screen time. Rose's burgeoning feminism is located in the moral gap created by the inability of the wealthy patriarchal class to control the behavior of the lower-class masses within the confines of the ship. In addition, the filmic device provides historical illumination of the new class consciousness and rebellion that occurred in early twentieth-century America as a result of increased immigration, pervasive labor unrest, and oppressive corporate practices.

The steerage party is a raucous, roaring spectacle, unlike anything Rose has ever seen. Although the revelers comprise various diverse ethnic groups communicating to one another in their native tongues, the music is that of a traditional Irish *ceili.* In stockinged feet, Rose clogs with Jack, joins in a snakedance with the others, and swigs down pints of lager. Taking a long drag from a cigarette, she proceeds to demonstrate sheer willpower and determination by hiking up her skirt and slowly lifting herself toward the ceiling, her entire body balanced on the tips of her toes. This moment is the genesis of Rose's transformation. Contrary to the limitations that are placed on her by being a woman in a patriarchal society—limitations symbolized by a tightly corseted body constricted in movement, shape, and level of exertion—Rose has begun to defy her confinement. She emerges from below deck a different person. And although Hockley and her mother threaten her, the die has been cast for her inevitable rebirth.

With each successive descent to the lower levels of the Titanic, Rose increasingly questions her own identity. Her mother warns that by interacting with the lower classes, she is threatening to destroy their family's social and financial stability: "This is not a game. Our situation is precarious. We are left with a lot of debt, hidden by a good name. Our name is all we have. Cal is a good match." Although she does not want to see her mother forced into becoming a seamstress, Rose's shipboard journeys below have exposed her own commodification to her awareness. Her body is the valued currency, and marriage is the vehicle that will ensure the maintenance of her mother's lifestyle. While Young Rose, fertile and beautiful, is considered a valuable possession because she can ensure the promulgation of the Anglo-Saxon upper class, her mother is perceived to be past her prime. As a widow, she has only her daughter's highly sought-after qualities to barter for her own survival. The fiancé has replaced the father. Rose protests: "It's so unfair." Mrs Bukater Dewitt: "We're women. Our choices are never easy." Rose is financially dependent, but she is also a valuable symbol of economic production and exchange.

Although for a brief interlude Rose becomes resigned to her cultural destiny, her feeling of entrapment is pervasive. Jack becomes a medium through which she measures her own situation. She knows that she will die if she does not break free. In a reinterpretation of the traditional hero–fair maiden story, Jack tells Rose that "only she can save herself." No more prophetic words are spoken in the film. Rose breaks free from the bonds of her class and gender by utilizing what she realizes to be her most valuable asset: her body. On the final night of the short voyage, she unabashedly guides Jack into her inner sanctum, the symbol of traditional feminine domesticity aboard the ship, the sitting room, intended to be a replication of the home in which women are hidden from society. The huge safe that houses the valuable necklace is just a smaller version of the room itself, meant to protect the privileged woman's virtue. Surrounded by her precious Picasso, Degas, and Monet paintings, she disrobes and orders Jack to draw her "like one of your French girls—wearing this, only this," as she points to "The Heart of the Ocean" framing her neck.

For the first time in her life, Rose is in control of the situation. She uses her body in defiance of strict moral codes. She is supposed to be "safe" and contained in the sitting room, locked away from prying eyes. Instead she gains powerful exposure. As she hands Jack a coin, a token of her own evolving empowerment and the restrictive culture she is abandoning, she says, "Last thing I need is another portrait of me looking like a porcelain doll. As a paying customer, I expect to get what I want." As Jack sketches her, she remains focused intently on his eyes gazing at her because she has commanded it. Her eyes never flinch, and she grows confident and stronger before us. The scene fades from the intense azure of Young Rose's stare to the sparkling watery eyes of Old Rose, who whispers, "My heart was pounding the whole time. It was the most erotic moment of my whole life." This is also the moment that the girl is beginning to live in her own skin, exploring the power that resides within and using her voice and body to transform herself.

The consummation of Rose and Jack's love for one another coincides with the beginning of the end of the ship. At 11:40 P.M. on the night of April 14, 1912, the "unsinkable" Titanic hit a gigantic iceberg in the middle of the frigid waters of the North Atlantic. By 2:20 A.M., less than three hours later (less time than it takes to view the Cameron film), the symbol of man's ability to conquer nature fell slowly to the ocean floor where it would lie undisturbed for more than seven decades. Its legend would be created almost immediately, and "the sinking of the Titanic [would become] our century's first collective nightmare" (Heyer ix). In the final hours, Rose descends several more times to the interior of the ship's womb, and with each journey, she sheds still more of her upper-crust cloak.

The upper deck is mad mayhem as the grand Titanic begins to break in two and descend toward destruction. Distress flares are sent up to signal other ships that might be able to assist. Rose has very little time to assess the transformation that she has undergone, but with the resounding thunderclap of the flares that streak behind her head, lighting up the sky then fizzling to black against the stars, she makes decisions that will forever seal her fate. First she refuses to get on the lifeboat with the other women and turns to meet her death with a dignity that has nothing to do with "class." Running after her, Hockley calls her a "whore," and she replies in a steady voice, "I'd rather be [Jack's] whore than your wife."

Rose must save Jack, indeed. When he is accused by Cal of stealing the diamond necklace (a material symbol of imperialism and oppression), Rose's decision is not about whom to believe but about her own future. She must choose between retaining the traditions of her past or defying her own class and all that it is predicated on. Jack has been shackled beneath decks and is still there as the water floods in. "I'm tired of being polite!" she screams at the elevator attendant who refuses to lower the cage for her. In an act seemingly more natural to contemporary hard-body sci-fi heroines, Rose fights her way through the rushing glacial liquid that is pouring through the ship's corridors. Now without corset, but still in proper lady garb, hair loose and dangerous, Rose dangles from the ceiling pipes and makes her way to where Jack is shackled and helpless. After pummeling a man who tries to impede her progress, she wields a huge ax and hacks Jack's way to freedom. This act of female defiance represents the pivotal transformation of not only the character but also of her historical sisterhood who, during that same time period, were marching, picketing, and being jailed for wanting the right to vote. The two young lovers, in traditional action-flick style, fight their way through numerous impediments to once again reach the upper decks.

Once there, Jack tries to force Rose to get into a lifeboat, while callous Cal says only, "My God, look at you—you look a fright" and cavalierly drapes her with his coat, which contains the huge blue diamond in its pocket. Assured that Cal has arranged for Jack to escape on the other side, Rose agrees to get into a boat. As the lifeboat is lowered, she sees Jack on deck realizes that Cal has lied. Staring into Jack's eyes, Rose realizes that this descent is not one of self-discovery but instead represents a recuperation of her heart and body back into patriarchal society. As the boat skirts past the final lower deck, Rose grabs onto the deck rail. In another feat of bodily strength and sheer willpower, she hoists herself back onto the ship.

If this final act seals the fate of the lovers it also, and more important, signals Rose's total transformation as a new-breed heroine—one who, though representing a bygone era—embodies the power of woman within a womanly physique. Here, our understanding of the historical event and the culture of the time are known to us through a mass-mediated image. And that image relies on the iconic centrality of Rose.

As a priest administers the last rites and cries out, "The former world has passed away," the Titanic begins to descend into the ocean. When the tremendous force of the water snaps the ship in two, it gasps a final sigh and is swallowed by the Atlantic. Miraculously, Rose and Jack, along with more than seven hundred other passengers, survive the sinking of the Titanic. They cling to life on debris collecting in the frigid ocean, experiencing firsthand what has been called "the end of an era." Purplish, frozen bodies litter the disaster area, bobbing in their lifebelts, a testament to modern man's ultimate hubris and conceit. Progress, technology, invention, and all of modernity are now called into question, and the Titanic is an ode to the unpredictability and often senselessness of life. But Rose is not a long-suffering heroine of old. She survives the sinking, having come too far on this short journey to be stopped now. She has made decisions that we know will affect the remainder of her life and, we can imagine, will influence other women with whom she comes into contact. In their final moments, she promises Jack that she will "never let go," and through Old Rose, we know that indeed she never does lose sight of her own strength and power. We can imagine that her energy and courage will become the inspiration for many other women to strive for their own freedom.

With the sinking of the Titanic, Rose has changed from a privileged yet disenfranchised adolescent, forced to conform to models of femininity, to a woman who must choose her own path of liberation—from girl to goddess. Aboard the segregated rescuing ship Carpathia, Rose chooses to huddle with the masses on the steerage deck. Giving her name as "Rose Dawson," she not only honors Jack in death, but denounces what her inherited name represents: her social class and her past. The self-sacrifice once required of her has now been replaced by self-discipline and self-expression.[6] We now understand that the worn and aged photographs that Old Rose travels with are testaments to her post-Titanic life. Rose does not wither away pining for her lost, dead love, but instead lives life to its fullest. She becomes a stage actress, she straddles a horse at Coney Island, she gets married and has children.[7] The "mediatrix" even becomes an aviatrix, evident from the photo that shows her confidently standing in full pilot garb in front of a small plane. She also becomes a member of the first generation of American women to cast a vote. And now, of course, she is the narratrix of this filmic tale.

At the beginning of the film, Rose is self-conscious and vulnerable, seeing herself as others do. But by its completion, she has undergone a personal revolution. As the film draws to a close, it is Old Rose who once again dominates the story. In one final act of independence, she heads for the stern of the explorer ship, a chilly reminder of her attempted suicide on the Titanic more than eight decades before. With her bare feet and brightly painted red toenails, she climbs the railing. She looks at her withered reflection in the calm sea, and with a small sigh, throws overboard the precious "Coeur de la Mer" necklace. The past is dead, available only in recollections. All of history is allegorical and a matter of fragmentary interpretations. But Rose, as a new-breed heroine, at once young and beautiful and old and weakening, is strong of womanly body and heart. She represents our past, our present, and perhaps even our mass-mediated future as we now remember the Titanic tragedy through her eyes.

NOTES

I would like to express my appreciation to Dr. Jeannie Ludlow, Bowling Green State University, for her guidance and insightful suggestions during the writing of this essay. I would also like to thank my dear friend and mentor, Dr. Jeffrey Chown, Northern Illinois University, for his continuous support of my work. This essay is dedicated to the memory of Dr. Martha Cooper (1954–2000), Northern Illinois University, an extraordinary educator who will forever inspire me.

1. The number of victims and survivors continues to be debated. The ship made a number of stops before it headed out to sea from Southampton, England. It is likely that unaccounted passengers got off and on, and that there were stowaways who were never officially listed.

2. Most film reviewers and op-ed writers simply credited the film's success to the romantic storyline, which attracted young crowds smitten by DiCaprio. Winslet, however, was the subject of much personal derision, even though her performance was nominated for an Academy Award for Best Actress. Writers on both sides of the Atlantic were merciless about her perceived weight gain after the film's release and about her performance within the film, critiques that largely focused on her appearance.

3. The ambiguous position of Anglo-American girls during the time period, who were from the Victorian "Cult of True Womanhood" social stricture to the public sphere, was a cause for much cultural anxiety, according to Lynne Vallone and Claudia Nelson. The protean quality

of the Girl is described as "simultaneous subject, object, and opponent of cultural classification" (5).

4. The treasure hunt for materials still trapped in and near the *Titanic* introduces real-life issues of undersea excavators who face legal and ethical battles to determine whether submerged ships are legitimate underwater archaeological sites or watery graves that should be left undisturbed.

5. It is important to note that the footage of the *Titanic* wreckage is real. Cameron made twelve trips to the ocean floor, thirteen thousand feet deep, exploring and filming in and around the ship.

6. In Victorian and Edwardian ideals, white upper-class women were associated with self-sacrifice, while men aspired to forms of self-discipline. Rose challenges these notions throughout the film, ultimately throwing off the shackles of social expectations.

7. Rose also subverts the feminine ideal by becoming a stage actress and earning her own income, which effectively positions her as working class.

WORKS CITED

Baty, S. Paige. 1995. *American Monroe: The Making of a Body Politic.* Berkeley: University of California Press.

Biel, Steven. 1996. *Down with the Old Canoe: A Cultural History of the Titanic Disaster.* New York: W. W. Norton.

Fraisse, Genevieve, and Michelle Perrot. 1993. "Orders and Liberties." In *A History of Women in the West: Emerging Feminism from Revolution to World War,* vol. 7. Cambridge, MA: Belknap Press of Harvard University Press.

Heyer, Paul. 1995. *Titanic Legacy: Disaster as Media Event and Myth.* Westport, CT: Praeger.

Murray, Steve. 1997. " 'My Chick Flick' Says Tough Guy Cameron." *The Atlantic Journal and Constitution,* 14 December: K6.

Seger, Linda. 1996. In *When Women Call the Shots.* New York: Henry Holt.

Vallone, Lynne, and Claudia Nelson, eds. 1994. *The Girl's Own: Cultural Histories of the Anglo-American Girl, 1830–1915.* Athens: University of Georgia Press.

chapter 11

Pretty in Pink? John Hughes Reinscribes Daddy's Girl in Homes and Schools

Ann De Vaney

Between 1984 and 1986 teens went to the movies in unprecedented numbers, seeking what to them were engaging, powerful representations of themselves and laughing at satiric depictions of everyone else in five films directed by John Hughes. *Sixteen Candles* (1984), *The Breakfast Club* (1985), *Weird Science* (1985), *Pretty in Pink* (1986), and *Ferris Bueller's Day Off* (1986) caught and exaggerated the specific vernacular, dress, and behavior of suburban, white, middle-class adolescents at school and home. Indeed, in the mid-1980s, the reception of these films by Hollywood's primary consumers—teenagers—in movie theaters and in homes exceeded Universal Pictures' modest prediction of their success. When released, each of the five films remained nationally among the top thirteen highest-grossing films for ten to twenty weeks, while a few ranked within the top five for a number of weeks (Top 50 Chart, 1984, 1985, 1986). One might say that during 1985 and 1986 at least one John Hughes film was always screening at a movie theater somewhere across the country.

Strangely enough, Hughes's 1980s films are still being rented at phenomenal rates. What continues to secure the attention, admiration, and loyalty of teens and many young adults? Southern California high school girls whom I interviewed in 1999 were avid Hughes fans; they and their friends rented his films repeatedly. One girl told me *Pretty in Pink* was her favorite film; she had rented and viewed it thirty times. Several of these teens, acting sophisticated, said in front of one another that viewing Hughes's films was "really retro," meaning they watched in order to laugh at the dress and speech of the characters. But in my observation, that ironic gap was bridged when they actually viewed the films. They were captivated and did not laugh at anything that was not designed to elicit a laugh. Currently,

201

fans can visit multiple websites for these 1980s films: *Pretty in Pink*, *Sixteen Candles* and *The Breakfast Club* have sites constructed by fans that are visited frequently. There are also John Hughes websites on which fans chat and chart his career.[1] When I asked my male and female graduate students in the Midwest—some of whom had been teens in the 1980s—about John Hughes films, they were effusive in their praise, many admitting they still rented *The Breakfast Club*, *Pretty in Pink*, and *Sixteen Candles* and remembering with particular fondness their first viewings while in high school. Even though they had obtained a critical analytical distance, the Hughes oeuvre had a particular cachet that obscured their skills. They did not believe nostalgia drew them, but thought Hughes had captured life as they knew it in 1980s high schools.

By the 1980s, women's spaces at home, in classrooms, and in workplaces had become extremely politicized. Why then were these films, filled with stereotyped gender roles, so popular? And how could these films obscure the critical vision of adults who had first viewed them as teens? The unprecedented and continued popularity among a broad and diverse teen audience might suggest that Hughes's film language constructs a subversive and resistive discourse, that Hughes provides opportunity for adolescents to seriously explore the angst-ridden time between childhood and adulthood. I contend he does not. Promised such an exploration, 1980s and 1990s girls watching *Pretty in Pink*, *Sixteen Candles*, and *The Breakfast Club* are allocated instead, as remedies for the emotional problems and powerlessness they experience, a sugar pill of frilly bedrooms with makeup and hair ribbons sans computers. Further, they are offered mean-spirited adult female roles to play. As the 1980s body politic sought to rein in the female body that had been unleashed by the sexual revolution of the 1960s and 1970s, so too did John Hughes reinscribe that domestic ideal of remaining within the ruling confines of the family, of continuing to be Daddy's girl. In safe bedrooms, kitchens, school hallways, homerooms, and libraries, his girls act up and act out their adolescence, taking care of Daddy, wearing pink, not showing much skin, attending dances in school gyms, and being no threat to the patriarchal status quo of family or school. Hughes's girls perform white, neoconservative teen sex roles and offer a powerful invitation to girl viewers to do likewise.

I will refer generally to Hughes's 1980s teen films to delineate the roles of women and girls, but I will perform a close reading of three of the most popular, *Sixteen Candles*, *The Breakfast Club*, and

Pretty in Pink, to consider the subject positions he affords filmic girls and explore the invitations to subjectivity he offers his female viewers.[2] Particular attention will be given to how Valerie Walkerdine's notion of "daddy's girl" is reinscribed and to the concept of sex roles as performance (Butler).

The depiction of rebellion and the burgeoning sexuality of teens has been a perennial problem for Hollywood, especially when it comes to presenting female adolescents, since representing the tension between innocence and sexuality is fraught with moral overtones in U.S. society. Even today the new production of *Lolita* could not find a theatrical distributor in the United States.[3] For decades directors took refuge in domestic comedies and lighthearted musicals for adolescents, such as the films created for the teenage Shirley Temple, Judy Garland, and Sandra Dee (Douglas). John Hughes's teen star, Molly Ringwald, follows in the footsteps of those adolescent heroines who represented a vision of American girlhood that was acceptable to a broad spectrum of filmgoers. Hughes's films are as formulaic as were teen comedies and musicals of the late 1930s, 1940s and 1950s. He often takes refuge in comedy, as did his predecessors, but unlike them stays within the guarded visual geography of the home and school. His narratives ostensibly allow teenage viewers to feel powerful laughing at caricatures of adult teachers, school administrators, and family members. Hughes's movies also owe their popularity to an ostensible exploration of independence and rebellion, though this exploration is routinely contained within safe domestic and school boundaries. In several of his movies Hughes shines a unique light on young women, creating important leading and supporting roles for them.

In representing teens, Hughes adopts a formulaic set of visual codes (of behavior and dress)—for instance, princess, geek, jock, and "Mr. Popularity." There are additional categories for parents, teachers, high school administrators, grandparents, "special students," and people of color. The princess, for example, usually acts in an aloof manner, the geek awkwardly, and the jock with machismo. Hughes authenticates his codes by incorporating the vernacular of middle-class, white, suburban Midwest 1980s teens. His target audience not only reads these codes with facility but transfers them from film to film, so that Hughes need not elaborate all the signs of a particular code but in later films can evoke it with a phrase or a piece of clothing. A geek in a Hughes film, for example, is usually recognizable by his large eyeglasses and mismatched clothes. Two types of intertextuality exist here. First, Hughes mimics and exaggerates the codes present in the text of the vernacular and everyday dress of his suburban, white American 1980s teen characters, so there is intertextuality between their everyday discourse and the discourse of the film itself. Secondly, there is intertextuality that spectators can respond to with little prompting as they read the codes from filmic text to filmic text (De Vaney). Hughes films are not just melodramas; central characters do have the capacity to change in an appealing way, although the changes are formulaic: the heroine realizes that the "geek" is a sensitive fellow underneath his odd veneer and befriends him; the popular rich boy realizes the superficiality of his class behavior and "falls for" the heroine, socially a step below him.

The teen discourse in Hughes films is gendered, classed, raced, and sexual in nature, in short, neoconservative. In this essay I will explore the manner in which Hughes reinscribes neoconservative values on contemporary girls by offering them the promise of insight but giving them only the smallest kinds of rebellions within safe geographies of school and home. I borrow Michel Foucault's idea of the power of social and governmental institutions to induce normative behavior in citizens. Hollywood is just such an institution, and Hughes films, in particular, can be seen to legitimate a female role that is convenient for the continuation of a certain way of men ruling. Foucault notes that the pedagogical institution since the eighteenth century

> has multiplied the forms of discourse on the subject [of sex]: it has established various points of implantation for sex; it has coded contents and qualified speakers, speaking about children's sex, inducing educators, physicians, administrators, and parents to speak of it, or speaking to them about it, causing children themselves to talk about it, and enclosing them in a web of discourses which sometimes address them, sometimes speak about them or impose canonical bits of knowledge on them, or use them as a basis for constructing a science (about sex) which is beyond their grasp. (1978, 32)

These discourses are represented in films about teens and articulated in the functioning of social institutions governing teen lives in the United States, such as schools and families. Those institutions are armed against burgeoning sexuality and "on the lookout" for deviance. Public school rules and advice to parents of adolescents emphasize the regulation of children's behavior, particularly in the areas of male-female relations, and the structuring of subject positions that American teens must occupy. (While many American parents and educators believe that teen behaviors are natural, psychological, and universal phenomena, those outside the United States have different expectations of their adolescent children and function within disparate discourses.) Teenage life in the United States continues to be depicted as one fraught with dangers, a time when children act on emotion alone and lose the ability to reason and in which girls get pregnant and boys can turn to delinquency. Popular and scholarly discourses perpetuate these depictions. As they negotiate these covert but oversexed discourses of regulation, teens are pushed into subversion and resistance by, among other tactics, structuring subversive discourses that dare to challenge totalizing concepts of their identities. Some of the ongoing fascination of John Hughes's films for young viewers is provoked by his exploration of precisely those subversive discourses. But although Hughes authorizes his characters to speak openly of sex, scatological topics, and breaking rules, apparently garnering power for the speakers and their teen spectators, he lets his filmic discourses circulate within fairly safe geographies so that no real derangement is produced.

Since Hughes writes abundantly about sex, it might appear that he taps into Foucault's idea of multiple discourses on the science of sex, but abundance here is neither diversity nor complexity. Sexual discourses permeate all of Hughes's teen films, yet his adults speak seldom and politely about sexual matters, thereby constructing great silences on issues vital to their children. His teens construct subversive discourses in which they leap gleefully into the linguistic breach of adults, breaking the silences of their elders in utterances that are likely to delight teen and young adult viewers. In *Sixteen Candles* boys talk about how to get the panties of the heroine Sam (Ringwald) as proof of sexual intercourse with her. Ted, the "geek" (Anthony Michael Hall), brags that he can accomplish this feat and in fact does, without sexual intercourse. Here Hughes authorizes his young male characters to articulate a specific old macho discourse, classed and white, that exists on college campuses. Hughes girls, on the other hand, are more covert in their sexual discussions, sometimes writing things they will not utter, or speaking in code. In *Sixteen Candles*, Sam is secretly completing a sexual survey given to her by a friend. Under the lax gaze of a teacher, she fills in the form answering such questions as, "Have you ever done it?," "What was it like?," and "If you haven't done it, who would you pick to be your 'first'?" These passé codes represent an inflexible gendered approach to teen sexual discourse, one that supports the taboos of adults. Even though there is explicit spoken language in the panty scene and overt written language in the survey scene, these incidents uncover biases sanctioned by conservative, traditional discourses: it is impolite for females to speak openly about sex; boys will be boys. These discourses act to instruct and thereby regulate adolescent lives by offering models for the performance of sex roles, yet teen viewers respond as if these complacent scenes were imaginative rebellions.

In the only Hughes scene in which males and females talk about sex together, five characters sit on the floor in a library in *The Breakfast Club*. This heart-to-heart talk, this loosening of tongues, can occur only after the children have smoked marijuana. The dialogue is revealing. Claire, the "princess" (Ringwald), who has been inferring that she is a sexual sophisticate, is verbally stripped of her pretensions by John (variously labeled as a "delinquent" or "criminal") (Judd Nelson). In the first half of the film Andrew, the "jock" (Emilio Estevez), fought John, who was looking up Claire's skirt and touching her, to defend Claire's honor in a scene that had overtones of upright males protecting women from criminal rape. The vulnerability of women is present in the heart-to-heart sexual talk. After Claire divulges her virginity, she admits both that she is saving herself for someone she "really" loves and that she intends to be monogamous. The conclusive statement about sex, however, comes when Allison (Ally Sheedy), the "basket case," enters her opinion. Speaking of sex as a double-edged sword, she says, as would many reactionary men when discussing women, "If you don't, you're a prude; if you do, you're a slut. If you don't, you want to and can't. If you do, you wish you didn't." And to Claire she says, "You are a tease."

These are John Hughes's words articulating biased gender values that have been and continue to be sanctioned by Hollywood, words by which many men regulate the behavior of women. I asked my informants to weigh in on this scene, since it is one that lovers of *The Breakfast Club* always cite as "realistic." Boys, they indicated, are teases also; this activity is not limited to girls. A guy may approach a girl from a different group (clique) and feign interest in her when actually he is pretending. Guys are sex objects too and "use their sex" as do girls. While the white girls I spoke with did not condone the behavior of their male classmates, they offered complex accounts of interaction between adolescent girls and boys. This complexity is absent in the Hughes oeuvre. In the panty scene, the survey scene, and the library dialogue, Hughes allocates power to his male characters and seldom allows it to circulate in relations among people. The only compromise is the co-opting of a girl, Allison, into a patriarchal discourse.

Another Foucauldian issue, surveillance, is at play in Hughes teen films. Most of his narratives are set in safe spaces and give special emphasis to safe geographies where teens are under surveillance—classrooms, gyms, locker rooms, libraries, shop classrooms, halls and lockers, principals' and vice principals' offices, bathrooms, janitors' storerooms, teen bedrooms, and kitchens (Foucault 1979). Most Hughes plots are advanced by the ability of his teens to escape scrutiny in these guarded locales. They pass notes in classrooms, conduct business in bathrooms, sneak into storerooms and shop classrooms. At home they throw wild parties while parents are absent or while wealthy, neglectful parents are present. And they perform all these filmic activities under the gaze of captivated viewers who cheer them on. Sometimes Hughes's teens escape in cars, or within stores, once in a bar, but they never travel far from home; they never leave the suburbs. Yet while Hughes's heroes are romantic, Huck Finn–like characters in some ways—that is, individualistic, not joining groups, and anti-intellectual—they do not venture out to explore the world, as did Huck. When the Huckish Ferris Bueller decides to play hooky he takes the longest trip of any of the Hughes characters and travels from suburbia to downtown Chicago. For teens there is a frisson in viewing people under guard escaping the scrutiny of their surveillers because such action shows them how to negotiate power and provides power while viewing. Ultimately, however, putting such escapes on screen is an empty gesture. Hughes's young protagonists stay relatively close to home even when they transgress.

Even under surveillance boys are offered more subject positions than are girls in the Hughes oeuvre, a significant fact for girl viewers of these films. In *Bodies That Matter*, Judith Butler collapses the space between the concepts of sex and gender that had been widely accepted in feminist circles, instead viewing sex as a performance, an act that starts on behalf of the child when she is in utero. Social roles are mimicked for girls as well as boys, and speech, clothes, and behavior become props in this life drama. Adolescent girls in a time of uncertainty in their lives flock to performances by teen girls as guides in the attempt to negotiate their gendered positions. But Hughes's young women are conventional models, whether they are central or peripheral characters. They inhabit frilly bedrooms strewn with clothes, with dressing tables and ample mirrors but no desks or computers as the boys' bedrooms have. Indeed, with the exception of one scene, girls are not depicted studying and do not express interest in knowledge or careers. In Hughes's starkly anti-intellectual treatment of girls, only one, Andie (Ringwald), the heroine of *Pretty in Pink*, is interested in studying. While Hughes's boys are often preoccupied with sexual issues, his girls are always thinking and talking about male-female relations. The typical Hughes girl does not contemplate her relations with girl friends as do current teens on television but has unexplored relationships with girls in which conversations are only about boys. She is a stock Hollywood romantic stereotype who always gets her man.

The Hughes oeuvre is also about appearance. Along with girls' talk about boys comes talk about clothes. His heroines are usually dressed in "Annie Hall" outfits that they have either sewn or "put together," while his peripheral women are dressed in uniform clothing befitting their social class. Clothing is involved in the satire of social class and ostensibly Hughes appears to be recommending an eclectic, creative mode of dress for young women. But in Hughes films, resistive discourse misses a certain complexity—the sort described by Walkerdine:

> When I had no money for clothes as a teenager I derived great pleasure from going to Derby market to buy cheap pieces of material with which to make my own. Indeed I was proud of the way I could sew in ways that wealthier girls could not and that my clothes were often more spirited and dramatic than theirs (I was always a great fan of shocking pink!). I think it makes a travesty of what was a culturally and psychically complex act to call this resistance. (52)

Hughes makes a minimal move to depict his heroines' independence by casting them as outsiders, by allowing them cultural knowledge to pass along to their fathers, and by dressing them in eclectic clothes. The implication in *Sixteen Candles* and the overt statement in *Pretty in Pink* (in which the heroine, Andie, is poor) is that these individualists eschew fashion and can assemble or design and sew their clothes, thereby making their own fashion statement. By the 1980s, however, hippies had made eclectic dressing a fashion cliché, and female viewers could tell that Molly Ringwald was actually dressed in expensive eclectic clothing. So, Hughes undermines this message of pluck and ingenuity and, as Walkerdine so aptly notes, appropriates it from a "lower" class as only a superficial form of resistance. It is precisely this commercial strategy, this bait, that appeals to young female customers consuming Hughes films while planning a wardrobe.

As girl spectators are not only planning but playing with a notion of identity when they view these films, the character emphases can be significant in girls' development. One relationship is always present and subtly emphasized: a special bond between father and daughter. In the three films I read closely, fathers are depicted as somewhat caring and mothers are either absent or too preoccupied to truly care for their daughters. Andie is the heroine of *Pretty in Pink*, Sam of *Sixteen Candles*, and Claire, with Allison, in *The Breakfast Club*. Andie's mother has died and Andie fills the role of caretaker for her father, cooking for him, picking up his clothes, and urging him to look for a job. In the opening scene of the film, Andie awakens her father and has trouble getting him out of bed. She makes him promise to seek a full-time job. Yet, this working-class dad and all of Hughes's working-class white men, here and elsewhere, are depicted in an exceedingly sympathetic manner. Andie's father, Jack Walsh (Harry Dean Stanton), does display his love for her and concern for her welfare, but Hughes panders to the audience for sympathy for Jack throughout the film. This tactic is most evident in one scene when Jack speaks privately to a boy, variously called Duckie or Phil (Jon Cryer), who is obsessed with Andie.[4] Duckie tells Jack he wants to marry Andie and Jack asks if Andie knows how Duckie feels. Jack then shifts the focus of the conversation to himself and claims that he "loved like that once" and still does, but that Andie's mom "split." A narrative in which a mother is absent and a daughter assumes the caretaking role for the father is a perennial strategy in melodrama and was popular in old Hollywood films, especially westerns. But the presence of this technique and similar strategies in 1980s films creates a patriarchal valence that echoes the paternalistic values underpinning the supposedly subversive teen sexual discourse.

In *Sixteen Candles*, Sam's family forgets her sweet sixteen birthday, yet it is her father who remembers the next day and comes to apologize and wish her a belated happy birthday. He intuits that this oversight is not the sole cause of her malaise and elicits a confession from her that she is enamored of a handsome, popular senior who "doesn't know she exists." He "understands" and comforts her, trying to put the issue into perspective. "That's why they're called crushes," says he, indicating that infatuations are emotionally oppressive. In *The Breakfast Club*, Claire's father drives her to the Saturday detention, having failed to satisfy her expectations by arranging that she be released from this punishment in which she will have to join the "defectives." For Claire "defective" is synonymous with delinquent, and she yells before leaving the car, "I am not a delinquent." In all of these father-daughter relationships we can see the girls slide between childlike and mother- or wife-like behavior with their daddies. This changeling behavior, as Walkerdine calls it in reference to Shirley Temple and Little Orphan Annie, provides filmmakers with an opportunity to represent female behavior as childlike or adultlike, without confronting the sexual tension of adolescence. The sexual discourse may be hidden for the comfort of the adult spectator but is implied in the adult behavior of the filmic girl.

Although this essay is not about adult females, Hughes's representations of them provide future subject positions for his filmic girls. Mothers, for instance, are either absent or visible for only a few moments onscreen. In *The Breakfast Club*, a mother brings her son to detention and threatens him with punishment if he ever repeats "this performance." Viewers later learn she is the shrew who pushed him beyond his limit to obtain high grades, causing him to become suicidal. Other mothers in this film are simply topics of conversation in which they are depicted as neglectful: one is an alcoholic and another allows her spouse to abuse her son. Female teachers are invariably mean or uncaring, grandmothers are presented as "out of touch with reality," and Sam's older blond sister and a church organist are presented as dumb.[5] One searches in vain for sympathetic portrayals of adult women in his films. It is telling that in the thirty films Hughes wrote from 1982 to 2000, mothers are absent, preoccupied, neglectful, or uncaring. This can be seen especially in the case of all the National Lampoon films, the *Home Alone* films, the teen films of the 1980s, *Mr. Mom* (1983), and the remake of *Miracle on 34th Street* (1994).

During the 1980s when academic and professional doors were opening for women, and when *Roe v. Wade* was the law of the land, Hughes elected to depict his women as described above and his girls as under the rule of their fathers, intuitive men who advise their daughters about male-female relations. Such stereotypes have a time-honored position in Hollywood and on television shows with which Hughes grew up ("Father Knows Best" [1954] and a Hughes favorite, "The Honeymooners" [1955]). If Hughes's oeuvre is a popular cultural form of a patriarchal discourse that contains and constrains

Daddy hands his princess her lunch in *The Breakfast Club*.

the subject positions afforded women and girls, the speakers within the discourse emphasize that fathers have control over the bodies of their wives and daughters. In the 1980s Hughes was hardly alone. He was an important part of political and popular discourses that articulated a backlash against women's rights.

In an interview with Jack Corliss, Hughes said he liked to write from the female point of view because so many current teen comedies were about males and sex. He believed that the sixteen-year-old group was not being well served by people of his generation, the baby boomers, and indicated that his teen films enrich the youth culture: "I'm not going to abandon the youth of America. They're the ones who support the industry, yet are not always well served by it. A youth picture does not have to be synonymous with exploitation" (Greenberg 19). He aims to redress this wrong with his films. Strangely enough, many people I interviewed in the 1980s and 1990s did not feel exploited and spoke of the realistic nature of Hughes's films. I observed them laughing as they watched, yet afterward the codes of "realism" dominated their discussions, as though the films had been straight representations, not parodies.

One aim of a "realist" narrative is to urge the audience to share, rather than feel superior to, what stands for an authentic experience

of the hero or heroine. On the other hand, when Hughes parodies
people by use of ridicule and derision he is placing himself in a position of superiority and inviting those who laugh also to feel superior
to those ridiculed. When Hughes wrote films such as *National Lampoon's Vacation* (1983), he did not break out of the form of parody
and satire but allowed all the characters to be laughed at; his audience did not identify with but felt superior to everyone onscreen. But
in the films I am discussing here, he excuses his central characters
from parody. By doing this he allows these characters, as well as the
audience, to laugh at all those around them in the film. This mixing
of forms is a powerful technique, providing for a double laughter and
a double superiority. The audience can laugh and feel superior both
as an external, viewing audience and as they place themselves in the
shoes of the central characters vis-à-vis laughable marginal characters. (The receptive disposition of the spectator of parody is an ironic
one, but forms of viewer identification with "realistic" characters
are associative [Jauss].) In this way teen viewers feel that they are ne-
gotiating positions of power while viewing. One young boy told me
that he loved Hughes's films, because they "were a great revenge."

John Hughes fans, then and now, were so delighted to see themselves represented on the screen in a manner that was not freakish or
silly that they were, and are, enamored of his oeuvre. Indeed, Hughes
broke media ground by depicting teens more seriously than they had
hitherto been presented. He created a genre about and for teens that
mixes forms of realism, parody, satire, and musical video for the
generation raised on MTV and accustomed to mixing and matching
image and form. His imitators are legion in Hollywood and on television. Teen television dramas, in fact, have begun to include more
gender-equal roles for girls and boys. As a measure of the influence
of *The Breakfast Club*, we can note a recent episode of "Dawson's
Creek" (1998), the plot of which was similar to the storyline of *The
Breakfast Club*. This was a tribute to John Hughes, not a parody of
his work. Hollywood, however, has not opened the subject positions
for girls in current teen films but has concentrated on increasing the
amount of sexual and scatological parody.

In teen films, Hollywood appoints itself as speaker for teens,
vying with parental speakers and reauthorizing itself to speak to
adolescents about their lives. By sanctioning the Hughes discourses
I have described here, Hollywood disperses its power of surveillance
and participation in sexual discourses. Film speakers—girls, boys,
mothers, fathers, teachers, and administrators—are authorized to
enunciate the concepts and values of a retrograde, classed, white,

patriarchal discourse. Girl spectators watch the Hughes girls in eclectic clothes act out their identity in nonserious pursuits while remaining faithful to their daddies. Such performances of sex (Butler) need not be imitated by spectators in order to be believed as serious and real. The popular cultural presence of cultural diversity and gender fluidity does present a challenge to a certain way of tacitly ruling young citizens in the United States. Hughes's work is a defusing response to that challenge. But since resistance is the métier of teen discourse, adolescent spectators may eventually contest these retrograde representations.

NOTES

1. http://members.aol.com/XanderUbi/hughesretro.html;
   http://www.blkbox.com/~draper/ringwald/home.html
2. Released in April 1984, *Sixteen Candles* was the first film written and directed by John Hughes. Because Sam's sister's wedding is scheduled for the day after Sam's birthday, her parents forget about it. This oversight establishes the plot, but the storyline is propelled by a familiar love triangle. Sam "moons" over a senior, the unattainable rich Jake, while the geek, Ted, stubbornly pursues Sam. The plot unfolds at a school dance, at a "free-for-all" party in Jake's house, and at a church where Sam is the maid of honor in her sister's wedding. Sam gets her man.

   The Breakfast Club was the second film written and directed by Hughes. The five main characters, "jock," "geek," "delinquent," "princess," and "basket case," assemble in the school library for a day-long Saturday detention. Their punishment is under the surveillance of the vice principal, a traditional overseer of conduct and discipline in U.S. public schools. In sympathy with the miscreants, John Hughes opens this film with David Bowie's lyrics, "And these children that you spit on,/ As they try to change their world,/ Are immune to your consultations." The plot is advanced by subversive dialogue that constitutes a discourse of resistance. The students escape surveillance for the last third of the film; they locate and smoke marijuana, break into a choreographed musical number similar to a music video, and have a heart-to-heart talk with one another about parents and sex. In this section realism and fantasy are mixed formats Hughes employs to hold his audience.

   Pretty in Pink was written and produced by Hughes but directed by Howard Deutch under the supervision of Hughes. (Deutch's only prior directorial experience was on MTV.) In this film, Andie is a lower-middle-class student in an upper-middle-class school, and another love triangle propels the plot. Duckie, the "geek," is hopelessly in love with Andie while she is likewise disposed to an unattainable popular rich student, Blane. Andie lives alone with and takes care of her father because her mother deserted the family. The story relates Andie's struggles in securing Blane as a boyfriend.

3. See Kristen Hatch, "Fille Fatale: Regulating Images of Adolescent Girls, 1962–1996" in this volume.

4. Duckie exhibits classic obsessive behaviors and yet Andie and her father think these behaviors are cute. Hughes wants viewer sympathy for this scary behavior.

5. For his diverse audience, Hughes fashions a female subjectivity that limits and confines, that does not address diversity. In spite of civil rights gains in the 1960s and 1970s his films are also retrograde in another way. When people of color or handicapped persons appear in his 1980s films they usually have no relation to the plot but are simply the butt of Hughes's obvious visual and verbal taunts. The small woman (Zelda Rubinstein) who plays the organist in *Sixteen Candles* asks foolish questions and actually rattles when she walks. In the same film a young female student (Joan Cusack) with a neck brace appearing briefly in a couple of scenes is the object of laughter when she attempts to drink from a water fountain and later from a beer can. In *Ferris Bueller's Day Off,* when a Latino car attendant (Richard Edson) takes the keys to Ferris's Ferrari to park the car, Hughes breaks the narrative form by having Ferris (Matthew Broderick) look directly at the audience. His look within the context of this scene means, "Should I trust him?" Evidently not, according to Hughes, because the attendant does take the Ferrari on a joy ride with his African American colleague (Larry Flash Jenkins). But extended derogation is saved for a young Asian character, Long Duk Dong (Gedde Watanabe), who has an important role in *Sixteen Candles.* Hughes elicits laughter at this Asian boy's speech patterns, clumsy behavior, and dumb responses to other characters. Hughes's cruel treatment of these characters is consistent in the 1980s films. Neither people of color nor physically challenged persons are ever depicted sympathetically. By stripping them of filmic power and representing them always as objects of derision, Hughes locates himself within a discourse that is intolerant of any kind of difference.

WORKS CITED

Butler, Judith. 1993. *Bodies That Matter.* New York: Routledge.
Corliss, Jack. 1986. "Growing Pains." *Time,* 3 March: 83.

DeVaney, Ann. 1987. "The World of John Hughes." *Framework, A Journal of Images and Culture* I: 16–25.

Douglas, Susan. 1994. *Where the Girls Are: Growing Up Female with the Mass Media.* New York: Times Books of Random House.

Foucault, Michel. 1978. *The History of Sexuality: An Introduction,* vol. 1. New York: Penguin.

———. 1979. *Discipline and Punish: The Birth of the Prison.* New York: Random House.

Greenberg, J. 1984. "Universal Signs Hughes to 3-Year Pact." *Variety,* May 2: 19.

Jauss, H. R. 1982. *Aesthetic Experience and Literary Hermeneutics.* Trans. M. Shaw. Minneapolis: University of Minnesota Press.

Top 50 Chart. 1984. *Variety,* May 9–June 13..

———. 1985. *Variety,* March 5–May 22.

———. 1986. *Variety,* June 25–October 1.

Walkerdine, Valerie. 1997. *Daddy's Girl.* Cambridge, MA: Harvard University Press.

chapter 12

Pleasures and Problems of the "Angry Girl"

Kimberley Roberts

You've got power, Veronica. Power I didn't think you had.
JASON DEAN IN *Heathers*

Veronica Sawyer's teenage "power" in *Heathers* (1989) is a direct precursor of the 1990s popular feminist groundswell known as *girl power*, a structure of belief and a set of consumer practices that center on the individual teenage girl's power to effect change in her universe. Moreover, Winona Ryder's performance presages what I would like to call the "angry girl" genre of the 1990s, or, the body of film where teenage girl anger is articulated specifically as a weapon against gender crimes. In 1996 alone, for example, we see in this genre Annette Haywood-Carter's *Foxfire*, Jim McKay's *Girls Town*, and, most important for the purposes of this paper, Matthew Bright's *Freeway*, in which a girl protagonist makes it her personal mission to defeat a serial killer who victimizes women and girls.[1] In other words, many film heroines of the girl power era are pissed off and ready to do something about it—they are fighters who combat the forces against them, unapologetically and often violently.

The connections between these two phenomena of mid-1990s American culture—the "angry girl" in 1990s film and the widely popular girl power "movement"—are not coincidental. They are mutually constitutive, even if at times they are also at odds. As I will argue, even though a film like *Freeway*—the "angry girl" film par excellence—does suggest a shift in the way girls are portrayed in the 1990s, the girl power phenomenon cannot always fully account for the heroine's angry outbursts. Central to my discussion will be this tension between girl power as a politically viable force and as mere lip service to a certain set of appealing ideals. One of the pressing

217

questions I will ask of girl power is whether, in fact, there is space within its philosophy for girls to articulate and own their anger. For although the girl power era indicates a certain time of empowerment for girls, it is important to remember that anger is still largely taboo. In fact, most girls learn early on to deny their rage and instead express themselves through more acceptable modes of femininity. As Lyn Mikel Brown puts it:

> The pressure for girls to split off their anger is enormous and the rewards are clear. The girls who do so, however, risk losing the capacity to locate the source of their pain and thus do something about it; they risk losing the potential for a once ordinary, healthy resistance to turn political. Without anger there is no impetus to act against any injustice done to them. If we take away girls' anger, then, we take away the foundation for women's political resistance. (13)

For this reason, looking at the ways girls' anger is represented in film will say much about just how accepting our culture has become about female power and resistance to sexism. Likewise, investigating how these representations fit into the girl power ethos will give us a better sense of how powerful such a feminist youth movement can hope to be.

Girl Power

In part, girl power is the manifestation of a decade-long fascination with teenage girls and girlish things—one that started with the feisty resurrection of the term "girl" in the early 1990s by members of the musical and zine-based movement Riot Grrrl. Arguably a more radical and overtly political movement than girl power, Riot Grrrl represents a kind of pre-lapsarian girl power: that is, a discourse and set of practices somehow largely outside the commercial and media-saturated realm. Riot Grrrl possesses the political muscle often lacking in girl power; it also has the cohesion of a bonafide youth culture.[2] As one early manifesto states:

> [Riot Grrrl is important] BECAUSE we need to acknowledge that our blood is being spilt, that right now a girl is being raped or battered and it might be me or you or your mom or the girl you sat next to on the bus last Tuesday, and she might be dead by the time you finish reading this . . . BECAUSE a safe place needs to be created for girls where we can

open our eyes and reach out to each other without being threatened
by this sexist society and our day-to-day shit. (Kearney 154)

Those who identify with Riot Grrrl, therefore, are aware of the forces
against them—of their doubly marginalized position as youth and
as women. Girl power, on the other hand, represents the tamer,
more palatable version of Riot Grrrl—a version largely created by
the media. The focus for girl power is on "feeling good"—on tapping
into individual power as opposed to focusing on the forces curtailing
it. As one twelve-year-old girl puts it: "It means equality . . . that
girls are strong, each one in her own way." (Lemish 164)

But more important, the phrase girl power reflects the changing face of feminism: the notion perpetuated in the popular press
and elsewhere that feminism has abandoned its so-called puritanical
roots and has "evolved" into a politics of pleasure. As one of the Spice
Girls states their mission in coining the phrase: "We're freshening up
feminism for the 90s. . . . Feminism has become a dirty word. Girl
power is just a 90s way of saying it" (Douglas 21). A woman can
do it all, the reasoning goes—wear a miniskirt *and* command a six-
digit salary, enjoy her boyfriend's chivalrous attentions *and* initiate
sex. Some feminist scholars, who are justly worried that this change
guts feminism of its political muscle and thus track girl power with
skepticism, call the 1990s the "postfeminist" era. On the other hand,
anti-feminist writers like Tad Friend of *Esquire* magazine see this
change, which he calls "do-me" feminism, as one aspect of a long
overdue makeover.[3]

As with most media-hyped phrases, however, girl power is mul-
tivalent. It has absorbed everything from girls' friendships to their
fashion sense. In fact, its commercial capital has so defined it that the
intersection between philosophy and consumerism is very blurred
indeed. In terms of its relationship to actual teenage girls, girl power
carries a commercial message, in that it signals their emergence as
a powerful economic force. With the immense popularity among
teenage girls of films like *Scream* (1996) (which grossed $103 mil-
lion at the box office upon its initial release), bands like the Spice
Girls (whose single "Wannabe" sold 1.8 million copies in the United
States alone), and television shows like "Buffy the Vampire Slayer"
and "Sabrina the Teenage Witch," the economic clout of adolescent
girls is not so difficult to calculate. The number of teenagers in the
United States is on the rise for the first time in fifteen years, and their
ranks are growing at a faster rate than the overall U.S. population.

Moreover, according to one market research firm, teenagers will spend an estimated $84 billion of their own money this year. Clearly, teenage girls aged thirteen to seventeen—88 percent of whom "love to shop" according to one consumer survey—represent a viable market (Munk 33). The larger question, however, relates to how the two sometimes contradictory facets of girl power—its role as heiress to the second-wave feminist movement on the one hand and its connections to an increasingly commercialized girls' culture on the other— are connected. In other words, why, aside from and in addition to its almighty consumerist ethos, does girl power resonate with adolescent girls in the 1990s?

In part, girl power appeals because of its relevance to a teenager's life. Girls today are well aware that their concerns are frequently overlooked in contemporary feminist discourse. As one adolescent girl writes:

> I was stuck in the middle. I was changing. I wasn't a woman, but I wasn't a little girl. I wanted to play with dolls, but then I wanted to go out and meet guys. I wanted all these clothes, but then I wanted toys, too. . . . It was a lot of changes. I was really stuck in the middle, that's how I felt. I don't know if my mother understood that or if she remembers how that feels. (Cassidy 40)

Not only do some girls today feel that older women have typically ignored them as conscious subjects, they are also quite clear about the ways they are different from "older" feminists.[4] The "new" girl power feminism—as defined by postfeminist websites, in anthologies like Barbara Findlen's *Listen Up. Voices from the Next Feminist Generation* (1995), and by the Spice Girls' liner notes—fits more comfortably with the current self-conceptualizations of teenage girls, particularly in terms of pleasure (the old feminists didn't let you wear makeup), sexuality (the old feminists were puritanical), and empowerment (the old feminists claimed victim status). Although these representations of earlier feminist positions are myopic, even blatantly inaccurate, nevertheless today's postfeminism looks quite different from the feminism of the 1970s and 1980s. And yet, girl power also seems to espouse the most sacred 1970s feminist tenets, such as the power of group solidarity and inner exploration. As the Spice Girls say, "Girl power is when . . . you believe in yourself and control your own life" (Press 61). This sounds much like the early consciousness-raising of Betty Friedan.

Clearly, girl power is full of contradictions. For the remainder of this chapter I will look to *Freeway* to explore how girl power suggests simultaneously a politics of action and a politics ultimately unconcerned with social justice. But before doing so, I want to make one caveat. Although the significance of girl power for "real" girls seems crucial to any understanding of its force as a political movement, I am interested here in the ways this popular and media-driven movement affects representation, in particular, the way it filters into and is produced by various conceptualizations of teenage girls in film. As Jon Lewis points out in his study of teen films:

> [Teen] films provide at best the principal artifacts of youth culture; at worst, they offer proof positive of the hegemonic effect of "the culture industry" (the argument that the media not only produce texts for consumption, but ideology for consumption as well; the argument that culture is yet another product of postwar industry). Given such a dialectic, one cannot study culture without attending to the representations of that culture in the media. (3)

Thus, even though the film I am analyzing here is not exclusively targeted at teenage girls as the ideal audience, it does use the teenage girl as a means to convey certain messages about power, authority, and the status of contemporary feminism.

Freeway: The Angry Girl Has Arrived

As an updated version of "Little Red Ridinghood," *Freeway* highlights the interlocking oppressions facing teenage protagonist Vanessa Lutz (Reese Witherspoon) and the survival strategies she adopts to fight them. From the outset, the film marks her as the epitome of alienated and disenfranchised youth. Vanessa is a welfare kid—young, poor, and daughter of a junkie/prostitute (Amanda Plummer) who is unable to protect her from the sexual advances of her stepfather (Michael T. Weiss). But Vanessa is not helpless; she is precocious and resourceful. As we travel with her through the concrete landscape of Los Angeles, we watch her evade the big bad wolf—in this case, a therapist-turned-serial killer (Kiefer Sutherland) who stalks the freeways in search of young girls to rape, mutilate, and murder. We also witness the lives of other semi-literate teenagers whose paths have led them to drugs, sex, and guns. And throughout, we see the adult world around Vanessa fail her: the police do not believe her, the courts will not protect her, and she is left to fight back on her own. And fight back she does. In *Freeway*, we see a female character who fights physically, who uses weapons, and who, by her own admission, "has a problem with anger." Gone are the days of passive/aggressive "female" modes of fighting or even the accidental violence of some other feminist film heroines such as Thelma and Louise. Vanessa Lutz represents a new brand of teenage heroine—one who purposefully attacks her oppressors, from Bob the serial killer to the guards at her juvenile detention center.

Although I could focus on any number of girl power films, I am choosing *Freeway* precisely because it so blatantly codes an adolescent girl's angst as anger.[5] Moreover, Vanessa's angry outbursts function in the film specifically to disrupt audience expectations regarding her class, race, and gender position. Of course this is not to say that her anger is always subversive but rather that these filmic eruptions do different cultural work depending on the context. For example, Vanessa's aggression might unsettle stereotypic expectations regarding age and gender while simultaneously mitigating the film's qualified class radicalism—most young girls do not make or use deadly weapons, nor do they fight mano a mano, as Vanessa does several times in this film. Despite the obvious pleasures young feminists (in particular) experience while watching an angry girl kick ass, this film and other "angry girl" films like it do not automatically ensure radical political intervention.

Freeway does, however, portray the American teenage girl as fundamentally and justifiably angry. This, in turn, coincides with other popular narratives of girlhood perpetuated in the media. As one *Utne Reader* cover describes today's girls, they are "Dissed, Mythed, and Totally Pissed" (Brown 4). It is, in fact, Vanessa's intentional anger that makes her particularly satisfying as a girl power heroine. She does not approach violence with ambivalence or as a last resort as did Veronica Sawyer. She embraces it by saying things like, "I'm pissed off—and the whole world owes me," as she threatens to shoot a john, but instead locks him in the trunk of his car. She challenges conventional gender codes by showing that she is not just angry, she is also willing to do something violent about it. Moreover, the angry girl generally—and Vanessa in particular—is significant and pleasurable precisely because the expression of anger has hitherto been the unspoken domain of men and boys. The long history of the angry youth in film, canonized by James Dean, has by and large been a male story—one where the individual is valorized and set in conflict with the traditional mores of his parents and the larger society.

Moreover, this trope of the "lone wolf" is not just an issue of filmic representation. Sociologist Barbara Hudson describes how this narrative of adolescent rebellion is gendered—how the very word "adolescent" seems synonymous with the kind of rebellious behavior we expect from types like James Dean. She argues that adults seem to expect both girls and boys to act out in adolescence in very specific and similar ways; yet at the same time girls have the added pressure of measuring up as young ladies. Thus, her research indicates, girls are generally deeply confused and psychically torn by this developmental process. For example, in order to move properly into womanhood, girls are expected to "relate" well—to form lasting ties and to act with emotional maturity—while, on the other hand, they are encouraged as adolescents to "lighten up"—to break with their parents and to rebel against societal constraints until they can find their own place within the system. This leaves most teenage girls in a classic double-bind; they believe that their rebellious feelings make them improper as "young women" and, conversely, that their status as young women requires them to leave rebellious adolescence behind before they have really experienced it. Most often girls choose the latter scenario, primarily because it is much less threatening to the dominant cultural system. As Hudson writes: "Since femininity is the 'master discourse' in the sense that it is the status of femininity that teenage girls are aspiring towards and the status of adolescence that they are aiming to leave behind, being dismissed [by adults] as adolescent is more dangerously subversive of femininity than being 'womanly' is of adolescence" (51). In other words, if a girl identifies with the "rebellious" facets of adolescence, those coded "male," she is in fact resisting the mechanism by which the dominant culture works to interpellate her as a female subject.

For this reason, the feminist viewer can greatly enjoy the experience of watching Vanessa as she defies societal norms and expresses her fury—as she literally kills the killer with her bare hands—for in so doing she is also resisting socialization as a respectable "woman." She embodies the potential for subversion of gender norms because she is a liminal figure—not quite woman, not quite child. She is still full of potential in ways that full-grown women cannot be, since they must undergo the arduous and ambivalent process of unlearning socialized behaviors. *Freeway*, accordingly, makes none of the concessions we can see in the feminist classic *Thelma & Louise* (1991). The main characters in that film represent a contrasting model of how full-grown women respond in film when extremely angry. If we think about their scenes of daring, where both women are alternately elated and horrified by criminal actions they have committed, we see how difficult it is for women to own their tendency toward violence. The initial attempted rape of Thelma is crucial in setting up the justification for all their future actions. Moreover, the audience relies on the tension between the pair being in danger and being dangerous. But Vanessa, moving from the status of victim (young, impoverished, illiterate, alone) to that of self-determined aggressor fighting the misogynist, elitist serial killer, becomes the ultimate feminist avenger. As she explains to the police investigating the case, "I just knew that if I let him go he would go out and kill some other girl—and that would've been my fault. And I couldn't have lived with that. Never. No way." Vanessa appropriately delivers her vengeance with her boyfriend's handgun— a gift he gives her at the film's opening. Ironically this generous act gets him killed in the very next scene when he is left unable to defend himself in a drive-by shooting.

One of the most intriguing aspects of *Freeway* is the way it implicitly asks the audience to celebrate Vanessa's revenge and to take pleasure in her acts of violence, a pleasure derived from seeing girls break out of stereotypical gender roles. As Kirsten Lentz argues:

> Women's knowledge of, aptitude with and willingness to use guns affords a pleasure familiar to feminists: the female subject masters with utter competence a "masculine" practice, attitude and/or domain. . . . This pleasure clearly participates in the liberal narrative of "gender role" transgression. But the fact of the deadliness of guns . . . complicates this liberalism. (374)

In other words one might argue, particularly in the wake of incidents like the Columbine shootings, that celebrating the violence perpetrated by Vanessa is not a feminist move but an instance of buying into a masculinist mode, one that causes more problems than it solves. However, I would agree with Lentz that it is the fantasy of power these girls project that is so deeply satisfying. These films do not suggest that violent retribution is a viable option in "real life." As Carol Clover puts it when discussing rape-revenge films: "It goes without saying that the notion of women going around New York putting bullets through male chauvinists has everything to do with fantasy and little to do with reality" (142). Yet, as *Freeway* and other angry girl films (as well as the women's lives they fictionally represent) make clear, the criminal justice system rarely protects women and girls from sexual predation and even more infrequently punishes the perpetrators of these predatory crimes. For this reason, even violent revenge can resonate for female audiences.

Along with encouraging this form of audience identification, *Freeway* also uses structures of address that ask the viewer to understand Vanessa's anger as class rage. It is no coincidence, for example, that Bob the serial killer is also a highly paid therapist who lives in a gated community in the Los Angeles suburbs with his "skipper wife" (as Vanessa calls her) played by Brooke Shields. Vanessa is as enraged by her class status as she is by her position as a young woman in a male-dominated society. As Bob puts it when she uncovers his identity: "I call people like you 'garbage people.' And I assure you, Vanessa, you are one of them. . . . People like me don't go to the gas chamber. The chance of somebody like me going to prison is absolutely nil." *Freeway* thus highlights the way systemic oppression operates in quotidian life. As it turns out Bob's assessment of the way the criminal justice system works is right on the mark. When Vanessa attempts to kill him but somehow he miraculously survives, she, not he, is the one put on trial. Because of Bob's class and educational privilege, the police refuse to believe Vanessa's story that the upstanding psychologist is in fact the I-5 killer. In this topsy-turvy game of "Will the real criminal please stand up?" *Freeway* also points to the bourgeois fear of urban space and to the perception that the disenfranchised masses are those we need to fear. Unlike many other mainstream Hollywood films and television series that frequently strike a reactionary note vis-à-vis the inner-city underclass (Joel Schumacher's *Falling Down* (1992), for example, or "NYPD Blue"), *Freeway* indicates that those with power are the real wolves, especially if you are a girl without financial or educational resources. In taking this stance, the film highlights one of the ways that girl power cannot make sense for a girl like Vanessa. Despite her best efforts to "believe in [her] self and control [her] own life" as the Spice Girls advise, Vanessa does not stand a chance when pitted against a criminal justice system that is inherently biased, a system that would convict rather than defend her.

And yet, as surely as there are radical moments where systemic gender and class oppressions is exposed and routed by the film, it also hits a reactionary note in its portrayal of the underclass. To account for the film's more conservative elements, we might posit that Vanessa's brash actions, as written and directed by Matthew Bright, are not the workings of a feminist and class-aware avenger but merely occasions for the viewer's classist voyeurism. Vanessa's outrageousness can only find narrative expression *because* she is a member of the underclass—and because she represents a satisfying bourgeois fantasy where her actions constitute a transgressive celebration of the working class. With her overt sexuality and propensity for cathartic emotions, she cannot be contained by middle-class social decorum. However, this formulation also seems overly simplistic. For as John Hartigan explains in "Unpopular Culture: The Case of 'White Trash,'" when the "white trash" image is called forth—as it most certainly is in *Freeway*—it does not function rhetorically as a celebratory identity miraculously freed from bourgeois cultural norms but as a pollution of the white racial order that must be exorcized. He asserts that in its standard derogatory usage, " 'white trash' is used to name [and I would add to exclude] . . . those bodies that exceed the class and racial etiquettes required of whites if they are to preserve the powers and privileges that accrue to them as members of the dominant racial order in this country" (320). According to Hartigan's formulation, a character like Vanessa would serve to contain the white audience's anxiety about racial pollution—an anxiety evoked by the spectre of an underclass that is white. Moreover, as all name-calling does, labeling somebody "white trash" asserts difference and maintains boundaries, not just between whites of varying class positions, but also between the white poor and the non-white middle class. And here the film provides an interesting intervention. Despite the film's reliance on signifiers of "white trash"—the fact that Vanessa's grandmother lives in a trailer park, for example, or that Vanessa speaks with an inexplicable southern hillbilly accent despite the fact that she has lived her entire life in Southern California—Bright seems to be evoking this rhetorical identity not to solidify the boundaries between black and white, rich and poor, but rather, to make them "less" discrete. In fact, the film suggests that intra-racial solidarity might be a means to dismantle class- and race-based hegemony.

The negotiation comes through most clearly in the portrayal of Vanessa's relationship with the African American cop, Mike Breer (Wolfgang Bodison). When Vanessa is first interrogated by the police detectives assigned to her case, she appears small and vulnerable in her orange "murderer" suit; yet she is also at her angry best. She complies when the two police officers ask her to recount her criminal record, and as she catalogues her offenses—shoplifting, arson, soliciting—Breer responds with lecherous, smirking interest. Self-consciously voyeuristic, the film asks us to identify with Breer in this scene; we, as "respectable" viewers, are equally titillated by Vanessa's transgressions—both by the way she bucks gender normativity through her criminal actions and by the way she refuses to play by the rules of middle-class respectability.

Yet, when Breer asks her if she is just doing what comes naturally (soliciting) she flies into a rage, goads him with the epithet "nigger," and clocks him with a metal chair. Thus, as in most of the other similarly violent scenes, her anger is figured specifically as a response to sexism and classism. But because the opening scene of *Freeway* shows Vanessa engaged in a long, open-mouthed kiss with her African American boyfriend Chopper (Bokeem Woodbine), and because subsequent scenes reveal that by all accounts he is the one person in her life who actually means something to her, it is clear that Bright is not portraying Vanessa as a stereotypical racist. Instead, through name-calling Vanessa focuses attention on the affinity between herself and Breer; in effect, she recognizes that just as Breer can strip her identity to a stereotype by reading her as "white trash," so can she reduce his middle-class existence by calling him a "nigger." When he responds with outrage she saucily says, "So what? You don't like being called a nigger? So I don't like being called a natural-born whore. So there." Whereas Breer wants to establish a boundary between them by seeing her as the money-grubbing "whore" who is beyond the pale, she exposes his vulnerability to show how their positions outside the dominant power structure are ultimately somewhat alike. His fierce need to legitimate his position as an African American member of the middle class also explains in part why he is the character who stands for oppressive and wrong-headed authority in the scene, as opposed to the white cop, Wallace (Dan Hedaya), sitting by his side. Despite Breer's attempts to distance himself from Vanessa, he cannot, as a black man, scale the social ladder through his middle-class job any more than she, an illiterate juvenile delinquent, can coast on her white prettiness. In fact, one could argue that he is in a far more precarious position; she can at least hope for the safety that passing allows.

Nevertheless, Breer's subsequent discovery of Vanessa's innocence—the fact that he is the one to crack the case and the first to believe in Bob's guilt—further functions to show the psychic and political allegiances between Breer and Vanessa. During a scene at Vanessa's high school when Breer is interviewing her friends, he does an abrupt about-face when he discovers that Vanessa's dead

Vanessa Lutz at her angry best, defying the wrongful authority of the Los Angeles Police Department in *Freeway*.

boyfriend was black. This bit of evidence, it seems, is enough to convince Breer of Vanessa's worth—of her potential for truth telling. She has become "authentic" to him through her relationship with an inner-city black man—a black man who bears some physical resemblance to himself. In fact, Breer becomes Vanessa's staunchest advocate—overtly venting his hostility toward Bob's high-class wife and hunting tirelessly for the evidence that will bring Bob down. Thus, in contrast to the earlier interrogation scene where Breer tries to distance himself from Vanessa by objectifying her and her exploits, eventually he seems to feel an affinity with her. Race (and poverty) do matter, he seems to suggest, even though up until this point he has been trying to deny such solidarity. Bright uses Vanessa's anger in the interrogation scene and Breer's process of discovery in the later scenes to highlight the kindred connection between Breer and Vanessa—to metaphorically think through the potential for shifting class and racial allegiances in 1990s urban America.

Freeway's interest in allegiances does not stop there, however. While Vanessa is fiercely individualistic for most of the film—and in that way lines up perfectly with the girl power ethos—she also learns to rely on other girls to help her through her various trials. Although she eventually strangles Bob in her grandmother's trailer in the final scene *without* the help of the police, the pivotal plot moment that sends her on this final quest revolves around girl bonding with her fellow inmate, Mesquita (Alanna Ubach). Initially the two are enemies in the youth detention center, but eventually they come to respect one another as they successfully plan and execute their escape. As part of a Latino gang and a convicted murderer, Mesquita represents yet another facet of the underclass of Los Angeles. Similar to Vanessa's relationship with Chopper, her relationship with Mesquita serves to highlight the allegiance she feels to other teenagers who have "been in the system"—others who are considered beyond the pale of middle-class respectability and law-abiding behavior. Vanessa's relationship to Mesquita, however, is also deeply connected to their position as women. The following scene occurs just after they have escaped the detention center and is set ironically in the backseat of Mesquita's boyfriend's car. Bright is playing with the assumption that all teenagers use "the backseat" for one thing and one thing only. In this case, however, the two girls are discussing their budding feminist awareness:

> MESQUITA: Caro, you're gonna think I'm sounding all feminist and shit. It's like, the one thing that I learned in jail is that girls gotta help out other girls. You know? Especially convict girls, cuz if they don't they'd all be fucking dead. You know?
> VANESSA: I hear what you're saying.
> MESQUITA: Okay.

Mesquita is well aware of the fact that nobody is going to watch out for girls—especially those without the standard support systems of school and family—except other girls. It is not only men and boys who stand by watching but other women as well. In fact, the film bears out Mesquita's suspicion in its depiction of adult women: they are either thoroughly enmeshed in the institutions that coerce girls—for example, the guards at the detention center—or they are too absorbed in their own lives to provide nurturance—Vanessa's mother. Intergenerational conflict—the sense that women, often feminist women in particular, are somehow failing girls—is one of the central tensions in girl power. And one of its inherent contradictions is this sense of the importance of girl bonding on the one hand and its fiercely individualistic rhetoric on the other.

It is interesting that this contradiction is in dialogue with some of the other widespread messages proliferated by mass culture about teenage girls and girl power. For example, teen magazines' emphasis on issues such as "the power of positive thinking" suggests that if you work hard enough you can achieve anything you desire. Likewise, the aspirational feminism espoused by companies like Nike projects a tough and powerful teen image; slogans like "Just Do It!" emphasize a kind of girlhood unhampered by class, gender, and racial biases. We need not worry about identity politics, this line of reasoning goes, because they are meaningless in a world dominated by individual achievement. In this sense, girl power relies heavily on the cult of the individual. Vanessa's status as a young girl without family who must rely solely on herself—and who is able through her own strength and ingenuity single-handedly to defeat Bob—also participates in this discourse of individualism.

On the other hand, the Spice Girls' liner notes—the ur-text of girl power, if you will—also emphasize the importance of one's "mates" and the need for girls to stick together. "Girls gotta help out other girls," as Mesquita says. Power, according to this formulation, is collaborative. It is strength born out of community, specifically out of a youth community. Vanessa's relationship with Mesquita also participates in this facet of the girl power ethos and suggests the necessity of solidarity among girls in particular in a culture that tends to value them very little.

Finally I return to the question I posed earlier: how do these conflicting representations of girls' strength and anger speak to our understanding of girl power as a contemporary feminist form? On the one hand, the new aggressiveness exemplified by Vanessa Lutz seems to dovetail nicely with a brand of feminism that promotes physical action over theorizing. She is the poster girl for certain third-wave feminist theorists who chastise older feminists for their supposedly anachronistic emphasis on the victimization of women. Vanessa, the film makes clear, is no victim. Simultaneously, however, the film undercuts this reading in the final scene just after she has killed Bob. We see her slumped over on the front stoop of her now deceased grandmother—her face tear-streaked and bruised; she is without family, without resources, and with nowhere to go. The film ends with her eerie laughter—and we are left wondering, where will she go next? She may have defeated the demon that was Bob, but the real demons of poverty, illiteracy, and a criminal record still exist. In fact, it is her very outlaw mentality—and her raging need to take things into her own hands in order literally to survive—that offers a critique of the ways in which girl power's tendency toward a "Just Do It!" ideology leaves those in the grip of systemic oppression completely outside the fold and, indeed, often further subjects them to it. Despite the bluster of her angry outbursts, we cannot help wondering at the film's conclusion, what exactly can this particular girl "just do"?

NOTES

1. Although there are strong, feisty female characters who serve as precedents to Vanessa, very few (aside from slasher film heroines) are American teenage girls. One notable exception is Hitchcock's Charlie in *Shadow of a Doubt* (1943), a teenage heroine who not only solves the central mystery of the film but also gets rid of the killer without the help of a Prince Charming. For aggressive women characters who fight back, see the *Alien* series (1979, 1986, and 1992) *Blue Steel* (1989).

2. As defined through the work of the Centre for Contemporary Cultural Studies in Birmingham, U.K., in the 1970s (the Birmingham School), youth subcultures are self-identified groups with "a sense of oppositional sociality, an unambiguous pleasure in style, a disruptive public identity, and a set of collective fantasies" (McRobbie 42). In other words, they adopt certain customs, relations, and material objects to create new subjective cultural meanings in opposition to the dominant culture. They are by definition both repressed and resistant. Typically, youth subcultures are specifically geographically located—for instance in the street—and display "integrated behavior, beliefs and attitudes" (Leonard 102). For more on youth subcultures see Willis; Hall and Jefferson; Hebdige; and McRobbie.

3. Tad Friend's article "Yes" sets up an overly simplistic opposition among contemporary feminists, pitting sexual-agency feminists like Naomi Wolf, Rene Denfeld, Katie Roiphe, and Camille Paglia against the anti-porn feminists Catherine McKinnon and Andrea Dworkin. Echoing Katie Roiphe's *The Morning After: Sex, Fear and Feminism on Campus*, Friend claims that "older" feminists like Dworkin and McKinnon have too long held sway on issues of sexuality within American feminist discourse, an assessment that not only ignores a long history of pro-sex activism within the feminist movement but also works to perpetuate intergenerational mistrust among feminists. He applauds the "do-me" feminists for their embrace of sexual agency—even as he simultaneously acknowledges that "do-me feminism is largely the preserve of a white female elite" (56), a critique I certainly second.

4. One notable exception to this claim would of course be the vast body of feminist literature on girls, body image, and eating disorders. See, for example, Mary Pipher's *Reviving Ophelia: Saving the Selves of Adolescent Girls,* Joan Jacobs Brumberg's *The Body Project,* Kim Chernin's *The Tyranny of Slenderness,* and Becky Thompson's *A Hunger So Wide and So Deep.*

5. There are several other girl power films from the mid-1990s I could have used in place of *Freeway.* See, for example, Annette Haywood-Carter's *Foxfire,* Jim McKay's *Girls Town,* Lisa Krueger's *Manny and Lo* (1996), Herbert Ross's *Boys on the Side* (1995), Peter Jackson's *Heavenly Creatures* (1994), Victor Nunez's *Ruby in Paradise* (1993), or Leslie Harris's *Just Another Girl on the I.R.T.* (1992).

WORKS CITED

Brown, Lyn Mikel. 1998. *Raising Their Voices: The Politics of Girls' Anger.* Cambridge, MA: Harvard University Press.

Brumberg, Joan Jacobs. 1997. *The Body Project: An Intimate History of American Girls.* New York: Random House.

Cassidy, Carol. 1999. *Girls in America: Their Stories, Their Words.* New York: TV Books.

Chernin, Kim. 1981. *The Obsession: Reflections on the Tyranny of Slenderness.* New York: Harper Colophon Books.

Clover, Carol. 1992. *Men, Women and Chain Saws: Gender in the Modern Horror Film.* Princeton: Princeton University Press.

Denfeld, Rene. 1995. *The New Victorians: A Young Woman's Challenge to the Old Feminist Order.* New York: Warner Books.

Douglas, Susan. 1997. "Girls 'n' Spice: All Things Nice?" *The Nation,* 25 August: 21.

Findlen, Barbara, ed. 1995. *ListenUp.: Voices from the Next Feminist Generation.* Seattle: Seal Press.

Friedan, Betty. 1963. *The Feminine Mystique.* New York: W. W. Norton.

Friend, Tad. 1994. "Yes." *Esquire* 121, no. 2, February: 48–56.

Hall, S., and Jefferson, T., eds. 1976. *Resistance through Rituals: Youth Sub-Cultures in Post-War Britain.* London: Hutchinson.

Hartigan, John. 1997. "Unpopular Culture: The Case of 'White Trash.'" *Cultural Studies* 11, no. 2: 316–43.

Hebdige, D. 1979. *Subculture: The Meaning of Style.* London: Methuen.

Hudson, Barbara. 1984. "Femininity and Adolescence." In *Gender and Generation,* ed. Angela McRobbie and Mica Nava, 31–53. London: McMillan.

Kearney, Mary Celeste. 1998. " 'Don't Need You:' Rethinking Identity Politics and Separatism from a Grrrl Perspective." In *Youth Culture: Iden-*

tity in a Postmodern World, ed. Jonathon S. Epstein, 148–88. Malden, MA: Blackwell.

Lemish, Dafna. 1998. "Spice Girls' Talk: A Case Study in the Development of Gendered Identity." In *Millennium Girls: Today's Girls around the World,* ed. Sherrie Innes, 145–67. Lanham, MD: Rowman and Littlefield.

Lentz, Kirsten Marthe. 1993. "The Popular Pleasures of Female Revenge (Or Rage Bursting in a Blaze of Gunfire)." *Cultural Studies* 7, no. 3: 374–405.

Leonard, Marion. 1998. "Paper Planes: Travelling the New Grrrl Geographies." In *Cool Places: Geographies of Youth Cultures,* ed. Tracey Skelton and Gill Valentine, 101–18. London: Routledge.

Lewis, Jon. 1992. *The Road to Romance and Ruin: Teen Films and Youth Culture.* New York: Routledge.

McRobbie, Angela. 1991. "Settling Accounts with Subcultures: A Feminist Critique." In *Feminism and Youth Culture.* New York: Routledge, 26–43.

Munk, Nina. 1997. "Girl Power!" *Fortune,* 8 December: 33.

Pipher, Mary. 1994. *Reviving Ophelia: Saving the Selves of Adolescent Girls.* New York: Ballantine Books.

Press, Joy. 1997. "Notes on Girl Power: The Selling of Softcore Feminism." *Village Voice,* 23 September: 61.

Roiphe, Katie. 1995. *The Morning After: Sex, Fear and Feminism on Campus.* Boston: Little Brown.

Thompson, Becky W. 1994. *A Hunger So Wide and So Deep: American Women Speak Out on Eating Problems.* Minneapolis: University of Minnesota Press.

Willis, Paul. 1977. *Learning to Labour: How Working Class Kids Get Working Class Jobs.* Westmead, U.K.: Saxon House.

chapter 13

The Nerdly Girl and Her Beautiful Sister

Timothy Shary

Young people are often occupied by intellectual pursuits; after all, most children between the ages of five and eighteen spend much of their time in school, acquiring not only the basic knowledge they may need to ascend to adulthood but also important social skills and coping strategies that are vital to surviving childhood. Yet when children are seen in American movies, they are most often depicted outside the classroom, and even when they are shown in school they rarely seem to have much interest in their studies. This pattern may not be so difficult to explain. Just as adults may not find entertainment in watching films about the daily drudgery of most people's lives, so children would likely resist films about the supposed enjoyment of school activities most of them probably find tedious or even odious.

The films that have nonetheless endeavored to portray young people within a school setting or exercising their intelligence in creative ways have yielded a number of interesting patterns: movie high schools after World War II became symbols of postwar excesses (whereas before the war, the rare ones seen onscreen symbolized proper cultural assimilation), with alienated middle-class kids derailed by an anomie utterly alien to adult culture;[1] high schools of the 1980s were suddenly filled with libidinous teens engaged in carnal contests (for example, *Losin' It* [1982], *Risky Business* [1983], and *The Joy of Sex* [1984]); science was a popular field of study for youth before the 1990s (as in *Real Genius* [1985], *The Manhattan Project* [1986], and *Deadly Friend* [1986]), but the scant studying that goes on in contemporary youth films is more likely to focus around the arts. Each of these patterns is revealing of changing cultural trends, as are a number of other patterns involving racial and class differences among school youth, the role of teachers, and the influence of parents.

One of the most compelling and pernicious patterns of school-age youth in films is reflected in the way girls are represented in comparison to boys. In real life girls are just as likely (if not more so) to excel in education, but the number of girls in movies who demonstrate intellectual proficiency is clearly fewer than the number of boys. Worse yet, smart girl characters are typically shown paying a price for their intellect, in the form of derision, self-contempt, or ostracism. Smart boys in films are also similarly punished, but they most often rise above their initial frustration and win acceptance while retaining their intellectual power. Most films actually suggest to girls that intelligence is a burden more than an asset; more valuable assets that tend to grant girls success (popularity and respect) are fashion sense, physical beauty, agreeable attitude, and the attainment of a boyfriend. The few films that have attempted to celebrate girls gaining power through knowledge have not been celebrated at the box office.

This essay demonstrates this substantial problem in the representation of young women through an analysis of "smart girl" roles in American movies over the past few decades. Along the way, I will make various comparisons to images of smart boys as well, but my argument hinges on the dichotomous depiction of girls (and here I generally concentrate on teenage girls) who have either been reduced to the stereotypical "nerd" role traditionally used to ridicule smart boys or been debased by another dilemma that generally diminishes their intellectual authority.

The nerdly image is one of gawky appearance, social discomfort, and personal confusion; virtually all characters so portrayed have as their main motive the transformation of their image from unflatteringly ridiculous to respected, and many boy characters achieve this, as in *Class* (1983), *Three O'Clock High* (1987), *Class Act* (1992), and *Angus* (1995). That nerdly girl characters often face greater obstacles, even though the same opportunities for transformation are available to them, indicates that if the movie industry—along with the glam culture of magazines and television—is aware of the difficulty girls have in managing their image it nonetheless persists in conditioning them to appreciate themselves (and each other) for their image, not their intelligence. This is an especially troubling development considering how many films appear to be offering empowering messages for girls when ultimately they still minimize the power of knowledge and emphasize the power of beauty.

Beauty is often the source of conflict for non-nerd smart girls, who usually get attention for their pretty looks and have trouble ne-gotiating their intelligence. Even the proud and stylish smart girl character who avoids stereotypical nerd codings finds that she rep-resents some sort of threat—to boys, to society, to herself—one that films alleviate by typically depicting her as poor, shy, neurotic, or irrational. Portrayed as a nerd or not, the smart girl does not appear well-adjusted and happy, whereas less intellectual girls in other films do, for example, *Valley Girl* (1983), *Girls Just Want to Have Fun* (1985), *Can't Buy Me Love* (1987), *Don't Tell Mom the Babysitter's Dead* (1991), *Clueless* (1995), and *American Pie* (1999).

The Evolution of Smart Girl Roles

Teenagers were an essentially uncharted population until after World War II, when gradually a separate identity for late adolescents began to emerge in popular media (thanks in part to the work of various developmental psychologists). Movies and the new medium of television offered a bipolar image of teens, who were either clean-cut good kids or roughhouse rabble-rousers in dungarees. The for-mer tended to listen to their parents, go to school, and speak with eloquent pride about their community, whereas the latter did all they could to disrupt their community, showing their contempt for authority and lack of direction (Doherty 1–16). Movies were more likely to showcase the rebels than was television, which catered to a more sensitive audience and thus highlighted the generally compla-cent adolescent in shows such as "The Adventures of Ozzie and Har-riet" (1952), "Father Knows Best" (1954), and "Leave It to Beaver" (1957). Some movies did strike a moral balance within a bipolar character, such as Jim Stark (James Dean) in *Rebel Without a Cause* (1955). Still, the majority of these young roles in both television and film were male, and few showed any intellectual promise.

By the 1960s, especially as youths raised their voices in the political turmoil of the decade, images of teens were becoming more complex as society continued to identify characteristics within the youth population that made kids seem distinct from adults. This led to not only more films about teens but more about teen girls, who were nonetheless often shown in negative terms, particularly when they appeared to have any intellectual ambitions. In *Splendor in the Grass* (1961), the promise of Wilma Dean (Natalie Wood) is ruined after she goes crazy from sexual and familial anxiety. *David and Lisa* (1962) featured Janet Margolin as a similarly troubled young woman, whose capacity for love is warped by her schizophrenic incapacity to deal with life. Pookie (Liza Minnelli) in *The Sterile Cuckoo* (1969) was a bolder, quirkier teen, but alas her spunky sapience was also not enough to save her from a breakdown. In *Last Summer* (1969), Catherine Burns played an unattractive smart girl who so disrupts a circle of friends that they eventually rape her.[2]

The 1970s were a relatively fallow period for teen films until the end of the decade erupted in a flurry of slasher-style horror films, as exemplified by *Halloween* (1978), which curiously began to showcase a new type of young heroine whom Carol Clover labels the "Final Girl," and whose "smartness, gravity, competence in mechanical and other practical matters, and sexual reluctance set her apart from the other girls" and make her an ironic match for the killer (40). Despite the potential power within the numerous Final Girl characters, and the fact that their skills ultimately save them, these roles were founded on the sustained torture of these same girls presented for spectatorial stimulation. The Final Girl's insights ensured that she would be the most abused character in any teen horror film, as her sadomasochistic drive to eradicate the killer guaranteed her continuing terror. This trend has continued in teen horror films ever since, notably the *Nightmare on Elm Street* series (1984–94) and the *Scream* trilogy (1996–2000).

There followed a distinct shift in teen films during the 1980s. Not only were many more being made (for reasons including the relocation of theaters to shopping malls and loosening moral codes for underage sexual activity), but more girls were appearing as protagonists. Yet few movies of the 1980s featured noticeably bright teen girls, and those that did soon revealed the split image of young female intelligence that persists in films to this day: nerdly girls are marginalized and non-nerd smart girls are suppressed. Conditions for nerdly boys were arguably much better. They enjoyed more visible recognition, especially after the success of *Revenge of the Nerds* (1984). Geeky boys had a veritable poster child in the persona of Anthony Michael Hall, whose prominent turns in *Sixteen Candles* (1984), *Weird Science* (1985), and *The Breakfast Club* (1985) brought a certain sensitivity to the nerd role; and they usually succeeded in overcoming the social and/or personal obstacles that their nerd status engendered.[3] Boy nerds did indeed exact a "revenge" on their oppressors through triumphing over the adversity that their intelligence apparently induced, or, as Joseph Gelmis put it in his review of the 1986 film *Lucas*, "The nerd is to the high school movies of the '80s what the rebel without a cause was to the high school flicks of 30 years ago: an unlikely hero" (5). This comment points to the latent advantage for boys of being a nerd, but Gelmis does not draw out the distinct *disadvantage* of appearing nerdly for girls. The title character of *Lucas* wins the respect of his peers after trying to prove his mettle in a football game; his admiring fellow nerd Rina (Winona Ryder) is left in the background, waiting timidly for him to realize that she is a better option than the kindhearted older cheerleader he has been fixated on.

Contemporary Nerdly Girls

Some teen films in the past twenty years have featured minor female nerd roles often secondary characters to male protagonists, as in *Lucas*, *My Science Project* (1985), and *Born to Be Wild* (1995), but only three have actually focused on a nerdly girl as the main character: *She's Out of Control* (1989), *Welcome to the Dollhouse* (1996) and *She's All That* (1999). Inclusive of these films, the image of nerdly girls has been used as shorthand for the torment that awaits smart women later in life if they do not find a way to become more physically attractive, and thus the narratives about nerdly girls are built on an inverted Pygmalionesque pathos, as the character attempts to redirect her intellectual sophistication to a social sophistication.

In fact, if the nerdly girl does not transform she faces a certain doom, as in *A Nightmare on Elm Street 4: The Dream Master* (1988), which offers the lone example of an African American nerd girl in all of youth cinema. Sheila (Toy Newkirk) has adjusted to her nerdly image (which is amplified by her being asthmatic), and so her fate is not to become a Final Girl but to perish at the hands of the phantom killer. *No Secrets* (1991) presents a nerdly girl within a trio of female friends who unwisely take in a dangerous drifter on a vacation. Despite her well-reasoned suspicions, Clare (Heather Fairfield) has such bewildering self-disgrace that she becomes increasingly infatuated with the villain, even after the other girls tell him to leave. Clare then goes after him dotingly, as if to demonstrate her daring and desirability, anticipating some sense of liberation that never comes. She does not perish at the hands of this killer but is left with the redoubtable recognition that she still is not as accepted as her two more attractive friends are.

She's Out of Control offers the strange equation of young female intelligence with paternal power as it focuses on the fears of

Doug (Tony Danza), father to fifteen-year-old Katie (Ami Dolenz), who wears the ubiquitous nerdly braces and incredibly thick glasses. Doug appreciates his daughter's dedication to her studies and her safely tepid relationship with the awkward boy next door. Then one day Doug's girlfriend takes Katie on a life-changing escapade— shopping for new clothes and contact lenses, getting a new hairstyle, and having her braces removed—that instantly, and thereafter effortlessly, makes Katie the obsessive object of every local boy's desire. Doug's control of his formally undesirable daughter is thus thrown into jeopardy, and much of the film glosses over the problematic pleasure that Katie finds in her new and superficial image to play up the humorous terror of a father facing his little girl's blooming sexuality. Of course, Katie's sexuality is activated through mere alterations in her appearance, after she sheds the symbols of her awkward adolescence. She then proceeds to run through the affections of various boyfriends with little regard for her feelings or theirs. Regardless of her intelligence before she was transformed, she does not stop to consider the consequences of her changes or her actions.

Katie does eventually show some resolve in resisting a potential date rapist, declaring that she will not lose her virginity to a guy who is not "special" to her, but by this point the narrative has clearly moved away from demonstrating her intellectual integrity to revealing her moral integrity, to showing that this "smart girl" has gained her greatest pride in being a "good girl,"—a pride that is even more important to her father. The story leaves Katie on a plane to Europe for a school trip, with her still awkward neighbor right beside her, suggesting a return to the originally safer relationship that her social ascent had let her abandon. It is as if she recognizes that Daddy was right all along now that she is, at last, back under control.

After a general shortage in American teen films during the early 1990s, when films about violent teenage boys were popular, *Welcome to the Dollhouse* presented perhaps the gloomiest prognosis for nerdly girls. Dawn Weiner (Heather Matarazzo) appears less intellectual than do past nerd characters: her seventh-grade outcast status is assured by her dressing in clothes that are more customary for third grade and wearing the trademark thick glasses. What makes Dawn a nerd to be reckoned with from the start is her intense anxiety about her image, which she recognizes but cannot seem to change. The other girls at school clearly dress differently and aggressively intimidate Dawn (one even forces Dawn to defecate while she watches, a complex psychological degradation that other films have never risked depicting), but instead of cowering into shyness, Dawn has learned to fight back or, more often, to vent her anger in other ways. Her saccharine little sister, appropriately named Missy (Daria Kalinina), is an easy target for much of Dawn's displaced contempt for her family and a culture that values femininity in delicate, coy terms—Missy prances about in a tutu and ingratiates herself to her parents with excessive innocence—and Dawn abhors Missy's blatantly puerile means of gaining attention. Dawn seems to have little interest in any such acceptance until she develops a crush on her older brother's friend Steve (Eric Mabius).

This crush makes Dawn consider her appearance even more seriously, as does the violent interest a delinquent classmate, Brandon (Brendan Sexton Jr.), shows in her. Brandon threatens to rape Dawn, but in an unexpected revelation he shows Dawn that he is more innocently attracted to her, even if he does not want anyone else to know. Brandon's sensitivity thus becomes an interesting foil to Dawn's: both students want the affection of someone who cannot provide it (Dawn tells Brandon she is in love with Steve, but she still wants to be friends), and both face the embarrassing discovery that the images they have developed deny them a sense of security and belonging. When Dawn makes her ultimate desperate plea for Steve to join her "Special People" club, he tells her that the term stands for "retarded," which is both a cruel way of rejecting her and a subtle way of indicating that Dawn has yet to resolve her naive and pathetic need for social validation. After Brandon runs away from home, Dawn realizes that Steve was unattainable and Brandon was uncontainable. In the end, instead of finding a way out, she must endure five more years of school.

Indeed, the film proposes that Dawn can only wait and hope for nature to bring better options, and that perhaps this powerlessness is integrally linked to her gender positioning: unable to capitalize on her smarts and savvy, the nerdly girl must hope for cultural change that will accord her a more respected status, since the changes she has made or can make on her own are clearly not recognized by those around her. Director Todd Solondz stated his own clarification of Dawn's essence as distinguished from her appearance: "This is not about an ugly kid. It's about a kid who is called ugly" (Cross 26). After Steve rejects her and Brandon runs away, a poignant closing shot shows Dawn within the confines of a busload of classmates, isolated

Dawn vents her anger by decapitating her sister's doll. *Welcome to the Dollhouse.*

and alone—much more so than the many male nerd characters in earlier films, who had at least won their crush's attention if not some friends.

She's All That in many ways offers a more insidious depiction of a teenage female nerd, in a plot that borrows directly from *Pygmalion*. Brainy Laney (Rachel Leigh Cook) is ridiculed by the popular kids for her artistic aspirations and her social insecurity, until popular jock Zack (Freddie Prinze Jr.) takes on a bet that he can change even this "loser" into a desirable girl. He does this not out of any affection but to save face after his girlfriend dumps him, which is why he accepts the task of not only romancing the wallflower but turning her into a prom queen. In this way an explicit transformation narrative is set in motion, in which once again an already pretty performer simply needs to doff her glasses to start looking attractive.

At first Laney shows an informed suspicion of Zack's intentions, which makes her seem confidently independent, yet she gradually gives in to the lure of being accepted, despite the fact that the popular crowd persistently resists her. In this way, the film is harsher than many of the previous nerd tales, for Laney so openly compromises her sense of identity in spite of herself that her efforts appear truly embarrassing. Further, Zack's unusual intelligence does not appear to impede his injurious manipulation of Laney. He boosts his inflated ego by being not only the motivation for her change but the organizer of it. This is somewhat alleviated by an ending in which Zack finally realizes that he has really fallen in love with her, yet Laney still retains the artificial appearance that he has desired all along, and though she may have gained some pride in winning the prize boy, she is still unaccepted and essentially unknown. *She's All That* suggests that its heroine is indeed all that—smart, comely, talented, caring, resilient—and concludes that such great qualities do not guarantee happiness without social and masculine endorsement.

One recent film offers an unexpectedly stinging statement on the current state of nerdly girls in American films. The protagonist of *Never Been Kissed* (1999) is not a teen but a twenty-five-year-old reporter named Josie (Drew Barrymore), who is assigned to return to her high school to do a special report. Josie is both terrified and thrilled by this prospect, for she still lives with the torment of being a nerdly girl and views the assignment as an opportunity to revise her identity. (Presumably her extra weight and braces made her unappealing as a teen; now only her shy smarts keep her from socially integrating.) Josie initially befriends the cast-off teen prodigies she would have allied with when younger, but she is more triumphant after being invited to join the school's popular elite after she learns to feign late-1990s coolness by wearing the right clothes and dumbing down. She even begins to overcome the dilemma of her repressed sexuality—which has been exaggerated by her peers—after she shares a crush with a teacher. Thus, her transformation is complete: she has been able to gain the love and attention she had been denied through showing that a nerd can reform. Armed with this confidence, she berates her cohorts at the school prom for not appreciating each other for who they really are.

There are obvious ironies in this message of acceptance, but the greatest is that it had been available to boy nerds since the 1980s in movies such as *The Breakfast Club, Lucas,* and *The Beat* (1988)—in fact, an almost identical scene was played out in *Can't Buy Me Love* with a boy nerd more successfully defending his fellow nerds—and these characters actually gained acceptance. As the 1990s closed, nerdly girls in American movies were still being told that their acceptance in society was unlikely: movies like *She's All*

That and *Never Been Kissed* were visibly demonstrating that for young women, being smart but unattractive is a dangerous combination of qualities that can only lead to grief.[4]

Non-Nerd Smart Girls

The number of films featuring socially attractive and confident smart girls has been greater than those featuring nerdly girls, but the vast majority have never been popular with audiences. Many of these films show their heroines initially using their intellect to their advantage until they encounter the negative consequences of their sagacity: men become suspicious of them, they become corrupted by their drive for perfection, and they feel disconnected from their peers. Unlike the nerd transformation that relies on physical change, most non-nerd smart girls transform by simply sublimating their intellect into achieving recognition for their attitude or style. Even in movies where a girl's intelligence is a structuring aspect of the narrative, either the smart girl is made to minimize her intellectual qualities or those qualities negatively affect her.

As with nerdly girls, non-nerd smart girls have been used to support male characters on whom the narrative focuses. Unlike nerdly girls, however, smart girls are the romantic objects of less intelligent boys, at least briefly, in 1980s films. *Pretty in Pink* (1986) offers something of a hybrid in Andie (Molly Ringwald), whose outcast status among her peers more clearly arises from her working-class background than her funky appearance and good grades. Andie's wisdom and wit seem to alleviate her lack of acceptance until one of the rich guys in her class becomes attracted to her, and then, like other excessively vulnerable smart girl characters, she compromises her self-respect (and a dear friend) to gain the affection of her popular crush.

Say Anything . . . (1989) is the story of just-graduated Lloyd Dobler (John Cusack), an aspiring kickboxer who rather impulsively decides to ask out the pretty class valedictorian, Diane (Ione Skye), a girl who has apparently been so absorbed in her studies over the years that she never made a single friend at school. Sheila Benson observes that Diane finds in Lloyd a "funny, tender, unquenchable optimist who is at the same time her passport to the real world" (1), and Lloyd's sincerity and affection soon become her means to the self-discovery that her doting father has always suppressed. Her father eventually grows suspicious of Lloyd's slack ambitions and coerces

Diane to break up with him, but this is a film where the smart girl's intellectual and moral integrity are *not* compromised. She discovers that her father is an embezzler and resolves to travel to England on a prized fellowship with Lloyd, who—she comes to realize—offers an emotional connection just as valuable as her academic pursuits. Further, despite Lloyd's pain on first being dumped by Diane, his desire for her is founded not on her looks or popularity but on a confident fulfillment rarely afforded to teens in films.

Alas, the breakthrough that *Say Anything . . .* appeared to inaugurate in 1989 was short-lived. Two more films soon followed featuring the smart girl and dim guy romantic pairing, *How I Got Into College* (1989) and *Cool as Ice* (1991), but the first film, like many to follow, made its smart heroine a neurotic overachiever who cannot enjoy herself; while the second was a vehicle for rapper Vanilla Ice, whose ego so overshadowed the smart girl his character falls for (Kristin Minter) that she was reduced to a mere prop. The fact that only a handful of 1980s films even featured attractive smart girls is appalling, although worse yet, these characters would remain equally rare throughout the 1990s.

The most disturbing pattern in the depiction of smart girls has been their image as corrupted by their own ambitions, a pattern that emerged only in the 1990s and was perhaps first evident in *No Secrets*. A more troubling example is *Just Another Girl on the I.R.T.* (1993), which is one of the rare features to focus on an African American young woman, the rebellious Chantel (Ariyan Johnson), a Brooklyn eleventh-grader filled with racial pride, street-tough attitude, and academic acumen. Yet after she unintentionally becomes pregnant, she makes matters worse by vacillating about what to do: she first contemplates abortion, then tries to cover her condition with baggy clothes, and ultimately delivers the baby with her boyfriend at her side. After impulsively abandoning the newborn in a trash heap, the two soon realize their mistake when the baby is rescued, and Chantel then plans to be a good mother while she pursues her educational and career goals.

Chantel is a refreshing girl character in that her attitude seems to naturally empower her resistence to conformity, and indeed, since this black female teen rebel is virtually unique in youth films, one can easily criticize the film's less-than-positive message about its protagonist. The question of why such an otherwise aware and assertive young woman would become so desperate as to consider infanticide demands closer consideration, if only because the film is calling attention to the difference between the academic and social struggles of high school and the more ambiguous and consequential struggles of adult life, which Chantel is not ready to face. Chantel is in her established element, mouthing back to her teachers and talking trash with her girlfriends, but no teenager, regardless of race, is ready to handle the responsibilities and requirements of parenthood, or so the film initially seems to suggest. Then with its ending, *Just Another Girl* implies that although the transition to adulthood is tough, one simply has to live up to it. As David Denby observes, Chantel "manages to triumph without losing or learning anything" (60). The film's title is all the more apt because Chantel is *not* just another girl that one would see in other teen films, until you consider that her intelligence and attitude are shown to flounder under the pressure of her moral problems. Such are the consequences for many otherwise smart girls in 1990s youth cinema.

Alicia Silverstone made two films in which she played smart girls before her bigger star turn in *Clueless* (1995), where her character seems to revel in her limited range of knowledge. In *The Crush* (1993) she plays Darian, whose intellect and salacious manner are at first attractive to an older man. When he rejects her advances, she dives into a downward spiral of deviance, if not psychosis. Her character in *True Crime* (1995), a Catholic schoolgirl predictably named Mary, is not as dangerous, although her curiosity about solving a local murder spree leads to her unknowingly befriending the killer, then even more improbably losing her virginity to him, and finally, after solving the murders, killing him. The film thus offers Mary as a smart survivor, yet takes advantage of her criminal insights by showing how they corrupt her.

Perhaps the most criminal depiction of young female intelligence can be found in the complex thriller *Wild Things* (1998), in which Sam (Matt Dillon), a respected high school counselor, joins two of his female students, Suzie (Neve Campbell) and Kelly (Denise Richards) in an extortion scam. Though Sam is clearly the oldest of the three and is ostensibly calling the shots, Suzie (a secret supergenius) turns out to be the one who is manipulating the other two, which is made more ironic by her low-class status and her assumed lack of intelligence. She also shrewdly employs her sexuality, as she enacts a pseudo-lesbian attraction to Kelly and disarms Sam with her ultimate lack of interest in him. Suzie's true perspicacity and determination render her the most dangerous and yet most sympathetic of the film's villainous characters, her concealed sense of purpose effectively transcending her supposed carnal anguish and allowing her to kill off her accomplices and succeed in a more astonishing crime than they had envisioned.[5]

In many ways, *Election* (1999) presents the most menacing portrait of young female ambition. The story begins with Tracy Flick (Reese Witherspoon), an overachieving high schooler running for student council president who sparks the ire of her advisor, Mr. McAllister (Matthew Broderick). He not only harbors a distorted attraction to her but fears that Tracy's implicit lust for power would only grow more monstrous if she won. As McAllister tries to thwart her efforts, Tracy engages in her own unethical conduct, raising the stakes of the generally inconsequential election to a validation of all her political dreams and personal desires: winning would not only verify her popularity, it would chase away her self-doubt. Like other morally challenged smart girls, Tracy wages her war of acceptance in solitary terms, losing sight of the reasons why she is striving to attain her goals. The election becomes a contest of wills between Tracy and McAllister, as the two navigate through a series of shifty schemes until his greater transgression of rigging the ballots ensures not only her victory but his self-destruction. The ending suggests that women like Tracy—who implicitly goes on to claw her way up through the ranks of the federal government—may become unconsciously sullied by their own drive to succeed and may fail to use their intelligence righteously, regardless of their intentions.

To be fair, there have been a few more enterprising roles for smart girls in recent American movies, although in each the protagonists continue to confront the problems of patriarchy and/or their own ambition, knowing full well the difficulties their intelligence brings. *Just One of the Guys* (1985) was one of the first in this regard, as it depicts a talented female journalism student who has to pose as a boy to earn an internship and is finally taken seriously as a writer as a result of her masquerade. By the film's end, however, she resorts to a more passively feminized role to secure a boyfriend. *Space Camp* (1986) features two attractive smart girls within a crew of teenagers who inadvertently become pilots on the space shuttle. One of the girls is racked by constant concerns about her skills, and both endure the misgivings of their male colleagues, yet they prevail in safely controlling the spacecraft. Unfortunately, such depictions of girls involved with science have been essentially nonexistent ever since. *Stand and Deliver* (1987) offers an especially inspiring story of smart girls (and boys) excelling in their schoolwork, since the teen characters are all underprivileged barrio youth, although the story focuses primarily on their dedicated teacher.

In the 1990s, a few more teen films would offer relatively positive depictions of smart girls, including *The Unbelievable Truth* (1990), in which a mildly neurotic but bright high school senior survives her strange family and an even stranger first love, and *The Incredibly True Adventure of Two Girls in Love* (1995), which not only offers one of the rare lesbian *and* interracial pairings in all of teen cinema, but also shows how the smarter African American character is able to gracefully help her white girlfriend finish high school.

And then there was *Hackers* (1995), which was the single film of the cyber-oriented 1990s to delve into the world of teens and their computers, thus perhaps indicating a general disinterest on the part of studios for dealing with the ever-threatening issues of youth intelligence in general. The story focuses on Dade (Jonny Lee Miller), an eighteen-year-old super-hacker who becomes attracted to fellow computer whiz Kate (Angelina Jolie), the most sexualized smart girl in all of youth cinema: her tight clothes, excessive makeup, and numerous make-out scenes with a dull boyfriend (whom she apparently uses for nothing but sex) give her less prominent computer skills an additional charge. She becomes an object of Dade's desire both on the level of intellectual competition (as when the two set up a hacking contest to see who is better) and in terms of alleviating his sensitive virginal status—she actually becomes his ticket out of juvenile cyber-fantasy and into mature masculine development. Kate is not only respected among her all-male cohorts, they are in awe of her prowess. After she helps her friends take down a corrupt computer operator, she pairs up with Dade, who convinces her to wear a revealing dress on their first date, suggesting that they have been able to "program" each other to their liking. For Dade this means bedizening Kate, but for Kate it means convincing Dade of her intellectual *and* sexual potency. Alas, this potent combination has not been presented positively for girls in any American teen film since.

The nerdly girl and her pretty but equally tormented counterpart are apparently still common fixtures in teen films and will likely continue to be as long as female intelligence is viewed with discomfort and resistance. These young female characters are still turning up in plots where the emphasis is on character transformation or confrontation with an unaccepting culture. Sadly, such narratives are in some ways true to the reality of patriarchal society, but why more films are not made about teen girls less tormented by their intelligence is a distinct mystery, especially as girls continue to gain prominence and power in popular culture. The association of girls' intelligence with ugliness, neurosis, intimidation, and immorality has only served to disenfranchise and discourage young women who aspire to great intellectual achievements *and* social acceptance. Films need to be made that show young women fulfilling these aspirations, as they do in daily life.

Notes

1. Jon Lewis makes a particularly harsh argument on the anomie of youth in films (35–55).
2. It is worth noting Hollywood's endorsement of these tragically tormented roles for young female stars: Wood, Minnelli, and Burns were all nominated for Oscars.
3. I cannot help but point out that Anthony Michael Hall went on to play the richest nerd in the world, Bill Gates, in *Pirates of Silicon Valley* (1999). Due to the resistance to images of intellectual women (and the career risks involved in portraying them), I do not believe a teenage actress would be cast to play a nerd in more than one film during her career, nor would she enjoy the success that Hall did in the mid-1980s. Thus far, none have.
4. Another 1999 film is worth mentioning in this regard: *10 Things I Hate About You* features an outcast girl whose supposed shame is not her intelligence or looks but her *feminist attitude.* She is so filled with haughty contempt for "misogynistic consumer culture" that she draws the ridicule of all around her, at least until she is systematically transformed by a paid paramour who unexpectedly falls in love with her. The story takes up *Taming of the Shrew* to showcase the difference between the protagonist and her younger, far more popular (because normalized) sister, and the most compelling aspect of this update is not the shrew's independent spirit but her more explicit conflict in balancing her contemporary politics with her tacit longing for conformist romance.
5. "Evil women" whose power arises from their sexuality and intelligence have been popular since at least the 1940s emergence of femmes fatale in films noir, and seemed to find a resurgence in the past generation as a reaction to women gaining professional power (for example, *Fatal Attraction* [1987], *The Temp* [1993], *Disclosure* [1994], and *American Beauty* [1999]). The fact that teen films have been recently demonstrating the supposedly corruptive effects of female intelligence and

sexuality suggests that this tradition is shifting its concerns (and fascinations) to a younger population of women.

WORKS CITED

Benson, Sheila. 1989. Review of *Say Anything. Los Angeles Times,* 14 April, Calendar: 1.

Clover, Carol. 1992. *Men, Women, and Chain Saws: Gender in the Modern Horror Film.* Princeton: Princeton University Press.

Cross, Alice. 1996. "Surviving Adolescence with Dignity: An Interview with Todd Solondz." *Cineaste* 22, no. 3: 24–26.

Denby, David. 1993. Review of *Just Another Girl on the I.R.T. New York,* 5 April: 60.

Doherty, Thomas. 1988. *Teenagers and Teenpics: The Juvenilization of American Movies in the 1950s.* Boston: Unwin Hyman.

Gelmis, Joseph. 1986. Review of *Lucas. Newsday,* 28 March, sec. 3: 5.

Lewis, Jon. 1992. *The Road to Romance and Ruin: Teen Films and Youth Culture.* New York: Routledge.

chapter 14

Maternity, Murder, and Monsters: Legends of Babysitter Horror

Miriam Forman-Brunell

The bad babysitter. This essay aims to illuminate this implicit yet pervasive characterization of female adolescent caregivers in American popular culture. Since the late 1960s, audiences have encountered numerous representations of babysitters that are overwhelmingly critical, often sexual, and frequently frightening. Although actual babysitting most often proceeds without a serious hitch, the problems inherent in it have been widely and sometimes wantonly exaggerated, as revealed on many levels from the pragmatic to the cultural. A study of the babysitter—as opposed to girls in other roles—requires specific attention to a variety of productions, some of which are pornographic or quasi-pornographic. Typically in popular and pornographic movies, made-for-television movies, and the preteen fiction these have inspired, the protean babysitter—whether represented as virgin or vixen, victim or villain—generates disorder by threatening the safety of children, the stability of family life, and the fidelity of marriage.

Inscribed on the culturally constructed babysitter is a wide-ranging discourse about female adolescents as self-absorbed, unpredictable, irrational, irresponsible, unreliable, inscrutable, unruly, unstable, incompetent, sexually irresistible, unrealistic, pleasure seeking, and profit hungry. Why have adolescent girls been represented as deceptively compliant and dangerously unreliable? What historical forces have informed these dominant cultural representations of adolescent caretakers? Do representations of bad babysitters lead employers to suspect theirs of wrongdoing? What impact might such representations have on modern American girls for whom babysitting is often the quintessential form of inaugural female employment?

Informed by debates in women's history, cultural history, family history, girls' culture, and feminist film theory, I argue that the trope of the adolescent babysitter has been shaped by the changes wrought by the sexual revolution, youth culture, and second-wave feminism. These profound historical transformations challenged older customs and traditional assumptions. They also raised new expectations and opportunities that unleashed cultural anxieties about the economic order and social and sexual disorder. A fundamental shift in family, feminine, and childhood ideals that recontexualized relationships between spouses, between the sexes, and between generations produced fears and fantasies about the future course of female adolescence. Changing definitions of femininity found expression in the cultural construct of the babysitter who has reflected, reinforced, exaggerated, and distorted our culture's ambivalence about gender roles since the 1960s (Douglas 13).

As Carroll Smith-Rosenberg has demonstrated about male adolescents during another tumultuous period in our nation's past, fears about a changing social order that challenges patriarchal power and adult authority give rise to popular imagery and folk legends. Beginning in the 1960s, the pop icon and folk figure of the bad babysitter emerged to mitigate feelings of powerlessness "by deflecting and partially distorting change and thus bringing it within the control of the imagination" (90). Such mimetic and semiotic "texts" as movies, fiction, and urban legends in which the bad babysitter is represented shed light on ambivalent attitudes, beliefs, and perceptions about adolescent girls. In her study of female adolescents in American movies before 1960, historian Georganne Scheiner has shown how girls were "problematized as signaling both generational change and societal instability in times of flux or crisis" (144).

Embedded in the liminal adolescent babysitter are attempts to contain conflict, change, and contradictory fears and fantasies about economic, sexual, and social issues. The babysitter is located at the ambiguous borders between culture and chaos, childhood and adulthood, girlhood and womanhood. The economically marginal babysitter launching her career as a wage earner exists only in the uncertain domain of house-as-workplace. Like Rosie the Riveter, the figure of the babysitter conveys "double-edged messages . . . of resistance as well as submission, empowerment as well as containment" (Dabakis 196). Will the babysitter support domesticity or try to destroy it? Will she undermine the work ethic that babysitting also represents or will she indulge in a leisure culture like her employers "out for the night"? Will the sexually nubile sitter seduce husbands and threaten wives?

Hired to keep the place clean and safe, the iconic sitter makes a mess out of living rooms and of lives. Hired to be the cop who maintains order, she becomes a criminal. Sitters are suspiciously watched, harshly criticized, unduly punished, and occasionally done in. Hired to provide safety, the babysitter is a magnet for maniacs. The male monster who stalks and threatens girls in popular movies and teen fiction represents a culture's ambivalence about the pursuit of female autonomy that babysitting—as a symbol of traditional gender roles and as a form of female employment and empowerment—represents. Ambivalence about the adolescent babysitter can be read in the mixed messages encoded in the many monsters that inhabit babysitter narratives and embody the culture's contradictions about women. For example, male monsters destroy both the domesticity that the sitter represents and the ideology that contains her. In the construct of the Other Monster, the murderous and mad babysitter similarly manifests both anti-feminist fears and feminist hopes.

Before World War II, "babysitting" as we know it today did not exist. Instead, "minding the children" was the ungendered activity of girls and boys, women and men, neighbors and kin. After the war, babysitting emerged as a "petticoat monopoly" dominated by white, teenage girls eager to supplement their allowance as workers. Yet postwar parents found much about their teenage sitters they did not like. Suburban couples railed against those who charged too much and cared too little about "Junior" and his fictitious sister, "Jane." Frustrations with self-absorbed teens shaped by a new youth culture and by wartime employment opportunities for teens and women found expression in numerous magazines and in the postwar classic *Sitting Pretty* (1948). In that popular movie, the teenage babysitter destabilizes family life and subverts gender roles: she prefers partying with friends over playing with children. Although the problems associated with hiring an adolescent girl who had been shaped by the "cultural practices of bobby-soxers" would persist throughout the 1950s, the innocuous role she played in the popular imagination was verging on change (Formanek-Brunell 61–82; Scheiner 143).

During the 1960s, increased suburbanization and mobility led to greater geographic isolation. Families were separated from a wider network of kin and had to turn to girls about whom they knew very little to care for their children. Occasional articles about kidnappers and child abusers warned parents not to trust "just anyone" ("Baby-

Sitter Is Murdered"; "Parents of Babies Warned"). In 1959, J. Edgar Hoover, director of the FBI, had urged parents to hire only the "reliable" ("FBI Director Hoover Warns"). But in the 1960s, apprehensions, suspicions, and parental guilt in suburbia's uncertain refuge were less likely to be expressed in the mass media. Instead, uncertainty found expression in the informal exchange of urban legends.

According to folklorist Jan Harold Brunvand, "the legends we tell, as with any folklore, reflect many of the hopes, fears, and anxieties of our time" (2). "Nobody really likes babysitters," who are a distortion of the usually obscured and often intense ambivalences felt by everyone—including children—about hiring adolescent non-kin (Bermudez). In the allegedly "true stories" that adults, adolescents, and children shared with each other, babysitters were now more likely to be depicted as frightening, not merely frustrating. One legend that circulated widely recounted the horrors of a babysitter high on drugs or alcohol. In her delirium, the babysitter bakes the baby she mistakes for an uncooked turkey. This legend about gender-role subversion addressed simmering cultural tensions about youth culture and social anxieties about childcare, the core issue that "gave rise to more controversy than almost any other family-related issue during the late 1960s and early 70s" (Mintz and Kellogg 222). Although guilt about leaving one's children with a stranger probably generated fear and paranoid thinking, parents nevertheless seemed to believe the stories they heard—such as this one. "My mother told me this urban legend when I was about 10," reported a University of California junior. "She swears it is true since she thinks she heard it from a sociologist" (Day). Parents like this mother must have wondered: Were other teenage girls in the neighborhood as deficient in good judgment, domestic skills, and maternal instincts as this cannibalistic one they had heard so much about?

Another legend casting girls in an unfavorable light that captured the popular imagination is known to folklorists as "The Babysitter and the Man Upstairs." In this supposedly true story, a stranger calls secretly from an upstairs extension to repeatedly ask the sitter: "Have you checked the children?" Though phrased as a question, it is really a reprimand from above to girls not doing their job properly and a commandment to act responsibly. But for adults, this tale probably reinforced fears about adolescent girls. Though she does call for help, she does not check the children. Because she is too absorbed in the television in most versions of the legend, she fails to hear or to help the children, who are slaughtered. In the end, the babysitter's negligence makes her nearly as dangerous as the maniac upstairs who is more vigilant than she is.

The success of this particular folk legend in tapping cultural anxieties about changing roles for women and girls contributed to its appropriation by the popular culture in the 1970s and 1980s. *When a Stranger Calls* (1979), about a teenage girl who unwittingly attracts the maniac who threatens her life and the safety of the children she has been hired to protect, is closely based on the urban legend. Other movies like *Fright* (1971), *Are You in the House Alone?* (1978), and the blockbuster *Halloween* (1978), which drew on similar narrative elements, relied for the turn of their plots on the avenging maniac who menaced teenage babysitters. Narrative conventions, dark theaters, and cinematic devices enabled spectators to experience the babysitter's subjectivity. Sometimes we see what she sees, and are thus enabled to identify with her fear of impending catastrophe. At other times, we share the leering gaze of the stalker, assuming the (uncomfortable and/or exciting) role of an accomplice to an obsessive, sadistic voyeur.

Parents/employers can feel the thrill of retribution at a safe distance because the monster who punishes girls is so deranged (Modleski 163). A revenge fantasy for girls who gab (and one that parents/employers could relate to in the days before "call waiting") is the maniac's symbolic inversion of the telephone. Fred Walton, who had a job answering telephones in the months before he shot *The Sitter* (the short he made before the full-length movie, *When a Stranger Calls*), made "the most of that fearsome modern weapon, the telephone," according to Janet Maslin (Maslin; see also Harmetz). In the hands of the maniac, the telephone is transformed from umbilical nurturance into a phallic tool for the intimidation, submission, and victimization of girls. In the material world of girls, the telephone served as an instrument of liberation and communication. The place of this new technological device in their lives had been the result of postwar consumer spending and aggressive corporate marketing. AT&T had even produced *The Baby Sitter* (c. 1960) a vocational film for high school students at the time in which phones never stopped ringing. Already by the 1950s, though, the telephone had become the babysitter's "tool of the trade" to be used in case of emergencies and for on-the-job sociability. A babysitter in one Tom & Jerry cartoon is so thoroughly absorbed in her phone conversation (about a boy, of course) that she doesn't notice that the baby has wrecked the household (*Tom, the Babysitter* [1993]).

But in a more sinister vein, filmmakers and latter-day writers of preteen fiction would utilize the telephone as a symbolic threat. On the cinematically inspired book jacket of *A Killer in the House* (Carroll), a phallic, blood-red receiver dangles from its cord (see also covers for O'Keane and Sumner). On the cover of *Baby-sitter's Nightmare*, one of a number of horror books about babysitters, a worried girl presses a red phone to her face even though the telephone plays no role in the book (Daniel).

These fictional babysitters have much in common with John Carpenter's serious and independent Laurie Smart (Jamie Lee Curtis); they are all transgressors. For example, Laurie thinks that she is playing by the rules, but the cultural ambivalence about the autonomy of female income earners that underpins this narrative will lead to her victimization. Often this contradiction between our desire that the teenage babysitter have autonomy and our fear of her independence is even inscribed onto her body. Though typically attractive, the sitter's breasts are often intentionally obscured by a stack of schoolbooks she clutches to her chest. These are markers of studiousness, seriousness, and scholastic aspirations. Iconic babysitters—high achievers, hard workers, and wage earners—are largely "nice" girls, that is, academically rather than socially successful. In fact, it is only because Laurie is "pure at heart" that her life will be spared in *Halloween* (Williams 27).[1] But Laurie will come precariously close to dying.

In contrast, a babysitter in *The Beast and the Babysitter* (Stevens) rejects a work ethic based on maternal self-sacrifice. She would rather read than babysit and is not industrious in the least. She blatantly shuns self-denial and deferred gratification. Instead of cleaning the stacks of dishes or playing with little Lewis while his younger sister naps, she is engrossed in a book. But when a bored and lonely Lewis wakes up his sister, Veronica angrily snaps her book shut and utters the expletive, "Oh, fudge!" (Stevens 4). Growing more impatient by the minute, and instead of attending to the baby, Veronica decides that now is the time to do the dishes, the domestic chore she has put off in order to read. Fear-inspiring babysitters are those like Veronica—for whom babysitting is not an apprenticeship in idealized domesticity. For the rest of the story, Veronica remains just where she wants to be: on the periphery.

Other iconic babysitters inspire fear because of the fantasies they arouse. The representation of the babysitter as an object of male sexual desire was first given expression in the 1960s by American

The babysitter and her charges menaced in *Halloween.*

fiction writer Robert Coover, author of "The Babysitter." Though unusual among other highbrow works of fiction included in the *Norton Anthology of Literature,* this canonical work gave expression to a sexual fantasy. With probable origins in the eroticized class relationship of the Victorian master and servant, this fantasy was revived and revised by the sexual revolution. In postwar America, not only were the babysitter and her employer likely to be of the same class, but the job itself made the babysitter less like an employee and more like an intimate family member. According to one expert, "Intimacy, in our society, is often eroticized," especially so among men (Stains 26).

In Coover's short story "The Babysitter" and in the 1995 movie version with the same title, a responsible and levelheaded teen (Alicia Silverstone) unknowingly entices her middle-class employer and several other men to imagine raping her and then to attempt it. *The Babysitter's Seduction* (1995) similarly traces the violent machinations of a seemingly ordinary (if not thoroughly obsessed) upper-middle-class husband who kills his wife in order to marry the virginal babysitter. "Of course, most of us [men] never act on our thoughts; we never cross the line. It's like a heavily patrolled border, and as a strictly practical matter, we're smart enough to know that if we happen to wander over, we're likely to get shot" (Stains 26). But the men in these movies do violate the incest taboo that shelters most real babysitters from unwanted male advances.

The babysitter in pornographic movies is a clearer projection of this particular erotic male fantasy. In *The Backdoor Babysitter* (1991), a "dirty old man" turns his voyeuristic gaze "towards sinful suburbia . . . [where] mock babysitting has long been a favorite activity." Though the movie has little to do with the fantasy, the caption next to the suggestive image of seventeen-year-old Vicki on the video box cover of *Jailbait Baby Sitter* (1978) reads: "Don't let daddy drive her home!"[2] In *The Governess* (1993) Linda masquerades as "the au pair from hell" in order to seek vengeance on her employer, Mr. Prentice, a philandering father and sexual abuser who got Linda pregnant when she was just a girl. Now grown up, she's "come to score . . . and settle a score" by destroying his marriage and family. Of course we get to watch her have sex with his wife (who eventually leaves him), his son, and his chauffeur (who runs off with his daughter-in-law).

Young women with sexual agency who leave a path of destruction are both arousing and awesome. The box cover of the hardcore porn video *The Babysitter* reads, "Danielle has always fantasized about making love to Mr. James. One hot night her dreams come true." The babysitter in *The Babysitter* (1969), in a soft-porn movie about the tension between male temptation and doing the right thing, is a highly sexualized young woman eager to satisfy her passion for pleasure. She has been influenced by 1960s youth culture, sexual revolution, self-liberation, and nascent feminist ideology. In the southern California suburban home where she is babysitting, she smokes pot and dances topless to psychedelic rock music. Candy (Patricia Wymer) loves music, she later explains to her intimacy-starved employer trapped in a troubled marriage, because it is like sex. That Candy is permitted to express her sexual potency is partly for her sake as well as to arouse desire among viewers. This female object, as Laura Mulvey might argue, is to be consumed like candy by the male spectator.

Over a late-night snack Candy explains how she wants "to have fun, feel things, be free!" Candy represents the dangers that the new morality, which emphasized self-fulfillment, posed to traditional family sacrifice. She effortlessly seduces a man who ought to know better: a prosecutor, father, and husband. That husbands turn to sexy sirens, even underage ones, is often blamed on wives who cause marriages to sour, as is the case here.[3] In the end, husband and wife reunite and free-spirited Candy nonchalantly moves on to the next guy, the next job. As sexually passionate as her namesake, Candy is a brunette instead of a blond in *Weekend with the*

Babysitter (1970), another movie about male exploration of sexual boundaries. Repudiating restrictive gender norms, neither babysitter is about to become a wife or mother any time in the near future. Dreams come true or fears run amuck?

A girl like Candy knows her own mind; but fears that teens could neither control their own imagination nor master their own behavior were also projected onto babysitters. The fantasy lives of fictionalized babysitters often overwhelm their ability to trust their own perceptions, think rationally, and act responsibly. Because Jenny in R. L. Stine's novel *Babysitter,* the first of a four-book series, is easily frightened, we question her credibility. Because she doubts herself, we cannot trust her perceptions. Because Jenny makes one bad decision after another, we are unable to rely on her to do the right thing. She babysits even though "some creep in a ski mask was breaking into homes and beating up baby-sitters" and she has received menacing phone calls (Stine 16). "Are you all alone in that big house? Well, don't worry. Company's coming" (62). Jenny does make the promise to control her "wild" imagination, satisfying her rational mother (a legal secretary) who thinks that her daughter is too much of a dreamer; but it is a promise Jenny cannot keep.

Not so with boys in children's literature. They are unmistakable representations of male power: confident, responsible, resourceful, fraternal, and entrepreneurial. For example, the teenage protagonist of *Henry Reed's Baby-Sitting Service*, Henry Reed, is enormously ambitious. "Here I am fifteen," Henry laments, "and I'm not even started on a career, much less a fortune" (Robertson 18–19). The son of a diplomat, Henry has much in common with other fictionalized males, such as Carl the dog (a rottweiler) in a popular children's book series and Jerome the alligator. Boys' active dominance is often represented by their high standing in the food chain. Like Henry and Carl, Jerome uses his intelligence ("an idea") to heroically outwit the ten practical jokers in his charge and prove himself as a babysitter, and, of course, as a young male.

Like boys, middle-aged single women and survivors of male violence in movies like *Halloween 20* are levelheaded, if a bit driven. Jill Johnson (a more mature Carol Kane than the teenage babysitter she had played in *When a Stranger Calls*) is the director of women's services on a college campus in *When a Stranger Calls Back* (1993). In an attempt to help out a psychologically troubled coed (Julia Schoelen) who survived an assault five years earlier while babysitting, Jill tracks down the attacker. In the penultimate scene, he is brilliantly camouflaged as a graffitied brick wall, a possible reference to his origins as an urban legend. But in the end, it is the portly detective (Charles Durning), not Jill, who shoots to kill. The last we see of Jill and the coed, they are battered but shoulder to shoulder on hospital gurneys in a chilling representation of sisterhood and survival.

The only teenage babysitters in movies of the 1980s who are allowed to exercise female power are truly deranged and not merely troubled ones like the coed. Those that are out of control and out of their minds stand as powerful representations of monsters in their own right. Representations of babysitters (as well as nannies) were shaped by anti-feminist fears about socially and sexually rebellious girls and women, the impact of child abuse, and rising divorce rates (Fischer). According to *People Weekly* at the time, "The hired hand that rocks the cradle may belong to an unstable, even dangerous, baby-sitter" ("When the Bough Breaks"). Joanna (Stephanie Zimbalist), the teenage vixen in *The Babysitter* (1980) who is unhinged by her murderous passion and "monstrous female sexuality," speaks to the anxieties generated by these discourses (Creed).[4] Like other psychotic monsters in postmodern horror films, she violently disrupts the everyday life of an ordinary family she threatens. She plots her seduction of Dr. Benedict (William Shatner) and takes over the daily responsibilities of family life neglected by alcoholic Mrs. Benedict (Patty Duke). Though her husband is suspicious, Mrs. Benedict is oblivious to Joanna's strange behavior. The girl "borrows" Mrs. Benedict's sexy negligee and plays with snakes (the classical symbol of evil). Crazed Joanna is plotting murder just like other dangerous babysitters who infiltrate American families made dysfunctional by inadequate wives and mothers.

There was no shortage of teenage monsters just as threatening and thrilling as Joanna, who represented both anti-feminist fears and feminist ideas about new possibilities for women. Given that they were caught between these conflicting notions, monstrous madness was their only option. For example, Diane Franklin plays a menacing babysitter in the television movie *Summer Girl* (1983). Many like her are emotionally unbalanced products of "broken homes" in a society especially anxious about the psychological effects of divorce. In the television movie *The Sitter* (1991), Nel (Kim Meyers) is illegitimate and abandoned. Taken in by kin, she is an indentured servant to her abusive aunt. With her flowing golden locks, frilly apron, ballroom gown, and yearning for Prince Charming (she memorizes romantic movie dialogue), Nel seems like a modern Cinderella.

However, although she appears innocent (she dons an English nanny outfit when she babysits in a hotel), Nel is insane. Unable to distinguish romantic fantasy from reality, she is delusional, dissociative, and sadistic. Nel stands in sharp contrast to Marilyn Monroe's portrayal of a far more pathetic young woman in the prefeminist original version, *Don't Bother to Knock* (1952).

Even preteen fiction aimed at girl readers became similarly populated with depraved sitters.[5] In Stine's *Attack of the Beastly Baby-Sitter*, a mutant rat girl transforms young boys into rodents. In *Babysitter IV* (Stine), because Jenny's mother fails to serve as her mentor, Jenny ends up identifying with an aggressor—the vicious employer who beats up babysitters. She places menacing phone calls to a babysitter then kidnaps a baby she threatens to kill. At the tragic conclusion of Stine's four-volume series, Jenny is thoroughly transformed into a raving maniac. Margo, however, is even more bizarre, violent, obsessive, sexually aggressive, deceptive, manipulative, and murderous in *Beware the Baby-Sitter* (William) and in the "Sweet Valley High" book series sequel, *The Evil Twin* (Pascal).

Although not all iconic babysitters are insane, many are suspected of being so. Alice becomes a suspect in the *Baby-sitter's Nightmare* when all the houses where she babysits are robbed and a babysitter is also found dead. Janaan is another sitter who is falsely accused of murder in Alane Ferguson's *Show Me the Evidence*. The significance of all of these representations lies in what fears and fantasies they reflect but also in their impact on expectations and perceptions of adolescent girls, especially in caretaking roles. Janaan is a fictional character in a mystery but the unwarranted suspicion that she is a child abuser is dead-on. According to Leslie Margolin, who researched the nuanced language used by social workers, babysitters are often assumed by investigating officials to be culpable of child abuse. In their official reports, social workers devote more attention to describing the abuse than the suspect's "intentions, feelings, and interpretations of what happened" (Margolin 60). Regarded as "perpetrators" as opposed to "suspects," babysitters are presumed to be malicious. For example, one social worker's

> unusually graphic style of presentation gave the bruises a special status. They were no longer simply bruises but were now defined as out of the ordinary, strange, and grotesque. By removing the bruises from everyday experience, the stage was set for redefining the babysitter who supposedly did this to the child. *In this manner, a person whose social*

status had been taken for granted could now be seen as potentially
suspicious, foreign, and malevolent. (Margolin 60, emphasis added)

Just as generations of babysitters since the 1960s have taken
their first steps toward income and independence, they have been
provided with and represented in prescriptive tales and a surfeit of
frightening scenarios to fuel the imagination (see Ury 81–92). One
Internet movie reviewer recalled that when she was a girl, *When
a Stranger Calls* scared her and all her babysitter friends (Bloomley). Twenty-three-year-old Cindy recalled hearing babysitting stories that "really scared me and although I kept on babysitting I never
once fell asleep before the parents came home" (Zimmerman). After hearing a scary story about a babysitter when she was a girl,
Cynthia was too afraid to babysit (Pierce). But perhaps, as Isabel
Cristina Pinedo has argued, horror films produce for "female spectators a pleasurable encounter with violence and danger" (6). Perhaps
girl spectators—especially the many who do not like to babysit—
identify with the rebellious, monstrous, or subversive sitters they
see. Perhaps there are others who enjoy the representations of sexual
agency.

However, the fears and fantasies they see enacted on movie and
television screens are not necessarily ones to which girls lay claim.
The frustrations and fantasies that go along with the only job for
which girls qualify by virtue of their sex go both ways. Given employment opportunities other than babysitting, girls often prefer to
flip hamburgers than babysit. Perhaps it is because of the horrors of
babysitting, as they see them. In qualitative studies conducted by
researchers since the late 1970s, girls have complained, of course,
about the low pay and hard work. But they also do not like irresponsible employers who call or cancel at the last minute, pay by check,
and bounce checks. Some employers depart in a hurry, and others
arrive home later than expected, sometimes drunk. Although some
men accept the fatherly role of taking the sitter home afterward, sitters complain about sexual harassment (Stains 26).[6]

A combination of labor needs and market demands has contributed to the fact that since the mid 1980s, teenaged babysitters
have become increasingly scarce while preadolescent ones have become more abundant. While teenage girls have been widely vilified
since the 1960s as we have seen, preadolescents have been idealized
in the Baby-sitters Club (BSC) book series and popular movies since
the mid-1980s. Shaped by a fledgling *girl power* ethos, this multi-

valent form of commercialized postfeminism that empowers fiction-alized babysitters appeals to real girls. That the BSC work ethic also professionalizes preadolescents has made them appear far more at-tractive than the potentially threatening teenager down the block.

Notes

1. Alice Fleming in *Baby-sitter's Nightmare* is also a good girl whose life will be saved because of her sexual purity.
2. Other pornographic videos include *Perverted: The Babysitters, Part One* (n.d.) and *New Babysitter* (1995).
3. See also *The Babysitter* (1980) and *The Babysitter* (1995).
4. Films with monstrous females in caretaking roles include *The Hand That Rocks the Cradle* (1992) and *The Guardian* (1990).
5. There is horrific Crissy in *One Evil Summer (Fear Street)* (1994).
6. See also babysitter backseat seduction in *The World According to Garp* (1982).

Works Cited

"Baby-Sitter Is Murdered in Bronx Rooming-House." 1958. *New York Times,* 19 November: 68.

Bermudez, Martin. 1987. Legend I Urban Belief B3B3. November 1. Folklore Archives. University of California, Berkeley.

Bloomley, Betsy. Betsybloom@juno.com.

Brunvand, Jan Harold. 1981. *The Vanishing Hitchhiker: American Urban Legends and Their Meanings.* New York: W. W. Norton.

Carroll, J. H. 1995. *A Killer in the House.* New York: Harper Collins.

Creed, Barbara. 1993. *The Monstrous-Feminine: Film, Feminism, and Psy-choanalysis.* New York: Routledge.

Dabakis, Melissa. 1993. "Gendered Labor: Norman Rockwell's 'Rosie the Riveter' and Discourses of Wartime Womanhood." In *Gender and American History Since 1890,* ed. Barbara Melosh, 182–204. New York: Routledge.

Daniel, Kate. 1992. *Baby-sitter's Nightmare.* New York: Harper Collins.

Day, Michelle. 1990. Legend I Urban Belief B3B3. December 1. Folklore Archives. University of California, Berkeley.

Douglas, Susan. 1994. *Where the Girls Are: Growing Up Female with the Mass Media.* New York: Random House.

"FBI Director Hoover Warns on Strange Baby Sitters." 1959. *New York Times,* 21 December: 17.

Ferguson, Alane. 1989. *Show Me the Evidence.* New York: Bradbury Press.

Fischer, Lucy. 1996. *Cinematernity: Film, Motherhood, Genre.* Princeton: Princeton University Press.

Formanek-Brunell, Miriam. 1998. "Truculent and Tractable: The Gendering of Babysitting in Postwar America." In *Delinquents & Debutantes: Twentieth-Century American Girls' Culture,* ed. Sherrie A. Inness, 61–82. New York: New York University Press.

Gilson, Kristin. 1998. *The Baby-sitter's Nightmare.* New York: Harper Collins.

Harmetz, Aljean. 1979. "Cheap and Profitable Horror Films Are Multiplying." *New York Times,* 24 October.

Margolin, Leslie. 1992. "Deviance on Record: Techniques for Labeling Child Abusers in Official Documents." *Social Problems* 39 (February): 60.

Maslin, Janet. 1979. "Killer on Little Cat Feet." *New York Times,* 12 October.

Mintz, Steven, and Susan Kellogg. 1988. *Domestic Revolutions: A Social History of American Life.* New York: The Free Press.

Modleski, Tania. 1986. "The Terror of Pleasure: The Contemporary Horror Film and Postmodern Theory." In *Studies in Entertainment: Critical Approaches to Mass Culture,* ed. Tania Modleski. Bloomington: Indiana University Press, 155–66.

Mulvey, Laura. 1975. "Visual Pleasure and Narrative Cinema." *Screen* 16 (autumn): 6–18.

Orgel, Doris. 1985. *My War with Mrs. Dalloway.* New York: Viking Penguin.

O'Keane, Bernard. 1995. *Lights Out.* New York: Harper Collins.

"Parents of Babies Warned on Sitters." 1952. *New York Times,* 30 January: 12.

Pascal, Francine. 1993. *The Evil Twin.* New York: Bantam.

Pierce, Cynthia. 1991. Legend I Urban Beliefs B3. September 30. Folklore Archives. University of California, Berkeley.

Pinedo, Isabel Cristina. 1997. *Recreational Terror: Women and the Pleasures of Horror Film Viewing.* New York: SUNY Press.

Robertson, Keith. 1966. *Henry Reeds Baby-Sitting Service.* New York: Viking Press.

Smith-Rosenberg, Carroll. 1985. *Disorderly Conduct: Visions of Gender in Victorian America,* 90–108. New York: Oxford University Press.

Scheiner, Georganne. 2000. *Signifying Female Adolescence: Film Representations and Fans, 1920–1950.* New York: Praeger.

Stains, Laurence. 1993. "Nanny Dearest." *Men's Health* 8 (September): 26.

Stevens, Kathleen. 1989. *The Beast and the Babysitter.* Milwaukee: Gareth Stevens Children's Books.

Stine, R. L. 1989. *The Babysitter.* New York: Scholastic.

———. 1991. *The Babysitter II.* New York: Scholastic.

———. 1993. *The Babysitter III.* New York: Scholastic.

———. 1995. *The Babysitter IV.* New York: Scholastic.

———. 1997. *Attack of the Beastly Baby-sitter.* New York: Scholastic.

Sumner, M. C. 1995. *The Evil Child.* New York: Harper Collins.

Ury, Allen B. 1996. "The Case of the Very Bad Baby Sitter." In *More Scary Mysteries for Sleep-Overs.* 81–92. New York: Price Stern Sloan.

"When the Bough Breaks." 1992. *People Weekly,* 24 February: 60.

William, Kate. 1993. *Beware the Baby-Sitter.* New York: Bantam.

Williams, Linda. 1996. "When the Woman Looks." In *The Dread of Difference: Gender and the Horror Film,* ed. Barry Keith Grant, 15–34. Austin: University of Texas Press.

Zimmerman, Cindy. 1971. Legend I Urban Beliefs B3. December 3. Folklore Archives. University of California, Berkeley.

chapter 15

Bubblegum and Heavy Metal

Frances Gateward

In 1997 the release of a period fantasy film hit the islands of Japan like a tsunami. A critical and popular success, the epic featuring a girl character in a pivotal role broke all existing box-office records. The film was seen by over thirteen million viewers during the first six days of its release, and within six months, it was estimated that one out of every ten Japanese citizens had gone to the local multiplex to see it.[1] This was not James Cameron's juggernaut *Titanic* but *Mononoke Hime* (Ghost princess/*Princess Mononoke*), written and directed by Japan's master of animation, Miyazaki Hayao.[2] Recognized as one of the best films of the year by the prestigious journal *Kinema Jumpo,* coming in second to Imamura Shohei's *Unagi,* *Princess Mononoke* is visually dazzling and narratively complex, a provocative and ambiguous allegory concerning human progress and its effects on the natural environment. The critical acclaim and popularity afforded Miyazaki's animated masterpiece is neither unusual nor unexpected in Japan, the largest producer of animation in the world. For in Japan, anime, the term used both in Japan and the West to refer to Japanese animation, generates approximately 55 percent of domestic box-office revenues and is a respected art form free of the stigma that in the United States characterizes animation as entertainment for children.[3]

In this essay I examine the origins and characteristics of the rich, fascinating, and immense world of anime, providing the context for my main concern—the construction of girls. My particular interest is in the realm of science fiction and fantasy, genres that are defined as male in both Japan and the United States but are curiously inundated with female protagonists in anime.

Anime 101

The recent phenomenon of *Pokemon*—the animated series (1998), the feature films (1999 and 2000), the toys, and the myriad ancillary products—caught many Americans by surprise. Pikachu and the other one-hundred-and-fifty-plus cartoon figures enjoyed a popularity of great magnitude, saturating kinderculture to such a degree that grade-school children were characterized as obsessed.[4] Many Americans, invoking racist and nationalist sentiments, likened the influx of the Pocketmonsters to cultural invasion, mistakenly suggesting that this was the first anime series broadcast in the United States to capture the imagination of children and the wallets of their parents.[5]

Japanese animation debuted on American television over three decades before, in 1963 with Tezuka Osamu's "Tetsuo Atom/Astro Boy," broadcast for the most part on independently owned and operated UHF stations. The series, featuring the adventures of a crime-fighting robot boy, was followed by others such as "Gigantor," "Marine Boy," "Kimba the White Lion," and, of course, "Speed Racer".[6] Importation continued through the years, bringing to American television screens "TranZor Z," "Star Blazers," "Battle of the Planets," "the Macross/Robotech" trilogy, "Dragonball," and "Sailor Moon"; and to the silver screen the postmodernist science fiction features *Ginga tetsudo three-nine/Galaxy Express 999* (1979), *Akira* (1998), and *Kokaku kodotai/Ghost in the Shell* (1995). Though these titles represent only a small percentage of what is available to American audiences—there are hundreds of titles and anime is much easier to find in the local video rental outlet than are live action Japanese films—they do reveal some of the field's common characteristics, among them origin, a diversity of genre, serious themes, and similar character design.

The term *anime* is a fairly new linguistic twist, coming into use during the 1960s. The previous term for Japanese animated film, *manga eiga*, refers to the source of its origin, *manga*, black-and-white serialized publications often likened to comic books. Unlike American comic books, which are consumed by a rather small and select audience, *manga* are read widely in Japan by boys, girls, men, and women. In 1980 over 1.16 billion copies of the book-length comic magazines were purchased, representing 27 percent of the total books sold (Schodt 12).[7] Though *manga* have historically been strictly divided along gender lines—with *shonen manga* for males and *shojo manga* for females—it is not uncommon these days to find that many cross over. Women are as likely to write and draw *manga* enjoyed by boys as men are to author titles for girls and women. Though not all anime productions are adapted from *manga* titles, the majority of them are, and the relationship between the printed narrative and the animated version is a circuitous one. If a published *manga* is successful, it is adapted into either a television series or an OAV/OVA (original direct-to-video animation available for purchase) and then produced as a feature film. In most instances the basic story remains the same, but sometimes it is serialized across media. If the latter case is true, the story can then be adapted back into a *manga,* television, or video series. Of course, it is also possible for a title to begin as either a film or in video form and then end up as *manga.* (Some titles even have sequels, prequels, spin-offs, and SD [super-deformed] versions: parodies of well-known anime that feature popular characters in miniaturized form, like toddlers with chubby bodies and large heads.)

Animation in Japan, and indeed around the world, is often treated with more mainstream intellectual appeal and critical respect than in the United States, where, with a few exceptions, it is deemed an entertainment form for children and adolescents. The state of animation in the United States is due to a number of factors: most animated feature films released in the United States are marketed as kid flicks; most animated programs on television are scheduled during time slots designated for children's viewing (weekday afternoons and Saturday mornings); most lack any semblance of aesthetic value; and most hold little intellectual currency. In Japan, a great number of animated television programs are broadcast during prime-time viewing hours. OAVs make it possible for series to contain more (and heightened) violent and sexual content. Animated features for mature audiences are released on a regular basis, and anime covers a wide range of genres that appeal to varied groups—sports, domestic drama and comedy, erotica, crime/police action, salaryman, horror, working women, fantasy, science fiction, romance, martial arts, and war. Certainly one of the appealing aspects of anime, to both native viewers and international *otaku* is the pervasiveness of serious and sophisticated themes, even in children's titles—unrequited love, crises of faith and religious belief, ethical dilemmas about the use of violence, *giri ninjo* (tension between duty and personal inclination), and death.[8] The expiration of the protagonists' family members and companions, often by violent means, and even the deaths of the protagonists themselves are quite normal.

Astro Boy and the entire Sailor Scout team of "Sailor Moon" were killed in their respective television series, though not in the American versions. The dichotomy between Japanese and American audiences' expectation of animated fare is a major point of contention between Japanese producers and American distributors. "Astro Boy" was cancelled after only one season of broadcast in the United States because of its increasingly violent content. When "Gatchaman" was adapted for American television, and changed into the series "Battle of the Planets," it was dramatically altered: "The program was not merely adapted into English; about a third of each episode was removed and new animation added. Most of the alterations were necessary to make "Battle of the Planets" as a children's program, since "Gatchaman" was an adult drama with bloody fight scenes and risqué humor. The original mood of violence and tension was lightened considerably" (Patten 11). More recently, confused American parents eagerly took their children to see *Princess Mononoke*, but once the film began, they promptly escorted their children out of the theater. They expected a Disney-like spectacle but were confronted instead with a violent, bloody, and sometimes horrifying feature, with motifs of demonic and supernatural possession as well as scenes of war and decapitation, certainly for mature audiences only.[9]

For American audiences, one of the most disconcerting aspects of anime, even those with thematic emphasis on grave issues and topics, is the manner in which characters are drawn. Though historical dramas such as *Hadashi no gen/Barefoot Gen* (1983), a tale about the bombing of Hiroshima seen through the eyes of a boy who survives the atomic blast, and *Hotaru no haka/Grave of the Fireflies* (1988), the story of a boy and his younger sister's struggle during World War II, feature characters with more normalized features, most people in anime are rendered unrealistically. It is common to see the thin, angular bodies for both males and females associated with *manga*. Frederick Schodt notes that "the males are often so thin and wispy in appearance that they can be distinguished from females only by their clothes and somewhat larger feet" (92). Males and females also share the characteristic oversized eyes and vibrantly colored hair (pink, blue, orange, purple) arranged in gravity-defying styles that would put most New Wave pop stars to shame. The adaptation of the Western convention of "Bambi-like orbs," for both Asian and non-Asian characters, emerged after World War II and is often attributed to the acceptance of Western styles of beauty and the influence of American animation. Yet it is also possible to

Sailor Moon travels through the Black Dream Hole to save Chibi-Usa in *Bishojo senshi Sailor Moon Super S: The Movie.*

consider the stylization as an aesthetic one; it first appeared in the *shojo manga* that featured stories of romance and female fantasy. Artists employed the technique to better communicate emotion. (*Manga* rely more on graphics than language.) In anime, quivering, glistening eyes more effectively suggest a struggle of emotions than cliché dialogue does. In titles depicting battles of good versus evil, the smaller the eyes the more insidious the character.

The similarities between males and females in hairstyles, facial features, and body type are often mirrored in characterization as well. Stereotypical, gendered behaviors are frequently reversed: women and girls exhibit courage, strength of will, aggression, ambition, and sexual desire; men and boys are timid, passive, and overemotional. The males in anime are much like those of the American genre of the woman's film. As Doane describes them, "The genre does seem to require that the male character undergo a process of feminization . . . they are attentive to detail, minute incidents, and the complexities of intersubjective relations. They often attempt to read the woman's face for its hidden meanings in the same way that women are consistently taught to read faces, to decipher motives" (116). These switches in gender roles occur not only figuratively, realized through emotion and behavior, but also literally, with actual physical transformations, the most famous example being *Ranma 1/2*, (1989) where a high school boy turns into a teenage girl whenever he is splashed with cold water. Gender expectations are such in anime that the presence of transvestites, transsexuals, and homosexuals is treated as mundane. Schoolgirls have crushes on *sempai*, their senior classmates, usually rendered as more sophisticated and more beautiful. In both *Battle Skipper* (1995) and *Gunbuster* (1989), when the adolescent protagonists first encounter their crushes, the scenes resemble the banal constructions of melodramas and soap operas: the swelling of nondiegetic romantic music, cross-cutting between close-ups of longing and desire, and soft focus. Anime stylizes the moment even more, as the younger girl's eyes will bulge, her face blush, and her expression become goofy. The object of her affection may be caught in a freeze frame, twirl about in slow motion, and be showered by softly falling rose petals. In *Project A-ko* (1986), a movie considered a parody, infatuation becomes the focus of the narrative. The relationship between two high school girls, A-ko and C-ko, inseparable since they were toddlers, is threatened by the actions of B-ko, who swears that she will have C-ko for herself. Every morning before school, B-ko meets A-ko en route and challenges her to a battle to the death. The weapons chosen and ensuing destruction escalate as the narrative progresses.

The permeating gender twists presented in anime are an intriguing and perplexing aspect, for as both David Desser and Annalee Newitz point out, American *otaku* are overwhelmingly male. Perhaps even more striking is the fact that they avidly consume genres that are perceived as women's genres in the West (Newitz 4). Desser attributes the interest to the sexual confusion and formation of sexual identity of adolescence (American consumers of anime tend to be of high school or college age) and Newitz to idealized romance in the old-fashioned sense. "Young American men become fans of romantic comedy anime because these narratives present a form of heterosexual masculinity which is not rooted in sexual prowess, but in romantic feelings . . . perhaps attempting to escape the hypersexuality of their own media culture by reimagining romance as a relationship which goes beyond the purely sexual" (6). But romantic relations are not always so innocent, for explicit sex and sexuality permeate.

Pretty Soldiers for Justice

Adapting to shifts in *manga* and in the culture at large, anime artists brought forth a new type of anime in the mid-1980s—the magical girl genre. Its ascendancy in the 1980s led to its domination of anime in the 1990s. Typified by girls and young women with supernatural, psychic, or alien powers, the genre marks a historical moment of crisis in Japan: the rise of women's movements.[10] As Gina Marchetti points out, "There is a very important link between genre and ideology. Particular genres tend to be popular at certain points in time because they somehow embody and work through those social contradictions the culture needs to come to grips with and may not be able to deal with except in the realm of fantasy" (187). This is especially true in regard to science fiction and its speculative cousin, fantasy, genres that reflect contemporary social concerns and anxieties, solving or making them more palatable by displacing them into the future or toward other or alternative worlds of existence. We find in titles like *Nausicäa* (1984) a girl who can save the residents of a valley by communicating with the giant insects that have overrun the postapocalyptic world; in *Vampire Princess Miyou* (1988) a protagonist who does battle with demon-like creatures that threaten humanity; in *Zenki* (1995) a schoolgirl/Shinto priestess who protects her village; in *Sailor Moon,* the "pretty soldiers for justice," a team of six schoolgirls (Sailor Moon, Sailor Venus, Sailor Jupiter, Sailor Mercury, Sailor Mars, and Sailor Chibi) who have the ability to tap the power of the cosmos for the cause of good; and in *The Adventures of kotetsu* (1996) a girl who is "sugar and spice and itchin' to slice." This last is a coming-of-age tale about a girl who, with a magical *Katana* (sword), engages in combat with zombies and street punks. On one level, these titles, and the dozens of others that make up the genre, present a new type of action heroine (in step with movements for gender equality) with these characteristics: intelligence, resourcefulness, courage, the valuing of female camaraderie, a refusal of the physical limitations that hamper women's and girls' lives, and resistance to conformity.[11] However, all of these profound and positive aspects are drastically contradicted in a number of ways. First and foremost is the fact that these girls do not actively seek their power. They are either born with it or are found to be the "chosen" of a higher power. Some, like the protagonist in *Iczer 1* (1995) even reject it, and a failure to act results in needless death and destruction. Even more disturbing is something that is considered a staple of the genre: the eroticization of the female body, problematized further by *kawaii*, a value on cuteness that infantilizes teens and young women.

Recently a new and troubling youth subculture materialized in Tokyo: *kogaru* or high school girls. Referred to as Ko gals, the culture is defined by high school girls who dress up in modified school uniforms that highlight their sexuality—unbuttoned or low-cut shirts and skirts short enough to leave their underwear exposed. They parade through the streets seductively, actively teasing older men, sometimes engaging in prostitution. Harada Masato's 1997 feature film *Bounce Ko Gals,* shot in a documentary-like style, contains scenes of such girls selling their underwear to specialty shops where men go to buy them, appearing in underground erotic films, and taking money from unsuspecting businessmen tricked into thinking they will receive sexual favors in exchange. This phenomenon is not lost on anime producers, as one is almost guaranteed to see magical girls exposed—shots of underwear and ripped clothing or scenes of dressing and showering, none of which functions to define character or progress the narrative.

The series and movies of *Sailor Moon* are the most derivative. Why? Because the uniform of Japanese schoolgirls most resembles sailor suits, and those worn by the fourteen-year-old Sailor soldier and her colleagues are very short, coming just below what viewers can imagine as their panty lines. As Grigsby points out, sailor suits are common in erotic *manga* and Japanese pornography, and there are adult male fans as well as girl fans. Grigsby has found that pirated editions of "Sailor Moon" are exchanged in underground circles in Japan, videos in which the sailor girls are raped by men or engage in lesbian sex.[12] Thankfully, no such violence occurs in legitimate versions of the anime title, nor do sex scenes that objectify the girls for the pleasure of the viewer. *Sailor Moon S* (1994) does present some narrative elements that reveal some of the reasons for the anime's popularity with girls, reminding me immediately of the Spice Girls: individualized characters with distinctive personalities (Sailor Jupiter as the tomboy; Sailor Chibi as the "baby" of the group;

Sailor Mercury as the "smart one," etc.); genuine concern for each other; the ability to be physical while retaining traditional femininity; and a realization of the power of collective action (to defeat the evil Ice Queen they must act as a team).[13] The potential radical impulse of "Sailor Moon" is never realized, however, because the girls are too highly sexualized. They are presented as immature. Their favorite activity when not crime-fighting is shopping, and, as many have noted, they obtain their power through the use of jewelry and makeup. They transform from ordinary schoolgirls into their superheroine personae by holding jewelry in the air and, in the Japanese version, yelling "Makeup!" (During the conversion process, fingernail polish and lipstick magically appear on their nails and lips.)

Demon/Devil Hunter Yohko (1991) is another example of contradictory anime. The virginal, teenage protagonist Yohko faces a dilemma of sexuality. She is caught between her mother, who urges her to enjoy sexual pleasure (giving her daughter condoms to use), and her grandmother, who insists that Yohko remain chaste. Yohko is given an opportunity to engage in intercourse and she takes it, going to a hotel with an interested schoolmate. In a graphic scene, they undress and he proceeds to fondle and suck her breasts, much to her pleasure. As her partner moves to assume the missionary position, Yohko's grandmother bursts through the wall to interrupt the couple. It turns out that the matriarchal line of the family are demon-hunters—the grandmother the 108th and Yohko the 109th. A generation was skipped because Yohko's mother lost her virginity before her powers could mature.

Once Yohko's powers are developed, she will be free to enjoy her sexuality. A demon appears, Yohko learns to use her special gifts during the heat of battle, and, defeating the demon, takes her place as the 109th demon-killer. This movie, working as an allegory, suggests to viewers that teen sexuality, specifically teenage girl sexuality, is a monstrous force (embodied in the demon) that needs to be contained and that the traditional values of the grandmother are to be adhered to, not the more modern mores of the mother.

Science Fiction

Though the work of some science fiction authors such as Ursula Le Guin, Philip K. Dick, Frank Herbert, Octavia Butler, and William Gibson has received well-deserved critical and theoretical attention, science fiction, like animation, is still treated with derision in the

United States, especially science fiction films. As Vivian Sobchack notes in her examination of science fiction films, "Myths about the genre abound," such as that the films "cannot possibly be as thoughtful, profound, or intellectually stimulating as SF literature, and that because of the nature of the medium itself film is incapable of dealing with the ideas as effectively as does literature" (1993, 24). Again, much of the public perception of science fiction films has to do with the targeted demographic and marketing. There have been a few "adult" science fiction films through the years, more recently *Contact* (1997), *Event Horizon* (1997), and *Sphere* (1998), but overall, sci-fi films are constructed to appeal to a more juvenile audience, despite their MPAA ratings—for example, *Jurassic Park* (1993), *Independence Day* (1996), *Men in Black* (1997), and *Star Wars Episode I: The Phantom Menace* (1999). Japan, however, takes its science fiction very seriously. The nation is both the largest producer and the largest consumer of science fiction in the world. In Japanese science fiction *manga*, live-action film, and anime the characters offer tragic figures within narratives that are complex and pessimistic, often denying audiences the happy ending required in the West.

As Sobchack reminds us, science fiction gives us a "poetic mapping of social relations as they are created and changed by technological modes of 'being in the world' " (1988, 229). We can see in science fiction anime Japan's cultural anxiety with shifts brought about by the advancement of technology, the emergence of Japan as a world economic power along with the advancement of capitalism, and the advent of gender-based equality. All of these issues are treated with ambivalence, for though the social upheaval resulting from these changes has benefited society, the changes have also caused much dismay.

One of the more interesting characteristics of sci-fi anime is the relation of women to technology. Women figure prominently and are linked to the hard sciences and mechanical invention much more closely than in American science fiction film and television. They are present as scientists and researchers, but much more as androids, cyborgs, and users of *mecha*.[14] Derived from the word "mechanical," the term refers to any type of machine but is used specifically to describe mechanized body armor, ranging from the hard suits in *Bubblegum Crisis* (1987) to the giant robots that characters control from within in *Gunbuster*. A crude version of this can be seen in the film *Aliens* (1986), when Ripley dons a loader to do battle with the queen alien. Examples in recent anime include the ultimate military weapons, female robots: in *Black Magic M-66* (1987); *Battle Angel* (1993)(where, in a nightmarish world of people being killed for their organs,[15] a female cyborg dies in an attempt to save a teenage boy); and *Ghost in the Shell* (1995) (a feature film about a female cyborg cop who is driven to question her humanity).

The association of the female with technology, especially the link between biology and machines, is one of anime's most fascinating yet confounding components. Both women and technology have historically been, and continue to be, deemed simultaneously attractive and abhorrent. The connection may represent a feminization of technology so that the male *otaku* can experience a mastery over two powerful, perhaps frightening dimensions of their daily lives—the opposite sex and science. On the other hand, the link can be interpreted progressively—girls and women in these tales embrace and demonstrate adeptness in a typically male-dominated field. Unlike the females in the magical-girl genre, the girls and young women in science fiction anime do not reject their power. They savor the strength and independence it provides, while at the same time understanding the responsibilities such power requires.

In the OAV series *Gunbuster,* Takaya Noriko, a student enrolled at the Okinawa School for girls, dreams of joining the multinational Space Corps so that she can follow in her father's footsteps, fighting with Earth's defense forces against the alien enemy that threatens to invade. This coming-of-age tale functions as an allegory. Noriko, who is neither the most skilled nor the most talented student in school, learns through hard work, study, and perseverance that it is possible to achieve one's goal, even if the goal is as lofty as saving humanity. Despite her ineptitude (she cannot adequately operate a robot fighting unit) she is chosen by "the Coach" to partner with the best student at the school, Amano Kazumi, and the pair of high school girls leave the planet for the ship Excelion. While in space Noriko is forced to mature. She experiences romantic love for the first time, but it is never fully realized. Noriko develops a crush on an older male cadet, Smith Toren, but he is killed in the first battle because she freezes in combat and fails to protect him. Noriko is left to grieve for him while also confronting her own mortality for the first time. Noriko, her shipmates, and the Terran forces eventually triumph, but not without costs: the humans use a "black hole bomb" to destroy the aliens, leaving the Earth and the solar system irreparably damaged (no doubt a reference to the atomic bombs dropped on Japan during World War II). Because of her tenure in space, Noriko

Sylia's hardsuit. *Bubblegum Crisis.*
Courtesy AD Vision, Inc.

loses all of the people she has loved on Earth. (Due to the use of warp
drive, there is a disparity between time on Earth and time in space.
Noriko and her "older sister" Kazumi return twelve thousand years
after their initial departure.)

Bubblegum Crisis, another OAV, also offers women who tri-
umphantly make use of technology, but they do so in a much more
adult-oriented form, for the world presented is grim, violent, and
pessimistic. Tokyo, destroyed in a massive earthquake, is replaced
by Megatokyo, the most technologically advanced city in the world.

Because Genom, the international corporation, has made Japan its base of operations, the nation has also become the world's greatest economic power. But things are not so good for all its residents: late capitalism has eroded the class system to the point where there are only the haves (those associated with Genom) and the have-nots (everyone else). Technological advancements have left the environment in an irrecoverable state so that the daily struggle to survive is made even more difficult.

"Boomers," synthetic biomechanical organisms designed for manual labor, frequently malfunction and go on rampages. The similarities with *Blade Runner* (1982) do not end there. One of the series' main characters is Priss, a rock singer who leads a band called the Replicants.[16] Priss and three other young women, who because of *kawaii* often seem more like girls or teenagers, lead secret lives as the Knight Sabers, a team of body-armored females who destroy Boomers and challenge the inhumane, profit-mongering Genom corporation. *Bubblegum Crisis* provides interesting cultural critique: Tokyo was devastated in World War II from carpet-bombing and recovered to become the business center of the economic tiger Japan. *Bubblegum Crisis* suggests that the massive economic and cultural changes affecting Japan, seen as progress, are made at the expense of human relations.

It is precisely anime's concentration on relationships that makes it so compelling. Rather than pitting girls against demons, alien species, or corrupt transnational corporations, the primary battles that take place within anime are struggles to construct identities that allow them to be true to themselves and to each other, recognizing and realizing their potential. This is accomplished most often as the girls negotiate the complex and sometimes puzzling nature of relationships between them and their parents, their teachers or mentors, siblings, lovers, other girls, and the world.

The "otherworlds" of Japanese animation, despite their ambiguous and sometimes contradictory messages, provide a valuable lens through which we can examine cultural issues and social change, especially for girls. Some titles may serve as alternatives to children's media in the United States, media in which few girls are permitted to experience adventure and exploration of both themselves and the world. In an increasingly globalized culture, media messages easily cross national boundaries and may provide possibilities and alternatives to the staid or retrograde images that flood contemporary American popular culture.

NOTES

1. For more information regarding the film's box-office success, see *Nikkei Industrial Newspaper*, July 29, 1997, and the *Sankei Sports Newspaper*, July 29, 1997.
2. Miyazaki, a *manga* artist as well as a writer and director of film, began his career in animation in 1963. He is best known in the United States for *Kaze no tani no Nausicäa (Warriors of the Wind/Nausicäa of the Valley of the Wind)* (1984), *Tenku no shiro Rapyuta/Laputa* (1986), *Tonori no Totoro (My Neighbor Totoro)* (1988), and *Majo no takkyubin (Kiki's Delivery Service)* (1989)—films which feature the adventures of girl protagonists.
3. See Yang, Gan, and Hong (1997).
4. The effects of the *Pokemon* phenomenon on children were the frequent subject of newspaper stories and national news broadcasts. Parents and child psychologists complained that children were exhibiting signs usually associated with gambling addiction.
5. For more on *Pokemon* obsession and lawsuits filed by parents see Estrich, Burkeman, and Lee.
6. Another link between Japan and the United States in terms of anime is a dispute regarding Disney's popular feature film *The Lion King* (1994), which is very similar to Tezuka Osamu's *Kimba*—a fact noted by Japanese cartoonists who complained that Kimba was the uncredited inspiration for the film.
7. The average length of a *manga* is usually three hundred fifty pages, though some are as long as six hundred.
8. Though a derogatory term in Japan, *otaku* (obsessed) is not as negative in the United States, where it is used specifically to refer to anime fans.
9. *Princess Mononoke* was distributed in the United States by Miramax, the adult, art-oriented subsidary of Disney. (In 1996 Disney, in a deal with Tokuma Shoten Publishing, acquired the world distribution rights to Miyazaki's Studio Ghibli productions.)
10. For more on the feminist movements in Japan, see Gelb and Palley (1994).
11. The protagonists of *Debutante Detective Corps* (1996), *Project A-ko*, *Battle Skipper*, and *Blue Seed* are notorious in school for their lateness. Though this might be seen as a failure to meet expectations and a lack of discipline in our culture, it may, in fact, be interpreted as reflecting an independent spirit in Japan. The educational system of Japan puts tremendous pressure on students from grade school through high school. Future success is based on exam performance, which determines entrance into the right schools and, later, into the right companies. It is not uncommon for children to study three to four

hours a day outside of school. The girls' lack of interest in following the rules and their nonchalant attitude toward the educational system could be seen as a rejection of traditional societal structures.

12. Animated sexualized violence also occurs in mainstream anime. The OAV series *F.O.B.I.A.* (1995) opens with a scene of stalking and violation. Two girls getting dressed in their school locker room are attacked by an alien with multiple penis-shaped tentacles, which are extended to enter their every orifice. We learn later that the alien creature has a preference for young girls. Another title, *Kite,* (1998) features a girl assassin, trained by a police detective, who is apparently frustrated over procedures that do not allow the system to catch and detain child molesters. But as the narrative progresses we find, through the use of explicit flashbacks, that he too is a child molester and may be killing other offenders to lessen his competition for victims.

13. See Cynthia Fuchs, "Too much of something is bad enough: Success and Excess in *Spice World,*" in this volume.

14. Most *otaku* attribute the term to *Mobile Suit Gundam,* which introduced the form of technology in 1979. Since then the anime title has spanned over twenty years, with eight television series, eight feature films, and four OAV series.

15. *Battle Angel* is even more horrifying in Japan, where organ transplants are normally rejected by the general populace. Traditional belief systems suggest that a person's salvation depends on his/her body being intact upon death, and that one's essence is present in internal organs. This may also explain why horror anime abounds with body horror, usually rendered as graphic, violent transformations or body invasions leading to feelings of revulsion and abjection.

16. Ridley Scott's film, an adaptation of Philip K. Dick's novel *Do Androids Dream of Electric Sheep?,* features a detective hunting down murdering replicants—artificial, malfunctioning life forms. One of these, played by Daryl Hannah, is named Priss. As in *Blade Runner,* Priss falls in love with an artificial life form while there is the suggestion that another member of the Knight Sabers (like *Blade Runner*'s Rick Dekard) might not be human.

Works Cited

Burkman, Oliver. 2000. "Pokemon Power." *The Guardian,* 20 April.
Desser, David. 1996. "Anime: Its Origins in Japan and Its appeal to Worldwide Youth." In *Pictures of a Generation on Hold: Selected Papers,* ed. Murray Pomerance and John Sakeris, 21–34. Toronto: Media Studies Working Group.

Doane, Mary Ann. 1987. *The Desire to Desire: The Woman's Film of the 1940s*. Bloomington: Indiana University Press.

Estrich, Susan. 1999. "Gambling with Pokemon." *The Denver Post*, 27 April.

Gelb, Joyce, and Marian Lief Palley, eds. 1994. *Women of Japan and Korea: Continuity and Change*. Philadelphia: Temple University Press.

Grigsby, Mary. 1998. "Sailormoon: Manga (Comics) and Anime (Cartoon) Superheroine Meets Barbie: Global Entertainment Commodity Comes to the United States." *Journal of Popular Culture* 32, no. 1: 59–80.

Lee, Felicia R. 1999. "Coping: Who's Afraid of the Pokemon Monster?" *The New York Times*, 24 October.

Marchetti, Gina. 1989. "Action Adventure as Ideology." In *Cultural Politics in Contemporary America*, ed. Ian Angus and Sut Jhally, 182–97. New York: Routledge.

Newitz, Annalee. 1995. "Magical Girls and Atomic Bomb Sperm: Japanese Animation in America." *Film Quarterly* 49, no. 1: 1–15.

Schodt, Frederick. 1983. *Manga! Manga! The World of Japanese Comics*. New York: Kodanscha International.

Sobchack, Vivian. 1997. *Screening Space: The American Science Fiction Film*. 2nd ed. New York: Ungar.

———. 1988. "Science Fiction." In *Handbook of American Film Genres*, ed. Wes D. Gehring, 229–47. Westport, CT: Greenwood Publishing Group.

Yang, Jeff, Dina Gan, and Terry Hong. 1997. *Eastern Standard Time*. Boston: Houghton Mifflin.

chapter 16

The Pixel Visions of Sadie Benning

Christie Milliken

> My dad said to me, "You know, I'm really worried that
> all your work is just going to be on one subject," Benning
> recalls, and I was like, "Yeah, my life." He makes [experi-
> mental] films. What are his films about? They're about his
> life. It just so happens that his sexuality isn't something
> people are going to label or talk about or say, "He's the
> heterosexual artist."
>
> SADIE BENNING, *The Advocate*, 1991

In December 1988, experimental filmmaker James Benning gave his
fifteen-year-old daughter a Fisher-Price PXL-2000 camera for Christmas.[1] Sadie Benning recounts this event as initially one of disappointment: "I thought, 'This is a piece of shit. It's black-and-white.
It's for kids. He'd told me I was getting a big surprise. I was expecting a camcorder'" (Masters). After witnessing a friend's injury at the
hands of a drunk driver as well as a drug-related shooting in her
working-class Milwaukee neighborhood a week later on New Year's
Eve, Sadie began to create a series of tapes as an extension of her
diaries, combining highly personal outpourings with fragments of
everyday life recorded (mostly) in her bedroom. By the next time she
journeyed to Los Angeles to visit her father, Sadie—who was born
and raised in Milwaukee by a single mother—had made three short
videos.

According to press accounts of her rise to prominence, Sadie's
father showed these first three tapes in a class he was teaching at the
California Institute of the Arts. From here, one of the students from
this class put her work into a festival he was organizing at the time.
The rest, as they say, is history. Eleven videos later, Benning emerged
from the gay/lesbian festival circuit in 1990 to quickly become one
of the most talked-about young videomakers in the United States.

She was also the youngest artist ever to be included in the Video Viewpoints Series at the Museum of Modern Art (1992), the Whitney Biennial (1993), and the Bad Girls and Bad Girls West exhibitions, respectively at the New Museum in New York City and the UCLA Wight Gallery in Los Angeles (1994). The critical acclaim accorded to the young teen led to her being awarded a $35,000 fellowship from the Rockefeller Foundation (1993) for a feature-length film, for which—at just nineteen years of age—she was also the youngest recipient of such prestigious funding.

Variously dubbed a "wunderkind," an "auteur of adolescence," and the baby-dyke "rescuer of the dyke dimension in queer cinema performance" (Smyth 1993, 21), Sadie Benning and her work are of particular interest in the context of this paper for the ways in which these bold, highly personal documents or essays (as they have been called) speak to this cultural moment.[2] I want to sidestep questions as to the merits of Benning's widespread recognition and reward in the face of a comparatively long history of lesbian film and video work that has remained largely ignored (or at least has received comparatively little attention). I also want to avoid any lingering questions of nepotism that circulate alongside Benning's critical/institutional cachet vis-à-vis her father's longstanding career and acceptance within the canon of structuralist, avant-garde filmmaking. Instead, I argue that Sadie Benning's self-(re)presentation or identity performances have developed their popular and critical recognition for the ways in which her work coincides with current strategies of gender performativity, a return to particularized experiences of the body, the politics of enfleshment, and the recent upsurge in the public visibility of and critical attention to "girl cultures" (of which this anthology is a part). This broad concept includes a wide range of subcultural practices that have proliferated in the form of recent independent and mainstream film/video releases as well as fanzines and zine culture, gay/lesbian/queer subcultural visibility, queer fashion, butch/femme resurgence, the rise of dyke hardcore punk bands as part of the Riot Grrrl movement specifically, and the ever-increasing contribution of strident, politicized young women to the contemporary music scene more generally.

Home Work and Adolescent Angst

Benning's first tapes, *New Year* and *Living Inside* (each made in 1989 and approximately four minutes in length), were made in her bedroom for herself with no thought of ever being shown publicly. *New Year* shows Benning simultaneously testing her equipment (surveying the contents of her bedroom and home) and defining a mode of self-expression. Fragments from "The Price Is Right" and a Raisin Bran commercial on television are juxtaposed with sensational tabloid headline images that acquire an abstracted quality as the camera scans left and right, up and down, never fixing on a complete, coherent headline. The camera roves past objects and surfaces: a snow cone of a nativity scene, a combat boot, the corners of her room. These seemingly random images serve as purposeful punctuation to a series of statements written on paper and slowly passed across the bottom of the frame. A note reads: "A friend of mine was raped by a black man," which is followed by an image of Comet cleanser and of a hand washing a kitchen sink. The story resumes as a title states: "Now she's a racist Nazi skinhead." These stories of rape, racism, drunk driving, crack-selling neighbors, and the decline of her neighborhood are juxtaposed with larger questions of existence. Another note reads: "It would be so easy to die," followed by the image of a hand quickly (and randomly) flipping through a deck of cards. These handwritten messages begin to take on both a life of their own and a status as found objects not unlike school notes passed surreptitiously among friends or fragments of paper torn from the pages of a diary.

This confessional, autobiographical tone has much in common with a longstanding tradition of women's autobiographical writing, here in the form of video diaries. While this form of video document harks back to identity-empowerment models of 1970s feminism, there is a decidedly contemporary spin on Benning's stance. As a self-professed "queer," Benning is clearly part of a younger generation of lesbians characterized by a movement from an emphasis on identity to an emphasis on performance. Among a number of critical theorists contributing to the field of queer theory more broadly, Judith Butler's work in particular has had enormous appeal for the ways in which it breaks with the rhetorical position of previous generations of gay and lesbian theorizations by erasing or at least troubling gendered sexual identifications. Butler distinguishes queerness from older gay and lesbian identifications more stringently allied with identity-laden notions of earnest authenticity, in that queer identity has an authorizing/playful/performative power offering an in-your-face inducement to have fun and make trouble. This invocation is especially evident in Benning's later work such as *Jollies*

(1990), *It Wasn't Love* (1992), and *Girl Power* (1992; dedicated to "bad girls girls girls everywhere"). The first of her video diaries to overtly stage her coming-out process, however, is *Me and Rubyfruit* (1989), a work many critics regard as a turning point prefiguring the more self-conscious, deconstructive, and performative aspects of her later work.

An obvious homage to Rita Mae Brown's cult novel, *Rubyfruit Jungle*, Benning deals directly with issues related to her sexual identity in this tape. In *Me and Rubyfruit*, she "comes out," as it were, without leaving the closeted confines of her bedroom. This piece incorporates home-movie footage of Benning as a child as she ruminates in voice-over: "I wonder how many lesbians were born today. . . . How many died never knowing who they were. How many sit married, feeling empty and wondering why. I can't say I know how many, but that doesn't matter, 'cause one identity robbed is one too many." The video resumes with an amusing dialogue established between Benning and the *character* evoked in her notes (though this distinction quickly blurs) as they discuss the prospect of marriage in an extended interchange borrowed directly from Brown's novel. Benning postures: "Why don't you marry me? I'm not handsome but I'm pretty," to which a scribbled note replies, "Girls can't get married. . . . It's a rule." A series of disparate juxtapositions follow: porn images of heterosexual couples, sex toy advertisements, a rabbit's paw key chain, Barbie dolls in an intimate embrace. After a series of close-ups of Benning and another girl kissing passionately, a hand lights a match in a quick imagistic metaphor.

One of the most interesting aspects of *Me and Rubyfruit* is the way in which it collapses a nostalgic evocation of Brown's novel onto a highly self-conscious performance of coming out. In this sense, by borrowing from a literary narrative, Benning's tape poses an interesting counterpoint to more traditional documentary tropes surrounding coming-out narratives and the consciousness-raising strategy of realist representation. While Benning's tactics are reminiscent of more traditional talking-head strategies, her appropriation and performance here make such confessional tapes markedly different. In direct address she says to the camera: "Look, if we want to get married we *can* get married. It doesn't matter what anybody says. Besides, Leroy and I are running away to be famous actors. We'll have lots of money. Clothes. And we can do whatever we want. No one tells someone who's famous what to do. Now ain't that better than sitting around with an apron?" These lines, again a direct quotation from *Rubyfruit Jungle,* underscore Benning's marriage of the act of coming out with the words of the novel's protagonist (including reference to her friend Leroy). The scratchy in-camera edits in this video are punctuated with small fragments of various songs by artists ranging from Patsy Kline to Rickee Lee Jones, another characteristic of Benning's signature style.

In an essay entitled "The Politics of Pleasure: Cross-Cultural Autobiographic Performance in the Video Works of Sadie Benning," Mia Carter reads Benning's cultural samplings—particularly her use of outspoken, politicized African American musicians like Nina Simone and Billie Holliday—as part of her enormous appeal to her adult audience:

> Sadie's story of personal development and consciousness-raising may be particularly appealing to the academic and critical audience because it is a narrative that unashamedly exhibits political passions, celebrates faith in activism and integrationist politics, and blends formalist aestheticism and agitprop. The teenage director shifts through the cultural and historical detritus of earlier times and presents her audience with an image of what is, for her character/herself—and what may be for the adult audience—a usable past, rather than one that is consigned to memory and a bygone era's political energies and promises. (757)

Carter sees Benning's appropriation of a wide range of cultural practices from high to low as something beyond the "adolescent thrill of shoplifting" (Romney 34) and more precisely as what gives Sadie's work its unique dynamism: "[O]n a symbolic level, mimicry and theft could be said to be the teenager's forte" (Carter 757). Carter frames her analysis of Benning's work in the context of autobiographic performance (making a careful distinction between *Sadie* the performed self and *Benning* the author/director [746–77]), but I would like to suggest another way of reading Benning's autobiographic confessions.

If Every Girl Had a Camera: Pixel Politics and Bedroom Culture

Ideologically, Benning's work offers a complex personalized politics that invokes feminism's support of individual, gendered experience as the authorizing force behind movement-inspired political advocacy. This may partially help to explain her critical standing within high art's institutionalized domain. But Benning's importance to gay/lesbian/queer youth primarily and teen girls additionally is a factor that cannot be underestimated. I am thinking particularly of the ways in which Benning's diaristic, essayistic contemplations ally with a longstanding tradition of diary writing—especially for girls— and also with much of the current writing in Riot Grrrl and teen zines, characterized by an appeal for acceptance and support among girls (gay and straight) under a common cause reiterated in the in-your-face mantra: "Revolution Girl Style Now!" that is so often invoked in Riot Grrrl literature and music.[3]

Born out of the punk scene around 1991, the Riot Grrrl movement represents a decidedly female appropriation of punk's already subversive cultural modes (hence the *grrr* in Grrrls). As a self-defined and highly self-conscious part of the more generalized "women in rock" phenomenon, Riot Grrrl subculture extends beyond the production and consumption of live or recorded music and the pleasure associated with the expression of subcultural styles, reaching into the realms of political strategizing and continually re-rehearsed self-definition through zine publication. In fact, the Riot Grrrl movement began in print—initiated by foxcore (women's hardcore) bands through fanzines dedicated to promoting women's cultural production in general and the formation of girl punk bands in particular. Riot Grrrls everywhere were encouraged to "get tough, get angry, and form their own bands" regardless of musical background or experience. Benning's association and identification with Riot Grrrl is widely known, not only because of her incorporation of their music into several of her videos (including Bikini Kill's "Revolution Girl Style Now" over the end credits of *Girl Power*), but also because of the formation her own grrrl punk band and the creation her own zine, *Teenage Worship*.[4] In most of Benning's tapes, but particularly beginning with *Jollies* in 1990, the extracinematic influences of Riot Grrrl are apparent.

Various studies of the gendering of subculture from Dick Hebdige and Simon Frith to Angela McRobbie help explain why girls historically have not participated as actively as boys in rock culture, both because of patriarchal restrictions on girls and because their pleasure and identity formation, in response, tend to take on a different form from that of boys. Joanne Gottlieb and Gayle Wald surmise:

> Social restrictions on girls, their limited access to the street and their greater domestic role make the public spaces in which subcultures are

acted out (clubs, the street, bars) prohibitive and exclusive for them. The street often poses as a threat to girls and women insofar as they are liable to male heckling, harassment or assault. . . . Therefore while male youth culture is public, oriented around the street, girls' culture often takes forms that can be experienced within the home, such as dressing up, or engaging in the creative consumption of mainstream pop idols, including fan-oriented visual materials such as magazines, photographs and, most recently, videos. (256)

With network television and film clips, scrawled messages, magazine and tabloid cut-outs, and bursts of popular music, Sadie Benning's videos celebrate the look, surfaces, and textures of day-to-day experience, inscribing the language of story, anecdote, oral history, and testimony as strategic performances. In this regard, her work is as heavily indebted to MTV as to underground film, video, and performance art aesthetics. The anti-tech aesthetic privileged by punk and Riot Grrrl culture is not only evident in Benning's use of music in the soundtracks for her tapes, but also finds its parallel in the obtrusive short-circuit sound of the camera itself; the frozen pixelated slashes of the in-camera edits characteristic of her early work and the chunky, almost cubist black-and-white video pixels characteristic of the medium.

Several critics have remarked on Pixelvision's ability to return an audience to nascent states. Jonathan Rosenbaum, for example, says: "The intimacy and the grainy look [of the technology] bring one back to qualities found in some of the earliest movies, made around the turn of the century—especially to the sense that images are emerging out of a primordial darkness and chaos" (36). Pixelvision has about half the resolution of standard consumer camcorders, and the actual image area during playback is smaller than normal, giving a squared-off variation on letterboxing. This gives an intimate, peepshow or *mise-en-abîme* effect of framing these grainy images with black on all sides.

As her work develops, Benning uses the qualities of her medium to great effect, particularly insofar as grain and resolution are concerned. When representing herself in extreme close-up as she begins to do in her second tape, *Living Inside,* for example, she appears to be at once both near and far from the viewer. As she confesses that she has not been to school in a week ("Somehow I can't bring myself to go. It's so useless to me now"), she moves the camera very close to her face, her nose, her eyes. Yet simultaneously Benning seems far away, as she turns her face to a side profile and blows bubbles with her gum, forming a silhouette that takes on an abstracted quality, distorted by the extreme angle and grain. In *If Every Girl Had a Diary*, (1990) her hand takes on a unique personality of its own, shot in extreme close-up with various movements against a murky black atmospheric background. At first her hand looks unequivocally like a hand, but its expression changes to an angry fist; a minor shift then gives it the appearance of a frowning, sullen face, first lyrical and distracted, then angry, then contemplative—almost sad—alongside her voice-over ruminations.

The raw quality and the subversive nature of Pixelvision is punctuated by the camera's remarkably cheap price tag against domestic-market camcorder technologies. Fisher-Price introduced the PXL-2000 camera in 1987. Originally sold to toy stores (at a retail price of about $100), the cameras were designed to be the "lightest, least expensive and easiest to use cameras on the market" and were targeted at the ten- to sixteen-year-old market. The camera records both video and audio on standard audio cassette tape at high speed (a ninety-minute tape will yield about ten minutes of video). Due to the high speed of the transport, images deteriorate rapidly when played through the mini-monitor included with the system and require rerecording onto standard videotape for any conventional hardware (including VHS playback).[5] Edits, made in-camera by rewinding the cassette (a technique very much in evidence in Benning's early tapes), are made glaringly apparent both aurally and through the frozen pixelated gashes produced on the screen.

Pixelvision has clearly attracted a large cult following, inspiring a body of serious work with an affinity for its idiosyncrasies. In this regard, the enthusiasm with which Benning's work has been met by an older generation of critics is not unrelated to the technology she uses. Benning's pixel visions—her very playful, investigative, even philosophical use of this technology—provide a perfect enactment of Pixelvision's promise: its use (by a kid) outside the confined institutionalized domain of the media lab at school or distanced from expensive camcorders that offer a more polished visual image. The art world's institutionalization of Pixelvision in general and Sadie Benning's institutionalization of it in particular can be read as toying with Fisher-Price's business of supplying kids with miniaturized simulacra of large-people products, insofar as the medium is both prized and utilized to a degree beyond what was originally intended.

Grrrl Products:
Poaching/Production/Consumption/Creation

Benning's recognition (and reward) within and beyond the hallowed halls of both academia and institutionalized art venues may indeed problematize her relation to Riot Grrrl culture which—despite some variation in its articulation across a range of subcultural practices— is vociferously resistant to mainstream co-optation. Nevertheless, Benning continually expresses a desire to attend to her youth audience and the particular set of problems she (and they) must face in an ageist, sexist, racist, homophobic, and classist culture. Benning ruminates on her meteoric rise to fame in the film/video festival circuit and beyond in a 1992 interview with Mark Ewert:

> I think the biggest strength in my work is that it exists, and I wonder about all the kids, queer or not, who sit at home, writin [*sic*] or whatever, that haven't gotten exposure, mostly kids are taught to think that their creations are not valuable—"Watch TV." "Worry about your appearance." It's mostly a freak accident (and partly fate) that I am in the position I'm in today. Just three years ago I can see myself throwing my tapes in the garbage. I was embarrassed. (4)

These comments reflect Benning's particular commitment to youth and youth activism. Indeed, one might argue that regardless of whether Benning is a role model per se, her work—its very existence—is a testament to the value of and need for creative expression experienced by young and old, rich and poor, agile and infirm. That young people are actively discouraged from participating in the (adult) public sphere and its cultural practices makes Benning's videos an inspirational example for resourceful young people profoundly compelled by cheap, low-tech, artisanal modes. (On this I am drawing from my own classroom use of her work as well as the shared experiences of so many of my colleagues.) What is particularly striking to me is the pedagogical potential proffered by Benning's pixel visions, which seems to extend beyond specifically female appreciations (boys love her stuff, too) to generational ones.

Nevertheless, while Benning appropriates much of the defiance associated with punk's angry, confrontational, disaffected-youth sensibility, the specifics of gender make Riot Grrrl altogether quite different. Mary Kearney traces the complex debates around Riot Grrrl's dialectical interchange between youth culture and radical politics in "Riot Grrrl: It's Not Just Music, It's Not Just Punk." Kearney argues that whatever stance one takes regarding the longevity of the movement (which some journalists say is over) or the particular innovation of its form of political activism (since Riot Grrrl has been charged with adopting a separatist mentality akin to lesbian-separatism of the 1960s and 1970s), this movement has created a "profound rupture in our understanding of adolescence, femininity, youth culture, and political agency" (93). Sadie Benning's diaristic videos are illustrative of precisely this kind of rupture. The charm of Sadie's performances and the nostalgic texture of her pixel visions enact for us the fear, frustration, rage, and exhilaration of both coming out and coming-of-age. In a sense, her queer emphasis on performance as opposed to identity-laden tropes is (in part) born out of the fact that her commodification within artistic and academic institutions at so young an age makes her a perfect, unprecedented illustration of an identity not yet fully formed. Sadie performs an identity in the making.

Although all of Benning's tapes—even those that increasingly take on a narrative trajectory—can be read as a form of documentary self-portraiture, what distinguishes these intimate investigations from more traditional documentary is the degree to which they engage with the multiple functions of film and video as simultaneously entertainment/ritual/art/fiction and (however we problematize this) reality.

What is particularly provocative about Benning's work is the degree to which her personal lens reflects and refracts the complexity of embodiment and its implications for identity and self-representation. Benning performs this "body politic" in works such as *Jollies* and *It Wasn't Love* in her countless metonymy of impersonations, from a femme girl in a big blond wig (whispering the words to Peggy Lee's rendition of "Fever") to a man shaving before the camera/mirror, a butch crossdresser, a cigar-smoking gangster, a 1950s crooner lipsynching to "Blueberry Hill," an outlaw/con posing for mug shots, and a young urban dyke with tattoos and piercings. *It Wasn't Love* develops a narrative trajectory that promises Hollywood but ends up in a fried chicken restaurant parking lot where Sadie and her girlfriend make out. "Permission? I forgot all about it," her cheeky/tomboy/outlaw/persona postures: "Trouble? I got in a lot of that!" This tape displays a more self-assured tone as Benning develops her use of hand imagery to highly sexualized effect. In a close-up curve of her hand the pixelated image is suggestive of a cunt, which Sadie manipulates, provocatively sucking her thumb to create an affect resembling a phallus/dildo; what one critic describes as "her most sensual, rude-positive sequence" (Smyth 1993, 58).[6] In a poignant juxtaposition of images, a slight change in position and camera angle reveals Sadie in a similar pose, only now she sucks her thumb like a child.

Repetition and Innovation:
Genre, Gender, and Coming-of-Age

The temptation to read Sadie Benning's work within the longstanding tradition of autobiography is obviously powerful, and that she culls much of the raw material for her videos from her everyday life is beyond a doubt. Even her recent featurette, *Flat Is Beautiful* (1998), which most directly resembles a work of fiction (Benning does not personally appear in the tape at all), has a young adolescent girl named Taylor coping with the loneliness and isolation of her tomboyish identifications and her crushes on girls as she negotiates her strained relationships with her preoccupied single mother, their gay roommate Quiggy, and her emotionally unavailable father (who is directly involved in the art world). That the tape displays Taylor as a working-class latchkey kid (played by Sammy Steel) coming of age in the late 1980s (signified by her Madonna posters, Michael Jackson videos, and the Atari video games she plays) and depicts familial situations closely resembling those extratextually known to be Benning's in part accounts for a viewer projecting Sadie's life onto the text. In a 1992 interview in *Queer World* Benning confesses:

> When I was around 9, I had a girlfriend, but the whole neighborhood thought I was a boy, because my name when I was growing up was Taylor, my middle name. I looked like a boy—skinny, short hair—dressed like a boy, played with boys. My best friend was a boy, and he was paranoid to tell the rest of the neighborhood his best friend was a girl, so he told everybody I was a boy, and I just kind of went along with it. I felt like a boy and I liked girls; I thought, "Well, this is fun." So I had a girlfriend for several months. She was eleven; my first kiss was with her. (Harris 33)

Flat Is Beautiful makes extensive use of crudely but evocatively drawn masks, which all of the characters in the video wear.[7] With interiors shot in her signature Pixelvision and exteriors shot in Super 8, the tape depicts Taylor's isolation and alienation in her tough Milwaukee neighborhood, the cruelty kids can inflict on one another, and her attempt to come to terms with her self-consciousness about her skinny, androgynous, menstruating body, her crushes on girls, and parental neglect. Curiously, the masks simultaneously conceal and betray emotion by metaphorically foregrounding the agonies of that transitional time between childhood and adolescence and the simultaneous public/private demands of this liminal space.

Given some of the antagonism Sadie has expressed toward her father in the past, the scenes between father and daughter in *Flat Is Beautiful* are especially poignant. Taylor and her dad are never shown together, and interact only through long-distance phone calls. In one scene, after she objects to meeting his new girlfriend during a (seemingly rare) occasion when they are scheduled to get together, he reprimands her for her obstinance: "Well look, Taylor, I do what I can. I really try to meet everyone's needs in my life. There are things to being an adult that you just don't understand. Deadlines to meet. Emotional strains. Financial strains. Logistical strains. . . . You know. I just flew back from Paris [from an art show]. It's not like going to the corner store, honey." Her father is placed against a background of swirling, parallel black and white lines resembling the brush strokes of a Van Gogh painting. Within his space, periodic cuts show us a coffee table that displays art catalogs (of Clemente, Salle, and Rauschenberg—perhaps his clients or colleagues) while Taylor's face/mask and body, framed against a stark white brick background, increasingly register her resignation and disappointment. The sadness of this scene is underscored by a recurring image of a goldfish that gradually swims toward the mouth of a cartoon image of an angry snarling dog pasted on the outside of the goldfish bowl.

Mia Carter and Chris Holmlund have examined Benning's work within the tradition of autobiographic and lesbian documentary tropes respectively, but I would like to offer another tradition within which her work might productively be framed. I have referred to Benning's work as visual essays, since, like the literary essay form, they straddle so many categories—autobiography, nonfiction, fantasy, argument, speech, and manifesto—that they seem to resist generic classification. Moreover, the autobiographical character of the essay—its placement of the "I" within the very substance of a topic; its coupling of both personal and social/historical/political exploration; its emphasis on dialogue, communication, and accessibility—allies with Benning's project. In an essay on radical feminist essayists, Ruth-Ellen Boetcher Joeres describes the form as by no means typically academic but rather "an anti-genre which combines Movement and Theory" (166). She points out that although an essay may serve as autobiography, it is neither an autobiography nor an autobiographical novel. Nevertheless, Joeres contends, "If one can generalize about the essay as form in any way, it is this involvement of the 'I' that is often paramount—even Montaigne introduced his essays by commenting 'I am myself the substance of my book' " (166).

Michael Renov proposes an adjectival use of the term essayistic instead of the "totalizing effect" suggested by the use of "visual essay" (8). He offers the essayistic as a "prescription for an ailing documentary tradition," with the power to unleash "the expressive dimension (ever in the embrace of the imaginary) and the inscription of the self in the discourse of the other" (9). Listing video works from a diverse range of artists including Jean-Luc Godard, George Kuchar, Bill Viola, Cecilia Condit, and Daniel Reeves, Renov describes how these works resemble the literary essay form insofar as they "resist generic classification, straddling a series of all-too-confining antinomies: fiction/non-fiction, documentary/avant-garde, cinema/video" (8). Had this essay been written a few years later, Benning's work would likely have figured into Renov's framework.[8]

I want to suggest not merely the adjectival use of "essayistic" with respect to Benning's videos, but specifically a radical feminist inflection of the essayistic. Applying Joeres's model for "The Passionate Essay" to Benning's work provides a useful analogy between the "polemical," "persuasive," and "overtly ideological" characteristics of both the literary and visual form of the essayistic. In her distinction between the radical-feminist essay and its more traditional form, Joeres goes on to state:

> If radical-feminist essayists have anything in common, it is their shared passion, their desire, their need, indeed the absolute imperative they feel to communicate and to use words as a stepping-off point to action. Unlike the essays of Bacon or Montaigne or even of E. B. White, their essays tend to reach out with questions, not necessarily give answers. They are unabashedly political in the broadest sense of the word. . . . They dwell on difference, between themselves and patriarchy, among themselves. On occasion, radical feminist essayists even mark the essay form with their difference, transforming the expected into something else, transforming a letter or an academic article or a speech into an essay. (168)

Part fiction and part fantasy, inflected by both documentary and avant-garde traditions and somewhere between film and video, Sadie Benning's pixel visions may be read as passionate essays that borrow something as well from the Griersonian documentary tradition, which sees cinema as the hammer of education and social change.[9] Benning herself admits to similar ambitions when she states in a 1991 interview: "I want to change the way things are" (Spiro 68).

Girl Power, for example, demonstrates the activist, collectivist-based nature of Benning's identifications. Promiscuously comingling images from documentary footage from the civil rights movement and the Vietnam War, a newsreel interview with a racist, homophobic Nazi Party leader, images of World War II bomber planes, fragments of text, and illustrations from dated medical manuals and sex education pamphlets alongside her own imaginative musings. Benning makes a video that has much in common with both the polemical persuasiveness of the radical-feminist essayist and the fever of Riot Grrrl. An intertitle that reads "Violent Youth Fierce and Furious" is followed by Sadie dancing savagely and angrily; and this is soon followed by a more contemplative pose as she says to the camera in direct-address extreme close-up: "When I was a baby, I'd stare up at the sky. I dreamt of flying away from here. Only, in my dreams, I could never fly away fast enough. So I built my own world inside my head: I had imaginary friends, make believe love. And when I sang, I became every member of the Go-Gos, Blondie, Joan Jett, Devo. I did it all."

Benning then adopts a Kerouackian pose as she ruminates about her rich fantasy life: "I traveled to faraway places and did as I pleased; fought the law and, of course, made my own rules. . . . When I was a kid, I took my shirt off, imagining I was just as powerful and just as sexy as when Matt Dillon did it for *Teen Beat* magazine." This voice-over is punctuated by a series of close-ups of Benning's lips, hummingbirds feeding, a bat flying in slow motion, an image of Matt Dillon, and Benning's playful self-insertion into a bisected image of Luke Perry—performing a curious analogue of pop icon appropriation and cross-gendered identification. The intersection of gender with star identity here resumes as Benning swaggers: "I rode my Big Wheel down the street, pretending I was Erik Estrada, rushing on my motorcycle to save the life of some girl who desperately needed to be rescued." This monologue is accompanied by home-movie footage of a little girl in a fluffy white dress, possibly Benning, riding her tricycle around a crowded living room.

From just a few of the examples I have cited here, I would like to point out a tendency for Benning to counterpoint her most bold, in-your-face Riot Grrrl dyketactics with a retreat to a very vulnerable, childlike self-imaging. It is interesting to speculate that this is what makes the work she produced as a teen so appealing and unthreatening against the more entrenched, politicized adult lesbian performance/identifications of Barbara Hammer, Julie Zando, and Su Friedrich. What the future holds for Benning with respect to both her creative output and the critical/institutional acceptance of it has yet to be borne out. Benning's disillusionment with her own rise to fame in general and with the institutional attempts to centralize or at least ventriloquize her marginalized status begs many questions. Nevertheless, that her contribution to artistic cultural practices is pronounced and important to a wide range of people—particularly queer youth and girls—is beyond a doubt.

NOTES

1. James Benning is best known for doing Midwestern landscape films and as a transitional figure between the structural film movement of the late 1960s and early 1970s (identified with filmmakers like Michael Snow and Hollis Frampton) and the experimental narrative (or "new narrative") movement of the later 1970s and 1980s (which reached its commercial terminus with Jim Jarmusch and Lizzy Borden). His better-known films include *8½ × 11* (1974, his first film to blend structuralism with narrative elements), *11 × 14* (1984, his first feature), *American Dreams* (1984), *Landscape Suicide* (1986), and most recently, *Deseret* (1996, which premiered at Sundance). He did a few collaborations with Bette Gordon in the 1970s including *The United States of America* (1975). IIis last three films have all been landscape films dealing with the history of the American Southwest.

2. Sadie Benning's output to date includes: *Flat Is Beautiful* (56 min.); *German Song* (1995, 5:49 min.); *The Judy Spots* (1995, 13 min.); *Girl Power (Part 1)* (1992, 15 min.); *It Wasn't Love* (1992, 20 min.); *A Place Called Lovely* (1991, 14 min.); *Jollies* (1990 11 min.); *If Every Girl Had a Diary* (1990, 6 min.); *A New Year* (1989, 4 min.); *Me and Rubyfruit* (1989, 4 min.) and *Living Inside* (1989, 4 min.). All of these works, except for *Flat Is Beautiful* and *The Judy Spots,* are distributed through the Video Data Bank in Chicago.

3. I want to point out that female misbehavior and specifically feminist misconduct has a long history of supporting irreverent, angry, and

thoroughly unladylike behavior. A similar point is made by Alexandra Juhasz in her essay, "Bad Girls Come and Go, But a Lying Girl Can Never Be Fenced In," which offers an insightful, historically grounded analysis of the Bad Girls feminist art shows in 1994, of which Benning's work was a part.

4. Reference to this zine and its first issue devoted to "Puberty" is made in her interview with Mark Ewert (3). Benning has certainly been much discussed in Riot Grrrl, teen, and queer teen zines, (she was recently the cover story of a Massachusetts-based zine *Femme Flicke*). Benning's association with Riot Grrrl's music scene continues with her participation in a band called Le Tigre which is fronted by Kathleen Hanna (of Bikini Kill) and includes zine writer/publisher Johanna Fateman. The band released its first album in November 1999 and currently has plans for an upcoming tour.

5. For an excellent overview of Pixelvision, including an historical analysis of its place in the history of "scientific revolutions in the history of film and video," see Erika Suderberg's "Form and Dysfunction."

6. There has been considerable effort to reclaim the word "cunt" both in lesbian subcultures and in Riot Grrrl writing and music.

7. *The Judy Spots* makes use of a cardboard cut-out named Judy, whose face/mask looks very much like those drawn by Benning for *Flat Is Beautiful*. Made for an MTV *Ms.* Foundation fundraiser titled "Ain't Nothin' But a She Thing" (after a Salt-N-Pepa song), *The Judy Spots* consists of five short installments: "Judy Goes to the Mall," "Judy Gets Mad," "Judy Hates Her Job," "Judy Has a Nightmare," and "Judy Feels Sad," which variously show the trials and tribulations of girlhood as Judy ruminates about crying in public, expressing rage, crass consumerism, and the insincerity of her public persona.

8. This comment was made by Renov several times over the course of a graduate seminar he taught on the essayistic in film and video in the spring semester, 1995. I would like to gratefully acknowledge Michael Renov's enthusiastic contribution to and support of ideas developed in this paper, an early draft of which was written for that class.

9. Grierson's notion of art as a hammer is an idea he derives from Trotsky. This metaphor is expanded in a 1940 essay titled "Art In Action," in which Grierson states:

> "They tell us that art is a mirror—a mirror held up to nature. I think that is a false image, conceived by men in quiet unchanging times. In a society like ours, which is even now in the throes of a war of ideas and in a state of social revolution of the profoundest nature, art is not mirror but a hammer. It is a weapon in our hands to see and to say what is right and good and beautiful and hammer it out as the mold and pattern of men's actions" (cited in Evans xiii).

WORKS CITED

Boetcher Joeres, Ruth-Ellen. 1993. "The Passionate Essay: Radical Feminist Essayists." In *The Politics of the Essay: Feminist Perspectives,* ed. Ruth-Ellen Boetcher Joeres and Elizabeth Mittman, 151–71. Bloomington: Indiana University Press.

Brown, Rita Mae. 1973. *Rubyfruit Jungle.* New York: Bantam Books.

Butler, Judith. 1990. *Gender Trouble.* New York: Routledge.

Carter, Mia. "The Politics of Pleasure: Cross-Cultural Autobiographic Performance in the Video Works of Sadie Benning." *Signs* 23.3 (1998): 745–69.

Evans, Gary. 1984. *John Grierson and the National Film Board: The Politics of Wartime Propaganda.* Toronto: University of Toronto Press.

Ewert, Mark. "Interview with Sadie Benning." *Mirage* August 1992: 2–4.

Frith, Simon. 1987. *Art into Pop.* New York: Methuen.

———. 1996. *Performing Rites: On the Value of Popular Music.* Oxford: Oxford University Press.

Gottlieb, Joanne, and Gayle Wald. 1994. "Smells Like Teen Spirit: Riot Grrrls, Revolution and Women in Independent Rock." In *Microphone Fiends: Youth, Music and Youth Culture,* ed. Andrew Ross and Tricia Rose, 250–274. New York: Routledge.

Harris, Elise. "Baby Butch Video." *Queer World* 15 November 1992: 22–23.

Hebdige, Dick. 1979. *Subculture: The Meaning of Style.* New York: Methuen.

Holmlund, Chris. 1997. "When Autobiography Meets Ethnography and Girl Meets Girl: The 'Dyke Docs' of Sadie Benning and Su Friedrich." In *Between the Sheets, in the Streets: Queer, Lesbian, Gay Documentary,* ed. Chris Holmlund and Cynthia Fuchs, 127–43. Minneapolis: University of Minnesota Press.

Juhasz, Alexandra. 1999. "Bad Girls Come and Go, But a Lying Girl Can Never Be Fenced In." In *Feminism and Documentary,* ed. Diane Waldman and Janet Walker. Minneapolis: University of Minnesota Press.

Kearney, Mary Celeste. "Riot Grrrl: It's Not Just Music, It's Not Just Punk." *Spectator* 16.1 (Fall/Winter 1995): 83–95.

Masters, Kim. "Auteur of Adolescence." *The Washington Post* 17 October 1992, D1: 7.

McRobbie, Angela. 1991. *Feminism and Youth Culture: From "Jackie" to "Just Seventeen."* Basingstoke: Macmillan.

———. 1994. *Postmodernism and Popular Culture.* London: Routledge.

McRobbie, Angela and Mica Nava. 1984. *Gender and Generation.* London: Macmillan

Renov, Michael. "History and/as Autobiography: The Essayistic in Film and Video." *Frame/work* 3.2 (1988): 6–12.

Romney, Jonathan. "Honey I Shrunk the Kit." *New Statesman and Society* 12 November 1993: 34.

Rosenbaum, Jonathan. "Girl with a Camera." *The Reader* (Chicago) (November 1991): 10–11.

Smyth, Cherry. "Girls, Videos and Everything (after Sarah Schulman)." *Frieze* (January/February 1993): 21–23.

———. "Girls, Videos and Everything (after Sarah Schulman)." *Burn* (May 1993): 55–58.

Spiro, Ellen. "Shooting Star: Teenage Video Maker Sadie Benning Attracts a Youthful Audience." *The Advocate* 573 (March 26 1991): 68–69.

Suderberg, Erika. "Form and Dysfunction: Fisher-Price and the Cult of Pixel." *International Documentary* IX.4 (Winter 1990): 18–22.

chapter 17

She's Murder:
Pretty Poisons and Bad Seeds

Steven Woodward

> How wonderful to meet such a natural little girl! She
> knows what she wants and she asks for it. Not like these
> overcivilized little pets that have to go through analysis
> before they can choose an ice-cream soda.
>
> MONICA BREEDLOVE IN *The Bad Seed*

The great irony of Monica Breedlove's statement in *The Bad Seed* (1956), one of the first movies to concentrate exclusively on girlhood violence, is that the eight-year-old girl she is speaking about, Rhoda Penmark (Patty McCormack), is a precocious verbal trickster, a manipulator, a liar, and a murderer. We know that Rhoda is an untrustworthy brat from the earliest shots of the film where her saccharine performances to her father, mother, and doting "aunt" invoke rather than suspend our disbelief. However, at this point, we cannot guess at the full extent of her depravity. Even later, as we begin to suspect her of being a precocious murderer, her acts of physical violence are never seen onscreen: they come to us through the reports of others or through her own confessions delivered to her distraught mother. These confessions reveal that she is a violent psychopath who has already murdered at least three people in the short span of her life. Sensational as this film is, it is nevertheless original in portraying cinematically the idea that children are capable of great disingenuousness precisely because of their status as children, and that this capacity to mask one's motives reaches its highest potential in the female child, the killer girl.

The idea of the female killer has only been invoked at intervals by a film industry both eager to capture an audience and aware that the idea of the woman murderer represents an extreme problem in terms of audience perceptions about contemporary reality and audience desire. At times, that idea has simply been too alarming. *Pretty Poison* (1968) deeply unsettled its first audiences with its disturbing image—perhaps a reversal of the dynamics of *Psycho* (1960)—of a young man (Anthony Perkins) being outstripped in psychosis by his eager, pretty apprentice (Tuesday Weld) and as a result received only very limited release. Forms of violence are perceived as gendered. This view is supported by the fact that, statistically speaking, murder is very much the domain of men. However, the public perception of physical violence in general is that it is almost exclusively a masculine form of aggression, notwithstanding recent reports noting a marked increase in violent acts committed by girls and young women.[1] In the public mind, women and children remain outside the law: women above it, because they are the ultimate guardians of our moral code; children below it, because they have not yet had a chance to internalize that code.

On the other hand, the anxiety-provoking idea of a murderous female impulse has been a rich source for dramatic narratives. The idea of the woman-turned-killer has been much in vogue in recent American films (*Thelma & Louise* [1991], *Point of No Return* [1993], and *The Long Kiss Goodnight* [1996]). Such films depend on our assuming that female sexuality restricts women to emotionally grounded roles and functions. Pictures of female killers whose sexuality empowers them to commit violent deeds tap into the anxieties of both men and women about sexual equality. If women are to be equal to men, they must be able to kill, and the cinema (particularly the Hollywood cinema) has constructed a number of scenarios to address this quasi-fantasy. As Carol M. Dole has pointed out, however, "The film industry has had to balance the demand for stronger roles for women with the ambivalence of viewers (especially males, who make up so large a percentage of action fans) about the transgressive figure of the Woman with a Gun" and the castration anxiety she may provoke (12). We may discover, in these films, that women can kill just as well—as efficiently and cold-bloodedly—as men. In fact, they can often kill better, since the violence they unleash is so unexpected. But with a few exceptions (notably in Oliver Stone's *Natural Born Killers* [1994] and *U Turn* [1997]), the murderous aggression of screen women usually turns out to be sexually restorative and even morally redemptive. As Dole has observed of *Fargo* (1996), it "enables the female hero to have position, success, firepower, and domestic happiness all at once without threatening anyone" (19).

Escaping any such moral framework and hence disturbing and disrupting public perception (and being potentially more dramatic as a result) is the girl who kills. As Kathy Merlock Jackson has noted, "Boys and girls have been equally represented in popular movies," and "Little girls . . . are most frequently portrayed as good, self-reliant, and independent characters; they figure as capable, very much in control fix-its even more often than their male counterparts" (186). How extraordinary, then, that against this general use of the girl in cinema, depictions of that apparent oxymoron, the killer girl, would occasionally appear. This essay examines the framing of the girl killer in film narratives—How is she driven to kill? Must she learn to kill? How does she react to killing?—and considers whether that framing has changed over the period between *The Bad Seed* and *Fun* (1994).

The Bad Seed remains a landmark film, marking the emergence of the child monster in cinema. That that monster was a girl came as even more of a shock (see Jackson). In the film, Colonel Kenneth Penmark (William Hopper) and his wife, Christine (Nancy Kelly), live in a luxurious apartment with their blond-haired eight-year-old daughter, Rhoda. Colonel Penmark is called away at the beginning of the film on an assignment of unspecified length in Washington, and Christine is left alone with their daughter. Rhoda is adored by both her father and an elderly neighbor and family friend, Monica Breedlove (Evelyn Varden). To them, she is an entirely perfect being, though to the viewer and to her mother her polished manners and proclamations of love are somewhat saccharine (the falsity of her affections is quickly revealed in close-ups of her grimacing face and gritting teeth during hugs with her adorers).

We begin to see what lies behind Rhoda's veneer when one of her classmates, Claude Daigle, drowns while on a class picnic. Claude and Rhoda have been in direct competition for a penmanship medal, and Claude has won. When the boy's body is recovered from the lake, there is no sign of the medal, and both Miss Fern (Joan Croyden), the school's principal, and Claude's parents want to question Rhoda about the incident. After Mrs. Penmark discovers the medal hidden among Rhoda's things, she forces Rhoda to talk about her involvement. We discover not only that Rhoda is directly responsible for Claude's death, since she bludgeoned him with her shoe when he refused to give her the medal, but also that she has no remorse for her crime, blaming it on the victim. Mrs. Penmark takes the medal and drops it in the lake at the place where Claude

The child monster and her false affection in *The Bad Seed.*

was found, in the hope of protecting Rhoda. But in the remainder of the film, Rhoda confesses to killing an old lady by tripping her on the stairs and sets fire to the apartment building janitor, Leroy (Henry Jones), who pretends to have evidence of her involvement in Claude's death.

Although Christine Penmark is horrified and repulsed by her daughter, she soon begins to feel guilt herself. Although she is from a well-to-do family and her father, Richard Bravo (Paul Fix), is a prestigious writer and criminologist, she has long harbored the suspicion that she is not his daughter. Since Rhoda's childhood environment has been perfect, she suspects that there may be something bad in her blood, some evil that Rhoda has inherited from her. When her father comes for a visit, she confronts him with her suspicions and peculiar dreams of herself as a two-year-old, and he confesses that she is, in fact, the child of an infamous murderess. Although he tries to reassure her that murderous traits cannot be inherited, another visitor, Reginald Tasker (Gage Clarke), explains to her the theory of the "bad seed" or sociopath, the person without a conscience, who inherits and passes along this deficiency genetically.[2] Realizing that she is as guilty genetically as Rhoda is guilty morally, Christine decides to protect her daughter to the end. But after Rhoda murders Leroy—Christine sees him burned to death—Christine decides that the only protection she can offer is a long "sleep" for both of them, an act of murder/suicide, which is unsuccessful. As Christine is recovering in hospital from a self-inflicted gunshot wound, Rhoda, whose stomach has been quickly pumped free of sleeping pills, ventures out to the lake in the hope of retrieving the sunken penmanship medal and is there struck by lightning, an unconvincing cinematic clap of light and smoke. And there the film ends, though an additional title advises us coyly: "You have just seen a motion picture whose theme dares to be startlingly different. May we ask that you do not divulge the unusual climax of this story." Surely, though, there is nothing "unusual" about the cinematic justice meted out to Rhoda, just at a moment when we thought she had escaped punishment.

To some extent, *The Bad Seed* fits into a larger pattern of filmic visions of the kind identified by such critics as Jackson. She has examined the portrayal of children in film according to a pre– and post–World War II model. According to her, prewar American ideology was dependent on an image of the child as completely innocent. Children represent the future, which is, by implication, forever improving. But in postwar films, this entirely optimistic view was sullied, questioned, modified, and only occasionally reaffirmed: "The glories of childhood innocence were downplayed as demon children and tough, precocious imps inhabited the screen. These images no longer told of the dream [of a perfectible future]. Instead, they revealed societal fears; they foretold the nightmare" (9). Jackson notes that within this general pattern, *The Bad Seed* was indeed remarkable, proving "a real innovation for its time; never before had such an evil image of childhood appeared on the screen. . . . *The Bad Seed* made its mark as a box-office success, thereby providing the germination of a filmic image that would reach its peak in the 1970s: the child-as-monster" (112).

Furthermore, the film suggested that to some extent evil was inescapable. At the time of its appearance, most psychologists were inclined toward B. F. Skinner's ideas about the importance of environment and conditioning in creating human character (cf. Benjamin

Spock's *Baby and Child Care*). But this film implies that each generation may in fact be burdened with the sins of the past, that heredity is the most important factor (in a way totally unforeseen by earlier arguments about eugenics). This idea plays havoc with American notions of innocence, diligent application, and perfectibility.

Jackson's ideas help us see *The Bad Seed* as part of this emerging cynical vision. As she notes, the shock of such films depends on the apparent irrationality of the violence, and this shock has been heightened through an inversion in the social class of the child monster: "Although legal officials dealing with juveniles report that crime is more common among poor children, this is not the case in films: Monster children are almost always the products of upper- or middle-class families. These films, then, are commenting not on the state of child crime but on the corruption of mainstream American society" (186–87). However, Jackson fails to make much note of the gender issue that is such a prominent element in this film. While Rhoda could be seen as part of this larger pattern of middle-class demon children, she is exceptional in the disparity between her facade of feminine social decorum as the only child of an affluent and completely respectable American family and the savagery of her aggressions. It makes all the difference that this demon child is a girl. In her, the mask of femininity is layered over the mask of childhood innocence.

Interestingly, the sociopathic theory so clearly annunciated by Reginald Tasker in the film version of *The Bad Seed* offers a rationalistic explanation for Rhoda's behavior that should neutralize the gender connotations of the killer girl. She is, after all, not a killer *girl* but a killer *child*. Leroy torments Rhoda with the idea that they have electric chairs for children, "A li'l blue one for the boys, and a li'l pink one for the girls." But while the theory of sociopathy and Leroy's observation disrupt the most disturbing aspect in the idea of the killer girl—the implicit link between Rhoda's sex and her murderous impulse—other dialogue in the film reinforces the idea of female malice that is deathly powerful but also secretive and undetectable. In an early scene in the film, the discussion between Monica Breedlove, Emory, and Reginald Tasker of criminal behavior focuses exclusively on women sociopaths. They brood salaciously over the recent history of female murderers, in particular a nurse, Mrs. Alison, "that simply fascinating paranoidal female" who has poisoned a number of her male patients. And while Christine objects at this point in the film, saying she has no interest in such subjects—"I'm afraid I shy away from reading about such things"— she later asks Tasker about the history of the notorious, beguiling serial killer Bessie Denker and whether she was ever convicted for her numerous murders. As Tasker explains it: "Three juries looked at that lovely dewy face and heard that melting cultured voice and said she couldn't have done it." There are two possible implications to these discussions. On the one hand, the killer may hide behind the feminine mask: the figure of the nurse, epitome of nurturing; the beautiful woman, emblem of truth and justice, as well as beauty; the little girl, archetype of childhood's innocence. Indeed, as Lucy Fischer has pointed out, criminologists writing in the 1950s, like Otto Pollak, speculated that women's secretive nature likely concealed an abundance of criminal proclivities and actions: "Woman's role as a homemaker has provided her with many opportunities for murder and has assured that her murders will go unpunished" (271). On the other hand, and much more disturbing, femininity itself may some-how empower and direct the murderess. Feminine murders are all the more sinister because of their inscrutability and the possibility of a peculiarly feminine motive behind them.

The film encodes this idea of the mask visually: while we wit-ness a few examples of Rhoda's sudden violent turns and verbal abuse, her physical aggression occurs offscreen and is either reported by others or, later, confessed by her. Brutal female violence happens, but somewhere out of sight. To reinforce this inverted picture of the gender of violence even further, nearly all the men in the film are mild-mannered, deliberative (even the martial Colonel Penmark), and soft-spoken. Only the mischievous Leroy has enough of his own malice to recognize the same impetus in Rhoda.

Indeed, the gender implications of aggression are radically dif-ferent in the novel on which the film and the play are based, William March's *The Bad Seed*. In March's novel, the town in which the story is set is peopled with bizarre, violent, and sexually disturbing charac-ters. As a recent reviewer of March's novel commented, he "litters his novel with bad seeds" (Fasman 23). Leroy is not merely suspi-cious of children but is actively malicious toward them, giving one girl a dead rat wrapped up as a present. Other characters present a skewed sexuality, such as Monica Breedlove's incestuous yearning for her brother and her desire to mutilate both men and women. And when Christine discovers the truth about her own daughter, that truth represents a revelation not just about the presence of real evil in a few individuals and of a latent evil within herself but of an evil that pervades all humankind. Christine learns that

> violence [is] an inescapable factor of the heart, perhaps the most important factor of all—an ineradicable thing that lay, like a bad seed, behind kindness, behind compassion, behind the embrace of love itself. Sometimes it lay deeply hidden, sometimes it lay close to the surface; but always it was there, ready to appear, under the right conditions, in all its irrational dreadfulness. (March, quoted in Fasman, 23)

This implication, which was a major part of March's misanthropic view of human behavior and sexuality, is carefully sidestepped in the film version of the story.[3] Here, evil is clearly demarcated and can be clinically isolated, like the sociopath herself. Rhoda's delinquency is seen as an extremely isolated problem of female blood rather than a symptom of widespread social decay.

As I have pointed out, for the viewer of the film, Rhoda's violence is heard more than seen. It is represented in the false ring of her sweet talk with mother, father, and Monica, in the threatening tones of her exchanges with Leroy, and, only occasionally, in the grimaces she makes behind the backs of the admiring adults. Indeed, once this film identified the nature of female malice with Rhoda's false "sugar and spice" facade, many new narrative possibilities became available. As Fasman notes, "Rhoda, an intelligent, manipulative, thoroughly amoral girl, is an antecedent of that more celebrated intelligent girl-woman of mid-century American fiction, Lolita, created several hundred miles north at almost the same time" (23). Rhoda is an eight-year-old girl whose fits of rage resemble the tantrums of even younger children. By contrast, the filmic violence of pubescent girls would revolve around sexual issues, particularly Oedipal conflicts.

In *The Crush* (1993), we see what the amoral girl has become in teenage life. Her psychopathic energies are no longer directed toward academic achievement or childish desires. She has won or taken her academic accolades. Now she is intent on possessing a new treasure, a love object. *The Crush* is a dismal film by many standards, yet it offers an interesting vision of the adolescent bad seed, now grown into a pretty poison. Nick Eliot (Cary Elwes) drives his convertible along the freeway into an unnamed city (the film was shot in Vancouver). He has been hired as a columnist for an important magazine with an autocratic editor, but he is having difficulty locating a decent apartment. While driving through an upscale neighborhood, he almost runs over a teenage girl (Alicia Silverstone) who brazenly rollerskates into the street, then peers over her 'Lolita' sunglasses at him after he slams to a halt inches away from her. Eliot, evidently captivated by her charms, watches her as she skates back behind her house, then notices a sign on her lawn advertising an apartment for rent. Eliot's admiration for this girl, Darian Forrester, and his need for a place to live coincide; he takes up residence in the coach house behind Darian's family home.

But Darian is both sexually and intellectually precocious, and, driven by Eliot's obvious veneration of her charms, wants to become his lover. Unfortunately, Eliot's girlfriend (Jennifer Rubin) stands in the way, though Darian attempts to dispatch her by releasing a swarm of bees into her darkroom. Darian's father (Kurtwood Smith), on the other hand, seems blind to his daughter's burgeoning sexual desire. He constructs a full-size merry-go-round in the attic of the family home, an image of what he believes childhood should be, yet one that contains, quite perversely, images of that sexuality that he hopes to repress. While the ride is at rest, its horses appear charming and placid. Yet they soon become dreadful when the ride is in motion and they start their rhythmic plunging, with streaming manes, flared nostrils, and glaring eyes emphasized in close-ups. Indeed, the final scene of the film—one in which the daughter comes close to fulfilling the Oedipal quest/fate of killing the father—occurs in this attic space, with the merry-go-round whirling at full speed (and with Darian's childish and innocent friend, Cheyenne [Amber Benson], bound to the back of one of the beasts).

The narrative of the film, its cheap gloss on the Freudian roots of girlhood aggression, is not entirely fanciful. For the last half-century, the judicial system, informed particularly by psychoanalysis, has identified the cause of a whole range of girls' delinquent behaviors as sexual confusion. Indeed, as Rachel Devlin has noted (1998), the public perception that girls are generally good is not particularly accurate. Part of the reason for that perception is that girls' crimes seldom come into the public eye because they are seldom interpreted as public offenses and because the explanation for such crimes reflects on the immediate family instead of the social environment.

Devlin offers an interesting analysis of female juvenile delinquency in the 1945–65 period in the United States. Her contention is that in this period, the juvenile delinquent "became a site for the expression of cultural anxiety about the authority of the family generally and of fathers specifically" (84). In the postwar era, both male and female juvenile delinquencies were on the increase. Although female delinquency represented only a fraction of the problem, it came to compose a larger and larger portion of the total. While boys' delinquency was nearly always explained in relation to social and personal factors, girls' delinquency was framed in psychoanalytic terms, as a failure to successively negotiate the Oedipus complex. Male delinquency was an outcome of the failure of authority and discipline within the family; female delinquency was explained in much more equivocal terms as the failure of the father to participate adequately in the Oedipal drama of female adolescence. If girls transgressed the law, it was because they had not been able to assume the passive, masochistic, and erotic feminine identity that fathers' sexual admiration would require.

Furthermore, Devlin notes, because girls' crimes were seen as an outcome of identity confusion, they were frequently kept out of the public eye and the criminal courts. Many cases were dealt with by the police themselves, while others came before the Wayward Minor Court, which was "a social court or socio-legal tribunal" in which a judge interviewed the girl and, often informed by psychoanalytic interpretation of her conduct, recommended a course of action that precluded detention or other forms of punitive action frequently visited on boys (94).

The narrative of *The Crush* offers precisely the same interpretation of Darian Forrester's murderous intent as that underlying Devlin's analysis of delinquent girls. Though her father does not know it, Darian has been unable to sublimate the aggressive impulses of her childhood and directs them against any object that stands in the way of her finding a male admirer/father surrogate. *The Crush* is not exceptional in portraying this view of the motives of girlhood aggression. *Poison Ivy* (1992) and its progeny have kept this family drama at their center.

In *Poison Ivy*, Ivy (Drew Barrymore) lacks a family of her own and "invades" the wealthy family of her friend, Sylvie Cooper (Sara Gilbert). Sylvie's mother, Georgie (Cheryl Ladd), is a beautiful woman weakened and gradually wasting as a result of emphysema. Driven by the admiration of Sylvie's father, Darryl (Tom Skerritt), Ivy pushes the weak Georgie out of an open window—though the crime passes for a suicide—and claims Darryl for herself. Sylvie eventually realizes what really happened and, in a second struggle by the open window, manages to overcome Ivy, who falls to her death. Thus, the film is essentially a good daughter/bad daughter fantasy, with the transgressor clearly marked by her blond hair and siren-like femininity.

The Lolita figure is to this day the dominant image of the feminine form of aggressor. In her, beauty is not the image of spiritual goodness but a mask over corruption. Her aggression is delivered not through physical violence but through manipulation. Even clinical views of girlhood aggression hardly vary from this myth. At a conference held in Toronto in 1999, apparently the first in North America to focus on forms of female aggression, it was suggested that "after the age of 2 or 3, most girls stop displaying their aggression physically and learn through example to reinvent it in less detectable ways." Instead, girls develop "a 'sophisticated and insidious' form of aggression through false rumors, verbal abuse and premeditated manipulation" (Southworth A3). Although the idea of such manipulation is not news—soap opera plots have been built on such feminine wiles for decades—psychologists' recognition that it is potentially as damaging as physical violence seems to be entirely novel.

Strutting and Fretting

> Dear diary, I want to kill and you have to believe it's for more than just selfish reasons, more than just a spoke in my menstrual cycle.
>
> VERONICA SAWYER IN *Heathers*

Veronica Sawyer's (Winona Ryder) self-reflexive awareness that physical violence may be purgative and necessary, not just a selfish, momentary need or female vagary, is evident in a second strain of killer-girl films, which deal with the attempt to restore social and verbal sincerity through the recovery of physical violence. If girls' lives have been plagued with manipulation and deceit, then physical violence—aggression not masked by feminine wiles—might be restorative. This is the scenario concocted in *Heathers* (1989).[4]

The gender division of styles of violence is clearly demarcated in this film in about a clique of girls and an alien bad boy, new in town, who exhibits the quirky and unpredictable physical violence of the lone male. *Heathers* focuses on the social structure at Westerburg High, a school dominated by three "Heathers" (Kim Walker, Shannen Doherty, and Lisanne Falk) engaged in malicious tricks

to promote and maintain their popularity and domination over social life. Veronica Sawyer is their dubious apprentice, a girl only
half-indoctrinated in their ways. Depiction of the Heathers' feminine malice begins even in the opening credits as the girls play a
round of dream croquet toward some unseen goal, which turns out,
in the Wonderlandian last shot of the sequence, to be Veronica's
head. In the scene that follows, in the high school cafeteria, Heather
Chandler (Walker) instructs Veronica to write a fake love note to
the overweight and unfeminine Martha Dunnstock (Carrie Lynn), or
"Dumptruck," as they call her, and we watch the inevitable fallout
from this prank. Thus, within these first few moments, the idea is
clearly established that these girls' secretive or manipulative aggressions are essentially self-destructive, aimed as they are at members
of their own group (of friends) or at other girls that fail to meet a
feminine ideal.

That the Heathers are developing a masochistic ideal of femininity and an essentially passive and joyless sexual role for themselves is soon made clear. They yearn for sexual involvement as a
mark of feminine success and yet are repulsed by the crude fum-
bling and thrusting of the boys with whom they insist on becoming
entangled, either those from Westerburg High or, indeed, the more
sophisticated boys of Remington University. Although Veronica dis-
gustedly rejects the propositions of both groups, she is not merely
sexually repressed. After all, when the school's new rebel figure, Jason Dean (Christian Slater), or J. D. (perhaps aptly named after James
Dean), appears at her bedroom window one evening, she is delighted
to take "a walk with him," frolicking happily, without anxiety, on
the lawn of her family's sumptuous home. Jason's winning candor
has been demonstrated for us in that first scene in the high school
cafeteria, as a stark contrast to the machinations of the Heathers.
Approached by two dim-witted senior boys, Kurt Kelly (Lance Fen-
ton) and Ram Sweeney (Patrick Laborteaux), who can only muster a
"no faggots here" kind of harassment, he pulls a revolver from his
trench coat and shoots each in the head. Indeed, we do not realize
the shots are blanks until, in the next scene, Veronica reports, "All
J. D. did was ruin two pairs of pants."

If Veronica is responsive to the quirky style and rebellious spirit
of Jason Dean, it is partly because he offers her a means out of her
impasse. The film is, in the most essential way, about schooling in
gender, with Veronica choosing between the masculine, individualistic, unrepressed desire and anger offered by Jason Dean and the

feminine guile and manipulation offered by the Heathers. The feminine violence of social exclusion, she discovers, can be not only met in kind but subverted and displaced with masculine physical violence. Simply put, Jason will provide Veronica with the means to express her personal anger. When the two visit Heather Chandler in her princess's bedroom on the morning after the Remington University party, Veronica plans to feed Heather a bogus hangover cure, a mixture of milk and orange juice, that will make her vomit. Jason, however, proposes liquid drain cleaner as a substitute ingredient and actually dares the hungover girl into drinking it. No doubt, Heather's social and sexual "clog" is cleared, but the cure proves lethal. Thus, while Veronica is a witness and an accomplice to this murder, the narrative positions her so that she is not directly responsible: J. D. is the agent who acts on her feelings.

To reinforce this dubious idea, in the next scenes of the film, Veronica hears that Kurt Kelly has been spreading a rumor that he and Ram had a "swordfight" in her mouth and she decides to take her revenge. After arranging a tryst with them in the woods behind the school, Veronica shows up with J. D., gunning the two football players down with bullets which, according to J. D., break the skin and spill just a little blood. In fact, there is very little sign of any blood, but the two are most assuredly dead. And when Veronica confronts J. D. with his lie about the bullets, he counters: "You believed it 'cause you wanted to believe it. Your true feelings were too gross and icky for you to face." Jason enacts what Veronica can only feel and express inwardly in the convolutions of her diary entries. Her violent emotions must not be seen.

The feminine intrigues of *Heathers* not only denote social obstructions and defective relations but also indicate a morally corrupt society. Society here is too feminine in its repressions. Following the example of his father, a demolition expert who takes malicious pleasure in destroying what other people love, J. D. proposes to eradicate the corruption by blowing up the entire school and its occupants: "People are going to look at the ashes of Westerburg and say, 'Now there is a school that self-destructed not because society didn't care, but because the school was society.'" The students of Westerburg have learned their lessons too well and perfectly reflect the prejudices of the adult world. We know, by this point, that Jason's violence, too, although immediate, is actually confused and unfocused, reflecting his father's.[5] And Veronica has realized that J. D. is "not a rebel but a psychopath." He represents not just unrepressed emotion but a force of social disorder, even anarchy. Nor can she see any positive aspects in the "loving synchronicity" offered to students by one teacher who insists they join hands in front of television camera crews to mourn Kurt and Ram. As Veronica wryly observes, "I've seen J. D.'s way. I've seen Miss Pauline Fleming's way [note the feminine demarcation of this teacher as "Miss"]. And nothing has changed."

Schooled in these mechanisms for change, but nonplussed by the social arrangements that come out of them, Veronica must discover an alternative. She must fully accept the mantle of violence but use it for positive ends. Thus, in the crucial scenes with which the film closes, Veronica must battle with Jason in the subterranean depths of the high school to save this society that hardly seems worth saving. She must sever her alliance with him, transcending the previous conditions of social life (represented by the Heathers) and sublimating the morbid elements of individualism (represented in J. D.) in order to graduate. After she has wounded J. D., he emerges from the basement, his bomb now taped inside his trench coat, and blows himself up while Veronica calmly witnesses. As she strolls down the halls of Westerburg in the aftermath, she shows only a calm and unflinching confidence. The massive explosion has been adequate to blacken her face, frizzle her hair, and light her cigarette. But it has restored or even created a new emotional balance. She takes the ribbon of power from the hair of Heather Duke (Doherty), symbolizing her commitment to defining a new social order, and asks the wheelchair-bound "Dumptruck" to watch movies with her in place of attending the prom. By eluding formalities and other codes of exclusion and repression, Veronica manages to make violence meaningful and creative, reappropriating it for female use.

Signifying Nothing

> DEFENSE LAWYER: It's so incongruous, it's almost inconceivable.
> PSYCHOLOGIST: If anyone can change, it's a child.
>
> "KILLERZ," FROM "LAW AND ORDER," SEPTEMBER 29, 1999

Cases of girls killing seldom reveal such creative meanings as those demonstrated in *Heathers*. More often in popular filmic fiction, these are puzzling, inscrutable crimes beyond any frame of adult understanding. Resigning ourselves to logic, perceptions, and emotions unique to the mind of the girl who kills, we can only hope that she grows out of it. *Heavenly Creatures* (1994) and *Fun* probe the psyches of killer girls. The impetus in both is to try to explain incidents of girl murder, and both suggest that burgeoning sexuality is somehow at the root of their crimes—that it is the chemistry of two girls coming together, finding in their relationship a recognition of each other that is not offered by parents and other adults, that sparks their violence. In *Heavenly Creatures*, this moment of violence emanates from an erotic bond between two girls. In *Fun*, the unmotivated murder of an elderly woman serves as erotic bond, an ecstatic moment shared between two girls. In these films, girls commit murder precisely because they are girls.

Heavenly Creatures attempts to explain murder by taking the killer girls' point of view, using one girl's diary entries and letters between the two as narrative explication. The girls think they live in a leering and oppressive adult world. Fourteen-year-old Pauline and Juliet (Melanie Lynskey and Kate Winslet) form a friendship that crosses class boundaries. As both their families become aware, the relationship also threatens to transgress heterosexual norms. The compelling psychosexual involvement of the girls, figured onscreen in a medieval fantasy realm they create together, seems to be a positive force within the dull reality and mundane perversity of their parents' world. Clergymen, teachers, doctors, and parents attempt to displace the girls' fantasy but fail to do so. One girl's parents plan to divorce and leave New Zealand, and the other's, encouraged by the diagnostic gloss of a doctor, see an ideal opportunity to break up the budding lesbian relationship. But Pauline and Juliet resist this parental oppression, bludgeoning Pauline's mother to death.

In an interesting way, however, the film is misleading, since it is not simply about the championing of female fantasy over repressive patriarchy as the inclusion of much-repeated, visually bizarre fantasy scenes suggests. As sympathetic as much of the film is to the richness and vivacity of the girls' fantasy world, the actual murder of Honora Rieper (Sarah Peirse) is a bloody and fearful event, accomplished with a brick in a stocking dashed again and again against the screaming woman's skull. The girlish fantasy world with which we have been complicit, cannot possibly support, distance, or displace the graphic horror of this realistic moment. The murder itself happens in a space outside explication. And in the titles with which the film closes, detailing the trial, imprisonment, and release of Pauline and Juliet, it becomes clear that neither the justice system nor the narratives that support it could explain and, thus, prevent such a crime: "It was a condition of their release that they never meet again."

Fun concerns two teenage misfits, Hillary (Renée Humphrey) and Bonnie (Alicia Witt), whose pointless murder of an elderly woman, Mrs. Farmer (Ania Suli), is probed simultaneously by a prison psychologist, Jane (Leslie Hope), and an investigative reporter, John (William R. Moses). The John and Jane perspectives on the crime would seem to suggest that director Rafal Zielinski is exploring not just the nature of the crime but the impossibility of constructing an understanding of it from points of view that are both gendered and loaded with their own critical assumptions. After all, the girls reveal different aspects or tell different versions of their stories to these two adults.

The actual events of the day are not in question. Color footage and the girls' voice-overs gradually reveal their movements from the time their accidental meeting at a bus stop to their various manic antics and petty crimes, the murder of an elderly woman who could be their grandmother, washing blood out of Bonnie's hair in a gas station restroom, and the moment they fall peacefully asleep in Hillary's bed. We have a visual record of the events of the one day of Bonnie and Hillary's friendship. However, unlike *Heathers* or *Heavenly Creatures*, *Fun* gives us no special access to the motive or meaning of the murder for the girls themselves.

These girls do not face any immediate moral quandary that demands a response, violent or otherwise. Nor is there some fantasy realm for these girls within which their killing might be motivated. On the contrary, the prison sequences, intercut with the scenes of their short friendship, have a *cinéma verité* style, shot in grainy, handheld black-and-white. These stark images offer us little additional information, nor do the lines of questioning taken by John and Jane in their interviews with the girls add to our knowledge. John wants to turn Hillary into a victim, using extracts from her diary about her father's sexual abuse of her in the sidebars of his article and arranging for the publication of her poetry. And though he goads Hillary with the promise of an emotional catharsis—"This is your chance to tell the world how you really feel"—she will not be so easily taken in. Jane's needs are hardly less manipulative. She wants an explanation from Bonnie of her reasons and feelings about the murder. Refusing to believe the girls could have done it for fun, Jane insists that Bonnie will have to keep telling her story over and over again, "until you get it right." But ultimately, the explanation of the murder is hardly less hazy than Bonnie's definition of fun: "feeling things you've never felt before." John goes off to "connect the dots" or "fill in the blanks" of his evidence, while Jane can only lament, "Wish my job were that easy." Bonnie throws herself off a balcony and dies, and Hillary, moved to a different prison, faces the world alone.[6]

No doubt the crime here, as in *Heavenly Creatures*, depends on the peculiar chemistry of two girls. Hillary tells Jane about the special bond between her and Bonnie: "She didn't get to know me. We just knew each other right away. . . . When we met it was like a door opening. . . . And I knew we would always be together and nobody could get in with us." She later describes her peculiar sense of herself while with Bonnie: "It was like we were like werewolves that day."

But to be a werewolf is absolutely not to be a girl: the two identities are mutually exclusive. The werewolf is most typically viewed as a symbol of the irrational and sexual impulses of the man—grotesque fusion of wolf and human, murderous beast, ravenous cannibal, sexual predator (Carter). Even so, the werewolf helps us to encapsulate the meaning of the killer girl. For the girl who chooses to kill carries an impossible weight of moral responsibility, one that no boy or man killer ever carries in the movies. When the girl kills as girl, her action will be subject to the most thorough scrutiny and yet will remain inscrutable: unknowable, unjudgable, and therefore impossible to situate within the moral spectrum. Murder, indeed, reaches its full irrational potential with the killer girl, since the girl has been our magic mirror: her surface reflects only what we demand to see there, an idealized version of ourselves.

Notes

1. See, for example, Hull. As with most newspaper reports of female violence, this one emphasizes an apparent contradiction, describing the girls concerned as follows: "All four are bright, middle-class suburban high school students or recent graduates. At night, police said, the girls became gun-wielding bandits with no remorse" (E12). Hull emphasizes a kind of vampire syndrome: the girls' criminal natures emerged only at night, when they might be covered by darkness.

2. Jackson elides this important detail. She notes: "Bravo denies [Christine] could have inherited any criminal tendencies, saying that criminal children are always the product of their environment. Christine,

however, is convinced that she is responsible for bringing into the world a child with no sense of right and wrong, no guilt—in essence, 'a bad seed' " (111). In her analysis, Jackson fails to note that Tasker, a criminologist, expounds the new theory of inherited sociopathy to Christine, implicating her in Rhoda's crimes.

3. The sidestepping may well have occasioned, at least in part, by the Motion Picture Production Code then in effect, which enjoined that "No picture shall be produced which will lower the moral standards of those who see it."

4. *Heathers 2*, a sequel to *Heathers* by the same writer and director team of Michael Lehmann and Daniel Waters, and also starring Winona Ryder as Veronica Sawyer, was released in 2001.

5. That father and son mirror each other perfectly is made explicit through their inversion of roles. The father acts as son, for example, asking J. D. for help with his homework, while J. D. resolutely puts off the advances of this clamoring, surrogate son.

6. The idea of a change in Hillary's perspective is indicated visually, in the film's closing shots, by a switch between black-and-white and color, just at the moment that Hillary picks up a basketball among a group of fellow prisoners and nets it. The black-and-white footage has previously defined only the prison scenes, while color has been reserved for the "objective" view of the girls while they are at liberty. The switch is, therefore, highly ambiguous. It may suggest that Hillary is facing the reality of her situation (objective facts, social life, and responsibilities) or that she has gained some kind of psychic liberty, or both.

Works Cited

Carter, Angela. 1995. "The Company of Wolves." In *Burning Your Boats: The Collected Short Stories*. London: Chatto & Windus, 212–20.

Devlin, Rachel. 1998. "Female Juvenile Delinquency and the Problem of Sexual Authority in America, 1945–1965." In *Delinquents and Debutantes: Twentieth-Century American Girls' Cultures*, ed. Sherrie A. Inness, 83–106. New York: New York University Press.

Dole, Carol M. 2000. "Woman with a Gun: Cinematic Law Enforcers on the Gender Frontier." In *Bang Bang, Shoot Shoot! Essays on Guns and Popular Culture*, ed. Murray Pomerance and John Sakeris, 11–21. 2nd ed. Needham Heights, MA: Pearson Educational.

Fasman, Jonathan. 1999. "Violence of the Heart." Review of *The Bad Seed*, by William March. *Times Literary Supplement*, 26 March: 23.

Fischer, Lucy. 1989. *Shot/Countershot: Film Tradition and Women's Cinema*. Princeton: Princeton University Press.

Hull, C. Bryson. 2000. " 'Queens of Armed Robbery' Get 7 Years." *Ottawa Citizen,* 29 January: E12.

Jackson, Kathy Merlock. 1986. *Images of Children in American Film: A Sociocultural Analysis.* Metuchen, NJ: Scarecrow Press.

Southworth, Natalie. 1999. "Experts Report Girls as Aggressive as Boys but in Verbal Ways." *Globe and Mail,* 23 October: A3.

chapter 18

'Til Death Do Us Part: Identity and Friendship in *Heavenly Creatures*

Corinn Columpar

Navigating the territory between fantasy and reality, documentary and fiction, the ordinary and the extraordinary, Peter Jackson's 1994 feature *Heavenly Creatures* constructs an exhilarating world of formal excess and moral bankruptcy. The film's narrative, which chronicles a girlhood friendship so intense as to inspire matricide when the girls are threatened with separation, is based on one of the most sensational crimes in New Zealand's history and is informed by documents surrounding the crime and subsequent trial, such as court transcripts and psychiatric reports. Despite his commitment to historical accuracy, however, Jackson recounts the story of best friends Juliet Hulme and Pauline Rieper/Parker with a flamboyant and self-consciously dramatic visual style that evokes the emotional vicissitudes and fanciful reveries of adolescence better than any verbal testimony ever could.[1] While such expressive narration brings to life the unique imaginary universe that Pauline and Juliet conspire to create, it also allows for the emergence of a diegetic world that simultaneously invites and repels viewers and for the construction of a cinematic text marked by an ambiguous relationship to the "real."

In the opening sequence of the film three counterpointed layers of imagery serve to establish the complex vision of the film as a whole and to suggest both the horror and the logic of the girls' crime. The film starts with footage from an old travelogue that introduces the spectator to the setting, Christchurch, New Zealand, in the 1950s. Boasting such attractions as Canterbury University College with its impressive architecture, numerous flower gardens, and the spacious and popular Hagley Park, the newsreel portrays Christchurch as a clean, pleasant, wholesome community. This image is quickly intruded upon, however, by the shrieks of Juliet and

Pauline as they flee from the site in Victoria Park where they have bludgeoned Pauline's mother to death. This overlapping sound is followed by an abrupt cut to subjective shots of their frenzied ascent up a trail to the park's exit where, in the final moments of the opening sequence, they are met by a restaurant proprietor whom they implore for help, screaming, "It's Mummy! She's been terribly hurt!" Intercut with these shots of the immediate aftermath of the murder is a black-and-white fantasy sequence in which the girls are similarly running. In this case, however, they are on the deck of a ship, smiling, and yelling, "Mummy!" as they approach Juliet's parents who stand at the railing with their backs toward the girls. At the conclusion of this trajectory of images an intertitle states, "During 1953 and 1954 Pauline Yvonne Parker kept diaries recording her friendship with Juliet Marion Hulme. This is their story. All diary entries are in Pauline's own words."

This dense sequence of juxtaposed imagery and information creates certain thematic tensions that are central to the structure of the film as a whole. In pitting the brutality of matricide against, on the one hand, a self-constructed image of 1950s communal propriety and, on the other, the pursuit of a romanticized familial union, the film demonstrates both the horror lurking within the mundane and the manner in which reality and fantasy converge and diverge. That is, the film is from the start concerned with the relationship between the ordinary and the extraordinary and between the real world and the dream world of Pauline and Juliet. What is conveyed initially with three levels of imagery, however, is condensed into one level as the film progresses and the narrative goes back two years in time to the day of Juliet and Pauline's fateful first meeting. As the girls quickly develop a friendship they share stories of their childhood illnesses, engage in ritualistic ceremonies sainting their favorite popular entertainers, and invent parallel universes to which only they as self-proclaimed "heavenly creatures" have access. With its lush form the film replicates this adolescent world and, in the process, renders the ordinary extraordinary and allows fantasy to inhabit reality. These seemingly stable and discreet categories merge in a landscape surveyed by dramatic crane shots and populated by unicorns and fish store managers, by opera singer Mario Lanza and high school teachers, by members of royalty and marriage counselors. Furthermore, like the diegetic world of *Heavenly Creatures*, the film text itself is characterized by a degree of ambiguity for it presents itself as both history and fiction. With the intertitle that concludes the opening sequence and the subsequent use of Pauline's actual journal entries to narrate the film, Jackson lays claim to historical authenticity and alludes to the exhaustive research done before he and Frances Walsh wrote the screenplay. However, instead of opting for the "fine, self-effacing realist drama" for which one disappointed reviewer pleads (Romney 39), Jackson presents a film whose form is so excessive, so visible as to vitiate any claims to "objective" truth. In fact, however, it is Jackson's cinematic embellishment that seems to allow for a more sincere understanding of the crime at hand.

From the outset Jackson is interested in forging his own textual space for the telling of the story of Pauline and Juliet, and that space is the one between fantasy and reality, the ordinary and the extraordinary, history and fiction. That space is one that defies easy categorization. As a result, it is no coincidence that the relationship between Pauline and Juliet, which is the preoccupation of the film, is similarly ambiguous and likewise difficult to categorize. When Parker and Hulme were on trial in 1954 the nature of their relationship was the object of much public and professional discussion. Various psychiatrists reached divergent conclusions on the issue of whether the two girls were engaged in a physical relationship. The defense claimed that the girls were homosexual and thus, by definition of the times, mentally ill; yet it did so purely for the pragmatic purpose of strengthening its case, which was built around an insanity plea. Although the extent of their intimacy was never confirmed within the public discourse surrounding the case, Jackson's interest in the girls' relationship is not born of a desire to categorize or to discover how their affections for one another were or were not normative. In fact, Jackson has called the lesbian issue something of a red herring (Files 38), and, consequently, the film mocks any attempt to impose a label on the complex and multidimensional relationship that Pauline and Juliet forge.

In referring to this relationship reviewers of the film have employed a wide array of terms such as "conspiracy of affection," "growingly dangerous obsession," and association of two "soul mates" (Corliss, Mathews, Turan). While all of these phrases evoke the intensity and exclusivity of the friendship, Luisa Ribeiro offers the most trenchant description when she speaks of "Pauline's yearning for/to be Juliet" (34). While Pauline is more steadfast in her devotion initially since she looks to the bourgeois Juliet to help her

transcend her family's working-class status, the relationship between the girls is ultimately a mutual one characterized by both
identification and desire. As such, it confounds psychoanalytic accounts of relatedness that, working from a heterosexual matrix, assume those two processes to be mutually exclusive. The pleasures
that Pauline and Juliet share are many in number and shifting in
nature, just as the girls' very identities are fragmented and continually in flux. In exploring this dynamic multiplicity the film explores
the space between desire and identification and refuses to fix sexual identity in a way that would allow for a causal linkage between
the girls' criminality and intimacy. In other words, the film works
against any impulse to conflate the moment at which the friendship
turns from innocent to dangerous with some moment at which their
desire turns from "normal" to "deviant." Rather, what becomes
clear in watching *Heavenly Creatures* is that in order to understand
the crime that terminates the film and, by court mandate, the friendship, one must first understand the complexity of that friendship
throughout its duration.

In "Desperately Seeking Difference" Jackie Stacey explores the
interplay of identification and desire in relationships between women. Although her ultimate agenda is to conceive of a model of
spectatorship that does not consider female viewing pleasure as impossible or hopelessly compromised and compromising, her discussion yields important insights into ways women relate onscreen as
well. Writing in reaction to psychoanalytic accounts that assume
strictly heterosexual desire and homosocial identification, Stacey
argues for the possibility of a homoerotic desire between women
(between female spectator and female star and/or between women
on the screen) that is not masculine in nature or reducible to nar-
cissism. To flesh out her argument she turns her attention to *All
About Eve* (1950) and *Desperately Seeking Susan* (1985), two films
about one woman's obsessive fascination with another woman, that
explore "forms of otherness between women characters which are
not merely reducible to sexual difference, so often seen as the sole
producer of desire itself" (Stacey 1990, 370). According to Stacey,
both of these films engage in a play on similarity and difference as
they focus on a woman who aspires to be like another woman but
whose difference from her ideal is continually reaffirmed. That difference allows for a type of homoerotic desire that is not a lesbian
desire per se but enhances identification and produces a specifically
feminine pleasure.

Like Adrienne Rich's much-discussed notion of the lesbian continuum, Stacey's argument for a homoerotic element within female
friendships has been critiqued for de-eroticizing desire and de-polit-
icizing lesbian identity.[2] Teresa de Lauretis, for example, charges
Stacey with confusing narcissistic identification and desire and then
asserts a radical disjuncture between representations of female
friendship (where only identification is involved) and representations of lesbianism (where desire rather than identification is foregrounded). De Lauretis sees in Stacey's argument the same tendency
to conflate female homosexuality and female homosociality that informs "heterosexually conceived" depictions of lesbianism. Thus it
is with the goal of naming a specifically lesbian desire that de Lauretis imposes such a stringent taxonomy on films about relations
between women. Stacey answers de Lauretis's critique in a subsequent work by clarifying her project: "I am not de-eroticising desire,
but rather eroticising identification. I suggest that identification between femininities contains forms of homoerotic pleasure that have
yet to be explored. This is not to argue that identification is the same
as desire, or *only* contains desire, but rather to try to open up the
meaning of both categories" (Stacey 1994, 29).

Because of their divergent agendas the two thinkers reach an
impasse. While de Lauretis has a political stake in distinguishing
identification from desire and thus affirming lesbian sexuality, Stacey is intent on blurring the boundary between these two processes
in order to posit certain distinctly feminine pleasures that all women
potentially derive from the cinema and each other. Yet, given de Lauretis's concern with the invisibility of lesbians as social subjects,
it seems important to note that this theoretical polarization takes
shape around two films focusing on women who are definitively
heterosexual. *Desperately Seeking Susan* is the story of a dissat-
isfied housewife who, through identification with an ego ideal, is
liberated from her domestic role and enters a heterosexual relationship far more satisfying than her marriage. Secondly, *All About Eve*
is a fairly conventional representation of female rivalry in which a
starstruck young woman initially befriends and eventually comes to
displace the famous Broadway actress who is the object of her adula-
tion. Given Stacey's assumption that difference between women is
the only necessary precondition for the emergence of an element of
homoeroticism in films so heavily invested in a heterosexual economy of desire, it is not surprising that de Lauretis fears a consequent
erasure of lesbian desire and subsumption of lesbianism under the

rubric of female bonding. Furthermore, the films that Stacey uses as exemplary *are* primarily about identification—eroticized (Stacey) or narcissistic (de Lauretis).

Thus the following questions emerge: Must a film foreground lesbian existence in order to present homoerotic desire *qua* desire? Or is it possible for a film to thematize a homoerotic desire that does not displace but rather exists alongside heterosexual desire? In other words, are there certain films that point to a middle ground between de Lauretis's two categories in a more persuasive manner than the two Stacey discusses in "Desperately Seeking Difference"? In her book *In the Company of Women: Contemporary Female Friendship Films,* Karen Hollinger takes up these questions in a chapter devoted to the "erotic female friendship film." After positing the existence of certain "ambiguous lesbian films" that both suggest and disown a lesbian relationship at their center and thus present a dynamic interplay of identification and desire between women, Hollinger concludes that "the break between [de Lauretis's] two categories is not as decisive as [she] claims" (177). While Hollinger cites *Fried Green Tomatoes* (1991) as an example of this type of film, Chris Straayer turns her attention to the French features *Voyage en douce* (1980) and *Entre Nous* (1983) to explore the contradictory impulses and subversive potential of texts marked by such ambiguity. Straayer foregrounds the role of the lesbian spectator in creating meaning when she describes the films under discussion as "films that do *not* depict lesbianism explicitly, but employ or provide sites for lesbian intervention" (343). The textual sites that she invokes and explores illustrate bonds and looks that are shared by women and that hinge on some degree of lesbian desire, raise the specter of a lesbian relationship, and are thus available for eroticization.

Heavenly Creatures is a particularly interesting film to consider in the context of this middle ground held by the ambiguous lesbian film, for it both resonates with and diverges from the films discussed above in significant ways. In depicting Pauline and Juliet as physically intimate, *Heavenly Creatures* makes explicit what exists only at the subtextual level in *Fried Green Tomatoes, Voyage en douce,* and *Entre Nous,* yet it does so while holding the identity of lesbian in abeyance and constructing the girls' desires as multiple and shifting. As a result, sustained throughout Jackson's film is an interaction between identification and desire wherein neither process is privileged over the other and both are shown to be implicated in one another from the very start of the friendship.

It is on Juliet's first day at her new school that Pauline becomes aware of her. Pauline is immediately captivated by Juliet's precocious and irreverent manner, snickering when she corrects their French teacher and complimenting her earnestly when she devotes her time in art class to drawing St. George and the dragon rather than the subject assigned. Upon returning home from school Pauline rushes to the record player, puts on an old opera album from her parents' collection, and gushingly mimics the words spoken by Juliet earlier that day by describing Mario Lanza as "the world's greatest tenor." As she listens intently to the swelling music, she grips the album cover tightly, throws her head back, and wrinkles her nose in a moment of ecstatic appreciation that is intermittently interrupted by her father's distracting antics. In this scene Pauline's willful identification with Juliet incites a solitary pleasure, a temporarily objectless desire, a type of euphoria that is sustained in the ensuing months only by Juliet's presence. The next scene has Juliet and Pauline both sitting on the sidelines of their physical education class, trading stories about their childhood illnesses and resulting scars. Their likeness is established by matching shots that show them as bedridden children and that resonate with shots employed later in the film when Juliet must check into a sanatorium to recover from a recurrence of tuberculosis. Seizing on their status as outsiders as a point of identification and self-proclaimed superiority, Juliet declares, "All the best people have bad chests and bone diseases. It's all frightfully romantic."

These first two interactions serve to establish the dynamic of the girls' nascent friendship. They explore their similar interests and forge common passions, but almost always within the terms set by Juliet. The play on similarity and difference that Stacey discusses is at work here in that their lives parallel each other in certain gratifying ways (for example, in terms of their experiences with illness and their love of the macabre), yet their divergent class backgrounds create a fundamental difference, a gap between self and other that Pauline continually seeks to close. As a result, Pauline not only adopts Juliet's musical tastes but also falls in with any imaginative adventure Juliet proposes and insinuates herself into the Hulme family by accompanying them on vacation and calling the Hulmes "Daddy" and "Mummy." Despite her efforts, however, Pauline can never identify completely with Juliet, as evidenced by the texture of her accent, the inadequacy of her lone Mario Lanza album next to Juliet's plentiful collection, and the discomfort of Dr. Hulme in the face of what he perceives to be Pauline's "unwholesome attachment" to his daughter. Although this insurmountable difference may not translate inevitably into desire, it does create a distance that allows for desire between the two friends to emerge.

The complexity of the relationship and the extent to which the girls' interaction comes to define their individual identities is evident in the plethora of names by which each is known throughout the film. Juliet is alternately called Juliet, Giulietta, Julie, Antoinette, and Deborah while Pauline answers to the names Pauline, Paul, Paulette, Yvonne, Charles, and Gina. Each of the names is associated with a different institutional and/or interpersonal context, and, as a group, they show identity to be the mutable, provisional ineffability that, in the words of Diana Fuss, "becomes problematic in and through the work of identification" (12). While some of the names are significant only insofar as they attest to the girls' flair for drama and underscore adolescence as a time during which identity is even more fragmented and shifting than usual (for example, Antoinette and Paulette, the girls' chosen names for French class; and Julie and Giulietta, both of which are nicknames for Juliet used by Pauline on dramaturgically isolated occasions), others belie Pauline and Juliet's continual traversal of the boundary between fantasy and reality. In particular, it is in using the names Deborah, Charles, and Gina that they conflate the "real," empirical world with a chimerical world of their own design constructed around a fictitious kingdom named Borovnia and populated by various characters that they sculpt out of plasticine.

Pauline and Juliet first take up the respective roles of Charles and Deborah, the king and queen of Borovnia, when they play out a scene of Deborah/Juliet giving birth to Diello, a new heir to the throne that Pauline and Juliet want to introduce into their narrative. Their inhabitance of these roles is consolidated soon afterward when Juliet is quarantined in the hospital and the girls decide to write letters to each other as Charles and Deborah. From this point on in the film, Juliet becomes Deborah not only within the context of the friendship but also in the eyes of the spectator since the film's special-effect sequences representing Borovnia feature either Juliet or a plasticine figure in her likeness configured as the kingdom's first lady. Pauline's assumption of Charles's persona, however, is not as absolute, for she is never his embodiment within the film's visual economy and she comes eventually to be identified instead with Gina, an "amazingly beautiful gypsy." It is in this second identification that both Pauline and the spectator become fully invested, for not only does Juliet sculpt the figurine of Gina to look just like Pauline but she also calls her friend exclusively by the name of her Borovnian look-alike throughout the last quarter of the film.

While Pauline and Juliet's adoption of fictional identities demonstrates the coexistence and the eventual merging of reality and fantasy within the minds of both girls, the fact that Pauline's Borovnian identity shifts while Juliet's remains stable is telling. Given the disjunctures specific to her life, Pauline's identity is profoundly fragmented and continually in flux over the course of the film in a way that Juliet's is not. A survey of the many names by which she is known reveals what is at stake in this process of (self-)definition that leads inexorably to her plotting the violent murder that frames the film. Pauline's parents and the boarders who live in their family home address her by her middle name, Yvonne. Classmates, teachers, and the Hulmes call her Pauline, her given name and the name by which her real-life counterpart was tried, convicted, and relegated to infamy. Lastly, Juliet starts out the friendship using the nickname Paul, later invokes the name Charles, and finally supplants both of these options with the name Gina.

In some ways the film can be seen as charting an evolution from the given identity of Yvonne to the chosen identity of Gina, and it is this sense of progression that Ribeiro captures when she discusses Pauline's many names in terms of the themes of transformation and rebirth (37). To transcend her identity as Yvonne and all it is associated with—the family's working-class status, the domestic space, and, by extension, Pauline's plain mother—entails a movement away from the private space of her home. Pauline attempts to realize this movement by rejecting her own family and, obversely, idealizing the Hulme family and her place within it as, in her own words, one of "two beautiful daughters." Yet even more exclusive than the upper middle class to which the Hulmes belong is what one critic has called the "aristocracy of two" made up of the girls (Hoberman 59). While this class unto itself is built on Pauline and Juliet's sense of their unmatched genius and ability to inhabit the very same imaginative visions, its existence is affirmed each time they call each other by one of their many privileged nicknames. Thus Pauline positions herself outside her family and escapes her mundane life by taking refuge in this exclusive bond as well as in the fantasy world it engenders and the alternative identities it makes available. As the culmination of this escapist fantasy/reality, the identity of Gina the gypsy does indeed offer Pauline some degree of "satisfaction, however fleeting," especially insofar as Gina's status as a commoner allows Pauline to romanticize her own modest background (Ribeiro 37). Nevertheless, as tempting as it is to trace a trajectory of identification for Pauline, a narrative of self-realization that moves steadily away from the name Yvonne and all it connotes, Pauline cannot escape her family and her class background, not even by destroying her origins. Thus her continually shifting identity must be read in terms of not only transformation and rebirth but also multiplicity and fragmentation.

To understand the nuances of the various identities that take shape within the context of Pauline and Juliet's friendship, the various identities that are continually in flux and compete with those of Yvonne and, to some extent, Pauline for precedence, it is necessary to consider the issue of desire. For as much as the personae of Paul, Charles, and Gina speak to Pauline's campaign to transcend her familial lot, they also provide insight into the shifting nature of the girls' emerging desires. Diana Fuss posits the "fundamental indissociability of identification and desire" as she scrutinizes the evolution of the concept of identification in Sigmund Freud's work (12). Drawing on writings by Parveen Adams, Marcia Ian, Mikkel Borsch-Jacobson, and Freud himself that throw into question the tenability of any definitive distinction between these two concepts, Fuss asks, "What is identification if not a way to assume the desires of the other? And what is desire if not a means of becoming the other whom one wishes to have?" The paradigm Fuss constructs of identification and desire as not simply coincident but also inextricably entwined is corroborated by the relationship between Pauline and Juliet. Pauline's identification is so bound up with desire as to suggest a symbiosis between the two processes. More specifically, the way that she identifies herself and/or is identified by Juliet is contingent on the girls' continually shifting desire for one another and for various male relays.

Paul, Juliet's first nickname for Pauline, is significant in a number of ways. First, Juliet's use of it from the outset of their association serves to establish a friendly intimacy between the girls; secondly, since it is a derivation of Pauline and its coinage predates the founding of Borovnia, it is grounded in reality as opposed to fantasy, public space as opposed to private fiction; and, thirdly, it is a masculinization of Pauline's full name. This final aspect is particularly important because it is when Juliet calls Pauline by the name Paul for the first time that she interpolates her friend into a sort of heterosexual role play that initially structures their relationship. Having established a connection at school, the girls spend their first afternoon together outside of that institutional context on a day when Pauline rides her bike over to Juliet's home. Once on the grounds of the Hulmes' residence, Pauline stops to take in a view of the august house but is quickly distracted by the sound of Juliet laughing. She looks around to find Juliet standing on a small bridge and throwing flowers into the water below while costumed in a gown befitting a medieval princess. After Juliet catches sight of her friend, she interrupts her frolicking to yell, "Hi Paul!" and then enlists Pauline's help in capturing her brother who is dressed in the part of an evil prince. This scene is constructed to exploit the conventions of romance in that swelling, dramatic, nondiegetic music is paired with a shot/reverse shot sequence that employs a swiftly tracking camera to create a sense of breathless exhilaration and that establishes Pauline and Juliet as, respectively, bearer and object of the gaze. In naming "Paul" while engaged in a performance of hyperbolic femininity, Juliet constructs Pauline as the (good) prince to her princess and, thus, reinforces the conventionally masculinized and feminized positions the girls have taken up in relation to the act of looking and in accordance with cinematic convention, the act of desire.[3]

It is through this assigned role of Paul that Pauline enters not only the play world of Juliet and her brother on this particular afternoon but also the friendship that will claim virtually all of her emotional and intellectual energy for the next two years. The pattern established with this first visit to Juliet's home, a pattern characterized by Pauline's absorption in the sight of Juliet and Juliet's self-absorption in her imaginative reveries, persists throughout the first few months of their association. Furthermore, it is within this pattern and its consequent ordering of the gaze between the girls that desire and identification emerge as bound together for Pauline. This is demonstrated in a later scene that features the girls giving praise to a pantheon of their favorite stars.

In this scene Pauline and Juliet are outside at night, cutting pictures of celebrities out of popular magazines while sitting in front of a makeshift altar adorned with candles. After Pauline comments that she wishes James Mason would make a religious picture, Juliet declares that her father regards the Bible as a "load of bunkum" and that when she dies she will go to the Fourth World ("an absolute paradise of music, art, and pure enjoyment") rather than heaven. During this exchange Pauline is positioned slightly below Juliet so that the resulting shot/reverse shot sequence—which features shots of Juliet from a slightly low angle and shots of Pauline from a slightly higher one—literalizes Pauline's deference and Juliet's role as leader. After assuring Pauline that James Mason and Mario Lanza will eventually live in the Fourth World as saints, Juliet begins to place selected photos on the altar and to anoint each future saint by giving him a new name such as "This" or "Him" that Pauline then repeats. While Juliet's eyes never leave the altar in front of her as she engages in this improvised ceremony, Pauline's rapturous gaze, and thus words, are directed almost exclusively toward her friend. Even immediately after she offers up Orson Welles ("It") as her candidate for sainthood (only to have Juliet tear his photo off the altar and frantically declare him "the most hideous man alive") Pauline continues to watch Juliet fixedly. For Pauline the desire that undergirds this ritualized expression of teenage fandom is displaced onto Juliet, and the result is a relay of gazes that are alike in form yet divergent in content. The altar becomes a site where both homosocial identification and homoerotic desire are mobilized; even though Pauline follows Juliet's lead by mimicking her actions and words, she resignifies those actions and words in redirecting her gaze so that she is looking at, not with, Juliet.

While Paul does represent a masculinized or, at least, less feminized counterpart to Juliet's hyperfemininity, it is Pauline and Juliet's assumption of the identities of Charles and Deborah, respectively, that allows Juliet to fully inhabit her received notions of heterosexuality and Pauline to make performative her desire for Juliet. Elizabeth Cowie's description of fantasy as "a veritable *mise-en-scène* of desire" is thus borne out, since it is in the context of Borovnia that the girls explore their adolescent desires in an elaborate role play that they recognize as such (133). As the girls alternately identify themselves as Charles and Deborah on the one hand, and as Paul and Juliet on the other, they repeatedly cross the boundary between fantasy and reality. Yet the various identities and, by extension, the two realms to which they correspond remain separate, leading Pauline to describe her first letter to the bedridden Juliet in terms of two distinct selves: "I wrote a six-page letter as Charles. And a two-page letter as Paul." Nonetheless, as the role play continues, their fantasy world does bear on their reality in an increasingly more extensive and forceful manner, a fact made visually apparent by the film. Diello, the plasticine figure to whom the girls give birth

Worshipping at the altar of male celebrities.

mentally, artistically, and, at least in pantomime, physically comes to embody this interpenetration of fantasy and reality when in various scenes he suddenly appears as life-size and violently eliminates anyone who proves a nuisance to his creators. While Diello's transgression of Borovnia's outer limits does not eliminate the boundary between fantasy and reality (there is still something to transgress), it does initiate a destabilization or slow erosion of that boundary that is only fully realized in the last quarter of the film with the introduction of Gina, Pauline's second Borovnian persona.

The spectator first catches a glimpse of the fantasized Gina during a scene in which Pauline shows her collection of Borovnian figurines to John (Jed Brophy), a boarder living in her family's house. In commenting on the fact that Pauline resembles this beautiful gypsy, John intimates his attraction to her and, in the process, forges the association between Pauline and Gina that persists throughout the rest of the film. On her next visit to the sanatorium, Pauline excitedly tells Juliet of this burgeoning romance only to retract her words when Juliet, confronted with a rival for Pauline's attention and affection, becomes jealous and asks, "Is that why you haven't responded to my last letter?" In answer to this incriminating question Pauline mollifies her hurt friend by dismissing John as "only a stupid boy," thereby implying that the specifically feminine bond she and Juliet share is impregnable. In the ensuing weeks Pauline remains true to her words of reassurance. Even as she becomes involved with John and entertains his sexual advances, her devotion to Juliet only grows more intense. For example, while losing her virginity to John during their second rendezvous, Pauline copes by retreating into a Borovnian fantasy that brings her face to face with life-size versions of Charles and Diello and that culminates in her sighting Juliet/Deborah across a crowded room populated by various other plasticine characters. This sighting, which initiates an exchange of loving looks between the girls, is reminiscent of the one that takes place on Pauline's first visit to Juliet's home; in both cases, a shot/reverse shot sequence positions Pauline as initiator of the gaze and relies on Juliet's laugh to announce her presence. This time around, however, the romance into which Pauline is being interpolated is not heterosexualized or associated with her identity as Paul (or even, for that matter, Charles). This fantasy marks the first time that Pauline is called Gina (by both Charles and Diello). Consequently it initiates a new phase in her relationship with Juliet, one that is defined against the heterosexual encounter from which she is taking mental flight.

John is an important figure in the narrative because in inciting jealousy in Juliet and disillusionment in Pauline he serves as a catalyst for the changes that ensue in the girls' friendship once they are reunited, all of which are bound up with the name Gina. As is prefigured by the fantasy sequence discussed above, Pauline takes on this identity, finding within it some degree of stability as well as sway over Juliet. First, it is Juliet's jealousy that leads the girls to define their exclusive bond increasingly in gendered terms. As John's attempts to gain Pauline's attention inspire nothing but derisive laughter, Charles and Deborah's heterosexual romance takes a backseat to Gina and Deborah's less conventional commitment. While John renders reality and fantasy irreconcilable for Pauline, the fantasy of Borovnia is sustained within the context of Pauline and

Juliet's interaction. As much as Pauline tries to ignore John's presence during their sexual involvement, it eventually reasserts itself in the guise of a plasticine figure named Nicholas who repeatedly yells "Yvonne!" to get her attention until Pauline's escapist fantasy is entirely dispelled. This radical disjuncture between reality and fantasy or, to be more accurate, between Pauline's physical and mental realities, summarily represented in the contrast between the names Yvonne and Gina, is redressed with Juliet's recovery and subsequent return home. As the identity of Gina supplants the dual identity of Paul/Charles, fantasy and reality merge in a manner heretofore unseen in the film. Not only do the girls fail to distinguish between the empirical and the fictional (a condition that Pauline first fears and then celebrates as a sign of madness), but the film renders their dreamscape by integrating the two realms seamlessly at the level of the image.

The rewriting of Pauline's identity vis-à-vis Juliet/Deborah is bound up with a rewriting of the girls' desire. Although Pauline's intent gaze goes unreturned in the scene at the altar that features Juliet immersed in heterosexual hero worship, the circuit of homoerotic desire initiated by Pauline in this scene is closed later in the film when the girls become physically intimate after returning home from a screening of *The Third Man*. On leaving the movie theater the girls initiate a delightfully terrifying game of cat and mouse, running from a black-and-white Orson Welles whom they imagine to be lurking around every corner and shrieking hysterically all the while. After barricading Juliet's bedroom door against their fantasized intruder, they collapse on the bed exhausted and in a fit of laughter. At this point Pauline says in voice-over, "We talked for some time about 'It' [Orson Welles], getting ourselves more and more excited," and then, "We enacted how each saint would make love in bed." At this point a series of close-ups shows Juliet, Pauline, and two male relays involved in a night of sexual experimentation.

Initially a shot/reverse shot sequence shows Juliet lying on the bed with Pauline leaning over her, both of their faces bathed monochromatically in a bluish light. Pauline lowers her head and they kiss. When Pauline returns upright she morphs into Orson Welles, and Juliet gasps with anticipation. As Orson and Juliet kiss, Juliet remains tinted by the blue light while the image of Orson has the appearance of a sepiatone. Interestingly, when their faces come together in such a way that blue meets brown, it is Orson who appears more three-dimensional and naturalistic, while Juliet resembles a black-and-white film image. Next, Pauline is shown involved with Diello. Shots of Pauline lying back on the bed and lit in a naturalistic manner are intercut with shots of Diello aggressively waving his sword and then pulling Pauline into a Borovnian orgy where, through a masked cut, she is transformed into the plasticine Gina. After the camera tracks back to survey the tangled web of fantasized bodies, an image of Juliet's face looking down at Gina is superimposed over the dreamscape, which subsequently fades to black. Juliet then lowers herself and the two girls lie on the bed, kissing and caressing each other contentedly while bathed almost entirely in a naturalistic yellow/pink light. Over this image Pauline concludes her voice-over, saying, "We spent a hectic night going through the saints. It was wonderful, heavenly, beautiful, and ours. We felt satisfied indeed. We have now learned the peace of the thing called bliss, the joy of the thing called sin."

Crystallized in this scene is the complexity of the relationship between Pauline and Juliet. Fantasy and reality, heterosexual desire and lesbian sexuality, homoerotic desire and intimate friendship converge, intermingle, and mutate as a result of the manner in which Jackson represents and edits together the various phases of the encounter. The sequence is structured in such a way that two sets of shots featuring Pauline and Juliet engaged with each other serve as bookends for a middle section in which each girl is shown making love to—*and as*—a fantasized male partner. These two heterosexual interactions mirror one another in terms of the role each girl takes up therein and the male figure involved. First, both Pauline and Juliet appear in these interactions lying back on the bed, thus assuming a conventionally feminine (that is, less active) position vis-à-vis their partners. As a result, the obverse is also true in that they each identify/are identified with a masculine character when on top sexually. Within the terms of the film, Orson and Diello are complementary characters who bear a strong physical resemblance and forge a potent association between eroticism and violence, as a result fulfilling the same symbolic function within different imaginary universes. Thus, in engaging in the same sexual behavior with two embodiments of the same personage, the girls perform heterosexuality in an identical manner or, rather, a manner that bespeaks their identification with one another.

But this sequence also establishes the presence of a desire between the girls that exceeds these heterosexual scenarios. While the Juliet/Orson and Pauline/Diello pairings are constructed to resonate with each other, the two exchanges between Juliet and Pauline that initiate and conclude this "hectic night" diverge in such a way as to suggest the shifting and multidimensional nature of their involvement. The blue light that illuminates the faces and flattens the images of the girls at the start of the sequence serves to recall the black-and-white world of *The Third Man* and so to underscore the performative nature of their ensuing "enactment" of how each saint would make love. Furthermore, the shot/reverse shot pattern that is established with this initial interaction and that structures the rest of the sequence not only allows for an easy exchange of characters via editing, but also locates each girl in her own space and, by extension, her own fantasy. By the end of the sequence, however, the girls are lit in a naturalistic manner and are shown in a two-shot lying on the bed side by side with Pauline describing their experience as, among other things, "ours." This coda illustrates a sense of mutual recognition and profound intimacy between the girls that is visually set off from the preceding role play, and it makes palpable a homoerotic desire that undergirds their night of going through the saints. Furthermore, it suggests the extent to which desire and identification are implicated in one another. The multiple nature of the desires must be understood, at least in part, as a function of an ongoing negotiation of identity that allows for cross-gender identification (Pauline as Orson; Juliet as Diello) as well as Pauline and Juliet's assumption of the familiar and feminine identities of Gina and Deborah, respectively.

Although *Heavenly Creatures* represents homoerotic desire both indirectly (through the structuring of its gazes and the thematization of female bonding) and directly (as seen in the sex scene discussed above), it mediates against any impulse to label Pauline and Juliet's relationship "lesbian" or "homosexual." Unlike a film such as *Fried Green Tomatoes*, however, it does not do this to ensure the film's appeal to a mass market or to contain the ideological implications of a relationship/narrative from which men are displaced. Nor is it the case that the film's refusal to label results in the erasure of lesbian desire and/or preclusion of lesbian existence with which de Lauretis is concerned. Rather, in acknowledging desire between the girls without fixing their sexuality, the film divests that desire of its associations with the pathological. When Juliet returns from the hospital and the girls renew their friendship with an unprecedented fervor, Dr. Hulme becomes concerned about the relationship and suggests to Mrs. Rieper that she take Pauline to see a doctor lest she be developing in a "wayward fashion." Jackson presents the resulting consultation in an almost parodic fashion, making the doctor and Mrs. Rieper the mouthpieces for a bevy of dated stereotypes ("It can strike at any time, and adolescents are particularly vulnerable"), maternal platitudes ("But she's always been a happy, normal child"), and banal suggestions that serve only to inspire Pauline's wrath ("Perhaps you could consider spending time with boys?"). Furthermore, when the doctor names the unnameable, the camera focuses on his mouth with its crooked teeth and hesitant speech in an extreme close-up that renders his diagnosis of "h-h-homosexuality" absurd and utterly inadequate in light of the relationship's complexity. This refusal on the part of Jackson to invest the term homosexuality with any discursive credibility is highly significant in that it functions to undermine the persistent tendency to associate sexual "deviancy" and criminality within both cinema and the discourse surrounding the Hulme-Parker murder.

To make sense of the murder toward which *Heavenly Creatures* inevitably progresses requires not a categorization of the girls' desire but an understanding of how that desire is engaged in an ongoing and dynamic interaction with identification. After Juliet's parents announce their intention to divorce and the girls are threatened with permanent separation, Pauline hatches a plan to kill her mother so that she can escape her custody and run away with Juliet, her willing accomplice. While Pauline's journal entries and conversations with Juliet identify as the motive for their crime the girls' desire to leave New Zealand together (bound for either South Africa or Hollywood), their actions immediately after the killing suggest that something else is at stake. Were they serious about an imminent departure, they would steal away from the scene of the crime quickly and quietly instead of running from their deed, shrieking for help. Furthermore, their use of the passive voice in the plea, "Mummy's been terribly hurt," implies that they become so immersed in the drama of the event that they lose sight of their own culpability. Certainly their self-incriminating reaction could be, in part, a response to the shock of actual bloodshed, but it also points to an alternate motive. Pauline's mother is killed for the same reason that Nicholas (John's plasticine look-alike) is killed earlier in the film: as revenge for shattering Pauline's illusions by invoking the name Yvonne. Given Pauline's development and the evolution of the girls' relationship over the course of the film, the murder of Pauline's mother functions less as a bid for freedom than as a culmination of Pauline's campaign to abandon the identity of Yvonne in favor of that of Gina. Thus, matricide for Pauline constitutes an attempt to resolve her fragmented identity, to kill a part of herself by destroying her corporeal connection to the name Yvonne and all that it connotes. An identity in flux becomes an identity in crisis as she attempts to transgress unyielding class boundaries and maintain a provisional identity that is contingent on both Juliet's presence and the girls' shared fantasy/reality. Yet her attempt is futile. Ultimately, the girls' collective illusion, informed and fortified by a complex interplay of identification and desire, cannot be sustained. In fact, the act that was to unite them serves to separate them permanently—from one another, thus, from themselves.

NOTES

1. When Pauline was arrested for her crime it was discovered that her mother and father had never actually married, and, thus, she was charged with murder under the name Parker, her mother's maiden name. Given Jackson's focus on the events leading up to the crime, however, Pauline is known as Pauline Rieper throughout the film.
2. In "Compulsory Heterosexuality and Lesbian Existence," Adrienne Rich introduces the concept of a lesbian continuum that accommodates a wide range of female-identified experiences including not only lesbian existence but also female friendships, intrafamilial relationships, etc. In contending that all women move in and out of this continuum over the course of their lives, Rich creates a model of female connections that gives all women access to the personal and political power of woman-identification and to an identity forged outside the institutions of heterosexuality and patriarchy (see Snitow et al. 1983).
3. It is important to note, however, that with Juliet's assumption of the feminine position in this heterosexualized matrix comes no loss of narrative agency or authority since, as has been discussed, she is, at least for a while, in almost complete control of the girls' shared fantasies.

WORKS CITED

Corliss, Richard. 1994. "A Heavenly Trip toward Hell." *Time,* 21 November: 110

Cowie, Elizabeth. 1997. "Fantasia." In *Representing the Woman: Cinema and Psychoanalysis,* 123–65. Minneapolis: University of Minnesota Press.

de Lauretis, Teresa. 1991. "Film and the Visible." In *How Do I Look? Queer Film and Video,* ed. Bad Object-Choices, 223–64. Seattle: Bay Press.

Files, Gemma. 1995. "Those Difficult, Murderous Teenage Years." *Eye Weekly* (Toronto), 19 January: 38

Fuss, Diana. 1995. *Identification Papers.* New York: Routledge.

Hoberman, J. 1994. "Très Shriek." *Village Voice,* 29 November: 59.

Hollinger, Karen. 1998. *In the Company of Women: Contemporary Female Friendship Films.* Minneapolis: University of Minnesota Press.

Mathews, Jack. 1994. "Heavenly Creatures." *Newsday,* 16 November.

Ribeiro, Luisa. 1995. "Heavenly Creatures." *Film Quarterly* 49, no. 1 (fall): 34.

Rich, Adrienne. 1983. "Compulsory Heterosexuality and Lesbian Experience." In *Powers of Desire: The Politics of Sexuality,* ed. Ann Snitow, Christine Stansell, and Sharon Thompson. New York: Monthly Review Press, 177–205.

Romney, Jonathan. 1995. "Film: Murder Most Florid." *New Statesman and Society* 10 (February): 39.

Stacey, Jackie. 1990. "Desperately Seeking Difference." In *Issues in Feminist Film Criticism,* ed. Patricia Erens, 365–79. Bloomington: Indiana University Press.

———. 1994. *Star Gazing: Hollywood Cinema and Female Spectatorship.* New York: Routledge.

Straayer, Chris. 1995. "The Hypothetical Lesbian Heroine in Narrative Feature Film." In *Multiple Voices in Feminist Film Criticism,* ed. Diane Carson, 343–57. Bloomington: Indiana University Press.

Turan, Kenneth. 1994. "*Heavenly Creatures* a Devilish Delight." *Los Angeles Times,* 23 November: F1.

chapter 19

Too much of something is bad enough: Success and Excess in *Spice World*

Cynthia Fuchs

> We're proud to be girls. That's why we've got our lipstick and our miniskirts.
>
> MELANIE BROWN (SCARY SPICE), *New York Times*, February 16, 1997

In "Spice World," all things are possible. In "Spice World," girls are all powerful. In "Spice World," *girl power* is for real.

This miraculous place where girls want to be is made a larger-than-life reality in a movie called, appropriately, *Spice World* (Bob Spiers, 1998). The premise is sublimely simple. The original five members of the British pop music group the Spice Girls—Sporty, Scary, Baby, Posh, and Ginger—travel about London in their Spice-mobile for ninety minutes or so. They stop briefly for rehearsals, an alien encounter, military training, a party or two, and run-ins with managers, tabloid reporters, and fans. But for the most part, the Girls make the world around them theirs, absorbing and reimagining any potential obstacles (say, diabolical reporters or exploitative executives) in order to refashion their environment to suit their needs and desires: the Spice Girls shop, chat, eat, play, sing, dance, flirt, and, above all, support one another. In a word, they have fun. All this simplicity is deceptive, however. *Spice World* delivers exactly what its target viewers, girls aged six to fourteen, would seem to want: more of the Spice Girls. And apparently there can never be enough.

The dazzling fiction of *Spice World* demonstrates yet again that the Spice Girls are an extraordinary marketing phenomenon, almost preternaturally adorable and consumable. They appear to be as happy to be shopping as to be ogled at some swank gathering, as thrilled performing on stage at the Albert Hall before thousands of screaming fans as they are getting phone calls from their mums. Their delight

343

in their good fortune translates to their fans, who respond gratefully, as if receiving spiritual instruction. No matter that the Spice Girls are also, on occasion, reviled by the British tabloids, who run contests in which their readers select the Spice Girl who most annoys them. No matter that the Spice Girls are twenty-something women wobbling about on circa 1970s platform sneakers in mini-dresses so tight they are sometimes limited to baby steps. Their fans are loyal, their detractors are exhausted, and the Spice Girls abide.

This is the Spice Girls' most special gift, their persistence and resilience. Since their inception, the Girls have been ridiculed and repudiated, yet they absorb and refract the jokes and accusations and recontextualize their conspicuous imperfections to seem endearing and authentic. This gift is on full display in a documentary about their first U.S. tour, Ian Denyer's *Spice Girls in America: A Tour Story* (1999), released straight to video, which serves as an apt counterpart to *Spice World*, stylistically and thematically. Both movies, however, paint remarkably similar portraits of the excesses of "Spice World," the many ways that the Girls are consumed and consuming, unreal and surreal, excessive and never enough. This essay will focus on the strategies by which the group absorbs and recycles critiques in such a way that all complaints made about or against the Spice Girls become part of the marketing machinery. *Spice World*, the movie, is only a most extravagantly packaged instance of this process, exploring and exposing the complexities of an idea and ideal called "Spice World." Like Madonna or Michael Jackson before them, though in a more acute, hyperfragmented, near perfect "postmodern" form, the Spice Girls use disapproval as a vehicle to successful marketing, becoming more than any detractor might imagine. Persevering beyond conventional narrative structures, as perpetual products and performances, the Spice Girls—sans Ginger and looking forward to still more hits (of all kinds)—enthrall the girls who love and wannabe them.[1]

About Friendship

> Fundamentally, the Spice Girls are about friendship.
> EMMA BUNTON (BABY SPICE), *Entertainment Weekly*,
> JULY 17, 1998

The Spice Girls' sudden celebrity now looks—in hindsight—like a matter of cosmic convergence. Their self-promotional phrase *girl power* has come to convey a range of meanings for girls and those who would market images and products to them. Little could the Spice Girls know, when they fired their original managers and signed with Virgin Records under the stewardship of Simon Fuller, that they would be integral in changing the world's—or, more accurately, the global entertainment industry's—attitude toward girls.

In part the Spice Girls have been able to exploit the girl power "movement" because they act like, well, girls. That is to say, they perform according to prevailing social expectations of girls, as children (immature, impetuous, and unpredictable) and as sexual objects (sensuous, insatiable, and devoted to pleasing their men). Girls can believe they want to be like the Spice Girls, their older brothers or fathers can believe they want to do the Spice Girls, and their older sisters and mothers can debate the Spice Girls' place along a feminist continuum. These very different uses of the Spice Girls' self-conscious flamboyance demonstrate that their cartoon-like excess allows them to be read at sundry signifying levels. *Spice World* addresses and regenerates this multiplicity of meaning in a scene showing the Girls as petulant children, escaping the rigors of their preset timetable by jumping onto a speedboat for a quick tour of the Thames. Their patient handler, Deborah (Claire Rushbrook), explains to their anxious manager, Clifford (an especially sniffy Richard E. Grant), that they are "just having fun, you know, rock and roll," (this from a woman who wonders aloud what she's doing with her life, having already garnered degrees in "politics, philosophy, and economics" and is now spending her days "wondering whether Mel C is wearing the right Nike Airmax"). The generous-spirited wannabe Deborah "gets" the Spice Girls in a way that foppish fuddy-duddy Clifford never will. When he responds by twisting his face into a knot, Deborah asks, "Don't you remember being a kid?"

Spice World insists on recalling and caricaturing the joy associated with being a kid because and in spite of the fact that the Spice Girls' lesson in loyalty to friends has to do with an unmarried pregnant chum who asks them all to be godmothers, and, incidentally, present at the birth. While the Girls mouth idiot questions ("Do godmothers get stretch marks?"), for the most part they act out an understanding of their responsibility as friends and take that responsibility seriously. At the same time, the film makes much of their ecstatic girlishness, playfulness, and immaturity. Occasionally they pay a price for refusing to "grow up" (that boating scene ends with a dunking for a couple of Spice Girls and two of their adorable and trusting young girl fans—for which the Spices are roundly chastised by Clifford and then doubly punished by a tabloid headline in the next day's *Daily Event.*) But for the most part, they are depicted as female descendants of the Beatles, another British act whose members were beloved for their zaniness and easy-to-read status as types. Taking a cue from the Beatles, who were "the cute one," "the sincere one," "the shy one," and "the funny one," the Spice Girls assumed and adapted the name traps others had begun to apply to them: "the posh one," "the baby," "the scary one," "the sporty one," and "Ginger." *Spice World* refers obviously and repeatedly to the Beatles, taking off on the Fab Five's hijinks in *A Hard Day's Night* (1964) and *Help!* (1965) with fast-motion, skewed camera angles and bright color schemes. That the Spice Girls—at their ages—are passing for girls in *Spice World* is a joke, of course, and the film wields it as such, using their excessiveness to mock and argue against the traditional infantilization of girls.

Such infantilization—as it declines into rhetoric about children's innocence and need for protection—is even more dangerous than it might look. Henry Giroux argues that as children are "increasingly used as a moral yardstick" for legal and social constraints premised on their "protection," children's presumed innocence "appears both threatened and threatening" (33). Public concern over the lessons imparted by the Spice Girls to innocent girls—to wear makeup, short skirts, and midriff tops, or even to demand recognition and space to congregate with your chums—tends to be overshadowed in the promotional hubbub by the great inspiration provided by both the abstract idea and physical incarnations of girl power. Mel B and Mel C both look like they can kick serious ass, so Emma and Victoria's more traditionally feminine appearances seem less offensive. In *Spice World*, Baby Emma deploys her childish lollipop-sucking and general preciousness to get over on manipulable male authorities, playing them so they deliver what she wants. The other Girls see her skills and encourage her to use them: when a cop pulls them over for Victoria's incredible derring-do behind the wheel of the tour bus, the group pushes Emma to the front to beguile him with her big blue eyes and dulcet smile after their cleavages have failed to win their freedom. The point is, as you watch this scene, you're aware of all the shenanigans on the part of both the Girls and the cop. The Spice Girls' put-on innocence is not deceptive or threatening to an audience in on the joke from frame one. Instead, they epitomize what progressive goodness nice girls—even naughty nice girls—can wreak.

In this way, the Girls suggest the ways that girl power—as fantastic and surreal as it gets—might offer tentative hope for change in some not-so-distant future or even some girls' present. Derided as a bastardization of Riot Grrrl, originally intended as a specific assault on all that seems quaint and retro in "Spice World," originally "supposed to stick in the mainstream's craw," girl power also offers alternatives to status quo sexism and low expectations for girls (Press 60). It is even thinkable that the compromise and commercialism offered by "Spice World" are not the end of feminism. As Joy Press writes, the transformation of girl power into a rotating MTV product or advice columns in *Cosmo Girl* isn't just about surrender and retreat into a sugary haze. It is also possible that the images of singer-songwriter girls like Fiona Apple or tough hip-hop chicks like Eve and Pink, or even Britney Spears and other, even younger Spice Girl descendants, might "expand society's ideas about what is acceptable and what's possible for young women" (61).

What's possible for young women looks different after and even "during" the Spice Girls, as they hardly stay still long enough to seem substantial individuals. Indeed, the new solo careers—of Geri Halliwell (who has officially left the group and released an album in 1999 called *Schizophonic*), Melanie Chisholm (who released a solo project, *Northern Star* [EMD/Virgin], along with a new tough-girl look, in 1999), and Melanie Brown (who recently collaborated with Missy Elliot and The Artist, and whose solo hip-hop/funk hybrid record, *Hot,* was released in October 2000)—suggest that smart and long-range merchandising tactics are the norm. (Certainly this is the "norm" after the repeat and tie-in businesses of *Titanic,* but also after the perspicacious planning of start-up fashion-entertainment-sports businesses like WuTang and Master P's No Limit enterprises.) One-hit wonders will still come along, but calculation and precision marketing now dominate so-called "raw talent" in the processes of entertainment management. This is not to say that talent is irrelevant; it is to say that traditional veneration of talent as "authentic" or innate has evolved into a complex understanding of its constructedness, mythic value, and commercial appeal.

Ironically but also appropriately, the Spice Girls—so often berated for their obvious artifice—have been integral to this rethinking of the relationships between promotion and performance, self-expression and simulation. Indeed, *Spice World* is all about these interconnections. Alongside the film's incessant celebration of the Girls' darling naivete runs a second narrative, exposing and celebrating this pose as such, demonstrating the tenacious potency of girl power. The film creates a series of self-deconstructing myths, proclaiming the group's ferocious self-confidence and sense of independence. Coming on the heels of the more overtly aggressive Riot Grrrls, Courtney Love, and Alanis Morissette, the Spice Girls embody a highly marketable negotiation between separatist rage and submission to antiquated gender role expectations. They are presented as girls who don't compete with one another, who enjoy their own company, and who declare their disdain for traditional dating rituals: at a combination reception–press interview in *Spice World*, Baby says she wants to be able to order boys "like pizza." They are also girls who can shapeshift and experiment with gender roles when it suits them, posing as Marilyn Monroe and Wonder Woman, a guy from *Grease* and his sweater girl, Ursula Andress and Jackie O. They even exchange roles among themselves: during a photo shoot in *Spice World*, Ginger dresses up as Sporty, Posh as Baby, Sporty as Posh, and Scary as Ginger, a series of personality swaps that underlines the instability and theatricality of their identities, as well as the effort and time that go into creating each image, indicated by "comedic" time lapse cinematography.

The photo-shoot scene emphasizes the plasticity and transience of identity, the potential for perpetual transformation and self-creation allowed by faith in the tenets of "Spice World." Such instability sounds "postmodern," in the sense that it rejects closure and fixed definitions, or espouses relativity and borderlessness. However, as Susan Bordo writes, the "postmodern paradigm" for such mutable identities also effaces "material and social realities," encouraging "fantasies of rearrangement and self-transformation" that continue to privilege conventional, white notions of beauty (246, 247). *Spice World* does not put up much of a fight against such prescriptions, though Mel B's blackness is clearly central to the arguably racist construction of her persona as "Scary Spice," which includes ersatz jungle- and animal-print costumes, hair coiffed to look "wild," and her standard photo-pose, with mouth open to reveal her tongue piercing. Again, an excessive Spice Girl performance simultaneously absorbs and reframes the stereotype. While Mel B's participation in a predominantly white girl group is hardly a definitive answer to the combinations of racism and sexism that shape many lived experiences, it affords one alternative model to standard-issue "integrative" hierarchies, showing mutual respect and affection among the Girls and an apparent "color-blindness" among fans and observers.

But the photo-shoot scene in *Spice World* both exposes and exacerbates some problems with this alternative. Scary Spice's assumption of Ginger's sultry appearance and Baby Spice's incarnation of Scary's leopard-print costume and Afro wig both reveal the differences that race makes in femininity and sexuality. The sequence is quick: where previous shots show Mel C making fun of Victoria's cool pose, arranging her hair and sighing, "I'm *so* Posh!," or Ginger shuffling to the camera playing Sporty as masculine, Baby looks uncomfortable in her tight pants outfit, her eyes barely visible from beneath her hair. She slouches and moans, "Are we finished yet?" And Mel B looks ridiculous in a streaked red wig and fuzzy midriff top, flashing the peace sign and saying, "Blah blah blah, girl power, feminism, you know what I mean." A shot of Baby follows, as she gives up on the whole game: "Uhhh, God!" she says, and slumps off the set. The sequence is revealing, not because it tracks an activity in which all the Girls lose interest, but because this weariness and discomfort are especially pronounced in and illustrated by the swaps between Scary and others. Blackness is not a masquerade so easily executed by a white woman as Marilyn Monroe is, and feminist whiteness appears to be less comfortable for Mel B than Diana Ross (though, to be fair, she seems inconvenienced by the Ross-like red sequin gown, which is too elaborate and static). What is arresting about these revelations—abrupt and unremarked on as they are in the film—is that they reveal so much about the limits of self-expression and plastic identity.

With such audacious and plainly self-mocking moments, *Spice World* offers the Spice Girls not as perfect role models but as imperfect approximations of what girls might be or conceive of being. And currently, the possibilities are becoming more expansive and creative. *Rolling Stone*'s Jancee Dunn reports that these newly deemed consumer trendsetters (the usual marker is "since *Titanic*") seem mysterious and threatening to those customary movers and shakers, boys (or, more precisely, boys who have grown up—more or less—to run lucrative cultural institutions such as *Rolling Stone, Vibe,* MTV, and major record labels). Dunn calls girls "sophisticated and informed consumers," confident of their own tastes and futures, and fond of ritual (the primary example being mall-shopping, and according to Dunn, adolescent girls spend some $60 billion annually). While they may be bothered on occasion by conventional youth quandaries (nervousness about conformity and identity, familial and peer pressures), today's girls are also increasingly aware of their power to "dictate popular culture," while boys, according to one MTV suit, are feeling "disenfranchised because they don't have as many role models" (Dunn 110, 111). Likewise, Jon Pareles warns that "the season [Summer 1999] belongs to the kiddie-pop brigades," children aged five to thirteen, whose most salient sign of approval is not refined and readable applause, but a "high-pitched squeal from a mob of young girls" (1, 32). No doubt, this particular mob—so clamorous and changeable—is an alarming specter for established cultural discoursers like Pareles. Whether the squeal demonstrates "romantic fantasy" (when directed at boy performers) or "sisterly solidarity and fashion approval" (in response to girls), for Pareles it signals the decline of civilization into a most horrible abyss of endless "peppy, happy-faced pop songs" (1).

Such anxiety concerning the ascendancy of girl pop is typically couched as a somber interest in quality control, though it is clearly about the intersections of youth and desire as well. Although "there are five generations right now who consider themselves young," according to professional "trend consultant" Marian Salzman, the power to define youth and not-youth clearly lies with those in charge of production, distribution, and quantification (Dunn 111). Part of the apprehension surely has to do with an imminent changing of the good-taste guard: as people accustomed to pronouncing trends are displaced by younger people with divergent experiences and desires, the adults are no doubt feeling worried, less in control. This phenomenon, at the moment, has everything to do with target marketing and advertisers' recognition of girl consumer power, which was enforced and reframed by the Spice Girls. Dunn describes the "secret life" of her subjects as focused on MTV, boys, celebrities, clothes, and makeup: "They want brand names," observes an editor at *Teen People*, "especially designer labels. They've got money to burn, but they really want quality" (Dunn 118). Teen girls spend a lot of time in groups, they consult one another before they do their parents, they wear clothing that troubles their guardians, and they feel peer pressure to French kiss and go steady. In other words, today's teen girls are not so very different from those of previous eras. Only now, girls are more aware of their cultural clout, their ability to make decisions and to reject expectations. All this they have learned from the Spice Girls, if not directly, then from those artists, slogans, and fashions appearing in the Spice Girls' wake, from Britney Spears and the Backstreet Boys to Christina Aguilera and Jennifer Lopez.

There are any number of venues for selling music, fashion, and celebrity to girls, and most of them at least feign respect for girls' inscrutably mutable tastes and "issues." Certainly, one of the more visible post–Spice Girls venues is the preteen to adolescent girl–oriented magazine in the United States, from the adult spinoffs *Cosmo Girl* and *Teen People* to the relatively longstanding *Twist, Blast, Sizzle, Seventeen* (which has, in fact, been around for years, and pitched to twelve- to thirteen-year-olds more than actual seventeen-year-olds), *Jump, Teen, Teen Celebrity, Young & Modern, J-14, Teen Beat*, and *Tiger Beat.* All these magazines, many of them initiated since the Spice Girls, venerate heterosexual girlness as it is currently practiced in the United States and other places inundated by commercial hyperproductivity, including tips on makeup and clothing, advice on interacting with boyfriends and parents, and keys to pleasurable celebrity worship. To this last end, they tend to replicate the strategies deployed by the Spice Girls and fan mags or "special editions"—that is, they feature lots of pictures, candid and posed, frenzied and studied, and tidbits of information available in many other forms as well. Said tidbits might have to do with stars' favorite colors, foods, or designers (in the magazines aimed at slightly older girls), their backgrounds and families, or their guidance on dating or tasty recipes (often lifted from stars' mothers).

One of the more salient post-Internet corporate commercial strategies to come along in the past couple of years is MTV's *Total Request Live* (*TRL*), a daily show where viewers call in or email their votes for each day's top-ten countdown. As the magazine *Teen Celebrity* puts it, *TRL* represents a "total teen takeover," a show that asserts "the power of the people" (February 14, 2000, 37). That the show airs just as young viewers are getting out of school on the east coast only underlines the cynicism involved, encouraging kids to imagine their stake in what is calculated and available to consume. But the possibility arises in the calculations: the *TRL* choices are younger (Christina Aguilera was born in 1980, Britney Spears in 1981) and occasionally even more radical (in affect and message) than previous regular MTV rotations. And, these selections exemplify a new diversity in voters and voting options: kids cast their ballots as readily for Juvenile or Limp Bizkit as for Brandy, Jessica Simpson, or "Candy" girl Mandy Moore, and boys and girls alike defend their choices in public, in video inserts on the show, or in email "ticker tapes" across the bottom of the videos. Power to the kiddie-pop brigades.

Though the Spice Girls' swift rise came just before *TRL* and they have thus not yet been tested as vote-getters, their influence on the show's concept is clear. Not only did they clear the way for twelve-year-olds to imagine themselves with voices, more than once girl callers have cited "girl power" as their reason for voting for a certain artist or video performance. But what is most interesting about the *TRL* phenomenon—it is one of MTV's most popular shows, repeated during prime time and again on weekends, in "special editions"—is its apparent willingness to trust young, afterschool viewers to determine programming. This is not to say that choices are not preordained (voting possibilities are predetermined by MTV producers and executives, whose selections are never inadvertent), but it is to say that the process acknowledges—or, perhaps more accurately, intimates that it acknowledges—the significance of consumers' stakes in programming. Moreover, *TRL* reflects the practical reality that "authenticity," that old bugbear in music criticism and academic studies, is plainly comprehended by young music fans as a function of investment and interest. If you know enough about your favorite act, your vote is authentic and the act has real effects—on your taste, self-understanding, and context. As Michael Coyle and Jon Dolan observe, "The music industry is a difference-generating machine that operates by comparatively few discourses," and one of these, authenticity, "is not a quality but a way of affirming quality that now figures in many of the ways that audiences and performers use recordings in identity formation" (33).

This music industry is spoofed in *Spice World*, which represents business concerns as overdetermined and un-fun. Clifford's employer is the Chief, played by Roger Moore as a James-Bondish supervillain, shown alone in his hideaway, petting small animals and surrounded by high-tech gadgets, ceaselessly concerned with the bottom line. Obsessive and insecure, Clifford himself personifies the industry's most egregious narrow vision, as he is shown again and again lunching with Hollywood producers, checking his expensive watch, and hiding behind his tacky mirror sunglasses. One of his schemes involves a documentary of the Girls' busy days leading up to the Albert Hall show (here standing in for their first live show and so generating much nervousness all around), to be overseen by the director Piers Cutherton-Smyth (Alan Cumming), a self-important artiste who is continually setting up the perfect composition or hoping for the most compelling way to structure the film, say, a finale where the group breaks up. In the sense that he is waiting for this event rather than engineering it, he is slightly differentiated from the film's most visible miscreant, a bald, sneery tabloid photographer aptly named Damien (Richard O'Brien), assigned to create a scoop if none can be found. All these male characters—Clifford, Damien, The Chief, and Piers—are portrayed as destructively self-interested, unable to comprehend the beauty of the Spice Girls' somewhat disingenuous "message" that fame is great but inevitably fleeting and so not a viable premise for identity. Instead, the Girls perform a kind of collective self-reassurance for their fans, rejecting the men's anxious attempts to contain and control their "career" in favor of immediate pleasures.

My Future, My Past

> If you want my future, forget my past.
> SPICE GIRLS, "Wannabe"

What makes the Spice Girls model of identity and identification so seductive and odious at the same time is that it frankly celebrates the process of "selling out" with the caveat that if you never affect originality and authenticity, then you have nothing to lose in this process. That is, the Spice Girls make no pretense that they are anything other than what they have been called, a manufactured band rather than an organic one, a group put together through an ad in *The Stage* in early 1994, organized and trained by a former British boy band manager, Bob Herbert, along with his son Chris and partner Chic Murphy (Golden 13–35). But if the revelation of this back story was supposed to dampen the rather hysterical popularity of the Spice Girls (in 1997, upon the release of their first single, "Wannabe"), the result was, in fact, that fans did not care or knew as much already. And with this turn of events, the brilliant merchandising strategy behind the Spice Girls became clear to everyone, as it also became clear that there could be no scandalmongering or badmouthing of the group's talents, intentions, or origins. The Girls are proudly frothy and light, happy to be pop and to sell it ("Generation Next," their 1998 Pepsi commercial song, became a regular number in their live show repertoire). The Girls offer a story to counter the typical dismissal that they are the "female New Kids on the Block." Their version insists on their early assertiveness and decision to work as a team. Though initially conceived by Herbert as a girl band to be called Touch, along the lines of Boyzone and Take That, made up of a front person and backup singers, the Spice Girls ended up quite different in format and effects. After living and working together for nearly two years, the Girls renegotiated terms with their "discoverers" so that they were all equally performing and show-cased. Above all, the Spice Girls identified themselves as "friends," committed to one another and to their mutual success and excess.

The "manufactured band" tag remains mildly troubling, at least to the point that it generates responses from "Spice World," the metaphorical place where the Girls thrive, as well as *Spice World*, the movie. Steve Pond elaborates on the dangers of this tag in an article introducing the Spice Girls to his *New York Times* readers back in 1997: "Their bubble-gum music is undemanding, their marketing is so aggressive and their packaging so attractive that many already see them as the Monkees of the 1990s—the invention of musical Svengali" (H36). And yet the feared and expected backlash—to their overwhelming international popularity and obvious charisma, their lack of experience when they first came to the States (*Saturday Night Live* in April 1997 was their first performance with a live band, without lip-synching or recorded backing tracks), and their oft-remarked lack of authenticity and "talent"—never really happened. Or rather, its effects were minimal: "Spice World" continues.

The Girls' public responses to criticisms are typically ironic and charming, hyperartificial in ways that draw attention to the complex relationships between desire and performance, between subjectivity and belief. One of the most often repeated and likely apocryphal stories about the Spice Girls' early days has to do with the nicknames they were assigned—Posh, Sporty, Ginger, Baby, and Scary—by an ill-intentioned London tabloid as part of a campaign to discredit the band's music and reduce the Girls to "types." Instead of rejecting these silly names, the story goes, the Girls adopted them, thus identifying themselves as easily embraceable types, each with her signature characteristics, costumes, and props. Instead of turning off fans seeking icons with individuality and integrity, the audacious scheme has made the Spice Girls seem accessible, cute, and profoundly familiar, no matter how strange and excessive their self-demonstrations turn.

The origin story of the Spice Girls gets considerable ribbing in *Spice World* the movie, conceived and indeed consummated as a way to extend the Girls' initial fifteen minutes of fame. It works by elaborating and exaggerating the basic Spice premise that the Girls are interested in having fun—being girls—while everyone around them wants them to adhere to schedules and perform according to commercial needs. The film counters the "manufactured band" story with an alternative manufactured story, which occurs just as the

Girls are in crisis over Clifford's increasingly unreasonable demands. Angry at him during a rehearsal, they threaten to act out his worst nightmare, the breakup of the group. Later that night, the film shows them in various poses of remorse and nostalgia: miraculously, they simultaneously gather at the now-abandoned building that used to house their favorite fish 'n' chips joint. In a brief, idyllic, pre–Spice phenomenon flashback, the Girls appear as just girls, dressed in jeans and t-shirts, with slightly less makeup on their faces than usual, eating chips and drinking pop. Encouraged by the establishment's friendly but doubtful proprietor, the pre–Spice Girls gleefully expose their nascent talent by singing "Wannabe," using soda bottles for mikes and the joint's cheap chairs as props. The vision is quaint but serves a function, asserting that they were friends before they were stars and they will be friends forever after, because, as they are wont to repeat again and again, friendship never ends.

A World That Doesn't Really Exist

> I want my camera to take my audience on a journey into the mind's eye of the Spice Girls.
>
> DOCUMENTARY FILMMAKER PIERS, *Spice World*

You can read the entirety of *Spice World*—which has grossed some $77 million worldwide—as an ongoing tongue-in-cheek answer to critics of the Spice Girls' artifice. The film opens with a performance that is being recorded: under the credits, the Girls perform "Too Much": Scary looks into the camera and sings, "Love is blind as far as the eye can see," an example of the group's more arcane, not to say inane, lyrics. And yet the extent of seeing and the power of surveillance are primary themes in the film to come: as the Girls sing, the camera cuts between shots of them together and singly, to a control room full of video monitors, viewed from behind the shoulders and heads of mostly male producers and sound mixers, all business. At the end of the number, the camera shows that the Girls are performing for a crowd of mostly girls, who clap and cheer, positioned in the frame between the Spice Girls on stage and Clifford, who is standing behind the booth's glass wall. After the show, the Girls accuse their manager of not watching their performance, and indeed, previous shot/reverse shots have revealed that Clifford is concentrating on getting the reproduction, the commodifiable version of the performance, not on enjoying or participating in the present moment. And this, the love of performing and consuming performance, is what the film both celebrates and deconstructs, with Clifford acting as a kind of priggish and parsimonious Scrooge to the Girls' generous, optimistic spirits. Thus, he repeatedly reminds them of the work they have to do and schedules they have to maintain, as in, "There is the small matter of an extremely live gig on Saturday" or "I have an announcement: there's a press conference coming up that means smiling at the cameras and answering a lot of dumb questions, that is all." The Girls chafe at his disdainful and oppressive rule-making, and eventually they find a way to have their fun, be with Nicola (Naoko Mori) when she gives birth to her daughter, *and* please those who want to believe in them, their fans. In other words, girl power is exactly what it is cracked up to be in *Spice World:* a means of self-expression and self-fulfillment, and, even more important, a way to share your energy and general elation with the fans who have made you what you are today.

But "today" is already long ago, however recent it may seem—an unspeakable distance from Ginger Spice's unsettling defection and the four-member group's 1998 U.S. concert tour. Documented in *Spice Girls in America: A Tour Story,* this adventure seems, at first glance, to reverse the cartoonish exaggeration-and-hype strategy of *Spice World.* The film shows the tour city by city, with speedy time-lapse road imagery in between and location-setting shots to demonstrate moves from Los Angeles to Orlando to Chicago to New York. The film includes repeated backstage *sans*-makeup scenes, seemingly spontaneous shopping excursions, hotel room phone calls with family back home, and ostensibly frank interviews with road crew members (the percussionist, the lighting guy, the U.S. promotions manager, the caterer) and fans outside various venues (in Columbus, Ohio, a mother and daughter grin and fidget, pronouncing their fondness for the song "Mama," "because of the words").

It appears at first that this documentary carefully reinforces *Spice World*'s version of the Spice Girls as being all delightful, all the time. It celebrates their celebrity, in part by elaborating on established fictions of the Girls and of celebrity per se. In this rendering, audience and performer stakes in celebrity seem congruous, as if the Girls have as much investment in their stardom and excessiveness as any fan might. In his study of contemporary celebrity, Joshua Gamson asks, "If celebrities are artificial creations, why should an audience remain attached and lavish attention on their fabricated lives? How can stars be both true and false?" (48). *Spice Girls in*

America does not so much answer these questions as it elucidates and reveals some cracks in the grounds for such allegiance. In exposing the group's fractures and fallibility, the film only enhances their appeal.

Music director Simon Ellis observes early on in the documentary, "It's like spending your life in a world that doesn't really exist." And indeed, it is clear enough in *Spice Girls in America* that what you are watching does not exist: it is an excursion into a set of circumstances that are both bizarre and banal, where the girls embody and articulate sexual, material, and emotional desires, speaking for and to their fans. In other words, *Spice Girls in America's* version of their nonexistent world does not seem strange, but logical and revealing, even though nothing surprising is "revealed." The alternating talking-head/behind-the-scenes/stage-show format is familiar from almost any "concert" documentary, and yet the film is both self-conscious about its own fabrications (Madonna and Alec Keshishian's *Truth or Dare* comes to mind as a similarly self-aware text) and up-front concerning the extensive efforts required to sustain this world. The documentary, in other words, presents the Girls simultaneously as "real" (giddy, tired, grumpy, exhilarated, missing their mums) and spectacularly unreal (on stage and off, talking to and performing for the camera). Though clearly designed to appeal to fans who can't get enough of the Spice Girls as models and projections, the straight-to-video release is also fascinating as a portrait of the Girls in flux, dealing with the sudden departure of Geri Halliwell.

This event is surely crucial for the Spice Girls and their fans, as it literally rearranged the group and raised questions concerning their well-known "friendship is forever" mantra. As Benjamin Svetky puts it in *Entertainment Weekly*, Halliwell's decision to leave the group just weeks before the U.S. tour was disconcerting, to say the least, "effectively ending Spice life as we know it" (20). While his article recounts the reactions to the change and makes easy fun of covering the story, which involves listening to the music ("The horror. The horror"), it also shows, again, how the group endures, despite and because of such disaster and disrespect. Svetky observes that the "Spice Girls are a hugely profitable merchandising machine, one of the most successful marketing engines ever to roll off the pop-music assembly line" (21). Although the disparagement in such a description is clear, *Spice Girls in America* makes equally clear that the group members (and their management) understand, manipulate, even thrive on such predictable underestimation and reduction.

They are always able to turn it back around: "Look at all the nerves that we've picked," says Mel B cheerfully, "about girl power, about female rights."

The primary strategy for their success is their performance of a hypernormalcy. The Girls are like everyone else: alone and exhausted in their hotel room after a show, Sporty and Posh watch *Scream 2;* Sporty is nervous about performing for and meeting Madonna backstage; Baby carries pictures of her friends to every city and brings mum along for part of the tour ("I'm the worst critic," says Pauline Bunton proudly); Scary expresses amazement that "even in Katmandu they knew we [Scary and Posh] were pregnant"); Posh looks as bored as you are while she's on a car tour of LA's celebrity homes; and they all have their cell phones with them wherever they go. And Geri hangs over all of them, an ever-present absence, lingering in fans' minds ("My favorite was Ginger," says one Southern-accented fellow in Columbus, "She always wore the British flag"), in the Girls' conversations (Sporty says after Madonna leaves, "She asked me about Geri"), and visible in the music videos that screen behind them as they perform on stage for "2 Become 1" and "Say You'll Be There." And just so, the Spice Girls, it seems, will always be there. Mutating and reproducing, rotating off MTV and replaced by ensuing generations of girl pop acts, the Spice Girls seem irrepressible, preserved through action figures, lollipops, trading cards, music videos, and CDs. Combining complexity and simplicity, fiction and fact, success and excess, "Spice World" lives.

Notes

1. Halliwell retreated from the public and tabloid press, staying at her friend George Michael's home, and soon after was named the U.N. goodwill ambassador. She dedicated herself to "promoting safe sex in the Third World" and has had a star—a *real* star—named after her (Cassiopeia RA 01h 47m.61s D 55d 15'' 23.04'').

Works Cited

Bordo, Susan. 1993. *Unbearable Weight: Feminism, Western Culture, and the Body.* Berkeley: University of California Press.

Coyle, Michael, and Jon Dolan. 1999. "Modeling Authenticity, Authenticating Commercial Modes." In *Reading Rock and Roll: Authenticity, Appropriation, Aesthetics,* ed. Kevin J. Dettmar and William Richey, 17–35. New York: Columbia University Press.

Dunn, Jancee. 1999. "The Secret Life of Teenage Girls." *Rolling Stone* 825, 11 November: 107–21.

Giroux, Henry. 1998. "Nymphet Fantasies: Child Beauty Pageants and the Politics of Innocence." *Social Text* 16, no. 4: 31–53.

Golden, Anna Louise. 1997. *The Spice Girls: The Uncensored Story behind Pop's Biggest Phenomenon.* New York: Ballantine Books.

Pareles, Jon. 1999. "The Toy of Teenyboppers." *New York Times,* 11 July, sec. 2: 1, 32.

Pond, Steve. 1997. "Manufactured in Britain. Now Selling in America." *New York Times,* 16 February: H36–37.

Press, Joy. 1997. "Notes on Girl Power." *Village Voice,* 23 September: 59–61.

Svetky, Benjamin. 1998. "Tour Divorce." *Entertainment Weekly,* 17 July: 19–25.

Contributors

CORINN COLUMPAR teaches film studies and women's studies at Keene State College in New Hampshire and is in the process of completing a Ph.D. in women's studies from Emory University.

ANN DE VANEY is professor emerita of Curriculum and Instruction at the University of Wisconsin-Madison and a visiting professor at the University of California-Irvine. She is the editor of *Technology and Resistance: Decentralized Communications and New Alliances around the World* (2000) and *Watching Channel One: The Convergence of Students, Technology and Private Business* (1994).

LINDA DITTMAR is a professor of English at the University of Massachusetts-Boston, where she teaches film, literature, and women's studies. She is the coeditor of *From Hanoi to Hollywood: The Vietnam War in American Film* (1991) and *Multiple Voices in Feminist Film Criticism* (1994), and serves on the editorial board of *Radical Teacher*. She has published articles on film and literature in *Wide Angle, boundary 2, Novel, Mosaic, Iris,* and book chapters. Her special interests include minority discourses in film, both formally and thematically.

MIRIAM FORMAN-BRUNELL is associate professor of history and women's and gender studies at the University of Missouri-Kansas City. She is the author of *Get a Sitter: Fears and Fantasies about Adolescent Girls* (forthcoming, 2002); *Made to Play House: Dolls and the Commercialization of American Girlhood, 1830–1930* (1998); and the editor of *The Story of Rose O'Neill: An Autobiography* (1997). She is also the editor of the two-volume *Girlhood in America: An Encyclopedia* (2001), the co-editor of *The American Material Culture*

361

Encyclopedia (2002), and the reference series book editor of "Children and Youth in History and Culture" at ABC-CLIO.

CYNTHIA FUCHS is an associate professor in English, film, and media studies, African-American studies, and cultural studies at George Mason University. She is the coeditor of *Between the Sheets, in the Streets: Queer/Gay/Lesbian Documentary* (1997) and has recently published articles on hip-hop, the Internet, queer punks, and The Artist. Her essay on The Hot Boys appears in *Closely Watched Brains* (2001). She is a regular film reviewer for *Philadelphia Citypaper* and *Nitrateonline.com,* and is the film and television review editor for *Popmatters.com.*

FRANCES GATEWARD is assistant professor in the Unit for Cinema Studies and the Program in Comparative and World Literature at the University of Illinois, Urbana-Champaign. Her work has been published in numerous journals and anthologies including *Multiple Modernities: Cinema and Popular Media in Transcultural East Asia, Still Lifting Still Climbing: Contemporary African American Women's Activism,* and *Ladies and Gentlemen, Boys and Girls: Gender in Film at the End of the Twentieth Century.* She is the editor of *Zhang Yimou: Interviews* and coeditor of *Where the Boys Are: Cinemas of Masculinity and Youth.*

INA RAE HARK is the coeditor of *Screening the Male* (1993) and *The Road Movie Book* (1997), both with Steven Cohan, and the author of numerous articles on film and gender, and film and politics. She is a professor of English and the director of the Film Studies Program at the University of South Carolina.

KRISTEN HATCH is a Ph.D. candidate in film and television at UCLA. She is completing a dissertation on girls' erotic performance and the adult gaze from vaudeville to the present.

BELL HOOKS is the author of many books, including *All About Love: New Visions* (2001), *Feminism is for Everybody: Passionate Politics* (2000), *Ain't I a Woman: Black Women and Feminism* (1981), *Black Looks: Race and Representation* (1992), *Feminist Theory: From Margin to Center* (2000), and *Reel to Real: Race, Sex, and Class at the Movies* (1996).

MARY CELESTE KEARNEY is an assistant professor of critical and cultural studies in the Department of Radio-Television-Film at the University of Texas-Austin. Her publications include "Producing Girls: Rethinking the Study of Female Youth Culture," which appears in *Delinquents and Debutantes: Twentieth-Century American Girls' Culture* (1998), and "Girls Just Want to Have *Fun*?: Female Avengers in '90s Teenpics," which appears in *Pictures of a Generation on Hold: Selected Papers* (1996).

CHUCK KLEINHANS is coeditor of *Jump Cut: A Review of Contemporary Media* and director of graduate studies in the Radio/Television/Film Department at Northwestern University. His recent work includes articles on independent and avant-garde film and Hong Kong cinema.

LORI LIGGETT is a Ph.D. candidate in American culture studies at Bowling Green State University. Her research focus includes late nineteenth- and twentieth-century American women's cultural history. She is currently working on a project that explores the intersection of gender, ethnicity, and class within popular culture, labor, and media, and teaches at the University of Western Ontario.

CHRISTIE MILLIKEN is a Ph.D. candidate in critical studies at the University of Southern California School of Cinema-Television. She is currently completing a dissertation on sex educational film and video.

MURRAY POMERANCE is chair of the Department of Sociology at Ryerson University and the author, editor, or coeditor of numerous volumes including *BAD: Infamy, Darkness, Evil, and Slime on Screen, Enfant Terrible! Jerry Lewis in American Film, Magia d'Amore,* and *Where the Boys Are: Cinemas of Masculinity and Youth.* He is editor of the Horizons of Cinema series from State University of New York Press and, with Lester D. Friedman, coeditor of the Screen Decades: American Cinema/American Culture series from Rutgers University Press. His *An Eye for Hitchcock* is forthcoming in spring 2004.

KIMBERLEY ROBERTS is a Ph.D. candidate in English at the University of Virginia, specializing in feminist cultural studies, youth culture studies, and American literature. She is also the cofounder of the Young Women Leaders Program, a nationally recognized mentoring program for middle school girls based at the University of Virginia Women's Center.

TIMOTHY SHARY teaches film and television studies at Clark University in Worcester, Massachusetts. His articles on youth in cinema have appeared in various books and journals, and he is the author of *Generation Multiplex: The Image of Youth in Contemporary American Movies* (2002).

GAYLE WALD is assistant professor of English at George Washington University. She is the author of *Crossing the Line: Racial Passing in Twentieth-Century U.S. Literature and Culture* (2000) and has published in *Signs* on the "girl" in popular music culture.

ALLISON WHITNEY is a Century Scholar in the doctoral program in cinema and media studies at the University of Chicago. Her research interests include gender theory, immersive art installations, and the origins of IMAX cinema.

STEVEN WOODWARD is a student of children's literature, poetry, book history, and film studies. His Ph.D. thesis was on the British poet and children's author Walter de la Mare, and he has published papers on film, genre, and gender. He is assistant professor of film and literature at Clemson University.

Index

Pages with images are given in italics.